The Achievement of Christina Rossetti

The Achievement of
CHRISTINA
ROSSETTI

EDITED BY

David A. Kent

Cornell University Press

ITHACA AND LONDON

First published 1987 by Cornell University Press.

International Standard Book Number 0-8014-1937-9
Library of Congress Catalog Card Number 87-47548
Printed in the United States of America
Librarians: Library of Congress cataloging information
appears on the last page of the book.

The paper in this book is acid-free and meets the guidelines for
permanence and durability of the Committee on Production Guidelines
for Book Longevity of the Council on Library Resources.

IN MEMORIAM

CATHERINE MUSELLO CANTALUPO

Alike in the love poems and in the religious poems, there is a certain asceticism, passion itself speaking a chastened language, the language, generally, of sorrowful but absolute renunciation. This motive, passion remembered and repressed, condemned to eternal memory and eternal sorrow, is the motive of much of her finest work.

Arthur Symons, *Studies in Two Literatures*

CONTENTS

Contents

PREFACE

The idea for collecting essays on Christina Rossetti originated during the MLA Convention in Los Angeles, December 1982. Catherine Cantalupo, a recent Ph.D. from Rutgers, had organized a special session on Rossetti's devotional poetry and invited me to participate. Soon after arriving at the convention, however, I learned that Cantalupo was too ill to attend. Although we had only exchanged letters and spoken a few times on the telephone, her death in 1983 was a loss I felt in an unexpectedly personal way. With the concurrence of the other participants on that panel (Jerome McGann and Barry Qualls), I have therefore dedicated this volume to the memory of Catherine Cantalupo. Thanks to the editorial work of her husband, Charles, and of her thesis supervisor, Barry Qualls, it has been possible to include work by her in the collection. This essay shows us what Rossetti scholarship lost with her death.

The essays gathered here attempt a genuine reevaluation of a writer who the contributors believe has been unjustly neglected. The topics are diverse and the critical approaches varied. Rossetti is here addressed with the kind of serious attention almost entirely missing from writings on her work since the late nineteenth century, an attentive attitude well illustrated by the perceptive observations of Arthur Symons in the passage that provides the epigraph for this volume. For the convenience of the reader, the book is divided into three parts. I believe, however, that the division also serves to stress some important facts about Rossetti and her career. The first part addresses Rossetti's achievement as a major Victorian poet. In general, her poetry has eluded the attention of modern critics: these essays reveal the hidden complexity and consummate craftsmanship of her art. Furthermore, neither her work in prose (including her writings for children and her devotional writings) nor her cultural significance as a woman artist has received adequate treatment. The second group of essays demonstrates that the dimensions of her achievement are wider than has been assumed (and that the drama of her personal life, as seen in the new letters, was more intense). The third part builds upon the premises of the first two and focuses on Rossetti's struggle with other writers, both predecessors and contemporaries, to claim her own place in the Victorian literary world. The book as a whole illustrates that she achieved a position very different from that to which she has traditionally been relegated, and that our inherited image of her as an isolated, retiring spinster is, we are now beginning to realize, utterly inadequate.

Grateful acknowledgment is made to the British Library and Imogen Dennis for permission to quote from manuscripts of Rossetti's poems and to Yale University Library and Princeton University Library (Troxell Collection) for permission to quote from unpublished letters by Rossetti.

A number of people have been very helpful in the preparation of this volume. First of all, I thank my wife, Margo Swiss, who suggested the possibility for this kind of collection in the first place. I am also much indebted to Jerome McGann, whose kind encouragement to proceed then gave me the needed impetus to undertake the project. Bernhard Kendler of Cornell University Press has been a congenial and responsive editor. Martha Linke did outstanding editorial work, for which all the writers are grateful. Finally, William Whitla has given me "all good counsel" on many important occasions. In fact, all the contributors have cooperated in so many small ways it would be trespassing on the reader's patience to recite them. I simply wish to thank the authors for their support.

DAVID A. KENT

Toronto, Ontario

ABBREVIATIONS

Wherever possible, all references to Rossetti's poetry are to the first two volumes of R.W. Crump, ed., *The Complete Poems of Christina Rossetti: A Variorum Edition* (Baton Rouge: Louisiana State University Press, 1979 and 1986), and are indicated by volume number and page number. Other references to the poetry are from William Michael Rossetti's 1904 edition, as noted below under *PW*.

CS   Christina Rossetti, *Called to be Saints: The Minor Festivals Devotionally Studied* (London: SPCK, 1881)

FD   Christina Rossetti, *The Face of the Deep: A Devotional Commentary on the Apocalypse* (London: SPCK, 1892)

FL   *The Family Letters of Christina Georgina Rossetti*, ed. William Michael Rossetti (London: Brown, Langham, 1908)

LS   Christina Rossetti, *Letter and Spirit: Notes on the Commandments* (London: SPCK, 1883)

PW   *The Poetical Works of Christina Georgina Rossetti*, ed. William Michael Rossetti (London: Macmillan, 1904)

SF   Christina Rossetti, *Seek and Find: A Double Series of Short Studies of the Benedicite* (London: SPCK, 1879)

TF   Christina Rossetti, *Time Flies: A Reading Diary* (London: SPCK, 1885)

VDP   G. B. Tennyson, *Victorian Devotional Poetry: The Tractarian Mode* (Cambridge: Harvard University Press, 1981)

VN   *Victorian Newsletter*

VP   *Victorian Poetry*

VS   *Victorian Studies*

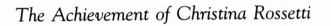

The Achievement of Christina Rossetti

JEROME J. McGANN

Introduction

"Of all decades in our history, a wise man would choose the eigh-teen-fifties to be young in."[1] This well-known judgment by the emi-nent historian G. M. Young reflects a widespread consensus not merely about that fortunate decade but about the entire period from 1850 to 1873—the "Age of Equipoise" as it has been called. In the words of another historian of the period, Sir Llewellyn Woodward, "few people growing up to manhood in 1870 could feel altogether in despair of their country."[2]

This was the same period in which Christina Rossetti established her poetic vision and reputation. Of course she was not a "young man," but then we have to imagine—do we not?—that social circum-stances in an enlightened country operate uniformly on the just and the unjust alike. However that may be, Rossetti negotiated the Age of Equipoise in a state of extreme antithesis. Woodward spoke for a consensus when he observed, "For leisure or work, for getting or spending, England was a better country in 1870 than in 1815."[3] This is a social, even a materialist, judgment with which many people living then agreed, and many scholars working now heartily concur. It is, in other words, an imaginable truth from a number of perspectives;

[1] G. M. Young, *Victorian England: Portrait of an Age*, 2d ed. (London: Oxford University Press, 1964), p. 77.
[2] See W. L. Burn, *The Age of Equipoise* (London: Allen & Unwin, 1964); and Llewellyn Woodward, *The Age of Reform*, 2d ed. (Oxford: Clarendon Press, 1962), pp. 630–31.
[3] Ibid., p. 629.

1

but from the perspective of Rossetti in 1869—when she wrote " 'They desire a better country' " (I, 195–96)—the better country lay, as Baudelaire once expressed it, "Anywhere Out of the World." For "The World" (I, 76–77) seen by Rossetti, was, as she described it in a sonnet of 1854, "a very monster void of love and prayer."[4]

The outward and visible sign of the inward and spiritual grace of this Age of Equipoise was the Crystal Palace Exhibition of 1851. Under this sign England launched herself into the second half of the nineteenth century armed with a faith in English virtue, a hope in unlimited material progress, and the charity of technology and capitalist enterprise. From her uncompromising religious perspective, Rossetti observed this complacency with indifference, contempt, or—sometimes—fear. Whatever the message the majority of her contemporaries read into the signs of the times, to her mind those signs meant only one thing: "Self-Destruction."[5] In the Age of Equipoise, Rossetti perceived the triumph of Vanity, a pattern of acquiescence not merely to "The three enemies" (I, 70–72) but to the illusory imagination that the Crystal Palace portrayed a great truth rather than a great deception.

Other voices of this period—Charles Dickens, John Ruskin, even Matthew Arnold—spoke to a similar purpose. Among the poets, one thinks especially of Rossetti's brother Dante Gabriel and of William Morris. But these men (Ruskin alone, perhaps, excepted) had to grow into their skeptical and critical minds, which they did not fully find until the Age of Equipoise had passed and the crisis of the subsequent years had descended. Rossetti's antithesis was inveterate and unswerving. From her earliest poems of the 1840s to her last poems of the 1890s, in works that were variously desperate, resigned, or uplifting, Rossetti set a face of flint against her fortunate age and the fortunate men who were born into it.

To understand the character—and finally the importance—of her antithetical position we have to distinguish it from that of certain others who took a dim or skeptical view of English progress and Victorian achievement. Liberal and conservative thought of the period alike repeatedly criticized the commercial spirit of the age. John Stuart Mill was skeptical of "the idol 'production' "[6] as early as 1829, and in

[4] "The World" is the first of three sonnets published by Rossetti under the heading "The three enemies" (I, 70–72).
[5] See the fifth section of poems (II, 260) in the last collection arranged by Rossetti herself, Verses (London: SPCK, 1893); it is headed "The World—Self-Destruction."
[6] Letter to Gustave d'Eichthal, October 8, 1829, in The Early Letters of John Stuart Mill, 1812–1848, ed. Francis E. Mineka (Toronto: University of Toronto Press, 1963), p. 37.

his monumental *Principles of Political Economy* (1848) he represented his ideal social order not as a capitalist one, but as a no-growth society. As he went on to observe in the same context: "I confess I am not charmed with the ideal of life held out by those who think that the normal state of human beings is that of struggling to get on; that the trampling, crushing, elbowing, and treading on each other's heels, which form the existing type of social life, are the most desirable lot of human kind."[7] The words might have been those of Thomas Carlyle, or John Ruskin, or Matthew Arnold, or Charles Dickens. The cash nexus and the profit motive seemed a dreary business to them all.

Nonetheless, however much these men criticized the materialism and capitalist spirit of the age, each was actively engaged in an effort to correct and improve what was evil or mistaken or faulty. In this respect they were all spokesmen for that central ideology of the period which is epitomized in those famous designations "The Age of Improvement," and "The Age of Reform." Ruskin, in many ways the severest critic of the times, spent most of his life and talents preaching to his contemporaries to reform their social circumstances. His imagination was dominated by hopes for the amelioration of what Wordsworth called "the very world, which is the world / Of all of us" (*Prelude* XI.142–43).[8] Like any capitalist, Ruskin was preoccupied with mortal and quotidian things when he said, "the question for the nation is not how much labour it employs, but how much life it produces." Nor was he thinking of the soul in its pilgrimage, but rather of the individual in society, when he added: "THERE IS NO WEALTH BUT LIFE. Life, including all its powers of love, of joy, and of admiration. That country is the richest which nourishes the greatest number of noble and happy human beings; that man is richest who, having perfected the functions of his own life to the utmost, has also the widest helpful influence, both personal, and by means of his possessions, over the lives of others."[9] For Ruskin "life" is human life in society, the true wealth of all nations.

Christina Rossetti was not a social reformer, she was a spiritual absolutist. Notorious for her reactionary views on most social questions, she observed capitalist and reformer with a similar skepticism. To her

[7]John Stuart Mill, *Principles of Political Economy*, 2 vols. (New York: Colonial Press, 1900), II, 261–62 (Bk. IV, chap. 6).

[8]The text used is *"The Prelude," 1799, 1805, 1850*, ed. Jonathan Wordsworth, M. H. Abrams, and Stephen Gill (New York: Norton, 1979).

[9]*The Genius of John Ruskin: Selections from his Writings*, 2d ed., ed. John D. Rosenberg (London: Routledge and Kegan Paul, 1979), pp. 269–70.

mind, both were literally on the wrong path, for each had set his feet in worldly ways and his eyes on worldly goals. Of course, Rossetti herself was actively involved, in the early 60s and perhaps before that as well, with the diocesan penitentiary at Highgate known as St. Mary Magdalene's, an institution, according to William Michael Rossetti, "for the reclamation and protection of women leading a vicious life" (FL, p. 26). We must not misunderstand her involvement in this work, however, which was directed to the spiritual improvement of these women's souls. This was not "social work" that Rossetti was engaged in, it was *spiritual* work, properly so called. Rossetti would not have set out to "reform" these women in order to transform them into productive and useful members of society. On the contrary, her object would have been to turn them away from a preoccupation with the world and the world's ways, to turn them toward their "true life." Rossetti's entire life and work compels us to understand her work at St. Mary's in this way. [10]

We want to be clear about such matters because they help us to understand the special critical force of Rossetti's verse. Gerard Manley Hopkins is a fine religious poet, and he stands with Rossetti in the orthodoxy that gives structure to his work. (In this respect, as we shall see in a moment, the work of both Rossetti and Hopkins stands apart from the religious poetry of Tennyson.) But Hopkins's religious poetry is quite unlike Rossetti's in that his best work always operates in a highly personal mode and style. His subjectivity is a convention of his form, just as that style is—again, unlike Rossetti's—"spasmodic." Christina Rossetti would never have permitted herself this sort of rhetorical display:

> No worst, there is none. Pitched past pitch of grief
> More pangs will, schooled at forepangs, wilder wring.
> Comforter, where, where is your comforting?
> Mary, mother of us, where is your relief?
> My cries heave, herds-long; huddle in a main, a chief
> Woe, world-sorrow; on an age-old anvil wince and sing—
> Then lull, then leave off. Fury had shrieked "No ling-
> ering! Let me be fell: force I must be brief". [11]

---

[10]As time passed, Rossetti's religious convictions grew somewhat less severe. She never swerved from her doctrinal views, but the tense negativity in her perception of worldly *vanitas* diminished. For a fine discussion of the subject, see Lona Mosk Packer, *Christina Rossetti* (Berkeley: University of California Press, 1963), pp. 324, 333.

[11]My quotations from Hopkins are taken from his *Poems and Prose*, ed. W. H. Gardner (Harmondsworth: Penguin, 1953). This poem (no. 65) appears on page 100.

4

At the back of Hopkins's "That Nature is a Heraclitean Fire . . ." are
the pyrotechnics of Byron or Donne:

> Across my foundering deck shone
> A beacon, an eternal beam.   Flesh fade, and mortal trash
> Fall to the residuary worm;   world's wildfire, leave but ash:
> In a flash, at a trumpet crash,
> I am all at once what Christ is,   since he was what I am, and
> This Jack, joke, poor potsherd,   patch, matchwood, immortal diamond,
> Is immortal diamond.

In sharp contrast, Rossetti's poetry is always nonpersonal (not exactly
impersonal) in the moderated style of Herbert, just as its address is
simple, cool, even at times severe.[12]
   I emphasize these differences between Rossetti and Hopkins because
they indicate why Rossetti's poetry involves direct social critique
whereas Hopkins's, characteristically, does not. In Hopkins we witness a personal psychomachia. Rossetti, on the other hand, is far more
reserved: the extreme conventionality of her imagery and stylistic
devices gives a peculiarly objective quality to even her first-person
poems, as if they dealt with typical events in the life of the soul rather
than with personal events from the life of Rossetti. As a consequence,
the field in which a Rossetti poem gets played out is objective rather
than subjective, and her work—again, unlike that of Hopkins—easily
moves into an open confrontation with "the world." We see this
confrontation very clearly in a well-known poem such as "A Triad" (I,
29) where three socially specific "types" of Victorian women are
weighed in Rossetti's balances and found wanting.
   Although we are not likely to miss the social character of a poem
such as "A Triad," the predominant type of Rossetti's work—that is,
her programmatic religious verse—can easily be mistaken for poetry
written in the interior and psychological conventions of Hopkins's
verse. This mistake is, I believe, largely responsible for the neglect and
misunderstanding of Rossetti's poetry. We will never really approach
the brilliance—the disturbing brilliance—of a poem such as "A better

[12]See Georgina Battiscombe, *Christina Rossetti: A Divided Life* (New York: Holt,
Rinehart and Winston, 1981), pp. 96–97, where she speaks of Rossetti's "gift of
allowing her imagination to dwell upon some experience, perhaps even a mere hint or
suggestion, taken from her reading or from her daily life, in this case ["Go from me,
summer friends"] from her work among 'fallen women,' and turning it over and over
until it changed into something personal to herself."

resurrection" (I, 68) until we understand how fiercely the poem is trying to annihilate all ordinary and personal attachments.

> I have no wit, no words, no tears;
>   My heart within me like a stone
> Is numbed too much for hopes or fears;
>   Look right, look left, I dwell alone;
> I lift my eyes, but dimmed with grief
>   No everlasting hills I see;
> My life is in the falling leaf:
>   O Jesus, quicken me.
>
> [ll. 1–8]

In the second stanza this condition of insufficiency is related even more directly to the sublunary world and its seasonal cycles. The "better" resurrection looked for is beyond the hope figured conventionally by the coming of spring. Rossetti wants something more than whatever it is that serves mortal beauty, something which—by all the measures we can understand or imagine, by all that our reason can conceive or our poetries create—is impossible: A life in falling leaves. Rossetti's strongest poems are always extinguishing themselves.

In the stanza I just quoted, a line such as "No everlasting hills I see" epitomizes this quest for mortal extinction. The words involve a witty play on a commonplace of the Christian lexicon: "everlasting hills." The line "says" that one does not see/is not seeing/cannot see such hills. Yet in a worlded perspective and lexicon, the phrase "everlasting hills" is a conventional figure for everything that seems most permanent and enduring: hence its appropriation by Christian writers. Rossetti's line assumes the natural basis for the Christian figuration, but it proceeds to deconstruct that figure, to insist that if the expression "everlasting hills" is to be *religiously* understood, it must be stripped bare of all its mortal association. So, literally, one does not and cannot see the everlasting hills, not in the eyes, not in the mind, not even in the imagination. They are beyond all those human devices and can be known, in the end, only through death and by faith.

This poem seeks for a better resurrection than merely an emergence from a state of psychic depression, loneliness, and aridity. The poet prays to be removed from the world altogether, to be transformed into an utterly unimaginable object: "A royal cup for Him my King: / O Jesus, drink of me" (ll. 23–24). It is the literalness of this kind of desire and its expression that is so striking. Such desires reach for something beyond all quotidian experience. The words seem to tell us what that something is, but the words are strange, even frightening, because they are not translatable into known terms and quantities. Such a poem flirts with what twentieth-century secular thinkers might call "surreality" because it moves so aggressively against every current of worldliness. Its surreality is an indictment of worldly language and worlded attachments, whether personal or social.

This surreal method and otherworldly approach are characteristic of Rossetti, as the following sonnet illustrates:

> Ah woe is me for pleasure that is vain,
>> Ah woe is me for glory that is past:
>> Pleasure that bringeth sorrow at the last,
> Glory that at the last bringeth no gain!
> So saith the sinking heart; and so again
>> It shall say till the mighty angel-blast
>> Is blown, making the sun and moon aghast,
> And showering down the stars like sudden rain.
> And evermore men shall go fearfully
>> Bending beneath their weight of heaviness;
> And ancient men shall lie down wearily,
>> And strong men shall rise up in weariness;
> Yea, even the young shall answer sighingly,
>> Saying one to another: How vain it is!
>> ["Vanity of vanities"; I, 153]

The poem begins as a first-person lament but quickly modulates into a narrative mode. By the sixth line the impersonality of its revelation is established, and it moves from that point to extrapolate the spiritual meaning of any form of mortal experience. Like so much of Rossetti's work, this is an implacable, even a frightening, poem, utterly devoid of sentimentality. In Hopkins, evil comes to us as suffering and pain, and courts our sympathy; in Rossetti, by contrast, evil is what Coleridge once called a "positive negation."[13] It is something pure, either terrible or horrible. By the same token, in this poem as in "A better resurrection," the "good" or desired condition is itself so alien to everything we know or can imagine that it too is extremely disorienting and often appears in strange and disturbing forms. Or the "good"

---

[13]"Limbo" (l. 38) in *The Poems of Samuel Taylor Coleridge*, ed. E. H. Coleridge (1912; rpt. London: Oxford University Press, 1960), p. 431.

toward which the speaker moves will be glimpsed in its absence, an indescribable condition of being: in Wordsworth's terms, something "longed for, never seen."

> O fair, O fair Jerusalem,
>   How fair, how far away,
> When shall we see thy Jasper-gem
>   That gives thee light for day?
> Thy sea of glass like fire, thy streets
>   Of glass like virgin gold,
> Thy royal Elders on their seats,
>   Thy four beasts manifold.
>   ["Now they desire"; *PW*, p. 187]

Here is a glimpse of heaven, but what is its import, and whence does it come? Rossetti is not our authority, of course, since this language is entirely appropriated. The language of revelations, it stands at an a priori remove from mortal experience. When such language finds a form of human utterance, words are materialized, but they appear to us as words that have escaped the possibility of our understanding them. They are human words, but because their referents are finally not human at all, they are emptied of meaning and acquire instead a portentous but obscure import. What is a "sea of glass like fire," or how can a city "have" such a thing? What are "streets / Of glass like virgin gold" or "four beasts manifold"? It does no good to reach back for original texts in Scripture or their exegetical and iconographical translations. Rossetti's poetry works precisely because it forces us to read everything *simply,* in literal ways; to seek and therefore not to find any human or worlded equivalents for what we read.

Thus, even when it is operating in structures of beatitude such as those I have been quoting to this point, Rossetti's is fundamentally a poetry of loss. In this respect the tone of her work is close to Tennyson's when he is exploring the territories of loss and unhappiness in a religious frame of reference. But if she and Tennyson are the age's best religious poets of loss, they differ sharply from each other in the way they manage their losses. The difference recalls those I have previously noted between Rossetti and such writers as Ruskin, only in this case the difference is more revealing still because both Rossetti and Tennyson saw themselves, and were seen, as "religious." From Rossetti's point of view, however, a poem such as *In Memoriam* is often anything but "religious," and her work—set beside it—constitutes at once a critique of its ideology and (thereby) a revelation of its disguised meanings.

These differences between Tennyson and Rossetti are nicely highlighted by the review of *In Memoriam* which appeared in the Anglican journal the *English Review*. Virtually the only early notice of Tennyson's poem which adopted a critical line, the review argued that the religious faith of *In Memoriam* was often suspect, or even worse. Its summary statement on this matter is somewhat startling in the context of the accolades that Tennyson was receiving in all the other journals: "We remain undecided as to Mr. Tennyson's faith, though we opine, that, strictly speaking, *he has none*, whether negative or affirmative, and advise him, for his soul's good, to try to get one!"[14] To the fideist mind of this reviewer, Tennyson's poem is evidently—even confessedly—founded on doubt rather than belief. In Tennyson's poem, the reviewer says, "It is most falsely . . . assumed . . . that the unbeliever in Christianity can possess a faith of his own, quite as real and as stable as that of the believer" (p. 90). Such an attitude strikes the reviewer as mere "vanity and folly" (p. 93), however, and it contributes to various specific doctrinal problems in Tennyson's text. The reviewer quotes, for example, the following verses as an instance of a position that is "simply and purely blasphemy":

> Though truths in manhood darkly join,
>   Deep-seated in our mystic frame,
>   We yield all blessing to the name
> Of Him that made them current coin;
>
>   [sec. 36]

What the reviewer objects to is Tennyson's assertion that the redemptive meaning of the Christ is not original with the life of Jesus. The "truths" incarnated in Jesus are, for Tennyson, "Deep-seated in *our* mystic frame" and not in the christological event. To an orthodox mind this position is indeed "simply and purely blasphemy." (To a liberal or Broad Church mind, of course, it is nothing of the sort.)

Rossetti's poetry offers a sharp contrast to Tennyson's because her theology never skirts what she would have regarded as dangerous

---

[14]Reprinted in *Tennyson, "In Memoriam": A Casebook*, ed. John Dixon Hunt (London: Macmillan, 1970), p. 94. The text for the quotations from *In Memoriam*, below, is *The Poems of Tennyson*, ed. Christopher Ricks (London: Longmans, 1969).

liberal positions. The difference is especially clear in the two poets'
radically opposite views about the nature of history, time, and the
place of human beings in "the world." One of the fundamental ideas
in *In Memoriam* is a Victorian commonplace I have already glanced at:
that human life is cast in a morally evolutionist scheme. This view
leads Tennyson to famous imperatives like that in section 118—
"Move upward, working out the beast, / And let the ape and tiger
die"—and to the reformist theology that dominates every aspect of
the poem. *In Memoriam* represents Tennyson's vision of a benevolent
spiritual dimension in human history that "smilest, knowing all is
well":

> And all is well, though faith and form
>   Be sundered in the night of fear;
>   Well roars the storm to those that hear
> A deeper voice across the storm,
>
> Proclaiming social truth shall spread,
>   And justice. . . .
>
> [sec. 127]

Rossetti also heard "a deeper voice across the storm", but to her it did
not proclaim the evolution of "social truth . . . and justice"; it promised the end of the world (a world which she saw as a self-destructive
mechanism) and the advent of an unimaginably different life in Jesus,
beyond all things that ear has heard, or eye seen, or tongue told.

Paradoxically, such an orthodox position gives to her work a direct
social import that we find only indirectly and as it were accidentally
present in Hopkins's verse. In this respect Rossetti and Tennyson are
comparable poets, though of course Tennyson's social ideas are the
diametric opposites, on all essential points, of Rossetti's.

II

"Next to the Bible," Queen Victoria once told Tennyson, "*In
Memoriam* is my comfort."[15] Odd as it may seem to say so, this critical
appraisal fairly epitomizes the way many readers still approach poetry
today—that is, for a confirmation of their most cherished beliefs,

[15]Hallam Tennyson, *Alfred Lord Tennyson: A Memoir*, 2 vols. (New York: Macmillan, 1897), I, 485.

attitudes, and opinions. Interpretation is, accordingly, the art of translating works of poetry into the "current coin" of whatever (ideological) realms we occupy. To practice hermeneutics is, more often than not, to appropriate inherited works of poetry to the ideological apparatuses—or "interpretive communities"—that are currently dominant.

One of the great virtues of Rossetti's poetry lies in its radical alienness. I suppose one could find today certain Christian souls who might aver, after the manner of the dear and honored lady, that Rossetti's poetry is their comfort and solace. But they are not many. Indeed, even in her own day Rossetti represented, in her severe orthodoxy, a retrograde and diminishing vision. The present and the immediate future belonged to the progressivist ideology that Tennyson inherited from certain lines of Romanticism and which he bequeathed to certain lines of Modernism and its aftermath. Rossetti is not incorporate with those lines of domination, but she is also alienated from most currently accessible forms of thought which would raise up a critique of the dominant lines. For this reason she tends to stand apart, unsubmissive to all ideological appropriation, an item we do not easily consume in our interpretations, a value we find it difficult to exchange.

Rossetti's poetry brings then a signal opportunity for critical understanding. Because her antithesis to her own social world does not readily translate into ours, none of our preconceptions—even our antithetical ones—are reinforced when we read through her perspective. Today we often find it easy to assimilate, antithetically or otherwise, the cultural products we call "Victorian"; but when we are asked to evaluate those products according to Rossetti's scales and measures, we experience an objective alienness duplicated at the subjective level in our consciousness and our sense of perspective.

This duplicated estrangement-effect is reproduced in the poetry as a network of secrets, ambiguities, and deceptive surfaces. The poems repeatedly offer scenes or events or reflections that initially appear simple and transparent but which, when observed more closely, begin to dissolve in the play of the verse—as happens, for example, in a poem such as "May" ("I cannot tell you how it was"; I, 51) or "The lowest room" (I, 200–207). Alternatively, the poem may plunge the reader into a *selva oscura* right away, as we see with a poem such as "From house to home" (I, 82–88), which begins as follows:

> The first was like a dream thro' summer heat,
> The second like a tedious numbing swoon,

> When the half-frozen pulses lagged to beat
> Beneath a winter moon.

That "first" and that "second" are never actually located or identified
in the poem. They remain cryptic words to the end and stand as signs
of the poem's own portentous yet, finally, mysterious tale. To read
"From house to home" is to enter a poetical labyrinth that seems to
wind itself out but which only winds itself up. In the end, we will be
able to interpret it, but only on the following conditions: that we
recognize the arbitrariness—the semiology—of the interpretation.

These difficulties arise because such a poem is keyed to the mysteries of a Christian faith. What is reliable in Rossetti's work is always its
religious ground. But that ground—according to Rossetti's ideology—
is explicable only in terms of a set of verbal locutions that are themselves ultimately beyond the human understanding of mortal and social beings. Consequently, the "solutions" to her poems characteristically appear in linguistic forms that themselves require interpretation. Unlike Tennyson, Rossetti insists that there is, absolutely,
no "current coin" for the (spiritual) truths that (ought to) matter to
us. Thus many of Rossetti's poems formulate interpretive keys that can
and should be applied either to themselves or to other poems in her
corpus. But the keys themselves appear to us in need of other keys,
and the doors they unlock, or the puzzles they resolve, only reveal
other doors and further levels of puzzlement.

This structural procedure operates in the "secular" poetry as well. A
brilliant example will be found in the dramatic lyric called "The hour
and the ghost" (I, 40–42). The poem comprises a set of statements
and responses by three speakers who are named, in the order in which
they speak, Bride, Bridegroom, and Ghost. Each one speaks three
times, and the poem gradually unfolds a strange love triangle.

In the initial stage of the drama the Bride appeals to her Bridegroom
to "hold me fast" because she is being drawn away from him by
another love—the "Ghost" in the poem, who calls to her to "come
home." Ghost and Bride were lovers before Bride married Bridegroom,
and the drama establishes Ghost as an otherworldly lover, whereas
Bridegroom is associated with domestic and quotidian values (see, for
example, lines 5–7 and 9–10). Furthermore, when Ghost says to
Bride, "Come with me, fair and false, / To our home, come home" (ll.
11–12), we recognize the reproach that dominates the dramatic situation. Bride has been "false" to Ghost; indeed, the latter's appeal
operates precisely because Bride is dominated by a sense of guilt.

The second sequence of three responses reinforces the initial situation. The appeal of Ghost operates more powerfully on Bride at this point, and the two male figures set forth their claims upon Bride, and the value of their respective loves. As readers we, like Bride, are led to greater sympathy with the appeal of Ghost, partly because Bridegroom is made to represent mundane and unromantic values, and partly because the issue begins to appear as a moral decision of great spiritual consequence. It is as if the appeals of Ghost and Bridegroom involved the very salvation of Bride's soul.

With the final sequence Bride makes a decision that only heightens the drama's tension and irresolution. Though she finally responds in a positive way to Ghost's appeal, in fact she gives her heart to him only equivocally. It is as if she had decided to stay in body with Bridegroom but fly in spirit to Ghost, whom she addresses directly for the first time in the poem:

> O friend forsake me not,
> Forget not as I forgot:
> But keep thy heart for me,
> Keep thy faith true and bright;
> Thro' the lone cold winter night
> Perhaps I may come to thee.
>
> [ll. 42–47]

Bridegroom hears her words and tries to pacify what he takes to be her troubled spirit. Ghost then delivers the poem's concluding speech, a shocking revelation of love as a permanent condition of culpability and suffering.

> O fair frail sin,
> O poor harvest gathered in!
> Thou shalt visit him again
> To watch his heart grow cold;
> To know the gnawing pain
> I knew of old;
> To see one much more fair
> Fill up the vacant chair,
> Fill his heart, his children bear:—
> While thou and I together
> In the outcast weather
> Toss and howl and spin.
>
> [ll. 51–62]

Love is a drama of faithless faith and cruel attachments, of fantastic obsessions or worldly indifference. Remembering or forgetting, being true or being false: in either case one finds one's self either in the slough of the world or the fire of an outcast existence. The poem concludes with an allusion to Dante's Paolo and Francesca which undermines the romanticism of Ghost's appeal, but its indictment of Bridegroom's world is equally definitive. Ghost speaks finally as a Satanic figure, but his indictments of Bride and Bridegroom are nonetheless telling. Bride is actually, he says, a "poor harvest" and a "frail" sinner because she equivocates her attachments. All three are, in their different ways, lost souls, and the poem's disturbing use of biblical language only reinforces the presence of a judge who operates in the work but who never appears (as it were) in person.

According to this poem, erotic love exhausts itself—in several senses—in its domestic and romantic options, at least when that love is heterosexually conceived. Furthermore, the allegorical configuration of the poem so generalizes the field of its application that this form of love and desire appears wholly unredeemable. Such a poem raises a fundamental challenge to any reformist or liberal ideology, whether religious or secular, since it leaves the mind with little room to maneuver for acceptable meanings. Erotic love must either be renounced altogether—an unimaginable project in itself—or it must be translated into forms of desire which are equally unimaginable or unspeakable.

This set of contradictory circumstances is nicely dramatized in one of Rossetti's strongest and most typical poems, "Memory" (first published in 1866 in "The Prince's Progress" and Other Poems and written in two stages, part I in 1857, part II in 1865). Like "From house to home" and many of Rossetti's other works, this poem (I, 147–48) presents a subject which remains unidentified throughout.

I

I nursed it in my bosom while it lived,
    I hid it in my heart when it was dead;
In joy I sat alone, even so I grieved
    Alone and nothing said.

I shut the door to face the naked truth,
    I stood alone—I faced the truth alone,
Stripped bare of self-regard or forms of ruth
    Till first and last were shown.

I took the perfect balances and weighed;
   No shaking of my hand disturbed the poise;
Weighed, found it wanting: not a word I said,
   But silent made my choice.

None know the choice I made; I make it still.
   None know the choice I made and broke my heart,
Breaking mine idol: I have braced my will
   Once, chosen for once my part.

I broke it at a blow, I laid it cold,
   Crushed in my deep heart where it used to live.
My heart dies inch by inch; the time grows old,
   Grows old in which I grieve.

In one sense the poem is a riddle we are asked to solve. What is this "it," this form of idolatry, that the poem's "I" nursed, interrogated, broke, buried, and over which—as part II of the poem emphasizes—the speaker now keeps a vigil of eternal devotion?

II

I have a room whereinto no one enters
   Save I myself alone:
   There sits a blessed memory on a throne,
There my life centres;

While winter comes and goes—oh tedious comer!—
   And while its nip-wind blows;
   While bloom the bloodless lily and warm rose
Of lavish summer.

If any should force entrance he might see there
   One buried yet not dead,
   Before whose face I no more bow my head
Or bend my knee there;

But often in my worn life's autumn weather
   I watch there with clear eyes,
   And think how it will be in Paradise
When we're together.

"Love" seems the most obvious answer to the riddle, but "love" as an answer is only a word; and if we seek to flesh out that word, to "world" it with Rossetti's life and even perhaps with one or another of her putative lost loves, we will find the poem escaping us. In the end the devoted object might be called the speaking I's lost Self (whatever that might be) just as the "I" is the lost self of that other Self. The conditions of these losses are as mysterious as their expression is here overdetermined—this is the "secret" of Rossetti's poetry of secrecy. And because the losses will be made good only "in Paradise / When we're together," the understanding of the losses shares the same incapacity which the poem represents as the experience of loss.

Lost experience, lost expression: such is the poetry of Christina Rossetti. Yet through all these worlds and words that "pass away" and are never enough, appear the figures of eternity—mysterious forms of language which, having no meaning we can understand, in that very fact break away and offer hope. When Rossetti writes about "Paradise" (I, 221–22) and "the Mother Country" (I, 222–24), her language may appear conventional, as we have seen. Unlike Hopkins or Tennyson, however, Rossetti does not struggle against such language or seek after current equivalents. In fact, her language can have no equivalents, for it is what the eighteenth century liked to call "the language of Adam": the language used before the fall and which we learn only through death. All of Rossetti's poetry yearns toward such a language, which it embraces for its evident and radical non-translatability. The language of a poem such as "Paradise" is a *purely* referential language, it has no lateral life at all. A locus of desire, its images do not suggest hidden levels or unexplored relations, they stand in a kind of meaningless concretion, pointing elsewhere:

> Oh harps, oh crowns of plenteous stars,
>   Oh green palm branches many-leaved—
> Eye hath not seen, nor ear hath heard,
>   Nor heart conceived.
>
> [ll. 38–40]

Curiously, or perhaps appropriately, the poetry that most closely resembles this is the work of Christina Rossetti's brother, Dante Gabriel. One thinks particularly of "The Blessed Damozel," which, like so much of Christina's work, draws heavily on Dante, certain early Italian poets, and the book of Revelation for its religious imagery

and paraphernalia.[16] Christina's bold and literalistic aproach to Revelation is especially interesting when compared with Dante Gabriel's,
as these lines from "The Blessed Damozel" illustrate:

> When round his head the aureole clings,
>   And he is clothed in white,
> I'll take his hand and go with him
>   To the deep wells of light;
> As unto a stream we will step down,
>   And bathe there in God's sight.
>
> We two will stand beside that shrine,
>   Occult, withheld, untrod,
> Whose lamps are stirred continually
>   With prayer sent up to God;
> And see our old prayers, granted, melt,
>   Each like a little cloud.
>
> [ll. 73–84]

Much of this imagery is drawn from Revelation: the stream flowing
from the wells of light recalls that "pure river of the water of life, clear
as crystal, proceeding out of the throne of God" (22:1); the lamps are
taken from Revelation 4:5; and the figure of prayers "each like a little
cloud" evokes Revelation 5:8 and 8:3, in which prayers and incense
rise up from the altar before God's throne.

But Dante Gabriel's literalism is finally very different from Christina's—in fact, is put in the service of an erotic heaven that she would
not construct in her poems and would never approve in her mind. As
she once observed of this poem by her brother, it "falls short of
expressing the highest view."[17] That judgment, so simple and yet so
severe, measures the distance separating their Pre-Raphaelite styles,
with their different heavens and hells.

Nevertheless, their respective commitments to an imagination of
heavens and hells measure an important similarity as well; for both
Christina and Dante Gabriel wrote from and lived in imaginations of

---

[16]For a good discussion of this aspect of the poem, see Dante Gabriel Rossetti, *The
Blessed Damozel*, ed. Paull Franklin Baum (Chapel Hill, N. C.: University of North
Carolina Press, 1937), especially pp. xxxi–xlvi.

[17]Quoted in ibid., p. xiii.

desire that found no social or worlded equivalents. In this imaginative aspect of their works we see the antitheses through which both dealt with their period, and by which they preserve their relevance in our own luxurious and imperial world.

III

The essays in this volume show that Rossetti's work, for all its strangeness, has, after many years of neglect, begun to find an audience once again. The authors approach her poetry from various points of view. My own approach might appear to some to lay an excessive emphasis on the religious dimensions of her work—to draw the poetry and the doctrine into too close a relation. To others the approach will surely seem altogether too secular, as if the religious dimensions of the poetry were to be treated aesthetically, or sociologically, or anthropologically. Yet others might think that these introductory remarks have not sufficiently emphasized the challenge represented by Rossetti's work for our society and its cultural institutions.

Readers who share any of these views are urged to press on. As the essays collected here illustrate, Rossetti's work is only beginning to be seriously re-examined at this point, and no one yet understands the full significance which that work holds, even for our own day. In my own view, she, along with her brother Dante Gabriel, speaks in a tongue that will seem remarkably clear to various types of postmodern sensibility. These homologies become especially plain when one reads the essays here by William Whitla, W. David Shaw, and Dolores Rosenblum, but they operate as well, it seems to me, in the pieces by Roderick McGillis, Betty S. Flowers, D. M. R. Bentley, and Diane D'Amico, in which feminist issues and certain related socio-historical questions are raised retrospectively for Rossetti's work but addressed immediately to us. The methodologies of these critics are quite various, but each author draws important intersections with issues that have a lively relevance for current literary and cultural studies.

The remaining essays here, with one exception, are more restrictively or scholastically conceived. The simple lack of basic scholarly materials is nicely highlighted in Antony H. Harrison's essay on Rossetti's letters. David A. Kent examines a traditional Rossettian topic—the relation of Rossetti's poetry to Herbert's—and Jerome Bump performs a similar investigation into Rossetti's Pre-

Raphaelitism. These are essential points of departure for anyone reading Rossetti's poetry, but heretofore they have not been examined with any real thoroughness. P. G. Stanwood and Linda Schofield are concerned to describe certain parts of Rossetti's work in terms of that single most important topic, her religious and devotional ideas. Finally, Catherine Cantalupo—the exception I mentioned above—has written a polemical piece that wants to read Rossetti from within. The critique of Romanticism in this essay, which proceeds from a recuperated Rossettian ideology, is, in my view, especially interesting since it operates outside all the dominant ideological lines licensed by our current literary institution.

Readers of this book will find that each of these essays sometimes moves along very different salients. Not all these scholars will be able to agree with what I have written, here and elsewhere, about Rossetti and Herbert and Hopkins, or about Rossetti's relation to the Tractarian Movement, or about religious ideas and Pre-Raphaelite connections. And I dare say that they disagree with each other on a number of important matters. I find such disagreements more comforting than not, however, just as I prize Rossetti's work perhaps most highly for the ideological antithesis it originally embodied and has since come to epitomize. The Age of Equipoise—like the Second Empire so trenchantly exposed by Baudelaire and, after him, by his mediator Walter Benjamin[18]—bears some disturbing similarities to our own. In all three, alienation achieves such institutional perfection, such exquisite and extreme forms, that the truest critiques of such alienation appear in rare and unexpected representations—odors of sanctity, flowers of evil. Rossetti had much to say in her Age of Equipoise, and her work descends into our own Spectacular Society with a corresponding freshness and relevance.

[18]See Walter Benjamin's "On Some Motifs in Baudelaire," in *Illuminations*, ed. Hannah Arendt (New York: Schocken, 1969), pp. 155–200; and his "Paris, Capital of the Nineteenth Century," in *Reflections*, ed. Peter Demetz (New York: Harcourt Brace Jovanovich, 1978), pp. 146–62.

PART ONE

ROSSETTI: POET

W. David Shaw

Poet of Mystery:
The Art of Christina Rossetti

Though the severe symmetry of Christina Rossetti's lyrics and their strict economy of means provide her with the comforts of a limit, these comforts are continually being eroded in her poetry. Chasms keep opening, and a power she can neither name nor comprehend is continually invading and breaking down the refuge of her chastened language and her spare, demanding forms. In examining some of the formal devices that Rossetti uses to repress the anguish of a harrowed heart and to define her vision of at-onement with Christ, I want to suggest how the instability of the forms generates a sense of mystery that protects Rossetti against both her desire for closure and her anxiety that closure may be premature.

Often the sense of mystery in Rossetti's verse comes from uncertainty about which of four dreams, which of four worlds, the poet is describing. Is the poem a waking fantasy like *Goblin Market*, or a nightmare within the fallen world, or a dream that disturbs the poet's soul-sleep, or a vision of at-onement at the end of time? At the nightmarish depth of Rossetti's world we may locate a hell of scorn, hate, and rejection in love; at the upper reaches an undisplaced vision of Christ's Second Coming. Between these upper and lower limits are the worlds of everyday waking experience and of innocence. In the third of these four worlds, the torments of a battered heart have been censored and repressed. In the fourth world, of innocence, everyday experience has been sublimated into the pleasures of an earthly paradise whose pastoral landscapes and gardens are perhaps the most familiar region of Rossetti's poetic geography. Though the earthly paradise

W. David Shaw

is sometimes envisaged during the soul's sleep (the sleep that the soul undergoes at death and which ends only at the Last Judgment), nightmares of rejection and loss may, as in any dream, suddenly shatter the poet's peace.[1] Dreams may provide a measure of comfort by sublimating traumatic experiences, or even by displacing a terror of last judgments and final things. But dreams are also notoriously unstable and elusive. Apocalyptic visions of at-onement with Christ may revert without warning into some new vision of hell, in which Rossetti's mended heart is once more battered down and broken.

Only "love," Rossetti says, can understand "the mystery, whereof / We can but spell a surface history" ("Judge nothing before the time," ll. 1–2; II, 295). By "mystery" she means something like a secret science or withheld truth, as John Henry Newman defines these difficult ideas in his Oxford sermons. As God's Providence speaks less openly the more it promises,[2] so Rossetti's private theology of reserve speaks more obliquely the greater the meaning it has to impart. Because there are heartbreaking reasons for Rossetti's excessive scrupulosity, her asceticism, and her shattered hopes, she needs to keep her private meanings hidden from all but understanding readers. What speaks to Rossetti from the far side of death is the mystery of Christ's love, capable of picking up her broken heart and offering such solace as he can. Less veiled or mysterious ways of exploring her anguish and at-onement with Christ might have exposed Rossetti's harrowed heart to the sport of scoffing and insult, to which Newman says any high road open to all men would have exposed the mysteries of religious faith.

Anguish and Repression: The Harrowed Heart

We can best grasp the anguish of Rossetti's harrowed heart by comparing some lyrics of despair with their original versions. The lyric

[1]For an excellent account of how, by its very oddity, the "historical backwardness" of such theologically conservative doctrines as "soul's sleep" ("psychopannyschism") and millenarianism helps the modern critic isolate sources of Christina Rossetti's unique poetic energy, see Jerome J. McGann, "The Religious Poetry of Christina Rossetti," *Critical Inquiry* 10 (1983): 127–44. In Rossetti's lyrics of apocalyptic vision, a sense of urgency is imparted by the millenarian impulses that John O. Waller studies in his essay "Christ's Second Coming: Christina Rossetti and the Premillenarianist William Dodsworth," *Bulletin of the New York Public Library* 73 (1969): 465–82.

[2]John Henry Newman, "The Nature of Faith in Relation to Reason," in *Sermons Preached before the University of Oxford* (London: Rivingtons, 1887), p. 215. In her

"A Nightmare" (*PW*, p. 333) preserves only a rigorously censored fragment of its five-stanza original, "A Coast-Nightmare."[3] Only the first four lines and the last four remain. The original "love" in ghost-land has been made into a mere "friend" (l. 1). And the surprising fantasy of sexual mounting, in which the lover rides the poet in a nightmare, has been canceled. All that survives of that erotic fantasy is the image of the poet as a damaged detritus, a blood-red weed, wrenched and tossed by the sea: "Blood-red seaweeds drip along that coastland / By the strong sea wrenched and tost" ("A Nightmare," ll. 3–4). Grotesque feminine rhymes, "ghostland," "coastland" (ll. 1, 3), and especially the mock-horrific "nightmare," "sight there" (ll. 5, 7), help Rossetti distance the terror by joking about it.

> I have a friend in ghostland—
> Early found, ah me how early lost!—
> Blood-red seaweeds drip along that coastland
> By the strong sea wrenched and tost.
>   . . . . .
> If I wake he hunts me like a nightmare:
> I feel my hair stand up, my body creep:
> Without light I see a blasting sight there,
> See a secret I must keep.
>   ["A Nightmare, Fragment"]

We learn that a friend has been lost. But is the loss of the friend the cause of the poet's being wrenched and tossed? Or would *he* have wrenched and tossed her if she had not *arranged* to "lose" him? And in what precise sense is the friend really "lost"? He is certainly not lost in the sense of being forgotten, for he clings to the poet's mind like a nightmare she remembers. Even the syntax is ambiguous. The final "See" seems to be a principal verb in apposition to "I see." But it could also function as an imperative verb, an injunction to the reader to "see a secret" that is both shown and concealed. In this censored fragment it is as if the secret of Rossetti's harrowed heart were both seen and not seen, both kept and not kept.

---

sonnet "Cardinal Newman" (*PW*, p. 280), Rossetti commends Newman's doctrine of reserve, praising him for choosing "love not in the shallows but the deep" (l. 6).

[3]For full bibliographical details, see H. B. DeGroot, "Christina Rossetti's 'A Nightmare': A Fragment Completed," *Review of English Studies* 25, no. 93 (February 1973): 48–52. Rossetti has torn two pages from the notebook in the British Museum (pp. 25 and 26 of Ashley MS. 1364, no. 2), and in line 6 "rides" has been changed to "hunts."

In revising a poem such as "I thought to deal the death-stroke at a blow" (*PW*, p. 289), Rossetti compresses the tenor of whole quatrains into single lines and phrases. In the first version[4] the source of her disaffection is made too explicit. She talks about her buried youth, the night that killed the noontide of her days, and she even becomes self-pitying. The revised version is more honest: we believe more in her efforts to keep a tight rein on her affections. Even when the poet seems to will her death, there is a contrary pull.

> 'Oh rest,' I thought, 'in silence and the dark:
> Oh rest, if nothing else, from head to feet:
> Though I may see no more the poppied wheat,
>   Or sunny soaring lark.'
>> ["I thought to deal the death-stroke
>> at a blow," ll. 5–8]

The concessive clause in the last two quoted lines evokes Keats's thought of becoming a sod to the high requiem of the nightingale, and it swells into a comparable revulsion against death.

The poet's return to life is first a straying of attention, a mental wandering (ll. 21–22), that links her rebirth with the visionary vagrancy of the first stanza. The linkage of rebirth and vagrancy by means of open vowels and matching metrical forms draws attention to an equally important difference.

> Then sit to hear the low waves fret the shore,
>   Or watch the silent snow.
>> [ll. 3–4]
> I felt the sunshine glow again, and knew
>   The swallow on its track:
>> [ll. 23–24]

---

[4]Preserved in Bodleian Library MS. Don. e. 1, notebook 9. In place of the concessive clause in lines 7–8 of the revised version, the qualification of "yet" in the canceled second stanza is rhetorical only:

> Once and for ever: lapsing without end,
> Lapsing and yet perpetually the same,
> Wave after wave, a current without aim,
>   Where should such current tend?

The lapse of the sea that is perpetually the same is not a real surge toward action but merely a fretful eddy in an aimless ebb and flow.

26

"Low," "shore," "snow" (ll. 3–4) are linked phonetically with "glow," "swallow," "on" (ll. 23–24), but there is some disproportion in the word lengths and sounds. Alliance is never mistaken for identity. The affinities of the semantic patterns in stanza seven, where the words at the head of the first three lines are linked anaphorically as well as phonetically, "All birds awoke," "All buds awoke," "Ah too my heart woke" (ll. 25–27), are more affecting because of the deceiving sameness. Words sound similar but disguise different meanings.

> All birds awoke to building in the leaves,
> All buds awoke to fullness and sweet scent:
> Ah too my heart woke unawares, intent
> On fruitful harvest-sheaves.
>
> [ll. 25–28]

"All birds" refers to the whole of a species. But it may not be the whole of the poet's heart that awakes. She laments that, unlike the birds, she "cannot build [herself] a nest" (l. 31). The poet expresses mingled elation and regret that only a part of herself should seem to be alive.

Though deeply personal suffering nourishes many of Rossetti's best lyric poems, that suffering is usually most affecting when, as in the lyric "Listening" (PW, p. 313), it has been most carefully displaced. Originally, this poem was part of a longer lyric called "Two Choices," whose last stanzas disclosed the anguish of one who had elected to become, not a "cushat dove" like the wife with downcast eyes whose "pulses fluttered" to hear her husband speak, but a cold and loveless spinster. In the canceled coda of the longer poem,[5] the graceful bough

---

[5]Preserved in fol. 13–15 of Bodleian Library MS. Don. e, notebook 9. The canceled sixth and seventh stanzas originally read as follows:

> He chose what I had feared to choose.
>   (Ah which was wiser, I or he?)—
> He chose a love-warm priceless heart,
>   And I a cold bare dignity.
> He chose a life like stainless spring
>   That buds to summer's perfect glow;
>
> I chose a tedious dignity
>   As cold as cold as snow;
> He chose a garden of delights
>   Where still refreshing waters flow;
> I chose a barren wilderness
>   Whose buds died years ago.

The original second and fourth stanzas were also deleted.

and tendrils of the vine to which the modern Eve is now compared (ll. 7–8) were harrowing metaphors, harsh images of barrenness and waste, prompting the thought that the buds in Rossetti's wilderness died years ago. The husband has chosen in his cushat dove the kind of wife Rossetti could never consent to become. From possible wisdom she declines to cold dignity, then to mere tedious dignity, which is cold as snow. Worst of all are the barrenness and blasted buds, especially when contrasted with the Eden of delights and refreshing waters—that paradise of soul's sleep—from which Rossetti, while alive, has chosen to remove herself. The poet has learned the values of a cold bare dignity in youth, but has had no opportunity to learn romance as she grew older. For her there is no "natural sequel of an unnatural beginning," only the frustration of emptiness and loss. Once we restore "Listening"'s deleted stanzas, we realize that its vision of a domestic Eden is the vision of an outsider. The poem represents either the "listening" or the eavesdropping of a soul in hell, or else the dream of someone who is sleeping at last.

Though the poet's self-censorship is strict, her heartbreaking pain cannot be permanently repressed. Indeed, in the next poem Rossetti wrote, the sonnet "Dead before death" (I, 59), all the displaced suffering surges forth. Its bitter outburst appalled William Michael Rossetti,[6] who might better have appreciated the cause of his sister's acrimony had he consulted the manuscript notebook in his possession, which reveals how the domestic paradise of "Listening" had originally been disturbed by countervailing reflections of chaos and hell. We expect the sestet of a Petrarchan sonnet such as "Dead before death" to resolve or at least mute the despair of its octave. But the sestet of this sonnet uses the echoing vault of the poet's despair to set up new linkages of desolating sound. Indeed, this sonnet refuses to honor, as it were, its own generic promise. Even after the expression of despair ought formally to conclude, at the end of the octave, the echoes of desolation continue to sound through the last six lines:

> All fallen the blossom that no fruitage bore,
> All lost the present and the future time,
> All lost, all lost, the lapse that went before:

[6]See William Michael Rossetti's note, PW, p. 479; "I am unable to say," he admits in a perplexed tone, "what gave rise to this very intense and denunciatory outpouring."

So lost till death shut-to the opened door,
So lost from chime to everlasting chime,
So cold and lost for ever evermore.
["Dead before death," ll. 9–14]

The harshness of the anaphoric triads (ll. 9–11) is relieved only by
the reverberating wail of open vowels. "Evermore" answers "everlasting" and "for ever," and "So" and "cold" answer a series of other open
sounds: "Ah," "All," and "lost" (ll. 1, 9–11, 14). While the triadic
"So," "So," "So" (ll. 12–14) remains rigid, the echoing "lost"s hud-
dle close together (l. 11), then become predictably expansive. The
contraction of the chiming "ever"s, converging in the final "for ever
evermore," reverses this expanding pattern. Because the speaker's despair persists, "from chime to everlasting chime," even after we expect
it to be resolved at the end of the octave, we find that these echoes
that refuse to cease are not crowded with meaning but are mere hollow
sounds like the echo of Sin's words in *Paradise Lost*, a reverberation of
loss, desolation, and death: "I fled, and cri'd out DEATH: / Hell
trembl'd at the hideous Name, and sigh'd / From all her Caves, and
back resounded DEATH" (*Paradise Lost*, II. 787–89).

To turn the hell of a stony heart into an Eden of renewal or rebirth,
Rossetti will sometimes make literal losses figurative. In the revised
version of the lyric entitled "May" (" 'Sweet Life is dead.'—'Not so' ";
PW, p. 320), Rossetti replaces an active first-person use of the verb
"to build" with a noncommital passive form of the verb "to freeze":

'Twixt him and me a wall
Was frozen of earth-like stone
With brambles overgrown:
["May," ll. 17–19]

Originally, in building a wall of stone between herself and her lover,
Rossetti had only her own stony heart to blame for their separation
and estrangement.[7] The funeral she watched was not just the funeral

[7]See Bodleian Library MS. Don. e. 1, notebook 9, fol. 55–57. The lyric was
originally entitled "A Colloquy." In the extensively revised second stanza we can see
most clearly how a love lyric has been turned into a nature poem. Initially the second
stanza read as follows:

But love is dead to me;
I watched his funeral:
Cold poplars stood up tall

29

of the "worn-out year" (l. 12) but the funeral of a lover for whose death she seemed personally responsible. By contrast, in the revised version the colloquy between two voices evokes an un-localized event, which cannot be given just one name, as it could in the first version, where a specific lover had died. In the dividing wall of frozen "earth-like stone" (l. 18) there is something now that exceeds the picture of a literal wall as a riddle exceeds its solution.

> 'But Life is dead to me:
>   The worn-out year was failing,
>   West winds took up a wailing
>   To watch his funeral:
>   Bare poplars shivered tall
> And lank vines stretched to see.
>   'Twixt him and me a wall
> Was frozen of earth-like stone
>   With brambles overgrown:
> Chill darkness wrapped him like a pall,
>   And I am left alone.'
>   ["May," ll. 11–21)

If the masculine third-person pronouns in this stanza refer not just to "Life" but to a lover who has died or from whom Rossetti is actually estranged, then the "earth-like stone" is less an image than a phantasm. The pictures in the stanza possess hallucinatory power. Their obsession with wailing winds, shivering trees, stretching vines, and earth-like stone is indeed strange. But as tokens of estrangement and suppressed guilt, these dark phantasms are understandable; it is no wonder Rossetti can never quite shake them off. By turning a poem about thwarted love and guilt into a triumphal nature lyric, however, Rossetti is able to displace self-blame. Restorative power comes not in the form of another lover but as a life force from nowhere, catching the poet off guard.

> While yewtrees crouched to see
> And fair vines bowed the knee
>   Twixt him and me a wall
> I built of cold hard stone
>   With brambles overgrown;
> Chill darkness wraps him like a pall
> And I am left alone.

> I meet him day by day,
> Where bluest fountains flow
> And trees are white as snow . . .
> ["May," ll. 2–4]
> He makes my branch to bud and bear,
> And blossoms where I tread.
> ["May," ll. 30–31]

Stirred into being by pregnant caesural pauses between "branch," "bud" and "bear" (l. 30), and by strong rhymes such as "flow" and "snow" (ll. 3–4), as compared with the weakly trailing feminine rhymes, "failing," "wailing" (ll. 12–13), this new power imposes itself stealthily but irresistibly. Bound by obligation and love to the spring-time scene as she never could be bound to another heart, Rossetti finds that her throttled affections also start to grow and bud.

Originally, the mother in the ballad "Seeking Rest" (PW, p. 296) was not a literal mother but Mother Earth, with whom Rossetti hoped to be joined in death.[8] In seeking the greater objectivity of a ballad, Rossetti decided to delete the suicidal longing of the child who knocks at earth's greening door and who implores her mother to admit her. But in no sense are the silences of the final version marked by neatness and composure.

> My Mother said: 'The child is changed
> That used to be so still;
> All the day long she sings and sings,
> And seems to think no ill;
> She laughs as if some inward joy
> Her heart would overfill.'
>
> My Sisters said: 'No prythee tell
> Thy secret unto us:
> Let us rejoice with thee; for all
> Is surely prosperous,
> Thou art so merry: tell us, Sweet:
> We had not used thee thus.'

[8]The earlier version is preserved in Bodleian Library MS. Don. e, notebook 6, fols. 22–26. A lyrical ballad that now begins with the mother's lament for the child originally opened with the following words of the child: "She knocked at the Earth's greening door. / O Mother, let me in," an echo of the old man's petition in "The Pardoner's Tale": "And on the ground which is my modres gate / I knokke . . . / And saye, 'Leve moder, leet me in'" (ll. 441–43).

My Mother says: 'What ails the child
    Lately so blythe of cheer?
Art sick or sorry? Nay, it is
    The winter of the year;
Wait till the Springtime comes again,
    And the sweet flowers appear.'

My Sisters say: 'Come, sit with us,
    That we may weep with thee:
Show us thy grief that we may grieve:
    Yea haply, if we see
Thy sorrow, we may ease it; but
    Shall share it certainly.'

How should I share my pain, who kept
    My pleasure all my own?
My Spring will never come again;
    My pretty flowers have blown
For the last time; I can but sit
    And think and weep alone.

                    ["Seeking Rest"]

"Seeking Rest" is a deeply disquieting ballad, partly because of what it leaves out. The breaks at the end of the poem, "I can but sit / And think and weep alone" (ll. 29–30), are too sharply and strikingly placed to be only rhythmic breaks. Like the breaks between the stanzas, especially between stanzas two and three, where incommunicable joy turns to equally unfathomable grief, the caesuras are designed to juxtapose actions and thus avoid plot and explanation. The child is autistic. In her inexplicable joys she is as totally isolated from her mother and her sisters as she is strictly alone in her immedicable woes. These are "woes that nothing can be done for," as Frost would say,[9] the woes of someone for whom "spring will never come again" (l. 27), "woes flat and final." Though grief is merely a blank in this ballad—the absence of a joy that has been—enough of the original loss survives to unnerve the reader and intimate an absence that is

[9]Robert Frost, preface to E. A. Robinson's *King Jasper*, in *Selected Prose of Robert Frost*, ed. Hyde Cox and Edward Lathem (New York: Holt, Rinehart and Winston, 1966), p. 67.

best expressed in silence, a silence of private mourning and unshaka-
ble reserve. Contrary to what the mother and the sisters assume, the
silences do not result from the absence of something nameable such as
spring. The child is silent because she has a mute sense of the larger
strangenesses of life. She is also in the presence of a nothingness, a
void, which successive stanzas of the ballad forcefully intimate but
which no inquiry or surmise of the mother and the sisters can successfully explain.

Like the child in "Seeking Rest," Rossetti finds there are mysteries
about which she can either say nothing or else too much. In "Winter,
my secret" (I, 47) cutting, eliding, and covering up are all a means of
preserving silence about such mysteries. Volleys of multiple rhymes set
off humorous chain reactions in the poem.

> Perhaps some day, who knows?
> But not to-day; it froze, and blows, and snows
> [ll. 2–3]

> Come bounding and surrounding me,
> Come buffeting, astounding me
> [ll. 15–16]

By the time we reach the fourth internal rhyme in the second example, however, the joking has ceased to be merely amusing. Prying
readers may be less hostile or bitter than the fierce Russian snows. But
Rossetti prefers to leave that assumption untested. Winter destroys,
she muses, and springtime renewals are precarious at best. Perhaps the
only time to reveal secrets like hers is late midsummer. These seasonal
images are non-naming figures for the secrets of Rossetti's inner
weather. As charades for the mysteries Rossetti has locked up, these
figures betray a Zen-like propensity to tease the reader. Rossetti jokes
about what frightens her and coyly hints that her secret may be the
absence of any secret after all.

"After Death" (I, 37–38), another lyric of repressed anguish, is one
of those strange poems that seem spoken from the far side of the grave.
Instead of dreaming of some earthly paradise, the poet finds her soul-
sleep is disturbed by a vision of her own funeral. The dead poet
overhears her male friend, and in the silence she knows that he weeps.
But the most affecting gestures are all imaginary. Far more is conveyed
by what the friend does *not* do than what he does.

> He did not touch the shroud, or raise the fold
> That hid my face, or take my hand in his,
>   Or ruffle the smooth pillows for my head:
> He did not love me living;
>
> ["After Death," ll. 9–12]

The negatives fall with appalling force and culminate in a kind of brutal assault. Yet into the friend's two repeated phrases, " 'Poor child, poor child' " (l. 7), which are the only words he speaks, words memorable in context but barely meaningful, Rossetti has managed to gather all the powers of language. By the end of the lyric, however, with the cruel admission "He did not love [her] living," the coldness of the grave has returned, and the poet's diction has been purified of all false or wrong surmise. The poem seems to progress toward sheer vacancy. What arrests this progress is the silence of the friend. There is no question of the poet's coming into the presence of his love. But there is no clear absence of affection either. His response may be pitying, or just noncommital. Most questions Rossetti is tempted to ask are simply unanswerable. And since we seem to be listening from the silence of a grave, the lyric's capacity to recede from its focused point of experience, the poet's funeral, to the context that expands around that funeral, discloses a capacity to extend our uncertainty into infinity.

In the sonnet "Remember" (I, 37), again a lyric of barely repressed pain but spoken from this side of the grave, Rossetti discovers that the most exquisite and refined torture is, not to be forgotten by her beloved, but to inflict suffering on *him*. Tactful concern for the lover now displaces any self-centered desire to live on in his memory. As we move from the remoteness of the silent land to the intimacy of the lovers' day-by-day planning for a future that will never come, the poem gradually domesticates the terror, and also increasingly uses phrases that have a two-way meaning.

> Only remember me; you understand
> It will be late to counsel then or pray.
>
> ["Remember," ll. 7–8]

If the phrase "you understand" modifies "remember me," it is harsh and admonitory. But if it attaches itself to the clause "It will be late to counsel then," as it is invited to do syntactically and by the semicolon after "me," then the tone is gentle and commiserating. Rossetti is

34

saying in effect, "It will not help to say anything then, not even to pray with you."

After Rossetti is dead, her lover may, like Wordsworth, be surprised by joy and forget his dead friend. And if he should remember, the pain of being momentarily unfaithful to her memory may be almost as harrowing as the original shock of learning she is dead. The moral injunction "Only remember" (l. 7), which is the principal command of the octave, becomes in the sestet a mere hypothetical condition.

> Better by far you should forget and smile
> Than that you should remember and be sad.
> ["Remember," ll. 13–14]

The "should remember" of the final line is no longer the "should" of moral obligation. It is now a mere subjunctive of possibility, a bare hint or suggestion, nothing on which the poet who is solicitous of her beloved's well-being is willing to insist. "Harsh towards herself, towards others full of ruth." That line (l. 5) from "A Portrait" (I, 122) seems to me the best single comment on the courtesy and ease with which the sonnet "Remember" absorbs the pain of death, turning self-regard into an exquisitely refined contest in gentility and tact.

The Genesis of Wonder: Marvels and Commonplaces

In an effort to give limits to experiences that escape all bounds and limits, Rossetti often manages to generate a sense of mystery out of commonplace refrains and repetitions, out of a bare depleted diction, and out of austerely simple stanzaic forms and metres. Ordinarily, the comfort provided by a predictable refrain helps protect the mind against invasions of powers it is helpless to control. But when a familiar refrain takes on unpredictable new meanings, as does the phrase "Astonished Heaven" in Rossetti's lyric "Her seed; it shall bruise thy head" (II, 295), the comfort of a limit is continually being broken down. By using changing grammatical functions of "astonished" Rossetti can create an *experience* of that very astonishment which is evoked by what is indefinite, unlimited—ultimately beyond the power of any single word to define.

Refrains are a familiar form of domesticating mystery, of trying to bring the strange into the orbit of the commonplace and known. First heaven is astonished at the miracle of man's creation: "Astonished

W. David Shaw

Heaven looked on when man was made" (l. 1). This is merely conventional wonder and is appropriately conveyed by an adjective modifying a noun. But the oracle about the second Adam astonishes heav-
en in a different sense. To define the typological mystery of the lyric's
title, which prefigures the victory of the second Adam over Satan,
Rossetti seems to use "astonished" as a transitive verb that turns
"heaven" from a grammatical subject into an object:

> Surely that oracle of hope first said,
> Astonished Heaven.
>> ["Her seed; it shall bruise
>> thy head," ll. 3–4]

But how can "heaven," as the author of "that oracle," be astonished
by its own invention? The absence of any commas in the 1892 version
of line 3, the use of two commas in the 1904 version, one before
"first" and one after "said," and the use of only one comma in the
version preferred by R. W. Crump, which is the version I have quoted
(II, 455), suggests the grammatical instability of the lines, which
waver in emphasis between the effect on heaven of the oracle's pro-
nouncement and the burden of the oracle itself. If we register the
latter emphasis, it is as if the stanza's last line circles back on the
opening phrase, making the oracle's content nothing less than the first
quatrain of Rossetti's poem.

Most astonishing is the third use of "astonished." In confronting
the mystery of a final transformation we might expect Rossetti to use a
subjunctive verb: "Till one last trump shake earth, and" astonish
Heaven. Instead, she writes "and undismayed / Astonished Heaven"
(ll. 10–11). Perhaps in the eye of God the Last Judgment has already
occurred. Or is the past tense of "astonished" used to remind the
reader of the instability of all time-indicators? "Astonished heaven"
may simply be a nominative absolute construction, syntactically severed from the phrases that precede, as the soul that awakes at the end
of time is astonished to find a disintegrating world fall away around it.
Or is "Heaven," along with "earth," another direct object of the verb
shake"?

> Till one last trump shake earth, and undismayed
> Astonished Heaven.
>> [Her seed; it shall bruise
>> thy head," ll. 10–11]

36

If so, why is there a comma after "earth"? And if Rossetti is saying that the trump did not dismay "astonished Heaven," why does she use the past tense to describe a future action? David A. Kent reminds me that the active grammar may restore to life a buried pun in "undismayed." The trump that "unmakes" earth is able to astonish but not undo an "un-dis-made" or undismantled Heaven, invulnerable, at the end, to the grand annihilation. The ever-present alternatives to any single interpretation come from Rossetti's conviction that God's vision of the end of time is not her own, and that each renewed insight about change will disclose deeper problems concerning a mystery she can never quite adjust to, a strangeness she continues to ponder with fresh wonder.

To create marvels out of commonplaces Rossetti shows in other lyrics that not even the comfort of a depleted diction, used in a lyric of bare notation, can protect the mind from sudden invasions of something unalterably real, something for which she seems not responsible and which is not her own invention. In the harsh stresses and spare trimeters of a lyric such as "A Christmas carol" ("In the bleak mid-winter") (I, 216–17) Rossetti seems to be making a song out of the fewest possible words. Nature has been stripped of its warmth and beauty, even as the substantives are stripped of their articles:

> Frosty wind made moan,
> Earth stood hard as iron,
> ["In the bleak
> mid-winter," ll. 2–3]

With the suppression of feeling comes a suppression of syntax and an elision of the verb "stood" before the preposition "like": "Water like a stone" (l. 4). Even the hardness of earth is made more austere by harsh triple stresses. As Rossetti deliberately approaches tautology, the language subsides into childlike incantation: "Snow had fallen, snow on snow, / Snow on snow" (ll. 5–6). The effect is bleakly seductive, as in Frost's snow poems, and it opens up an endless regress of winters, back to "the bleak mid-winter" of "long ago" (ll. 7–8).

In each of the three middle stanzas the poem suddenly shifts into high celestial drama, then returns to the simplicities of the manger scene. Alternating between the wonders of angelic veneration and the lowly homage of "the ox and ass and camel" (l. 23), it is as if Rossetti were trying to seal off the limits of "bleak mid-winter" from the disturbing entry of a God whom "Heaven cannot hold . . . / Nor earth sustain" (ll. 9–10). In the lowly "stable-place" (l. 14) and "mangerful of hay" (l. 20) Rossetti seems to be seeking the comforts of a limit, a sufficiency, which will protect her against sudden invasions of a force she cannot control. When God "comes to reign" a second time, all form will be annihilated and "Heaven and earth" themselves "shall flee away" (ll. 11–12). In the meantime the severe symmetries of the three middle stanzas help Rossetti deny the essence of what she labels, which is an experience of an infinitude no world or poem can quite contain.

> Our God, Heaven cannot hold Him
>   Nor earth sustain;
> Heaven and earth shall flee away
>   When He comes to reign:
> In the bleak mid-winter
>   A stable-place sufficed
> The Lord God Almighty
>   Jesus Christ.
>
> Enough for Him, whom cherubim
>   Worship night and day,
> A breastful of milk
>   And a mangerful of hay;
> Enough for Him whom angels
>   Fall down before,
> The ox and ass and camel
>   Which adore.
>
> Angels and archangels
>   May have gathered there,
> Cherubim and seraphim
>   Thronged the air,
> But only His mother
>   In her maiden bliss
> Worshipped the Beloved
>   With a kiss.
>
>   ["In the bleak
>   mid-winter," ll. 9–32]

The alternation between the immensities of heaven and the limits of earth contracts from two units of four lines each in stanza two to four units of two lines each in stanza three, as if in imitation of the downward mobility of God himself. Then the pattern expands again into two units of four lines each in the fourth stanza. But there the infinitude of a form-annihilating God is replaced by the cosmic commotion of "angels and archangels" and of "cherubim and seraphim" as they throng the air (ll. 25–28). As infinitude moves down from heaven to earth, nothing can forestall the always unsettling experience of having to confront the high in the low, the marvelous in the commonplace. More privileged than the crowd of "angels and archangels," whose busywork in heaven may prevent an observer from coming face to face with mystery itself, is the loving mother, Mary, who alone has power to dispel all human nervousness at trying to put an undiminished truth inside the comforting limits of a poem. Incarnation is a category for what cannot be categorized. But by exercising her prerogative as a mother in worshiping "the Beloved / With a kiss" (ll. 31–32), Mary, like Rossetti as she composes her art of the heart, can make the reader actually experience the sufficiency of finite love to a universe that is boundless.

The sudden exaltation of the lowly "maiden" (l. 30) prepares for Rossetti's insistence at the end of the carol on the sufficiency of a single unadorned word—the poet's "heart." The gifts of the magi and of the heavenly cherubim and the gifts of the poor coexist, both plainly established, now without conflict and in reciprocal dignity.

> What can I give Him,
>   Poor as I am?
> If I were a shepherd
>   I would bring a lamb,
> If I were a wise man
>   I would do my part,—
> Yet what I can I give Him,
>   Give my heart.
>   ["In the bleak
>   mid-winter," ll. 33–40]

After the dash, the poet catches her breath before offering her heart. She drops the "I" and repeats the verb. The poet is poorer than a shepherd, who at least could bring a lamb. And, like Mary, she has no wisdom. But at the end of the carol Rossetti's intimate offerings of her heart and her art are wholly congruent. The confidence sponsored by this congruence can be felt in the lyricism of the last verse, which implicitly rebukes the stiffness of the bleak opening stanza. Its trochees are at once rigid and lilting, spare and weighted. As one of those rare lyrics in which apparent artlessness seems the greatest achievement of the poet's art, "In the bleak mid-winter" is really a response to Mary's directive in the sonnet "All Saints" (*PW*, p. 148). The greatest gift Rossetti can give is poetry of etched austerity and unadorned words, a poetry expressing her love of God—an art of the heart.

A riddling lyric such as "Mirrors of life and death" (II, 75–79) presents a series of mere syntactic fragments in which no principal subjects and verbs appear after the first two stanzas. The poem consists almost entirely of epic similes requiring grammatical completion in each reader's mind. And as readers try to supply a subject for Rossetti's three quatrains of beheaded predication in another enigmatic lyric, "A life's parallels," (II, 105), they are made to realize that the definition of a mystery is a contradiction in terms. Because nobody knows what death means, any definition of death as a parallel to life is in danger of imposing the false comfort of a limit, thus denying the mystery. By using the negatives "Never on this side of the grave again," "Never despairing," "looking back, ah never!" ("A life's parallels," ll. 1, 9, 10) and by writing a poem that lacks a principal clause, Rossetti is able to defy poetic closure and keep the reader in uncertainty. In such poems she combines a disturbing sense of what is incomplete, unlimited, or boundless with a comforting sense of the limits imposed by simple stanzaic forms, by strict anaphora, and even by the promise of some last or final word, which is then withheld.

The Darkness of God: The Comfort of Limits and Invasions of the Infinite

How can a poet make mystery intelligible without destroying the mystery? And how can she contemplate commonplace things with fresh wonderment and questioning without annihilating their commonness? In a group of lyrics envisaging the end of the world, the end of the poet's life, and the darkness of God, Rossetti tries to familiarize mystery by imposing upon it the comfort of a limit. But in order to hold meaning in reserve and keep alive a mute sense of strangeness Rossetti is continually extending or breaking down the limits she imposes. In the lyric "Praying Always" (II, 304), it is the mystery of "forever," already latent in the commonplace adverb "always," which is first being limited to the measurement of a clock, then imperceptibly transformed into something immeasurable. The repeating phrase "The clock strikes one" (ll. 2, 7) is a time-indicator that localizes events "after midnight" and "after mid-day." But the third use of "one" terminates the action like a stop watch "after noon and night" (l. 11) when, in the final stanza, time stops altogether. Although the preposition "after" appears to be used similarly in all three phrases, there is in fact a profound disparity between the first two and the final "After"s. The first phrase of stanza three, "After noon and night," is not another adverbial phrase like "after midnight" (l. 1) or "after mid-day" (l. 6). Because this third phrase is introduced by a nontemporal preposition, by an "after" *after* all befores and afters, its meaning is not to be found in any dictionary.

> After noon and night, one day
>> For ever one
>> Ends not, once begun.
> Whither away,
> O brothers and O sisters? Pause and pray.
>> ["Praying Always," ll. 11–15]

Like Arthur Hallam's summons to Tennyson from "that deep dawn behind the tomb" (*In Memoriam*, 46. 6), the summons to all brothers and sisters is a summons that speaks to Rossetti from the other side of silence.

An end is necessarily external to whatever it ends. To approach such an end in her poetry, Rossetti must confront a speechless and untimely event. In several elegies that envisage the end of her own life, Rossetti mutes a frightful sense of what awaits her by using familiar diction and an ascetically simple syntax to provide the comfort of a limit. From seductive nostalgia for lost butterflies and larks, for example, Rossetti's lyric "Life and death" (I, 155) moves hesitatingly to the shrunken and the minimal. The rigid anaphora, "Nor hear," "Nor mark," seems imposed upon resisting lyric materials by some harsh fiat of the poet's will.

> Nor hear the foamy lashing of the main,
> Nor mark the blackened bean-fields, nor where stood
>> Rich ranks of golden grain
> Only dead refuse stubble clothe the plain:
> Asleep from risk, asleep from pain.
>> ["Life and death," ll. 14–18]

41

The tone is that of a physician investigating her own terminal disease, then stoically writing her report. In dropping the verb "mark" and the conjunction "that" before "where" in line 15, for example, Rossetti contracts the syntax until the simple paratactic phrases and the declarative sentences shrink almost to the infantile.

In other elegies Rossetti dignifies and mutes the horror of concluding by making death's defiance of limits an acceptable form of peace. The contracted commentary of an elegy such as "Sleeping at last" (PW, p. 417) is delivered in the voice of a poet already dead who uses the inhuman skeleton of grammar, phrases stripped of all principal verbs, until the ninth line. Severed by sharp caesuras and unattached to a grammatical subject, the phrases in the first two stanzas stand like epitaphs, in strict autonomy. Whatever change of contour may be registered at the center of each stanza, every successive epitaph erodes the formality of its internal rhymes by celebrating a victory of the same indefiniteness and void:

> Cold and white, out of sight of friend and lover,
>
> [l. 3]

> Sleeping at last in a dreamless sleep locked fast.
>
> [l. 7]

The refrain at the end of each stanza, implying in the tenseless eternity of its participle "Sleeping" a perpetual release for Rossetti, is at first sad and ironic, then therapeutic, and finally unstable in its meaning, capable of facing two ways at once.

> Fast asleep. Singing birds in their leafy cover
>   Cannot wake her, nor shake her the gusty blast.
> Under the purple thyme and the purple clover,
>   Sleeping at last.
>
> ["Sleeping at last," ll. 8–11]

Though Rossetti is deaf to singing birds, she is also invulnerable to gusty blasts. The internal rhymes, "wake her," "shake her" (l. 9), and the inversion of word order, which makes the second clause in lines 8 and 9 a mirror image of the first clause, remind us how reversible the meanings are. The prepositional phrase and present participle in lines 10–11 might logically modify the repeated pronoun "her" in the preceding line. But the period at the end of line 9 cuts into the syntax, severing the last syntactic unit from the body of the stanza. The poem has a curious way of going on after it has grammatically concluded. Even as it were in death, the speaker uses a final protracted participle as if to defy closure and to oppose a sense of limits.

In one of her most exacting lyrics of suffering and depletion, "'A bruised reed shall he not break'" (I, 67–68), Rossetti systematically erodes the comfort of a limit by making the end lines of successive stanzas decline from the modest to the minimal: "Alas, I cannot will" (l. 8), "I cannot wish, alas!" (l. 16), "I do not deprecate" (l. 24). Each time the soul seems capable of doing less. But at least the final negation is an affirmation in disguise. To deprecate is to negate, but to negate that negation is already to prepare for a reversal of the soul's will-less state. Though no self-activity may be possible, Rossetti can at least anticipate the first faint stirring of affective life.

We think that God will appeal to the soul's memory of the Crucifixion as a way of restoring the poet's love. He will chastise her by asking, how can *you* forget? But this is not what Rossetti's God says. Rather, if God was crucified for this will-less (though not unwilling) soul, the question to be asked is: How can *I* forget?

> For thee I hung upon the cross in pain,
> How then can I forget?
> If thou as yet dost neither love, nor hate,
> Nor choose, nor wish,—resign thyself, be still
> Till I infuse love, hatred, longing, will.—
> I do not deprecate.
> ["'A bruised reed shall he not break,'" ll. 19–24]

Over the expected platitude Rossetti has inscribed her own censorship of platitude. On behalf of the poet's bruised and damaged soul, God has already suffered too much to forget her now. Nor does he presume to criticize or minimize her anguish, for he has known the same anguish himself.

Everything depends on the power of contraction. The final line is the most contracted of all, for here the utterance of both speakers— God and the soul—is gathered into a single concentrated phrase. Indeed, for the first time in the poem God and the soul are able to speak in unison. The last line, "I do not deprecate," is equally in character for either speaker. Though readers are shocked, I think, to find "hatred" included in the catalogue of affective states God chooses to "infuse"—love, hatred, longing, will—it is part of Rossetti's hon-

W. David Shaw

esty that she should make God the author of her hatred of himself. "All poetry is difficult," as T. S. Eliot reminds us, "almost impossible, to write: and one of the great permanent causes of error in writing poetry is the difficulty of distinguishing between what one really feels and what one would like to feel."[10] In this lyric about bruised and broken hearts Rossetti is trying to find in life's most minimal offerings something residual that will suffice. In examining the depletions of a skeletal life—the renunciations of a soul that has perhaps renounced too much, Rossetti contracts language to the vanishing point. But even as the refrains decline from the modest to the minimal, Rossetti shows how the last trace of a false refuge or comfort must be broken down and abandoned. Her exacting honesty makes her exhaustion harrowing, but that honesty is also part of her greatness as a poet.

Relief after Suffering: The Vision of At-Onement

In a fourth group of lyrics Rossetti combines two attitudes to God which are seldom found together. She speaks as if there were a divine attribute of justice that must be appeased. But she also shares the mystic's sense that the only atonement she has need of is an *atonement* or becoming one, with the divine nature. Too often in seeking the comfort of a limit, Rossetti builds a wall between herself and God. This wall can be broken down only when the poet learns to tutor her heart and discipline her affections. Only by achieving at-onement with God in the mystic's sense, can Rossetti understand how atonement in the traditional sense is possible.

In "Weary in well-doing" (I, 182) Rossetti must learn to make her life a chiasmus, a crossing-over from despair to hope, from brokenness and fragmentation to at-onement with God. But this crossing is at first a mere vexing: God simply crosses her will.

> I would have gone; God bade me stay:
> I would have worked; God bade me rest.
>
> Now I would stay; God bids me go:
> Now I would rest; God bids me work.
> ["Weary in well-doing," ll. 1–2, 6–7]

[10]T. S. Eliot, "George Herbert," *Spectator* 148 (March 12, 1932): 361.

The first two lines of the second stanza are the chiastic inversion of the first two lines of the first stanza. God's will seems an arbitrary reversal of everything Rossetti seeks. With the predictable mid-line caesuras in the first two lines and the strong breaks at the end of lines 3 and 4,

> He broke my will from day to day,
> He read my yearnings unexpressed
> And said them nay . . .
> ["Weary in well-doing," ll. 3–5]

Rossetti's emphatically rhymed tetrameters and dimeters compose a sequence of pauses filled by words. The caesuras are more than just breaks. They are cuts, deliberately inflicted to batter down and wound the heart. As Rossetti's broken will turns into a broken heart "tost to and fro" like damaged merchandise (l. 8), the mere deciphering of unexpressed desires becomes the more frightening terror of the doubting soul, who begins to question her faith in God.

The true chiasmus of a crossing over from emptiness to plenitude, from brokenness to true communion, comes only as a different kind of crossing—as a crossing of the line lengths in the final question:

> I go, Lord, where Thou sendest me;
> Day after day I plod and moil:
> But, Christ my God, when will it be
> That I may let alone my toil
> And rest with Thee?
> ["Weary in well-doing," ll. 11–15]

In the first three lines of stanzas 1 and 2, semantic units and line lengths coincide. The one-line units tend at first to isolate the "I" as a mere cipher confined to singular statements. But in the last stanza the line lengths of the semantic units begin to expand. The pattern of lines per semantic unit is 1, 1, 3 instead of 1, 1, 1, 2. The movement into the more spacious three-line unit provides a crossover from the individual to God. Through a slight augmentation of the two-line unit Rossetti shows how a soul that is broken and not at one strives for wholeness and at-onement.

In another lyric of crossing-over, " 'Love is strong as death' " (II, 164), the soul's initial neglect of God—it has not sought, found, or thirsted for God—sets the metaphorical terms for its own recovery of

45

at-onement. The searching, finding, thirsting God, who binds the perishing soul with love, repeats the metaphors of the first stanza, but with a powerful reversal of all they imply.

> "I have not sought Thee, I have not found Thee,
>   I have not thirsted for Thee:
> And now cold billows of death surround me,
> Buffeting billows of death astound me, —
>   Wilt Thou look upon, wilt Thou see
>   Thy perishing me?"
> "Yea, I have sought thee, yea, I have found thee,
>   Yea, I have thirsted for thee,
> Yea, long ago with love's bands I bound thee:
> Now the Everlasting Arms surround thee, —
>   Thro' death's darkness I look and see
>   And clasp thee to Me."
>
>   [" 'Love is strong as death' "]

The perspective changes as Rossetti turns away from the self-regard of the reiterated "me"s of the first stanza toward the welfare of "thee," the terminal rhyme word in the first four lines of stanza two. Both the capitalization of the final "me" and the change in speakers indicated by the punctuation suggest that the second speaker is God. But everything the second "I" says is also in character for the transformed soul of the opening stanza. Rossetti's attention is turned away from self-regard, focused instead on the omnipotent care of God, with whom she now seems at one.

Such refocusing infuses the verse with unprecedented new energies. The darkest fears in the lyric project a sense of protracted dying. The protraction is a result of using the spacious participial form "thy per-ishing me" (l. 6) to separate the two elements, human and divine, that the pronominal forms seek to join. But so appropriate is the changed perspective in the second stanza to both the transformed soul and God that by the end of the lyric, the poet and God, locked together by three binding verbs—"look and see / And clasp" (ll. 11–12)—can slip into each other. Lost in a coupling of pronouns, God and the soul are no longer divided, as they were at the end of the first stanza: "Thy perishing me." Now their union is celebrated by a syntactic convergence, by a fusing of "thee . . . Me" (l. 12) in an emphatic merging of persons.

Poems of quarreling and fractious debate usually set the terms of

46

their own resolution. A lyric of crossed wills may turn into a lyric of genuine crossing, but only if the poet's aimless questioning has a destination as well as a destiny. Even in a lyric such as "Up-Hill" (I, 65–66) the reader has a sense that the pilgrim's questions and the stranger's answers could go on forever. The inn is said to contain "beds for all who come" partly because the pilgrim is eager to rest and frames the appropriate question: "Will there be beds for me and all who seek?" (l. 15). Like a skilled Socratic ironist, the stranger withholds information. Instead of consolidating the mental level on which the pilgrim's questions are asked, the stranger's laconic answers are only as satisfactory as the pilgrim's questions. Better and fuller answers must await better questions.

The soul's ability to set the terms of its own recovery is nowhere more evident than in another poem of anguished crossing-over, the sonnet "Have I not striven, my God, and watched and prayed?" (II, 205), which rivals in intensity and despair the dark sonnets of Hopkins. The triad of alliterating verbs in the middle of the sonnet, "I grope and grasp not; gaze, but cannot see" (l. 7) recalls the leveling hammer blows of the opening line, with its polysyndeton and harsh triple stresses on the past participles: "Have I not stríven, my God, and wátched and praýed?" But this triad allows Rossetti to launch her final fearful question. When she is herself as God is now, out of sight and reach, will the God who has reduced her to nothingness in every other sense reduce to nothingness her shame as well? If so, the loneliness that has contracted her soul in the one-line questions of the sestet, generating the near insolence of her query "Is Thine Arm shortened that Thou canst not aid?" (l. 4), and using the strident internal rhyme "Face of Grace" (l. 3) to mock God's mere façade of godliness, has still to achieve that curious blend of intimacy and reverence which by the end of the sonnet must once more make her whole.

> Have I not striven, my God, and watched and prayed?
>   Have I not wrestled in mine agony?
>   Wherefore still turn Thy Face of Grace from me?
> Is Thine Arm shortened that Thou canst not aid?
> Thy silence breaks my heart: speak tho' to upbraid,
>   For Thy rebuke yet bids us follow Thee.
>   I grope and grasp not; gaze, but cannot see.
> When out of sight and reach my bed is made,
> And piteous men and women cease to blame

47

> Whispering and wistful of my gain or loss;
> Thou Who for my sake once didst feel the Cross,
> Lord, wilt Thou turn and look upon me then,
> And in Thy Glory bring to nought my shame,
> Confessing me to angels and to men?

One of this sonnet's curious features is the way it breaks at the end of the seventh line. The querulous self at the beginning is given only seven of the octave's normal eight lines, while the drive toward atonement occupies exactly half the sonnet. The spacious expansion of the final question, which occupies one more line than a conventional sestet, hesitatingly sets forth the search for wholeness. After the broken, halting syntax of the first seven lines, where the one-line anaphoric questions collapse into elliptical half-line confessions of heartbreak and despair, Rossetti is able to cross by the bold bridge of her spacious seven-line question to an imagined state of recovered wholeness and simplicity. This striking dramatic effect is lost in the sonnet's original manuscript version. Initially, the premature crossover at the end of line 5 made Rossetti's indictment of God too studied and rhetorical.

> Or is the load of one more sinner laid
> On Thee, too heavy a load for even Thee?
>   [ll. 5–6][11]

The anger is more desolating in the revised version, where it is allowed to break out into stark bereavement, "Thy silence breaks my heart," and then turn into an oddly abased but still reproachful prayer: "speak tho' to upbraid, / For Thy rebuke yet bids us follow Thee." In the final version all the steps of feeling are embodied in the short clauses, the sharp mid-line break after "heart" (l. 5), and in the strong end-line pauses. The chiasmus of the sonnet's last two lines, which encloses the phrases "my shame" and "me" between God's "glory" and the approval of his angelic witnesses, is a climactic crossing-over from nothing to all. The crossover ratifies and puts its seal, so to speak, on the syntactic and semantic drive of the broken-hearted petitioner who, though shattered and unwhole, also rediscovers the meaning of again being one with God.

---

[11]The original version, which appears in the notebook MS. in the British Library, is recorded by R. W. Crump (II, 410).

If there is nothing behind the mirrors of life and death but what we place in front of them, then only an active, loving self can ensure acceptable peace and at-onement after death. What, then, if Rossetti's nothingness in life should become a mirror image of the nothingness that awaits her on the other side of silence? Often Rossetti seems to be aspiring towards the condition of an exhausted bell jar. Is a soul that is passive, exhausted, depleted, truly able to assume a Christ-like identity? Will God intervene at the Last Judgment to make her broken heart whole? Or will he treat her as she has always treated her earthly lovers, as one who is proud, dismissive, cold?

These are some of the fears that murder peace of mind and that disturb Rossetti's visions of soul's sleep and apocalypse in poems such as her sonnet "Rest" (I, 60–61). Though Rossetti envisages a ceasing to be "until the morning of Eternity" (l. 12), her vision of a final crossover at the end of time is far less powerfully realized than her chiasmus of the grave, which frames the first two lines of the poem with an invocation of "Earth."

> O Earth, lie heavily upon her eyes;
> Seal her sweet eyes weary of watching, Earth;
>
> ["Rest," ll. 1–2]

Faith and hope rest on "evidence of things not seen." But what sustenance can they expect to find in a mere vacuum or void? Like the uncompromised austerity and leanness of the sonnet's diction, the spare degeneration of "a blessèd dearth" (l. 6), of an emptiness that nourishes, makes out of the ordinary and unenhanced a poetry of "sumptuous Destitution," to borrow Emily Dickinson's phrase.[12]

Rossetti finds that if God is to be merciful to her, she may have to create him in her own image. God may have to be severe with her now, just as she must be cruel with earthly lovers in order to be kind to them in heaven. Such is the oblique logic of Rossetti's elegiac dialogue between a woman and her suffering lover in "Doeth well . . . doeth better" (II, 315). The woman is lofty but tender, and includes the man in her plans: "Yet still she spoke of 'us' and spoke as 'we'" (l. 6). All the pathos of this lyric hinges on the refrain, whose impact changes each time it is used. "My love whose heart is tender" (l. 1) at first suggests fragility and the need for warmth: the moon "lacks light

---

[12]*The Poems of Emily Dickinson*, ed. Thomas H. Johnson, 3 vols. (Cambridge: Harvard University Press, Belknap Press, 1955), III, 952 (no. 1382).

except her sun befriend her" (l. 2). But the second time the refrain is used (l. 4), the tenderness seems to be cruelty in disguise. "'Let us keep tryst in heaven, dear Friend,' said she" (l. 3). Though this request seems cruel at the time it is made, the third stanza seems to justify it. At least in keeping her tryst, the woman has been faithful to her part of the bargain.

As in Wordsworth's elegy "A slumber did my spirit seal," statements are validated in ways that are as surprising as unforeseen. The last stanza proceeds in the same even tone, quiet and reasonable, yet implying the total destruction of the hopes the lover has nourished in the middle stanza.

> Now keeps she tryst beyond earth's utmost sea,
>   Wholly at rest, tho' storms should toss and rend her;
> And still she keeps my heart and keeps its key,
>   My love whose heart is tender.
>   ["Doeth well . . . doeth better," ll. 8–11]

The cold request, "Let us keep tryst in heaven," a seeming confusion of tenderness with cruelty when it is first made, is now validated by the inescapably literal fact of death, which puts the woman securely beyond earthly satisfactions. The calmness of the final stanza is the calmness of death. But the meaning of the third and final use of the refrain (l. 11) is uncertain. Does "love" modify "she" or "heart"? If the latter, then the man's heart is really the tender one. But if "love" modifies "she," and *her* heart is tender, in what sense is it tender? Does the speaker keep her lover more securely because she has denied him? Is heavenly love more sublime than earthly love because more sublimated? Perhaps the heart is too fragile a container for human love. If so, has the woman's "cruelty" in refusing to make the heart a vessel for earthly love been tenderness in disguise? It is as if every reading of such phrases is so true that any single reading must be false. The unstable meanings help preserve the lightly touched irony and surprise, refusing to make the irresolvable and the strange less mysterious than they are.

In another lyric of anticipated but deferred at-onement, "All heaven is blazing yet" (II, 317), Rossetti uses many connecting strategies— all part of the verbal sleight-of-hand and the contrived economy of means. The tremor of open vowels, including the four exclamatory "O"s, sends a quaver of barely supressed emotion down these lines. The tones range from the hopeful to despairing. Linking patterns of similar length and shape invite the reader to compare "O hope deferred, be still" (l. 12) with "O hope deferred, hope still" (l. 16). Lines 4 and 12 have the same shape, as do lines 5 and 6 and lines 13 and 14. Even the rhyme words in these similar pairs are nearly identical: "choose," "Will" (ll. 13, 14) and "chose," "will" (ll. 5, 6). The huddling together of repeated sounds is the shudder of a soul that laments what it has lost but that also resolves to gather up and concentrate its now diminished powers.

> All heaven is blazing yet
>   With the meridian sun:
> Make haste, unshadowing sun, make haste to set;
>   O lifeless life, have done.
> I choose what once I chose;
>   What once I willed, I will:
> Only the heart its own bereavement knows;
>   O clamorous heart, lie still.
> That which once I chose, I choose;
>   That which I willed, I will;
> That which I once refused, I still refuse:
>   O hope deferred, be still.
> That which I chose and choose
>   And will is Jesus' Will:
> He hath not lost his life who seems to lose:
>   O hope deferred, hope still.
>   ["All heaven is blazing yet"]

Linkages of shape and sound are most arresting when there is some disproportion between the members. Thus there are slight variations in the rhyme words, and the pattern of syntax in "be still" and "hope still" (ll. 12, 16) is only apparently identical. The first "still" is an adjective, meaning "quiet" or "serene," and the second "still" is an adverb, a synonym for "perpetually" or "nevertheless." Lines 5 and 6 are almost tautologies: "I choose what once I chose; / What once I willed, I will." Tautology is the most withholding of tropes, and part of Rossetti's private theology of reserve. But in lines 13 and 14, which bear a deceptive similarity to these analytic statements, the poet switches to a synthetic judgment. Now she adds in the predicate a meaning not given in the subject, an identification of the poet's will with Jesus' will.

The rhyme words "will," "still," "chose," and "choose" recur ten times in a sixteen-line poem. The shadow of depletion is on such chastened diction. It is as if a computer had been given a limited number of rhymes and instructed to produce a minimal narrative. The austere poetic economy extends to individual words such as "only," which pack maximum meaning into Rossetti's unlavish idiom by looking two ways at once. "Only" (l. 7) might mean "were it not for the fact that the heart in its aloneness is clamorous and unruly." Or it might mean that the heart and nothing but the heart "its own bereavement knows." Lines 5 and 6 produce chiastic inversions of each other: "I choose what once I chose; / What once I willed, I will." Lines 9 and 10 repeat the same syntactic pattern as lines 5 and 6, but use different accusative forms. Line 11 has approximately the same semantic shape, but there is some disproportion now in its greater length: "That which I once refused, I still refuse." Coincidence of syntactic units and line lengths concentrates the energy with astonishing economy of means. The final "hope deferred" (l. 16) is the hope of earthly joy, but what it hopes "still" is the hope of Paul. Renunciation and deferral are made more acceptable when they allow Rossetti to cross the divide that separates hope from Hope, the second of Paul's three Christian virtues.

In the lyric beginning "Lord, when my heart was whole I kept it back" ("'Afterward he repented, and went,'" II, 300), Rossetti wonders whether, now that her heart is broken, she can ever achieve at-onement with God. Why should God be expected to accept damaged goods? And yet God operates by love and is not bound by logic, she reflects. The broken heart she offers may also be most like God's, since his too was once broken on a cross. In the lyric "A heavy heart" (II, 305), the heart is at first the ponderous grammatical object of a transitive verb: "I offer Thee this heavy heart of me" (l. 2). In the last stanza the lightened heart is lifted, and it becomes grammatical subject instead of object.

> Lifted to Thee my heart weighs not so heavy,
> It leaps and lightens lifted up to Thee.
> [ll. 11–12]

In the final line, "Thy Face, me loving, for Thou lovest me," the first-person pronoun is twice framed by the divine "Thou" in an empathic merging of persons. The mirroring effect of the mid-line caesura and the chiasmus of "me loving, . . . lovest me" are devices of a poet who loves to handle varied grammatical elements, turning them over with fond and exact scrutiny. In finding the proper language of prayerful petition in "Sursam Corda" (II, 311–12), Rossetti also finds the means to lift up her heart, an action she is powerless to perform at the beginning of the lyric: "I cannot, Lord, lift up my heart to Thee" (l. 2). The proximity of "Lord" and "lift," and the remoteness of "I" and "lift," suggest who the real agent of the lifting must be. In a powerful chiasmus and an increasingly intimate progression of principal verbs, Rossetti implores God to take what she is powerless either to keep or give away:

> Stoop, Lord, and hearken, hearken, Lord, and do,
> And take my will, and take my heart, and take me too.
> ["Sursam Corda," ll. 8–9]

Of all Rossetti's poems on bruised or broken hearts, the lyric "Twice" (I, 124–26) is most affecting. It condenses most powerfully the repressions of both human and divine love and is therefore the riskiest of Rossetti's experiments in this genre. There is always a disquieting possibility that in experiencing the disappointment of her earthly love, Rossetti is simply rehearsing for a disappointment after death. Can religion entirely overcome the exhaustion, despair, and suffering reiterated in her secular lyrics? If God is as cruelly stringent as Rossetti, will her afterlife not be as resolutely chastened and impoverished as her present life? These are fearful questions for Rossetti to ask. She has staked all on God's love for *her:* she does not want to lose a wager twice.

"Twice" establishes a precarious but potent relation between the "You" of the first half of the lyric and the "Thou" of the second. Is God going to be any more generous or loving than the contemptuous "You" who coldly studied then rejected the proffered heart as he might have studied, then discarded, a flawed work of art?

> You took my heart in your hand
>   With a friendly smile,
> With a critical eye you scanned,
>   Then set it down,
> And said: It is unripe . . .
> ["Twice," ll. 9–13]

As in "A Fisher-Wife" (II, 109), in which the "heart sits leaden" in the fisher-wife's "breast" until brought into her "mouth" (ll. 4, 8), there is in this lyric a powerful interaction between figurative and literal meanings. Part of the human anatomy can be made to achieve metonymically what the whole body can never achieve: "You took my heart in your hand / . . . Then set it down, / . . . As you set it down it broke" (ll. 9, 12, 17). As the critical friend, who cannot really have loved Rossetti, handles the heart as he might handle a piece of pottery, the metonymy is made to come to life with shocking literalness and force.

The last three stanzas repeat the drama for a second time: two of the agents—Rossetti and her proffered heart—are the same, but God is substituted for the critical lover.

> This contemned of a man,
>> This marred one heedless day,
> This heart take Thou to scan
>
>> . . .
>
> I take my heart in my hand—
>> I shall not die, but live—
> Before Thy face I stand;
>> I, for Thou callest such:
> All that I have I bring,
>> All that I am I give,
> Smile Thou and I shall sing,
>> But shall not question much.
> ["Twice," ll. 33–35, 41–48]

In revising the original version of line 33, "This heart, contemned of a man,"[13] Rossetti seems too ashamed even to name her proffered gift. The heart becomes nothing more distinctive than a displaced object, a mere demonstrative pronoun detached for three lines from its proper referent: "This contemned . . . , / This marred . . . , / This heart take Thou to scan" (ll. 33–35). But even while intensifying the shock and pain of her earlier rejections, Rossetti now uses the altered refrain ("You took my heart in your hand" [l. 9], "I take my heart in my hand" [ll. 25, 41]), the new form of scanning and criticizing (which is now refining, not dismissive), the smile of God, which

[13]The penciled deletion of "heart" is noted by R. W. Crump (I, 273). For permission to quote from Rossetti's notebook manuscripts I am grateful to the British Library Board, the Bodleian Library of Oxford University, and Mrs. Imogen Dennis, who holds the copyright on the Bodleian manuscripts. (I am indebted to the Office of Research Administration at the University of Toronto for defraying these permission costs.)

replaces the cold stare of the friend, and the "I"'s singing instead of questioning to recall the correct other uses—not only in this lyric but also in other poems on bruised or broken hearts. "All that I am I give" (l. 46) harks back to the ending of "A Christmas carol": "I would do my part,— / Yet what I can I give Him, / Give my heart" (ll. 38–40). As Rossetti in her carol falters after the dash, she wonders if she will be able to make her offering and complete her song. Will the whole enterprise totter and come to ruin, as her heart has so often faltered and failed her? Even in the poem "Twice" the dash after "live" (l. 42) puts the outcome in doubt.

But Rossetti is saved by devices that are now familiar. In "A Christmas carol" the remote is made homely, an art of the heart, as biblical commonplaces are renewed and the ordinary becomes miraculous again. And in "Twice" the poet's simple promise to "sing" (l. 47) reverses the bleak ending of the third stanza: "Nor sung with the singing bird" (l. 24). Even the last line recalls and completes the meaning of line 22: "nor questioned since." Though the poet refuses to question in both instances, she does so for opposite reasons. "To question" in the third stanza was to be self-critical, or perhaps to question God's justice. Originally, Rossetti had lacked the heart to examine her own heart; she had not enough courage to be critical of others. Now she "shall not question much," not because she is afraid of any injustice she may expose, but because she is confident God's treatment of her will be just.

A poem such as "Twice" combines so many forms of mystery that each time we read the lyric it reveals a different facet. It allows us to review everything I have touched on in this essay: the anguish of Rossetti's harrowed heart; the possibility of her growth into wholeness and at-onement; the mystery of whether she can ever assume a Christ-like identity of her own; and the ultimate mystery of what will finally speak to her from the far side of death. A simplicity in complication characterizes this lyric's metaphors of situation. If one finds the art too ingenuous, then one simply does not care for Rossetti's kind of poetry. But then one would not, I think, care for George Herbert either: one would prefer Hopkins or Donne. In "Twice," as in Rossetti's best lyric poems, the mind and feelings move in harmony with the form. Only in less successful poems such as "Changing Chimes" (II, 329) will Rossetti construct a pun ("All men," "Amen," ll. 5, 10) in the mind only, without a corresponding change in her affections. Her best lyrics direct attention to the changing uses of a repeated phrase such as "Astonished Heaven" in "Her seed; it shall bruise thy head" or even to the repetition of a simple preposition such as "after" in "Praying Always." Only by following the slight adjustments of grammar, the hovering syntax, and the fluctuations of tone, can the reader enjoy Rossetti's complex play of meaning.

Some readers may feel that a lyric such as "Twice" should culminate in an act more impressive and less homely than the poet's taking her heart in her hand. But then, one realizes, this is an exact and powerful gesture. The offering of her heart is the most important gift she can make. The plain honesty of statement, intimating an almost mute depth of feeling, reverberates with the last line of "A Christmas carol," and has the same reassuring ordinariness and truth. The comfort of repeating syntactic and metrical patterns in a lyric such as "Twice" also helps the mind protect itself against invasions of powers it cannot fully control. But unless the poet remains open and vulnerable to such invasions, the removal of events from one side of the grave to the other may merely allow Rossetti's losses to expand into infinity. Her final vision of acceptable peace is a vision of a God who will redeem her imperfect love. He will not treat her the way she and her earthly lovers have treated each other. More immediate and poignant than the solemnities of her marriage feast in Revelation is Rossetti's vision in "Twice" of a divine lover, capable of picking up her broken heart and offering it such solace as he can. When the devotional poet stops looking at her brokenness and looks instead at the wholeness of Christ, she has already set the conditions for her recovery. Instead of remaining self-abased and depleted, Rossetti must learn to merge with God: she must trust that her broken heart will be acceptable to him and that she can find in her at-onement with him all the heart can wish.

D. M. R. Bentley

The Meretricious and the Meritorious in
Goblin Market: A Conjecture and an Analysis

Goblin Market is an enchanting and problematical poem. Its fantastic elements, its religious resonances, and its sexual undertones
have led to a wide variety of critical interpretations, as has the relationship between the poem's two sisters, who have been depicted
variously as Freudian children, figural types, practicing lesbians and,
most recently, as "sisters" in the feminist sense.[1] William Michael
Rossetti's hint, apropos the dedication of the poem to Maria Rossetti,
that some "particular" and unknown event occasioned the writing of
the poem (PW, p. 460), has provoked some writers to identify its two
sisters with Christina and the pious Maria and to associate its mysterious goblins with one or more of the men who may have prompted an
actual or contemplated "fall" on their creator's part.[2] This variety of
critical and biographical interpretations of Goblin Market seems to call
out loudly for an explanation of the poem that accounts for its various

I am grateful to the various colleagues and students at the University of Western
Ontario who provided ideas and suggestions helpful to the development of this essay.
    [1]See, for example, Dorothy Mermin, "Heroic Sisterhood in Goblin Market," VP 21
(1983): 107–18. Examples of other approaches to the poem listed above can be found
in Thomas Burnett Swann, Wonder and Whimsy: The Fantastic World of Christina
Rossetti (Francestown, N. H.: Marshall Jones Co., 1960), pp. 92–106; Marian
Shaulkhauser, "The Feminine Christ," VN 10 (Autumn 1956): 19–20; Maureen
Duffy, The Erotic World of Faery (New York: Avon, 1980), pp. 315–20; and the
notorious reprinting of Goblin Market with salacious illustrations in Playboy.
    [2]See, for example, Lona Mosk Packer, Christina Rossetti (Los Angeles: University of
California Press, 1963), pp. 141–52.

D. M. R. Bentley

elements and possibilities in a credibly reconciliatory manner—a simple but plausible proof, as it were, of its primary motivation and
purpose. Such, at least, was the thought that initiated the hypothesis
explored in this essay: the hypothesis that *Goblin Market* did not arise
merely from Christina Rossetti's well-documented concern with "fall-
en women" and their reclamation but that it was originally written as
an "exemplary tale made imaginative"[3] to be read aloud by Rossetti to
an audience of fallen women, perhaps in the company of the Anglican
Sisters with whom she associated herself at the St. Mary Magdalene
Home for Fallen Women at Highgate Hill. A superficial attraction of
this hypothesis is that it might explain the curious combination of
sexual and proverbial, Marian and Christological, affective and theological elements that constitute *Goblin Market*, as well as the very
presence in the poem of the wayward Laura and the saintly Lizzie. A
more recondite attraction of the hypothesis is that, by positing a
context of reading and listening for *Goblin Market*, it throws into relief
the extent to which the poem actually involves such aspects of reading
and listening as correctly interpreting "messages" and learning from
exemplary tales. Tempting as it may be to proceed directly to a discussion of the poem in the light of a possible intended audience of fallen
women and Anglican Sisters, our hypothesis must first be placed—
even if to its own detriment—in the context of known facts about the
genesis of *Goblin Market*.

I

On the evidence of the received chronology, which has *Goblin
Market* "composed April 27, 1859" (I, 234) and Christina Rossetti
beginning work at Highgate Hill sometime in 1860, it would appear
that our hypothesis is untenable, as indeed it may be. On close examination, however, the chronological table of events may seem uncertain enough to allow for the possibility that Rossetti was working at
Highgate Hill (or, it may be, on a related project) at the time she was
writing *Goblin Market* and that the hypothesis is at least logically
plausible. It is on the authority of Rossetti herself in two places—the
Dennis Notebook and a copy of the 1893 edition of *Goblin Market*—
that the poem is thought to have been written on April 27, 1859, and

[3]This is Oliver Elton's description of *The Prince's Progress* in his *Survey of English
Literature, 1830–1880* (London: Arnold, 1920), IV, 26.

58

it is on the authority of William Michael Rossetti, in a letter tran-scribed by Mackenzie Bell, that her work at Highgate Hill is presumed to have begun in 1860. To raise doubts about the absolute accuracy of the April 27, 1859, date, it is only necessary to take a practical rather than a romantic view of poetic composition. Is it likely that a highly accomplished poem of nearly six hundred lines was composed in one day? Is it not more likely that *Goblin Market* was composed over a considerable period of time, and that the April 27, 1859, in the Dennis Notebook is therefore arbitrary—the date of the poem's incep-tion, perhaps, or the date on which it reached a sufficient state of completion to warrant careful transcription? Lona Mosk Packer pro-vides some support for such speculations with the information that *Goblin Market* was transcribed, more or less in its final form, into the Dennis Notebooks over a period of more than nine months between March 21, 1859, and December 31, 1860,"[4] and further evidence is provided by Rossetti herself in her 1893 note: " 'Goblin Market' . . . was written (subject of course to subsequent revision) as long ago as April 27, 1859 . . ." (quoted in I, 234).

In view of this information, it is worth wondering whether the date of April 27, 1859, was not chosen by Rossetti as much for its spiritual significance as for its temporal accuracy. April 27 is the feast day of Saint Zita, the "patroness of domestic servants," who was "intensely devout and punctilious in her work . . . and spent much time visiting the sick and prisoners in jail"[5]—qualities that, as will be seen shortly, might have associated her with a poem such as *Goblin Market*. As G. B. Tennyson has observed, the dating of works "by reference to the appropriate feast day on the Church calendar" (*VDP*, p. 155) was a common practice among the Tractarians and their heirs in the nine-teenth century; in fact, Dante Gabriel Rossetti had in 1850 dated his own *Ecce Ancilla Domini!* March 1850 in reference to the feast of the Annunciation.[6] Be this as it may, there seems to be enough uncertain-ty surrounding the precise date of *Goblin Market*'s composition to necessitate a looser formulation of its genesis than has usually been proposed: though probably written largely in the spring of 1859, the poem may have been conceived earlier and completed later. That

[4]See Packer, *Christina Rossetti*, p. 421, n. 17.

[5]Donald Attwater, *The Penguin Dictionary of Saints* (Harmondsworth: Penguin, 1965), p. 348. Attwater bases his descriptions on Alban Butler's *The Lives of the . . . Saints* (1756–1759).

[6]As suggested by A. I. Grieve, *The Art of Dante Gabriel Rossetti: The Pre-Raphaelite Period, 1848–50* (Hingham, Norfolk: Real World Publications, 1973), p. 21.

Dante Gabriel turned his thoughts intensively to the fallen-woman theme between 1853 and 1858 (*Hesterna Rosa* and his two depictions of Mary Magdalene were executed in these years, as were the compositional studies for *Found* [1853–][7]), might suggest that the groundwork for his sister's poem was also laid at this time, a possibility supported by the chiasmic relationship between "Jenny" ("finished," according to William Michael Rossetti, "towards 1858, but again revised . . . in 1869")[8] and *Goblin Market*: not only does Christina's poem contain a Jeanie ("She thought of Jeanie in her grave, / Who should have been a bride;" ll. 312–13 and earlier) but Dante Gabriel's includes a cryptic reference to a goblin ("It makes a goblin of the sun").[9] These observations of course add little to those of the various critics who have discerned the connection between *Goblin Market* and the widespread interest in fallen women and related matters (such as awakening consciences) which was being given expression by various writers and artists from at least the late forties onward.[10]

In turning from the dating of the poem to the matter of when Rossetti began her association with the St. Mary Magdalene Home at Highgate Hill, the discussion enters what Margaret Sawtell calls the "uncharted time"[11]—the period from 1855 to 1861 when almost nothing precise is known about Rossetti's activities and ideas. What little is known comes primarily from William Michael Rossetti and one or two others. In his *Christina Rossetti: A Biographical and Critical Study*, Mackenzie Bell quotes a letter from William Michael which includes the information that "at one time (1860 to '70) [Rossetti] used pretty often to go to an Institution at Highgate for redeeming 'Fallen Women.'" William Michael continues, "It seems to me that at one time they wanted to make her a sort of superintendent there, but she declined"; and, he adds, "In her own neighborhood, Albany Street, she did a deal of district visiting and the like."[12] As notable as

[7]See Virginia Surtees, *The Paintings and Drawings of Dante Gabriel Rossetti (1828–1882): A Catalogue Raisonné*, 2 vols. (Oxford: Clarendon Press, 1971), I, no. 57 (*Hesterna Rosa*) and no. 64 (*Found*).

[8]*The Works of Dante Gabriel Rossetti*, ed. with Preface and Notes by William Michael Rossetti (London: Ellis, 1911), p. 649 (Notes).

[9]Ibid., p. 39.

[10]See, in addition to Packer, *Christina Rossetti*, Georgina Battiscombe, *Christina Rossetti: A Divided Life* (New York: Holt, Rinehart and Winston, 1981), p. 94.

[11]Margaret Sawtell, *Christina Rossetti: Her Life and Religion* (London: A. R. Mowbray, 1955), p. 51.

[12]Mackenzie Bell, *Christina Rossetti: A Biographical and Critical Study* (London: Hurst and Blackett, 1898), p. 54.

this for its (understandable) vagueness is William Michael's headnote in the *Family Letters* to the only letter written by Rossetti to any member of her family from autumn 1858 to autumn 1864.[13] The letter is dated October 25, 1861, and the pertinent part of the headnote reads: "The statement, 'I have promised to go to Highgate,' relates to an institution at Highgate for the reclamation and protection of women leading a vicious life: Christina stayed there from time to time, but not for lengthy periods together, taking part in the work.—The 'proofs' which she had to attend to must have belonged to her volume, *Goblin Market*, &c." (FL, p. 26). While incidentally associating *Goblin Market* with Highgate Hill, this headnote is, if anything, vaguer than the letter to Mackenzie Bell regarding the nature and chronology of Rossetti's "work" with fallen women; however, the accompanying letter, in which Rossetti notes that she expects "to be home again about the 13th [of November] if not before" (FL, p. 26), does indicate that, although she did not stay at the St. Mary Magdalene Home "for lengthy periods together," her stay on this occasion at least could have lasted for two to three weeks. That Rossetti's involvement with the work at the "House of Charity" (as she calls the St. Mary Magdalene Home in a note) was by 1860 quite intense is implied by a letter that William Michael quotes and dates as follows in the *Poetical Works*: "'Christina' (thus wrote Mrs. William Bell Scott in 1860) 'is now an associate, and wore the dress—which is very simple, elegant even; black with hanging sleeves, a muslin cap with lace edging, quite becoming to her with the veil.'" (PW, p. 485). Accepting 1860 as the year in which Rossetti both began work at the St. Mary Magdalene Home and became an "associate" of the Sisters of Charity who ran it, Packer and Georgina Battiscombe place such poems as "Cousin Kate" (1859; I, 239) and "'The iniquity of the fathers upon the children'" (1865; I, 164–78) in the context of her interest in "the unwed mother and the illegitimate child."[14] Packer, however, raises what she calls the "open question" of "whether the personal contact with the women at this institution [the St. Mary Magdalene Home] stimulated her interest in the social problem, or whether a previous interest led her to work with the women."[15] Recourse either to common sense or to Dante Gabriel's work of 1853–

[13]An earlier letter, the only one from 1854–1856 to 1858, is headed "H. H. [13 November, 1855]" and occasions William Michael's comment: "I do not now well remember where she was—possibly Hampstead Heath" (FL, pp. 23–24). Or possibly Highgate Hill?

[14]Packer, *Christina Rossetti*, p. 153.

[15]Ibid.

1858 or indeed to Packer's own notes indicates that this question is not really "open" at all: Rossetti must have been interested in fallen women and their problems well before 1860 and well before the writing of *Goblin Market*.

It is in a note to her chapter on the 1860–1863 period that Packer speculates about the direction in which Christina and Maria Rossetti were taken by their interest in fallen women and related matters. Packer quotes Canon Burrows of Christ Church, Albany Street to the effect that in 1852, probably through the "'expense . . . and exertions, of the Honorable Mrs. Chambers,'" there was started "'a house of refuge for fallen women . . . in Camden Street,'" which was "'probably . . . removed when Mrs. Chambers left the neighbourhood. What help we used afterwards to render to this cause,'" continues Burrows, "'was chiefly in connection with the Diocesan Penitentiary, St. Mary's, Highgate.'" Packer's comment on this statement is illuminating: "At one time Maria belonged to Mrs. Chambers' Young Women's Friendly Society, which attempted to provide recreation and religious instruction for servant girls on their Sunday afternoons off. This was probably the indirect route through which Christina eventually found her way up to Highgate Hill."[16] Since it would clearly be unrealistic to draw firm distinctions between "servant girls," "fallen women," and "unwed mothers," it would surely also be unrealistic to designate 1860 as a watershed year either for Rossetti's sociological or for her artistic concerns. The fanciful nature of its male protagonists, the "goblin" or "merchant" (l. 70) men, makes *Goblin Market* less realistic and more reserved than, say, "'The iniquity,'" but, as various critics have in fact perceived, it arguably arises from and addresses a similar set of concerns. But was it ever actually read to an audience at the Young Women's Friendly Society or at St. Mary Magdalene's, Highgate? The answer to this question can only be a grudging "perhaps" or a more speculative "possibly." The notoriously unreliable Violet Hunt has the Rossetti sisters "obsessed all their lives with [the] idea of moral salvage" and "reading aloud to sulky fallen women in grey-walled Homes at Highgate and in Portobello Road"[17] but whether such readings, if they ever took place (as does seem likely), included *Goblin Market* or simply, say, scriptural passages will probably never be known. It is thus on nearly the weakest of pre-

[16]Ibid., p. 422 n. 3.
[17]Violet Hunt, *The Wife of Rossetti: Her Life and Death* (London: John Lane, 1932), p. xii.

texts—a mere logical possibility—that the present conjecture must rest.

One public reading of *Goblin Market* prior to the poem's publication in 1862 is known to have occurred, however, and the circumstances and audience's response are worth recording here, if only for the light they shed on the reception of the poem in such a forum. In a letter of October 28, 1861, Rossetti's publisher, Alexander Macmillan, wrote to Dante Gabriel: "I took the liberty of reading the *Goblin Market* aloud to a number of people belonging to a small working-man's society here [Cambridge]. They seemed at first to wonder whether I was making fun of them; by degrees they got as still as death, and when I finished there was a tremendous burst of applause".[18] Not only does Macmillan's letter register the suitability of *Goblin Market* as a poem for reading to a relatively uneducated, possibly even illiterate, audience, but it tellingly charts that audience's response to the three, broad movements of the poem: the temptation of the two sisters by the "fruit-merchant men" (l. 553; a temptation that would likely seem less opaque to an audience composed of working women rather than working men); the deadly serious fall and sickening of Laura; and the recovery and happy ending effected by the heroic virtue of Lizzie.

Almost inevitably Macmillan's revealing reading of *Goblin Market* to a "working-man's society" recalls Rossetti's own distinction, vis-à-vis *The Prince's Progress*, between two audiences for her poem: a "general public" of "mean capacities" and a smaller audience of such "minds" as her own who could be expected to "catch . . . refined clues."[19] Without belaboring the hypothesis being advanced here, the point may be made that an audience composed of fallen women and Anglican Sisters—or, by the same token, of working men and educated readers—would contain something like the two groups distinguished by Rossetti as audiences for her later exemplary and imaginative tale. The point may also be made that the two audiences conceived by Rossetti for *The Prince's Progress* and posited by our hypothesis for *Goblin Market* are to an extent imaged by the two sisters in the earlier poem. Corresponding to the educated and, by definition, literate "readers" of the poem is Lizzie, the sister (Sister) whose moral reason enables her to interpret accurately such things as the

[18]Quoted in the introduction to *The Rossetti-Macmillan Letters*, ed. Lona Mosk Packer (Los Angeles: University of California Press, 1963), pp. 6–7.

[19]*Rossetti Papers: 1862–1870*, comp. William Michael Rossetti (1903; rpt. New York: AMS Press, 1970), p. 81.

goblins' fruit and her sister's illness and who, moreover, cautions Laura with the exemplary tale of Jeanie, a simulacrum within *Goblin Market* of the poem itself and its didactic purpose. Providing a focus in the poem for the self-recognition of the fallen woman/"listener" is Laura, the sister who allows her moral sense to be subverted by the materialistic erotics of the goblin men ("Come buy, come buy'") and hence permits her very life to be placed in jeopardy. Rescued from the fate of Jeanie by a sister's love and acquainted with deep remorse, a spiritually and physically regenerated Laura becomes at the conclusion of *Goblin Market* a wife, a mother, and (in another simulacrum of the poem's didactic aim) a teller of exemplary tales—a model of aspiration, that is, for anyone with the desire to change for the better and the belief that, with the help of "a sister" (l. 562) and the grace of God, good can be brought out of evil.

While the hypothesis of an original audience of fallen women and Anglican Sisters can hardly draw convincing support from the technical and formalistic features of *Goblin Market*, it might nevertheless be said that such aspects of the poem as its rescue plot, its exemplary nature, its optimistic conclusion, and even its affective style could well have been designed to complete themselves in an audience so constituted. Nor is the wonderful admixture of fantastic and metaphysical elements in Rossetti's "symbolic fairy story"[20] a combination that would have been inappropriate in the forum of a Young Women's Friendly Association or an Anglican House of Charity. By approaching such issues as male rapacity, sexual transgression, heroic virtue, and spiritual purgation indirectly, even diplomatically,[21] the "generalizing form" of *Goblin Market* allows the poem to perform its analytical, critical, congratulatory, and educative functions without appearing excessively personal or polemical. It could even be said that, in a manner akin to Tractarian reserve and Butlerian analogy,[22] the fantastic surface of *Goblin Market* serves a purpose of apocalyptic concealment—that is, it almost simultaneously conceals and reveals the poem's metaphysical subtext or overtext. Since enchantment very much gives way to education in the narrative movement of *Goblin Market*, it could also be said that its fantastic elements provide a brilliantly chosen means of achieving the emotional and imaginative

[20]Jerome J. McGann, "Christina Rossetti's Poems: A New Edition and a Revaluation," VS 23 (1980): 254.

[21]See ibid., p. 252.

[22]See G. B. Tennyson's superb discussion of these modes in the chapter "Tractarian Poetics" in *VDP*, pp. 12–71.

engagement that, in many of the most successful teaching situations (Christ's parables for example), precedes the kind of moral and intellectual awareness that can lead to self-analysis and to spiritual change. In fantasy, observes John H. Timmerman, "the reader uses the master-keys of the story to unlock ever-varying personal doors in [her] own life."[23] Although not writing specifically about *Goblin Market*, Jerome J. McGann astutely describes the demands the poem makes on any reader or listener: "For a morally committed artist like Rossetti," he writes, "multiple levels of meaning form part of a structure that tests the . . . powers of apprehension. Her poetic characters are themselves typically placed in situations where they are asked to distinguish the real from the illusory."[24] This description could easily be applied to *Goblin Market*'s readers and listeners, whether conjectured or critical, for as McGann says, "we too listen and try to detect the meaning of the words we encounter"[25] in a Rossetti poem. In whatever context it was or is heard or read, *Goblin Market* serves the Christian-humanist function of testing and strengthening, not merely an audience's reading skills, but also their moral and spiritual awareness. If it was not read at the St. Mary Magdalene Home, one cannot help but think that it should have been.

As the discussion now turns to a more detailed examination of *Goblin Market*, it does so, not in the hope of assembling internal support for the forgoing conjectures, but in the belief that the notion of a specific hermeneutical context for the poem in Rossetti's practical reenactment of Christ's ministry to Mary Magdalene may help to shed light on various aspects of her very complex masterpiece.

II

The first crux confronted in an encounter with *Goblin Market* is the meaning of the goblins themselves. By tradition, goblins are sinister beings who can lure humans into a realm of entrapment from which they are unable to escape.[26] While this traditional association may help explain Rossetti's choice of goblins as the vehicles for a tempta-

[23]John H. Timmerman, *Other Worlds: The Fantasy Genre* (Bowling Green, Ohio: Bowling Green University Popular Press, 1983), p. 8. I am grateful to Evelyn Dekker for drawing my attention to this book.

[24]McGann, "Christina Rossetti's Poems," pp. 241–42.

[25]Ibid., p. 242.

[26]See B. Ifor Evans, "The Sources of Christina Rossetti's 'Goblin Market,'" *Modern Language Review* 28 (April 1933): 156–65.

tion of deadly consequences, it does not fully explain the resonances and significances that gradually constellate themselves about the goblins in the course of the poem. Almost at the outset, before the young sisters Laura and Lizzie have been introduced by name, it is clear that the unfolding drama will involve "Maids"—that is, virginal, unmarried girls—and mysterious creatures whose reiterated chant of " 'Come buy our orchard fruits, / Come buy, come buy' " (ll. 3–4) has a prominently commercial note. The goblins' is a materialistic view of the world as a place of getting and spending, a view that can spring an ontological trap on the unwary, converting not just things but people into commodities. The sensual and sexual implications of the cajolings and fruits of the goblins soon become obvious to most readers not merely because of the "Maids/goblins" dialectic but also because of the suggestively human adjectives ("Plump," "Bloom-down-cheeked," "Swart-headed," "Wild free-born," [ll. 7–11]) applied to the fruits themselves. Surely an audience of "servant girls" or "fallen women" or "unmarried mothers" would have recognized almost immediately the sexual significance of the goblins and their fruit, a significance that the poet treats by analogy and with reserve but not—as the Freudian interpretations of *Goblin Market* would have it—without conscious awareness. The sensibility that created the goblins was that of a Victorian lady, a religious poet, and a social worker; the goblins' enacted enticings combine the concealment necessary for decency and the revelation necessary for the sexual nature of the unfolding events to be perceived in the proposed hermeneutical context of the poem. Also available to the ear in the goblins' enticing descriptions of their fruit are the biblical resonances of such words and phrases as "Apples" (the first-mentioned of the goblin fruits), "free-born" (Paul's words in Acts 22:28), "Fair eves that fly" (l. 18) and, later, "brookside rushes" (l. 33) that intimate subtly of other temptations and battles in the Old and New Testaments. To a lay person, particularly one participating through memory or fantasy in the enticings of the goblins, such biblical resonances might pass relatively unremarked. But to a consciousness alert to "refined clues," the consciousness of Rossetti herself or of an Anglican Sister, they would serve to associate the goblins with the Christian's three traditional and mortal enemies—the flesh, the world, and the devil—vanities which, it may be remarked, constitute the subject of a number of the "Devotional Poems" in the *Goblin Market* volume.[27] Considered more close-

---

[27]See, for example, "The three enemies" (I, 70–72) and "The World" (I, 76–77). The compartments in Rossetti's volumes ("Devotional Pieces" and non-devotional

ly, however, Rossetti's initial depiction of the cupidinous goblins and their "free-born" fruit, with its gestures toward Paul, might lead a theologically-minded reader to expect that a Pauline conception of sin will undergird the spiritual drama to follow. No doubt the emphasis on will in *Goblin Market* derives either directly or indirectly from Augustine[28] (who, of course, formulated the Christian will as a separate faculty), but such passages as the following from Romans 7:19–23 seem to speak directly of the conflict occasioned in Laura and Lizzie by the goblins and their fruit: "the good that I would I do not: but the evil which I would not, that I do . . . [because] sin . . . dwelleth in me. . . . For I delight in the law of God . . . but I see another law in my members, warring with the law of my mind, and bringing me into captivity to the law of sin."

When Laura and Lizzie are introduced by name in the second paragraph of the poem, they both apparently possess a knowledge of good and evil which is sufficient to enable them to recognize in the goblins and their fruit something dangerous and to be avoided. Although both sisters exhibit the physical signs of a Pauline conflict between spirit and flesh—"clasping arms and cautioning lips" versus "tingling cheeks and finger tips" (ll. 38–39)—their different physical gestures reveal their respective propensities to good and evil, or, it may be, their relative strength and weakness of will: Laura, exhibiting early signs of *akrasia*,[29] "bow[s] her head to hear," but the more socially-conscious Lizzie "veil[s] her blushes" (ll. 34–35). At the very moment when, in dutifully cautioning her sister against having commerce with the goblins ("'We must not look at goblin men, / We must not buy their fruits'"), Laura seems possessed of a social conscience, she is permitting her senses and her thoughts to be taken over by the "men" and "their fruits." The better to hear and see them she pricks "up her golden head," wondering aloud "upon what soil they fed / Their hungry thirsty roots" (ll. 41–45). Perhaps needless to say, the ambigu-

---

poems) are not watertight but, rather, dialogically connected: the non-devotional poems are dramatizations of moral and spiritual issues, and the "Devotional Pieces" are meditations on many of the same topics. The latter may thus be read in numerous instances as commentaries on the former and could have been used for such purposes in the context conjectured here for *Goblin Market*. In any event, a Rossetti volume is a more unified whole than many critics and editors have recognized.

[28]Several critics, for example Packer, *Christina Rossetti*, pp. 142–43, have noted the connection between Augustine's *Confessions* and *Goblin Market*.

[29]I am indebted to my philosopher friend C. Barry Hoffmaster for some stimulating conversations on Aristotle's treatment of the will in the *Nicomachean Ethics*.

ity in these lines of the "they" and "Their," both of which could refer either to the goblins or to their fruits, reinforces the sexual nature of Laura's curiosity. Laura is in fact in the process of committing the error described elsewhere in the *Goblin Market* volume in "One Certainty": she is allowing "The eye and ear" to be "filled with what they see and hear" (I, 72), thus rendering the mind all but incapable of focusing its thoughts on spiritual and moral issues. As if perceiving this danger, an agitated Lizzie reminds her sister of her moral duty—"'Laura, Laura, / You *should* not peep at goblin men'" (ll. 48–49, italics added)—and, in a telling gesture, exercises her will to control her own wayward members—"Lizzie covered up her eyes, / Covered close lest they *should* look" (ll. 50–51, italics added). As the auxiliary verb "*should*" in these quotations indicates, a Pauline battle is taking place in Lizzie between an attraction to evil and a desire for good. In the heat of this battle Lizzie not only retains her knowledge of good and evil, her power to make right judgments, but she also exhibits a strength of will that enables her first to close off her eyes (see no evil), then to "thrust a . . . finger / In each ear" (ll. 67–68) (hear no evil), and finally to flee the scene of the temptation (do no evil). The act of fleeing, of abandoning her sister to temptation, does not, of course, leave Lizzie blameless, for, as the analogue of *Paradise Lost* and the conclusion of *Goblin Market* alike affirm, people should stand by one another in times of trouble. And "curious Laura," choosing "to linger" and "wondering at each merchant man" (ll. 69–70), is indeed in trouble: with ears and eyes fully concentrated on the goblin men, she is quite incapable of exercising right reason to recognize evil and so save herself.

A sign of the impairment of Laura's reasoning abilities is her loss of interpretative skills. On first contact with the goblins she had been able to read their moral significance correctly enough to caution Lizzie in the auxiliary verbs of dutiful restraint: "'We *must not* look . . . / We *must not* buy'" (ll. 42–43, italics added). With Lizzie's departure, Laura's social and interpretative community disappears, and, with her reason impaired, she becomes merely a curious observer of physical shapes and sounds. Remarking the non-human, primarily bestial, physiognomy of the goblins—"One had a cat's face, / One whisked a tail, / One tramped at a rat's pace" (ll. 71–73)—she first fails to "read" these features at all and then, after one brief and correct reading of their sinister qualities—"One like a wombat *prowled obtuse* and furry" (l. 75, italics added)—she wrongly and dangerously misinterprets the significance of their voices:

> She heard a voice like voice of doves
> Cooing all together:
> They sounded kind and full of loves
> In the pleasant weather.
>
> [ll. 77–80]

The clichéd rhyme of "doves" and "loves" emphasizes the erroneous and delusive nature of Laura's thinking. Her interpretative failure becomes apparent if she is compared, for instance, to the speaker of "Jenny," a thoughtful reader of signs who continually attempts to discover the meaning of the sleeping prostitute within a teleological framework, using at one point the famous simile of the "toad within a stone"[30] to associate her with a primal, corrupting power ("Lust") that will be present in the world until the end of time. Laura, of course, refers the goblins to no such framework and, all evidence to the contrary, eventually addresses the "leering," "queer," "sly" brothers (ll. 93–96) as "good folk" (l. 116). It is no trivialization of Rossetti's poem to observe that Laura, lacking the interpretative skill and self-control of the speaker in "Jenny," becomes the victim in a drama that, for all its oblique, supernatural machinery, would have provoked many moments of self-recognition in an audience of streetwise Victorian working women.

Technically, the opening sections of *Goblin Market* are remarkable for their enactment, in sensual, incantatory, and cumulative (even hypnotic) rhythms, of the visual and aural appeal of the goblins and their fruit. From almost the beginning, with the invitation of the goblins to "'Come buy,'" the poem evinces an oral manner that converts even a reader into a listener, involving him or her in the gradual process of Laura's fall. Although John Ruskin objected to the irregularity of the verse in *Goblin Market*, Rossetti remained loyal to her chosen vehicle, perhaps in part because its compelling rhythms are emotionally involving (particularly when the poem is read aloud) and in part because its irregular form is perfectly matched both to the anarchic energies of the goblins and to the drama of free will that is central to the poem. Consider the centrifugal force generated by the superficially bewildering and irrational catalogue of similes that describe Laura's decisive movement toward the goblins:

---

[30]*Works of Dante Gabriel Rossetti*, p. 41. According to William Michael (ibid., Notes, p. 649), the toad passage "belongs . . . to the first draft of the poem"—i.e., the part written in 1847.

> Laura stretched her gleaming neck
> Like a rush-imbedded swan,
> Like a lily from the beck,
> Like a moonlit poplar branch,
> Like a vessel at the launch
> When its last restraint is gone.
>
> [ll. 81–86]

With the complicity of her own free will[31] Laura moves, the similes tell us, from a state akin to natural innocence to a state symbolized by the complex figure of the "vessel"—a boat without reason's captain, of course, but also a man-made receptacle destined for service and mastery. Such an extrapolation may seem to overemphasize the sexual-economic element in *Goblin Market,* but it gains support from the events that follow when "sweet-tooth Laura," now speaking in a "haste" that betokens her rash imprudence, confesses to the merchants her lack of money ("I have no copper in my purse, / I have no silver either") and accepts their suggestion that she purchase their fruit with "a golden curl" (ll. 115–25). In substituting for the absent "coin" (l. 116) a "precious" (l. 126) part of herself (and a sexually suggestive part at that), Laura accedes to a process of dehumanization and commercialization whereby she becomes simultaneously a buyer and a seller, a consumer and a commodity. The results of this transaction (which recalls the golden hair/golden coin dialectic in "Jenny") are immediate and pronounced: dropping a tear "more rare than pearl" (a conventional emblem of innocence) she "suck[s] and suck[s] and suck[s] the . . . / Fruits which that unknown orchard bore; . . . sucked until her lips were sore" (ll. 127–36). While many features of the description of Laura's fall—including the insistence on the "unknown" origins of the fruit and the observation that "men sell not such [fruit] in any town" (l. 101)—decently place the erotic significance of these events under erasure, as it were, there is no reason to doubt that Rossetti intended her protagonist's frenetic guzzling of the merchants' fruits to be understood in a sexual sense. It was, after all, commonplace in the Victorian period to equate childhood with Eden, and the loss of innocence that occurred at the eating of the apple with a sexual awakening.

It is unnecessary to follow in detail through the middle sections of

---

[31]See Packer, *Christina Rossetti,* pp. 144–45, for an astute discussion of the role of free will in the poem.

Goblin Market the spiritual debilitation of Laura that results from her eating of the goblins' fruit. Suffice it to say that Laura's experiences reveal that the fruits of the "unknown orchard" are not the fruits of the "tree of life" (l. 260). By her intercourse with the goblins, she no more betters her condition than did Eve; she merely trades off her innocence in favor of Job-like confusion (l. 139), dissatisfied cravings (ll. 165–66), and a host of deadly sins from gluttony (ll. 134–36), through envy (ll. 253–55), to sloth (ll. 293–96).[32] When Lizzie counsels her sister with "wise upbraidings" (l. 142) in the form of Jeanie's sad tale (ll. 143–62), the phrase " 'Twilight is not good for maidens' " (l. 144) speaks ironically to those who have understood the sexual nature of Laura's dealings with the goblins. When Laura replies by asserting that she " 'will / Buy more' " (ll. 167–68) fruit and marvels at how " 'odorous . . . must be the mead' " (l. 180) where they grow, a reader interested in the spiritual and psychological drama of the poem sees in her auxiliary verbs the language of a will dominated by *cupiditas* and a reason given over to fantasy. A gloss on the figures of Jeanie and Laura pining and dwindling toward death can be found in the prognostications of Paul in Romans 6:23: "For the wages of sin is death; but the gift of God is eternal life through Jesus Christ our Lord." An audience less attuned to theological issues, however, might see in the images of a Laura "sick in part" (l. 212) and "knocking at Death's door" (l. 321) and of a Lizzie seeking a "fiery antidote" (l. 559) to "poison in the blood" (l. 555) references to a more literally physical and sexual disease that would, indeed, have put "Jeanie in her grave, / Who should have been a bride" (ll. 312–13). Again, it would be underestimating Rossetti's social awareness, let alone that of her proposed audience, to place such matters over the horizon of the poem's meaning.

Shortly after Laura's fall there occurs one of the most strikingly pictorial passages in *Goblin Market*: the tableau of the two sisters, "golden head by golden head" (l. 184), sleeping together (as was a common Victorian practice) in one bed. As in the similarly pictorial description of Lizzie standing firm against the goblins later in the poem, the static (*ut pictura poesis*) quality of this double portrait suggests a stability that opposes itself to the anarchic and melodious (*ut musica poesis*) nature of the goblins. Not only does the double portrait

---

[32]An interesting parallel for this portion of *Goblin Market* can be found in "The Card-Dealer" (1849), in which Dante Gabriel alludes to the same passage in Job 10:22.

D. M. R. BENTLEY

of innocence and experience together laid recall the question, posed
by the speaker in "Jenny," of whether it would ever be possible for
"pure women" to gaze on an impure one,[33] but in imaging that very
possibility it confirms that, whatever differences separate Laura from
Lizzie (or fallen woman from Anglican Sister), innocence and experience can indeed associate with each other without damage to the
former. It is as if the love that exists between the alliteratively linked
Laura and Lizzie[34] is itself proof against the forces of evil, for as the
two girls lie "cheek to cheek and breast to breast / Locked together in
one nest" (ll. 197–98), the "lumbering owls" [forbear] to fly and "not
a bat [flaps] to and fro" (ll. 194–95). In insisting on both the similarity
and the dissimilarity of Laura and Lizzie at this point, the various
illustrative similes that describe them—"Like two blossoms on one
stem, / Like two flakes of new-fall'n snow" (ll. 188–89)—serve to
affirm the dichotomy *and* the community that exists between the two
girls: "One warbling for the mere bright day's delight, / One longing
for the night" (ll. 213–14). Lizzie and Laura are as different as day and
night, Anglican Sister and fallen woman, and yet, as members of a
community of women, they are also part of one another. Perhaps
Rossetti had the House of Charity at Highgate Hill particularly in
mind when, in the next movement of the poem, she depicted the two
girls rising together "when the first cock crowed his warning" (a

---

[33]See *Works of Dante Gabriel Rossetti*, p. 40. See also William E. Fredeman, *Pre-
Raphaelitism: A Bibliocritical Study* (Cambridge: Harvard University Press, 1965), fac-
ing p. 123, for an illustration of Rossetti's design of "Golden head by golden head" for
"Goblin Market" and Other Poems.

[34]McGann, "Christina Rossetti's Poems," p. 253, makes a similar point concerning
the alliterative connection of the girls' names but argues that Rossetti "does not draw
any moral distinctions between Laura and Lizzie." It is worth noting that the names of
the two sisters gesture in directions that are both similar and different—Laura's
towards Petrarchan love (the love of a sanctified woman) and Lizzie's—that is,
Elizabeth's (meaning oath of God)—towards Saint Elizabeth of Hungary, whose
renunciation of the world in favor of the cloister provided the subject for several
artistic works, sympathetic and hostile, in the decade prior to *Goblin Market*; see
Rossetti's "St. Elizabeth of Hungary" (*PW*, p. 150), a lyric that William Michael
dates "16 June 1852" and glosses (*PW*, p. 470) as a perhaps sarcastic response to James
Collinson's *The Renunciation of St. Elizabeth of Hungary* (1850–1851), itself a rep-
arative response to Charles Kingsley's negative treatment of the ascetic Elizabeth of
Hungary in *The Saint's Tragedy* (1848). William Michael also notes (*PW*, p. 477) that
the first and later ("21 November 1850") of the two sonnets in "A Portrait" (*PW*, p.
286) "was meant for Saint Elizabeth of Hungary, and was so entitled; Christina had
before then read with interest . . . *The Saint's Tragedy*."

reminder of Peter's denial of Christ and of his failure of duty), and proceeding to set "to rights the house," as well as to cook, sew, and talk "as modest maidens should" (ll. 200–209). Be this as it may, it is certainly true that, as *Goblin Market* proceeds toward the redemption of Laura by Lizzie, the connective love between the two sisters continues to be at least as important as the difference between their respective states or between any dichotomies (innocence and experience, sacred and profane love, fallen woman and saintly savior) that they might be thought to embody.

As Lizzie watches Laura's spiritual and physical decline, her sympathy for her sister prompts her to consider sharing her sorry plight (ll. 299–301), a road that, if taken, would have seen her following in Adam's footsteps after the fall of Eve and, in effect, letting all go by placing human love above spiritual duty.[35] Confronted by Laura's imminent death, however, Lizzie transcends the option of rehearsing the role of the first Adam and elects instead to follow the example of the second Adam: weighing "no more / Better and worse" (ll. 322–23)—that is, transcending the relativism of a simple-minded morality—she embarks with probity on an *imitatio Christi* that is not only a reenactment of Christ's atoning sacrifice but also an eloquent affirmation of a belief that a fallen Eve can, through the wedding of human love to a higher principle, become the redeemed Magdalene. Apparently recognizing that for evil to be exercised it must be confronted and contemplated, understood within the teleological framework that can lay it low, Lizzie goes at "twilight" to the goblins' domain and "for the first time in her life / [Begins] to listen and look" (ll. 326–28). Only when a pure woman's eyes and ears are thus opened, the speaker of "Jenny" might say, can the forces that produced her sister's fall and its contingent suffering be perceived and neutralized.

Lizzie's perception of the goblins is considerably more complex, anthropocentric, and morally determined than was Laura's: not only does she perceive their animalistic vitality as debasedly human ("Puffing and blowing, / Chuckling, clapping, crowing" [ll. 333–34]), she also perceives their facial expressions in terms of a deceptive sophistication: "Full of airs and graces, / Pulling wry faces, / Demure grimaces . . . " (ll. 337–39). Whereas Laura had been charmed and

---

[35]Cf. "Eve" in *"The Prince's Progress" and Other Poems*, I, 156–58. Given Rossetti's apparent dislike of *Paradise Lost* (see William Michael's *Memoir, PW*, p. lxx), it is tempting to see in both "Eve" and *Goblin Market* a residue of the Romantic penchant for rewriting Milton.

deluded by the resemblance between the goblin men and furry animals, Lizzie sees the creatures for what they are: little men who resemble the distasteful aspects of animals in their raucous, aggressive, and unctuous behavior. "Chattering like magpies, / Fluttering like pigeons, / Gliding like fishes," they hug, kiss, squeeze, and caress her (ll. 345–49).[36] But Lizzie's is a self-possessed, no-nonsense attitude. Interrupting the goblins as they extol the sensual pleasures of their fruit, she addresses them with those tried and true weapons of reason: irony, memory, and good manners: "'Good folk,'" she says, "Mindful of Jeanie: / "'Give me much and many,'" and she tosses them "her penny" (ll. 363–67). Few skirmishes either in the battle of the sexes or in the war against evil are easily won, of course, so it is hardly surprising that in the ensuing confrontation with the goblins Lizzie is subjected to an escalating barrage from the traditional weapons of evil and seduction: first comes fraud ("Such fruits as these / No man can carry" [ll. 375–76]), then insult ("One called her proud, / Cross-grained, uncivil" [ll. 394–95]), and finally force:

> They trod and hustled her,
> Elbowed and jostled her,
> Clawed with their nails,
> Barking, mewing, hissing, mocking,
> Tore her gown and soiled her stocking,
> Twitched her hair out by the roots,
> Stamped upon her tender feet,
> Held her hands and squeezed their fruits
> Against her mouth to make her eat.
>
> [ll. 399–407]

Whereas Laura's credulous and to an extent willful accession to the suggestions of the goblins would have provided a negative example to an audience of "servant girls" or "fallen women" of how easy, and therefore understandable, it is to be deluded by the agents of evil, Lizzie's behavior here provides a positive example of how, with ade-

---

[36]These lines may be indebted to the description of the attendants of Circe in *Endymion*, III. 500–503: " . . . all around her shapes, wizard and brute, / Laughing, and wailing, groveling, serpenting, / Shewing tooth, tusk, and venom-bag, and sting! / O such deformities!" (*The Poems of John Keats*, ed. Jack Stillinger [Cambridge: Harvard University Press, Belknap Press, 1978], p. 177), a possibility that permits the perception of the goblin men as the male equivalents of Dante Gabriel's *femmes fatales* of the 1850s and later.

quate foreknowledge, presence of mind, and strength of will, those same forces can be defeated. In the proposed hermeneutical context of *Goblin Market*, Lizzie's behavior in face of the goblins' aggression would doubtless have been seen as in the fullest sense exemplary.

The passage just quoted at length is followed by an extended and insistently pictorial description of Lizzie that employs the saintly and virginal colours of white, gold, and blue—the principal colors, as it happens, of Dante Gabriel's *Ecce Ancilla Domini!*—to lend an almost iconic force to the portrait. An audience of High Anglican Sisters and their associates would doubtless have also recognized in the description several conventional attributes of the Blessed Virgin:

> White and golden Lizzie stood,
> Like a lily in a flood,—
> Like a rock of blue-veined stone
> . . . . .
> Like a fruit-crowned orange-tree
> White with blossoms honey-sweet
> Sore beset by wasp and bee,—
> Like a royal virgin town
> Topped with gilded dome and spire
> Close beleaguered by a fleet
> Mad to tug her standard down.
> [ll. 408–21]

Obvious to the meanest capacity is the pun here on "standard" (as well as the implication that when anything virginal keeps its standard high it will remain untraduced, not to say "impregnable"). Less obvious in its complexity is the simile of the orange tree: referring Lizzie's stand against the goblins to an Edenic realm outside the cycles of linear time (whose movement has been emphasized from the first line of the poem), the co-present fruit and blossom of the orange tree may also be taken in their traditional senses as emblematic of bridal purity and marital fecundity, and so as proleptic of the domestic scene at the conclusion of *Goblin Market*. Also notable for its complexity is the simile of the "lily in the flood": in its association with the Virgin and with Easter, the "lily" is an emblem of both purity and sacrifice; and of course the "flood," like the resolutely Marian tenor of the passage, serves to locate Lizzie at a point of turning, a watershed, between evil and good. To a High Anglican nun reading or hearing the poem in its original context, the image that Lizzie represents—of courage and patience in the face of evil and in the cause of good—would have seemed both true to life and typologically inspirational.

It is important to a full understanding of *Goblin Market* to recognize the symmetry that exists in the poem on either side of Lizzie's voluntary and heroic act. Both Laura and Lizzie, on returning from their confrontation with the goblins, are described as not knowing "was it night or day" (l. 139 and l. 449). But this repetition only alerts the reader or listener to the essential differences and contrasts between the events before and after the still point of Lizzie's trial. Whereas Laura, in rashly succumbing to the goblins, had left behind her "golden curl" and come away with "one kernel-stone" (l. 138)[37] of their fruit, Lizzie, in patiently enduring their assaults, loses nothing of herself and returns even with "her penny . . . in her purse" (ll. 452–53). Whereas Laura's self-abasement leaves the goblins unscathed and herself spiritually debilitated, Lizzie's "resistance" leaves "the evil people / Worn out" (ll. 437–38) and herself gladdened with the "inward laughter" (l. 463) of a triumphant exorcist. The most important aspect of the inverted parallel between the encounters of the two girls with the goblins is that, by virtue of her heroism, Lizzie functions as a mediator of grace, transforming the "juice" of the goblins' fruit (a thing of its own nature indifferent) from a "poison" (l. 555) into an "antidote" (l. 559) or, to put the matter differently, consecrating an agent of evil so that it becomes a force for good. The eucharistic implications of this transformation or consecration are especially explicit when Lizzie, her face covered with "juice," echoes Christ's words at the Last Supper: " 'Eat me, drink me, love me,' " she tells Laura, " 'make much of me: / For your sake I have braved the glen / And had to do with goblin merchant men' " (ll. 471–74). Although Lizzie's role in *Goblin Market* as a type of the Virgin Saint and as an example of the *imitatio Christi* is complex, it is not opaque; indeed, it would probably have seemed perfectly transparent to the Anglican Sisters of the interpretational community for which the poem was arguably intended.

As we examine the penultimate section of the poem, the section describing Laura's regeneration, we must constantly bear in mind that, in helping to achieve her sister's rehabilitation, Lizzie gives her nothing she did not have at the beginning of the poem; Lizzie simply assists in restoring and enlightening faculties (reason, will) and qualities (love, duty) that Laura possessed in some measure originally and lost

---

[37]See McGann, "Christina Rossetti's Poems," pp. 274–75 for a fine discussion of the "kernel-stone" in relation to the "fruit of bad trees" in Matthew 7: 15–20.

in some measure at her fall. *Goblin Market* is the work of neither a
Pelagian nor an Arian but of a poet in the Anglican middle way
between Calvinistic determinism and Catholic sacramentalism. To be
sure, Lizzie serves as a mediator of grace in Laura's regeneration, but
Laura changes for the better because, far from being totally depraved
or alienated, she also has within her the will to change and the
remnants of her pre-fallen self. The very thought that Lizzie has
"'tasted / For [her] sake the fruit forbidden'" (ll. 478–79) elicits from
Laura an empathetic and self-castigating response—"'Must your light
like mine be hidden . . . Undone in mine undoing?'" (ll. 480–82)—
that is sufficient to initiate the process of compunction and regeneration. "Shaking with anguish, fear, and pain" (l. 491), she avails
herself of the benefits of Lizzie's Christian heroism:

> She clung about her sister,
> Kissed and kissed and kissed her:
> Tears once again
> Refreshed her shrunken eyes,
> Dropping like rain. . . .
>   [ll. 485–89]

Nature and grace, far from being at strife, are simultaneously present
at the inception of the process that, in the three paragraphs that
follow, takes Laura through the painful stages of repentance, remorse,
and purgation which the penitent must necessarily endure to achieve
true regeneration and salvation. As her revulsion for the fruits of evil
gives way first to loud and self-castigating lamentation and then to
strong intimations of freedom from sin (ll. 493–506), Laura becomes
subject to an increasingly violent scene of conflict between the purify-
ing "fire" of God's law and the "lesser flame" (ll. 507–9) of sin's law.
Little imagination is required to appreciate the effect on a contrite and
self-analytical audience at Highgate Hill of Rossetti's vivid portrayal of
Laura's movement toward the bitter self-recognition of "Ah! fool, to
choose such part / Of soul-consuming care!" (ll. 511–12). Here perhaps more than anywhere else in *Goblin Market* the reader becomes a
participant in the poem's spiritual drama: the battle is not for Laura's
soul but for the listener's. Just as earlier the virtuous and suffering
Lizzie had recalled Christ and the Blessed Virgin, so here the remorseful and contrite Laura recalls the redeemed prostitute who gave her
name to the St. Magdalene Home at Highgate Hill, an association
that would hardly have been lost on the poem's conjectured audience.

When, "pleasure past and anguish past" (l. 522), Laura falls at last into sleep, the action of the poem clearly echoes and reverses her previous fall toward sin and death. "Is it death or is it life?" (l. 523) asks the narrator in a moment of suspense that would work to good effect in a reading context. The answer, of course, is the succinct and gladdening "Life out of death" (l. 524) that issues in the penultimate section of the poem in what, for the poem's original audience, must have been an inspiring depiction of Laura's spiritual and physical regeneration:

> Laura awoke as from a dream,
> Laughed in the innocent old way,
> Hugged Lizzie but not twice or thrice;
> Her gleaming locks showed not one thread of grey,
> Her breath was sweet as May
> And light danced in her eyes.
>
> [ll. 537–42]

If evidence in support of the hypothesis presented in this essay were to be sought in these lines, it might be found in Laura's restrained attitude to Lizzie. This attitude, it might be argued, reflects the humility of a Christian social worker who, while not wishing to be totally self-effacing as an agent of redemption, would neither wish her charges to underestimate the efficacy of their own will to change for the better nor want them to forget the paramountcy of God's grace, working mysteriously even in a sleep such as Laura's, to bring the most prodigal daughter to herself (see Luke 15:17).

With Laura's hard-won and painfully achieved return to "the innocent old way," *Goblin Market* does not so much come full circle as indicate the possibility of placing a once wayward but now regenerated girl back into society at a higher level of experiential and moral awareness. With spiritual salvation and psychological transformation come the defeat of alienation and the possibility of social reintegration. So it is that the final paragraph of the poem, set "days, weeks, months, years" (l. 543) later, finds Laura and Lizzie safe within the domestic circle: both are "wives / With children of their own" (ll. 544–45). This optimistic conclusion of *Goblin Market* would have provided for the conjectured audience of the poem a romantic hope, a confident affirmation that personal disaster can indeed be overcome and unblighted happiness achieved. The poem's change in focus from youth to adulthood, with all its contingent responsibilities ("mother-hearts beset with fears, / . . . lives bound up in tender lives" [ll. 546–47]) is supported by a stylistic shift into composed, even austere, cadences far removed from the "iterated jingle / Of sugar baited words" (ll. 233–34) which had issued from the goblins. Betokening the spiritual and psychological composure of the reformed Laura—the convergence in her psyche of desire and duty—is the repeated "would" that governs and paces the description of her homiletic and hortatory activities: "Laura would call the little ones / And tell them of her early prime . . . Would talk about the haunted glen . . . Would tell them how her sister stood / In deadly peril to do her good . . . Would bid them cling together . . . " (ll. 548–61). In this simulacrum of the didactic function of *Goblin Market* itself, the repeated "would"'s speak of responsibilities willingly and habitually undertaken.

At the culmination of the poem's concern with will and duty, there thus stands a right-thinking Laura who draws on her own past experiences, as well as Lizzie's, to emphasize the importance of community and mutuality. Conscious by virtue of those experiences that the domestic circle and the human family must perpetually defend itself against forces that would "tug [its] standard down," Laura joins "hands to little hands" (l. 560) and speaks the poem's final, stirring lines:

> ". . . there is no friend like a sister
> In calm or stormy weather;
> To cheer one on the tedious way,
> To fetch one if one goes astray,
> To lift one if one totters down,
> To strengthen whilst one stands."
>
> [ll. 562–67]

The hermeneutical context for *Goblin Market* conjectured in this essay of course dictates that the word "sister" here would have been heard as a pun on "Sister." Viewed from such a perspective, Laura's closing speech has both a universal and a topical application: " 'the tedious way' " is at once the wearying path of quotidian life and the difficult way of Christian virtue; the tendency to go " 'astray' " and to totter down are references both to general backslidings and to particular falls; and the strengthening help provided by a " 'sister' " refers both to the support of a family member and to that of a religious community. The shift in grammatical structure in the final line from the " 'To . . . if' " pattern of previous clauses to the " 'To . . . whilst' " of " 'To strengthen whilst one stands' " suggests that, however strong a person is or becomes, a fall is always a possibility, and thus continuing moral and spiritual support is always a necessity. Such support would characterize any bonded community; no doubt it particularly characterized Mrs. Chambers's Young Women's Friendly Society and the St. Mary Magdalene Home at Highgate Hill.

It is a commonplace of Rossetti criticism to argue that the poet's puritanical sense of the vanity of things and her millenarian focus on the life to come frequently resulted in poems tending toward a repudiation of life and a longing for death. Molly Mahood, for example, remarks that "Christina Rossetti . . . tries to live on a single plane of existence, rejecting outright the temporal for the eternal; but by reason of this failure to understand the nodal function of human life, her rejection of a God-given world and her striving after an inaccessible heaven end only in the inertia and death-wish which were diseases of her age."[38] In *Goblin Market,* these tendencies are more than balanced by the implication that what matters is the use to which the things of the world (goblin fruit, human sensuality) are put and by the emphasis on living, working, and teaching in the world. The God-given, post-fallen, and post-incarnational world is what men and women choose to make of it: things and people can be bought and sold (the goblins), or they can be consumed and craved (Laura), or they can be consecrated and redeemed (Lizzie). By definition, a sacramental vision of reality such as Lizzie's involves not a rejection but an elevation of sensuality—its dedication to a higher purpose—hence the combination of sensual gratification and eucharistic reference in Laura's redemptive eating, drinking, and loving of her sister. Nor is it surprising or inconsistent that a poem by an Anglo-Catholic humanist, a deeply religious social worker who in the end rejected the call of the cloister, should conclude not by focusing on either a community of ascetics or a society of materialists, but by affirming procreative marriage and, with that background understood as a given, by confirming the humanistic and educative importance of the affection and responsibility of mother for child and sister for sister. As a result of its concern, both obvious and conjectured, for specifically female moral and social problems, *Goblin Market* has wide-ranging feminist implications. Neither those implications nor, indeed, the poem's female focus should obscure from a twentieth-century reader the larger religious and social framework in which *Goblin Market,* as much as, say, *Pilgrim's Progress* or *The Rape of*

[38]Molly Mahood, *Poetry and Humanism* (New Haven: Yale University Press, 1950), pp. 37–38. I am grateful to Tracy Ware for calling my attention to Mahood's book.

the Lock, locates itself. For Rossetti, women can and must play an enormous part in securing for themselves and for their children a social order that is better if only because more aware of the sort of materialistic and ontological traps that can be set and sprung "in groups or single, / [By] brisk fruit-merchant men" (ll. 240–41). But the "little hands" that Laura joins together in defense against the brutal, dehumanizing, and spiritually desecrating forces that encourage men to become goblins and women to become commodities are the hands, surely, of both girls and boys—the hands of a future generation of sisters and brothers. Responsibly affectionate men are conspicuous by their absence from the lives of Lizzie and Laura. *Goblin Market* does not preclude the hope that they will not be so in a future generation.

WILLIAM WHITLA

Questioning the Convention:
Christina Rossetti's Sonnet
Sequence "*Monna Innominata*"

In her late teens Christina Rossetti explored the formal poten-
tialities of the sonnet in the *bouts-rimés* exercises she did to rhyme
schemes suggested by her brother William.[1] Indeed, the whole family
was involved in writing sonnets (or in writing generally), partly encouraged by their poet-scholar father (himself famous as an *im-
provisatore*), partly to extend their own literary skills. On the cover of
each of the four issues the Pre-Raphaelite journal, *The Germ* (1850),
William Michael printed his sonnet, "When whoso merely hath a
little thought," the most obscure and pronominally awkward effort of
the circle. He later composed his own sequence, "Democratic Sonnets," written in 1881 but not published until 1907.[2] Dante Gabriel
Rossetti's *The House of Life*, published in 1870 and extensively revised
for *Ballads and Sonnets*, 1881, was one of the most famous and difficult
sequences of the century, and among the Rossettis' friends sonnet-
writing became almost a passion. Sequences were published by Elizabeth Barrett Browning (*Sonnets from the Portuguese*, 1850), George
Meredith (*Modern Love*, 1862), William Bell Scott (*Outside the Tem-*

[1]See R. W. Crump, "Eighteen Moment's Monuments: Christina Rossetti's *Bouts-
Rimé* Sonnets in the Troxell Collection," *Princeton University Library Chronicle* 33
(Spring 1972): 210–29. Four sonnets appeared in 1847 in *Verses by Christina Rossetti
Dedicated to Her Mother*, privately printed in London by her grandfather, Gaetano
Polidori; they were "Tasso and Leonora," "The Rose," "Sonnet. Lady Isabella," and
"'Vanity of Vanities.' Sonnet." Each rhymes *abba abba cd cd cd*.

[2]See Leonid M. Anshtein and William E. Fredeman, "William Michael Rossetti's
'Democratic Sonnets,'" *VS* 14 (1971): 241–74.

ple, 1875), and Swinburne (*Dirae*, 1875), to name only a few who built on the earlier Romantic rediscovery of the sonnet and the sequence.[3] It was Dante Gabriel Rossetti himself who coined the term "sequence" for a formal cycle of sonnets, and he gave it currency in 1881 when he used it as a subtitle to his own *House of Life:* "A Sonnet-Sequence".[4]

Aside from many separate and paired sonnets, Christina Rossetti published some six sequences during her lifetime, and another was issued posthumously. In August 1881 Macmillan issued *"A Pageant" and Other Poems*, which included four sequences: "Monna Innominata: A Sonnet of Sonnets" (fourteen sonnets), "Later Life: A Double Sonnet of Sonnets" (twenty-eight sonnets), "The thread of life" (three sonnets), and "If thou sayest, behold, we knew it not" (three sonnets). Of all of her sequences, "Monna Innominata" (II, 86–93) has attracted most acclaim from readers, but even that is not to say much since Rossetti's sonnets have been given little critical attention. Early reviewers noticed the sequence favorably, and polite things have been said about it in all books on Rossetti. In recent years it has been the subject of a few articles, two chapters in theses, and one full-length study.[5]

[3]See William T. Going, *Scanty Plot of Ground: Studies in the Victorian Sonnet* (The Hague: Mouton, 1976). Going notes that over 250 sequences were written between 1800 and 1900, and he provides a useful chronology of them. Arunodoy Bhattacharyya has examined the Romantic sonnet in *The Sonnet and the Major English Romantic Poets* (Calcutta: Firma KLM, 1976). Full details on the extensive literature are contained in Herbert S. Donow, *The Sonnet in England and America: A Bibliography of Criticism* (Westport, Conn.: Greenwood, 1982).

[4]Dante Gabriel Rossetti first used the term in writing to Hall Caine, who was preparing an anthology: see T. Hall Caine, *Recollections of Dante Gabriel Rossetti* (London: Elliot Stock, 1882), p. 244. But see also *OED*, s.v. "sequence" I, 1c: Gascoigne, *Posies* (1575): "three sonets in sequence." A first version of Rossetti's *House of Life*, consisting of fifty sonnets and eleven songs, appeared in his *Poems* of 1870; a completed version of 101 sonnets was issued in *Ballads and Sonnets* in 1881.

[5]See T. Hall Caine in *Academy* (August 27, 1881): 152; Theodore Watts-Dunton in *Athenaeum*, no. 2811 (September 10, 1881), pp. 327–28, who praises Rossetti's fluency, freedom from artificial constriction, and "Shakspearean [sic] sweetness"; and *Atlantic Monthly* 49 (January 1882): 121. The book-length studies are noted in the standard bibliographies, such as that of William E. Fredeman, "The Pre-Raphaelites," in *The Victorian Poets: A Guide to Research*, ed. Frederic E. Faverty (Cambridge: Harvard University Press, 1968), pp. 284–93. Recent critical articles and dissertations include Wister Jean Cook, "The Sonnets of Christina Rossetti: A Comparative Prosodic Analysis" (diss., Auburn University, 1971; *DAI* 32: 6419a–20a); Stuart Curran, "The Lyric Voice of Christina Rossetti," *VP* 9 (1971): 287–99; Sister Hum-

WILLIAM WHITLA

Book-length works on Rossetti have almost always been obsessed with reading her poetry as veiled autobiography. Even the one extended treatment of the sequence has been deflected from criticism into hunting for the ghosts of supposed lovers which might be hovering between the lines of the sonnets. So although Harry Boynton Caldwell devotes considerable space to thematic influences, the sonnet form, and the conceits, when he comes to "the interpretation" he accepts the supposed autobiographical nature of the sequence and pursues the ongoing quest for "the identification of Christina's beloved."[6] Caldwell conjectures that certain lines refer to James Collinson, others to Charles Bagot Cayley, and that sonnet 1 could refer to either. Noting that Collinson's death in April 1881 was followed in August by the sequence, he asserts it to be a monument "to those hours with James Collinson and Charles Bagot Cayley which were dead in terms of historical event but which were alive in the heart of the poetess" (p. 88). But in 1963 Lona Mosk Packer identified a new ghost in the poem: she alleged that the sequence is "in the main a subjective expression of emotion rather than an exercise of the literary imagination in the form of a recognized poetic convention."[7] To Packer, the sequence represents "Christina's initial response to the Penkill experience" with William Bell Scott. But Packer's whole thesis is based on supposition and is without a shred of firm external evidence, as William E. Fredeman has decisively shown.[8]

bert McCann, "The Influence of the *Dolce Stil Nuovo* on the Poetry of Christina Rossetti" (diss., University of Wisconsin, 1978; *DAI* 39: 6145a); Helen H. Wenger, "The Influence of the Bible in Christina Rossetti's *Monna Innominata*," *Christian Scholar's Review* 3 (1973): 15–24; Ann Holt Wion, " 'Give Me the Lowest Place': The Poetry of Christina Rossetti" (diss., Cornell University, 1976; *DAI* 37: 1574a–75a); Ralph A. Bellas, *Christina Rossetti* (Boston: Twayne, 1977), pp. 71–73.

[6]Harry Boynton Caldwell, "Christina Rossetti's '*Monna Innominata*': Criticism, Tradition, Interpretation" (M.A. thesis, Vanderbilt University, 1961), Kentucky Microcards, Series A: Modern Language Series, no. 109. In a triumph of tenuosness, Caldwell asserts concerning sonnet 12: "It appears that Miss Rossetti takes the [Petrarch] line out of context to flatter another woman who is loved by Christina's beloved. Certainly this second woman is implied throughout Sonnet XII . . . and, therefore, we can safely assign at least this sonnet . . . to either Charles Bagot Cayley or James Collinson if we discover another woman involved in the life of one or the other" (p. 63).

[7]Lona Mosk Packer, *Christina Rossetti* (Berkeley: University of California Press, 1963), p. 224.

[8]William E. Fredeman, " 'From Insult to Protect': The Pre-Raphaelites and the Biographical Fallacy," in *Sources for Reinterpretation: The Use of Nineteenth-Century*

Questioning the Convention: *"Monna Innominata"*

Critical articles on Rossetti's sequence have drawn attention to specific areas of interest in the poem or to particular sonnets, to her indebtedness to the Bible, to Dante and Petrarch, or to prosody (Caldwell astonishingly says that she "follows the Italian sonnet form only in a broad sense," p. 69), while most writers summarizing the life and works have contented themselves with brief adjectival evaluations coupled with reductionist paraphrase or précis. No one has even made the conventional formalist appeal to complexity to demonstrate excellence, nor has the sequence been subjected to any kind of syntactic, New Critical, linguistic, or poststructural analysis. In a wider perspective, little theoretical or critical attention has been given to the on-going problem of any love-sonnet sequence, the effort to contain the agony of the persona within a highly structured art form, and the apparent contradiction that constraint implies. The contradiction can easily be removed by a biographical appeal to a context beyond the poem, as each poetic signifier is alleged to refer univocally to a specific person in the real-life experience of the writer, for example, Christina Rossetti. Or the contradiction can be suppressed by exalting the creativity and genius of the author, her effort to impose unity on disparate elements, to remove ambiguity in favor of disclosure of meaning.

Rossetti's late-Romantic composite lyric, embodying the subjectivity of the poetic persona inherited from Wordsworth and his contemporaries, resists easy biographical equation with real life, and posits ambiguity and concealment of meaning as two of its chief poetic strategies. Hence we are invited to read the poem not as a positivist statement about an existential experience, nor as a historicist re-creation of something from the documented past. The point of view is introduced and limited in a prose "preface" to the poem, but it is not explained there.

By deconstructing this preface (together with the glosses of William Michael Rossetti and others) to make it a necessary pre-text experience for us as readers, we can see how explanation is resisted even as the poem is introduced. Furthermore, we begin to perceive how the dialectical assumptions of the sequence, set out frequently in an implied debate form, are determined. This deconstructive exercise makes up the first section of this essay. The following section considers how

---

Literary Documents: Essays in Honor of C. L. Cline (Austin: University of Texas Press, 1975), p. 70; see also Fredeman's review of Packer's biography in VS 8 (1965): 278–80.

the sequence mobilizes the conventional Petrarchan prosodic patterns, and to what effect. The third section examines the Italian epigraphs to each sonnet. In the first edition (where no translation was provided), these epigraphs obviously assumed some knowledge of Italian and so necessarily limited the audience capable of appreciating the full impact of the poem. Even where a translation is provided, as in William Michael's edition of his sister's *Poetical Works* (1904), we are not informed of the sources for the epigraphs that point behind the sequence to the tradition alluded to in the preface. The epigraphs, in fact, allude to texts of many other poets, texts embedded in the poems from which the epigraphs are drawn. The appositeness of the epigraphs, or their formulation of a problematic poetics for the sonnet to which they are attached, provides an opportunity for intertextual exploration. Finally, in the last two sections, I look at the sequence itself, and especially at the convention of the love sonnet which is continually brought into the foreground only to be challenged and decentered by contradictions of form and content, and by a radical questioning of the very premises that are set up elsewhere in the poem.[9]

[9]The conventions of the sonnet sequence have been explored in an extensive critical literature that includes C. S. Lewis, *Allegory of Love* (Oxford: Clarendon Press, 1936); Lisle Cecil John, *The Elizabethan Sonnet Sequences: Studies in Conventional Conceits* (New York: Columbia University Press, 1938); Lu Emily Pearson, *Elizabethan Love Conventions* (London: Allen & Unwin, 1938); J. B. Broadbent, *Poetic Love* (New York: Barnes & Noble, 1964). For an index to the many studies of the courtly love tradition and its interpretation, see the articles and bibliography in *The Meanings of Courtly Love*, ed. F. X. Newman (Albany: State University of New York Press, 1968). Subsequent citations from the various sequences are from *Elizabethan Sonnets*, ed. Sir Sidney Lee, 2 vols. (Westminster: Constable, 1904).

The Rossettis' libraries held a number of collections of Elizabethan and later sonneteers, including at least the works of Wyatt and Surrey, Samuel Daniel, Michael Drayton, Giles Fletcher, Shakespeare, Sidney, and Donne, and David Main's *Treasury of English Sonnets* (Edinburgh: Blackwood, 1880), as well as a number of anthologies published after 1881: T. Hall Caine, *Sonnets of Three Centuries* (London, 1882); Henry J. Nicoll, *C Sonnets by C Authors* (Edinburgh: MacNiven & Wallace, 1883); William Sharp, *Sonnets of This Century* (London: Walter Scott, 1886). See Henry Southeran, *A Selection from the Library of the Late William Michael Rossetti . . . and . . . His Sister Christina Georgina*, Bookseller's Catalogue no. 67 (London, 1919), pp. 87–112; Henry Southeran, *Catalogue of Books* no. 827 (London, 1931), pp. 174 ff.; Bertram Rota, *Rossetti Family Books*, catalogue no. 180 (London, 1973).

Questioning the Convention: "*Monna Innominata*"

Deconstructing the Preface as Pre-Text

Beatrice, immortalized by "altissimo poeta . . . cotanto amante"; Laura, celebrated by a great tho' an inferior bard,—have alike paid the exceptional penalty of exceptional honour, and have come down to us resplendent with charms, but (at least, to my apprehension) scant of attractiveness.

These heroines of world-wide fame were preceded by a bevy of unnamed ladies "donne innominate" sung by a school of less conspicuous poets; and in that land and that period which gave simultaneous birth to Catholics, to Albigenses, and to Troubadours, one can imagine many a lady as sharing her lover's poetic aptitude, while the barrier between them might be one held sacred by both, yet not such as to render mutual love incompatible with mutual honour.

Had such a lady spoken for herself, the portrait left us might have appeared more tender, if less dignified, than any drawn even by a devoted friend. Or had the Great Poetess of our own day and nation only been unhappy instead of happy, her circumstances would have invited her to bequeath to us, in lieu of the "Portuguese Sonnets," an inimitable "donna innominata" drawn not from fancy but from feeling, and worthy to occupy a niche beside Beatrice and Laura.

This prose preface to "*Monna Innominata*" sets out a series of qualified assertions by the author as well as directions for the reader. In the first paragraph, by linking Beatrice to Dante and Laura to Petrarch, Rossetti has not only set up a context for her own poem, she has also tacitly acknowledged the tradition of the sonnet sequence (not unambiguously, as we shall see) and the dynamic relationship of her sequence with three or more other "texts": Dante's *Vita nuova* and *Commedia,* and Petrarch's *Rime.*[10] She also makes the interesting observation that Beatrice and Laura have paid a "penalty," one common to those who have been especially honored: they have become more remote—in her view, "resplendent with charms, but . . . scant of

---

[10]The *altissimo poeta* ("highest poet") appellation, here applied to Dante, is actually the greeting given Virgil by his fellow poets in *Inferno* IV, 80; and the second phrase, "with such a lover," refers to Lancelot in Francesca's story (*Inf.* V. 134). Rossetti used the first phrase, again referring to Dante, as an epigraph to her article "Dante, An English Classic" in *The Churchman's Shilling Magazine* 2, no. 8 (October 1867): 200–205.

attractiveness." Here Rossetti as critic has decentered the sonnet tradition from the poet or the poem to the muse, and has also radically revised Dante's own estimate of the muse's qualities. One implication of her comment might be that, in her sequence, less honor will produce greater attractiveness; another implication might be that Rossetti is questioning the convention concerning the poet's "donna." At the end of the first paragraph, then, the reader is prepared to expect a conventional sequence, spoken by a male to a female beloved who, because unknown and unnamed ("innominata"), and thus free of the "penalty" of fame and honor, might be more attractive and less remote than the celebrated Beatrice and Laura. Yet the decentering from poet to muse remains unsettling, and the title itself might suggest to the reader that the poem is even addressed to that unnamed lady.

Initially the second sentence and paragraph do nothing to put into question such a response, as Rossetti makes a historical observation about the unknown predecessors of Beatrice and Laura, establishing a parallel to the first sentence. But these predecessors are the beloved ladies of "less conspicuous poets," and they have paid the penalty of being nameless. By a circumlocution ("that land" for Italy) and explicit reference to simultaneous, conflicting spiritual and literary affiliations in a specific historical period, Rossetti alludes to that complex of events and ideas which constituted the subject of her father's life-work. Gabriele Rossetti explicated the works of Dante and his contemporaries according to an allegorical method that read the works and the history as having mystical significance, governed by arcane knowledge, and involving the Catholic Church, the Holy Roman Empire, such heresies as Albigensianism and Catharism, and the works of many of the troubadour poets.[11] But rather than proceeding further with a mystification like her father's, Rossetti displaces the reader's expectations in a different direction: "one can imagine many a lady as sharing her lover's poetic aptitude." This statement prepares us not just for a female muse of the convention, but for someone who is deeply involved in it as a participant: a lady who is not merely a passive object of adoration but is herself an active poet. And since she steps down from her pedestal to engage in the activity of poetry, the convention itself is put into question. We are thus prepared for a

[11]See Gabriele Rossetti, *Disquisitions on the Antipapal Spirit Which Produced the Reformation: Its Secret Influence on the Literature of Europe in General and of Italy in Particular*, trans. Caroline Ward, 2 vols. (London: Smith Elder, 1834); and E. R. Vincent, *Gabriele Rossetti in England* (Oxford: Clarendon Press, 1936), pp. 72 ff.

dialogue between a male poet and a female poet who share a "poetic aptitude." But we are not yet told who is the "author" of the poem. Further, we are informed that there may be a "barrier" between the two lovers, but even this possibility is set out in a series of qualifications and diminutions of that barrier which render it ambiguous if not obscure. Of course the traditional barrier in the courtly love convention was the marriage of the lady to another man. For Rossetti, however, the barrier is one that *"might* be . . . held sacred by both" (italics added). This phrase may possibly define the barrier, or possibly suggest that it *might not* be held sacred by both.

The qualification continues with the conjunctive adverb "yet" followed by the trope of litotes, here displayed as a double negative with an amplification: "yet not such as to render mutual love incompatible with mutual honour." The barrier itself is introduced syntactically almost as an afterthought, and that afterthought is further extended by the "yet not such" collocation. Accordingly the barrier, or possible barrier, or perhaps sacred barrier, whether to one lover or both, not excluding mutual love and allowing mutual honor—or at least not making the love and honor incompatible—*might* be imagined as a condition existing between the lady as poet and the beloved as poet: a considerable evasion of directness. Nothing in the poem unambiguously explicates the nature of that supposed barrier so rhetorically set out in the preface. The barrier is a block or gulf; the poem that "contains" it is, like the preface, a decentered labyrinth.

Only in paragraph three is the reversal of the reader's expectation which begins in the second paragraph completed. Rossetti's perspective is finally clarified by the conditional "had such a lady spoken for herself." Each of the sentences and paragraphs begins in the same way, with the ladies, but each continues very differently. In the first paragraph, Beatrice and Laura, sung by great poets, have paid the penalty; in the second, we are told that the heroines were preceded by unknown ladies sung by lesser poets; in the third, such a lady is imagined as speaking for herself. We are now more fully prepared for the questioning of the convention of the sonnet and the sequence which Rossetti's own sequence will present. But again there are qualifications (another "might"), and Rossetti's conclusion to the conditional clause is not, as might be expected, the following poem, but an allusion to the attractiveness of the lady developed from paragraph one. The terms have shifted, however. In the first paragraph the conceptual contrast is between "resplendent with charms" and "attractiveness." The second pairing is in the reverse order, which we must realign as "dignified" and "tender." When the donna-poet speaks or writes (or "sings") her own poem, her self-revelation ("the portrait left us") might appear less resplendent with charms (or less dignified) and more attractive (tender) than—what? The comparison here is not with Beatrice or Laura, but only with "any [portrait] drawn even by a devoted friend." The function of "even" is to set at a remove the claims of friendship as well as of passionate love. Those claims are possibly less accurate delineators in portraying "attractiveness" than the poet's own voice (*poeta loquitur in propria persona?*), another reversal or questioning of the convention that holds that the lady is presented exclusively and accurately and in erotic detail by the male poet (who, it must also be acknowledged, is required by the convention to delineate his own portrait as well).

The preface "concludes" or rather ends, since closure is resisted, with an ambiguous reference to Elizabeth Barrett Browning and her sonnet sequence. Again we are invited to make an intertextual comparison, but the terms of that comparison are unclear. Are we to think that if Elizabeth Barrett had been unhappy in her marriage she would then have been able to write a better sequence than she did, relying not on fancy but on feeling; and that only then would such a sequence's "donna" be the equal to Beatrice or Laura?[12] It would be truly astonishing for so exceedingly reserved, self-conscious, and polite a person as Christina Rossetti to make such a suggestion about another poet whom she admired and whose husband she knew. A wholly different significance comes from the passage when we regard the remark as an intertextual assertion: if Elizabeth Barrett had been only unhappy, instead of happy and unhappy, or instead of only happy, she would have been invited by her circumstances to give us a text about an unnamed lady (whom Elizabeth Barrett could not name, being only unhappy) drawn from her own *feelings*, unlike Rossetti who, apart from her happiness or unhappiness (never alluded to in the preface), must rely on her *fancy*. That is, Elizabeth Barrett's writing was a mimesis of the real world; she was in the circumstance not of fiction ("fancy") but of reality ("feelings"), and her poems directly address her lover, Robert Browning. An unhappy love would have given or allowed ("invited") Elizabeth Barrett to present a mimesis of

[12]Such is the interpretation given to the passage by Lona Mosk Packer: "If Elizabeth Barrett Browning had had an unhappy instead of a happy love, Christina suggests, she might have written genuine poetry springing from deep feeling rather than literary poetry resulting from cultivated art. The supposition is that Christina regarded her own work, rooted in strong feeling rather than in conventional literary attitudes, as the product of an unhappy love" (*Christina Rossetti*, p. 225).

a fictive world, a fancy for the imagined situation, say a semi-historical one of a *donna innominata,* the one that Rossetti posits, and to which Rossetti can bring the craft of fancy, because she is not introducing any feeling for an unhappy circumstance of reality into her role.

That the passage was open to such positive misreading is clear from Rossetti's letter to her brother, Dante Gabriel, about the equivalence Hall Caine had drawn from the sentence (happy is to fancy as sadness is to feeling) and which he misapplied to Elizabeth Barrett:

> I am much pleased with [Mr. Caine's] *Academy* article, though sorry that he seems to have misapprehended my reference to the *Portuguese Sonnets.* Surely not only what I meant to say but what I do say is, not that the Lady of those sonnets is surpassable, but that a "Donna innominata" by the same hand might well have been unsurpassable. The Lady in question, as she actually stands, I was not regarding as an "innominata" at all,—because the latter type, according to the traditional figures I had in view, is surrounded by unlike circumstances. I rather wonder that no one (so far as I know) ever hit on my semi-historical argument before for such treatment,—it seems to me so full of poetic suggestiveness. [*FL,* p. 98][13]

The preface, then, opens up the "semi-historical argument" and sets up an intertextual dialogue to be pursued in the poem with "the traditional figures I had in view" and suggests that the treatment is potent with "poetic suggestiveness." By way of contrast, William Michael's comment on the preface moves the reader outside the interrogative text to the enigmatic and private poet and her intentionality:

> To any one to whom it was granted to be behind the scenes of Christina Rossetti's life—and to how few was this granted—it is not merely probable but certain that this "sonnet of sonnets" was a personal utterance—an intensely personal one. The introductory prose-note, about "many a lady sharing her lover's poetic aptitude," etc., is a blind—not

[13]William Michael Rossetti, in his own note to this letter (*FL,* p. 97) stresses the direct biographical reference: "What she says in her letter—that the speaker in her sonnets was not intended for an 'innominata at all'—is curious, and shows (what is every now and then apparent in her utterances) that her mind was conversant with very nice shades of distinction. It is indisputable that the real veritable speaker in these sonnets is Christina herself, giving expression to her love for Charles Cayley: but the prose heading would surely lead any reader to suppose that the *ostensible* speaker is one of those ladies, to whom it adverts, in the days of the troubadours."

an untruthful blind, for it alleges nothing that is not reasonable, and on the surface correct, but still a blind interposed to draw off attention from the writer in her proper person.[14] [*PW*, p. 462]

Directly and flatly contradicting the implication of the preface that the sequence comes from fancy not feeling, William Michael's note refers to the preface as a "blind" drawn down over the poet's self. The purpose of the preface (and here he agrees with his sister) is to "draw off attention from the writer in her proper person" to allow her to assume her persona. The critic's task is not to raise that blind (an act William Michael almost invites us to do), but to exploit the persona and "her" text, not Rossetti's. William Michael tries to recenter the text in veiled biography. He wants all the signifiers in the preface to be pointers alluding to one signified datum that he explicates as Rossetti's love for Charles Bagot Cayley. He wants the preface to be a pre-face (or a veiled face) and the pre-text a pretext. He presents himself and "how few" others as the possessors of a privileged and external truth, and the purpose of his "blind" phrase is to draw off the reader's vision to that image, to center it on that truth-behind-the-screen which all signifiers, rightly understood by him, render visible and objective. But to follow William Michael into his tempting "blind" alley is to lose the free play that the preface invites.

[14]William Michael identifies Christina's lover as Charles Bagot Cayley in his prefatory *Memoir* (*PW*, p. liii) and also in *Some Reminiscences of William Michael Rossetti*, 2 vols. (London: Brown, Langham, 1906), II, 311–15. Cayley (1823–1883) was born in St. Petersburg, the son of a Russia merchant. He was educated at King's College, London, and Trinity College, Cambridge. He devoted his life to philology and to his translations: of the *Divine Comedy* (1851–1855), the Psalms (1860), and Aeschylus' *Prometheus Bound* (1867), Homer's *Iliad* (1877), and Petrarch (1879). Around 1847 Cayley studied Italian with Gabriele Rossetti and became a friend of the family, a friendship renewed in the early 1860s when he proposed to Christina Rossetti and was rejected, very probably on religious grounds. Thereafter Rossetti and Cayley remained good friends, saw each other from time to time, and exchanged small presents and letters. In February 1883 (the year is William Michael's plausible conjecture), Rossetti wrote to Cayley accepting his suggestion that she should become his literary executor in the event of his prior death and ended with a reference to her "Dante article," giving him "a thousand thanks for the permission I craved" (*FL*, pp. 124–25), very likely for his permission to use his translation of Dante in her article for the *Century Magazine*. When Cayley died on her birthday in 1883 he left to her "the remainder of such books as have been published for me" and also "my best writing-desk," together with her letters to him, which she ordered destroyed (*FL*, p. 140). See also Gilbert F. Cunningham, *The Divine Comedy in English: A Critical Bibliography, 1782–1900* (Edinburgh: Oliver and Boyd, 1965), pp. 40–45.

Questioning the Convention: "*Monna Innominata*"

The preface introduces to us the text of a poem that is decentered by it, as well as to various kinds of intertextuality, a sharply redirected process of reader-response, reversed ideological expectations about conventional sex roles, a "semi-historical" interest, and a deconstruction of the sonnet tradition accomplished by questioning some conventions of the genre, the persona, and the lover-beloved relationship. The preface is almost a tract in deconstructionist and poststructuralist criticism. Our next task is to examine how the preface has prepared us for the sequence itself.

Prosodic Convention and Invention

By giving to the sequence the subtitle "A Sonnet of Sonnets" Rossetti draws the reader's attention both to the "stanzaic" form of each individual sonnet and to the overall structure of the whole poem in which each sonnet functions as a "line." Rossetti was clearly particular about the production of her book, as a letter to Alexander Macmillan regarding its layout indicates: "At any rate I may count (may I not?) on no 2 poems sharing pages or part pages, and on all sets of sonnets being treated as so many separate sonnets."[15] And in the first edition, the preface on page 44 faces the first sonnet, and each follows, one to a page, amply set out, with line indentations carefully arranged according to the rhyme scheme. Her concern that the "sets of sonnets" be printed as a single poem is reiterated two years later in a letter to an American editor: "My wish includes your *not* choosing an independent poem which forms part of a series or group, —not (for instance) . . . one Sonnet of "Monna Innominata." Such compound work has a connection (very often) which is of interest to the author and which an editor gains nothing by discarding."[16] And again, to the Macmillan firm in 1886 she repeated her resolve: "I now make a point of refusing extracts, even in the case of my Sonnet of Sonnets some of which would fairly stand alone."[17] In these refusals to dismember her poems she twice refers to the "*Monna Innominata*" sequence as a work to be printed whole, and so emphasizes her view that it should be read as a single text. So also the prosody makes a body for study, not when each poem is seen only in isolation, but when the text as a whole is set out.

---

[15]*The Rossetti-Macmillan Letters*, ed. Lona Mosk Packer (Berkeley: University of California Press, 1963), p. 137.

[16]Ibid., pp. 154–55, n. 3.

[17]Ibid., p. 154.

At the individual level each sonnet follows the Petrarchan or Italian form of the octave and sestet, often separated by a turn (or *volta*). The octaves display traditional and regular closed rhyme patterns (*rime chiuse*), *abba, abba*. But on the sequence level the variations in the octaves occur at significant structural, thematic, and intertextual junctures:

1–3	*abba abba*	regular octave
4	*abab bccb*	
5–6	*abba abba*	regular octave
7	*abba baba*	
8–10	*abba abba*	regular octave
11	*abba acca*	
12	*abba abba*	regular octave
13	*abba baab*	
14	*abba acac*	

It is immediately clear that the first quatrain in sonnet 4 is the only unconventional first quatrain in the sequence. Five of the second quatrains are nontraditional (4, 7, 11, 13, 14), and each of these is different. Hence the sequence displays a movement back and forth in the octaves between regular octave and the interspersed irregular octave, until the last two, which are both irregular:

$$3^r \quad 1 \quad 2^r \quad 1 \quad 3^r \quad 1 \quad 1^r \quad 2 \quad \text{(octaves)}$$

These alternations indicate a systematic interplacing of regular octaves with irregular ones. Regular octaves begin the first three sonnets (in the "octave" of sonnets), but further, the only wholly irregular octave comes at the end of the first "quatrain" of sonnets (sonnet 4), a sonnet that introduces the theme of debate, exemplified in its own alternating rhyme scheme. The second irregular quatrain (7) marks the halfway point in the sequence, balancing the two parts of it; and a theme of that sonnet is, appropriately, equality. The third irregular quatrain (11) marks the end of the first tercet of sonnets, and introduces a new rhyme in the second octave to distance the lovers' real agony from mere gossip. The final irregular quatrains occur in the last two sonnets or "lines" (13, 14) of the sequence, ending the formal structure of the octaves with a discordant note at variance with the tradition, and very much in keeping with the total interrogative stance of the sequence.

In the sestets of the sonnets the pattern is a great deal more com-

plex. In every sonnet the rhyme scheme departs from the most common Petrarchan model of *cde cde* (interlaced rhyme, *rima incatenata*).
Nor is the second most popular Petrarchan form (*cdcdcd, rima alter-
nativa*) used at all.[18] The third form used by Petrarch (in sixty-seven
sonnets) is used in two of Rossetti's poems (6, 12) and their quatrains
are also traditional in form: *abba abba cde dce*. One other conventional
form is used, the so-called French or Marotique sestet, beginning with
a rhyming couplet, followed, usually, by a closed quatrain (sonnet 9,
the beginning of the "sestet" of sonnets: *ccdeed*, the same scheme used
in Dante Gabriel Rossetti's "Love Sight"). In sonnet 9 the form sets
up a dynamic relationship between the *volta* in thought at the end of
the octave and the sestet with its conjunctions that illustrate the
tension between form and content and point the dialectical argument:
"and yet" (beginning of the sestet, and the start of the couplet in the
poem); "but" (at the beginning of the concluding quatrain); to "so" at
the beginning of the second last line. All the other sonnets show
considerable invention:

1	*abba abba*	*cdd ece*	
2	*abba abba*	*cdd ccd*	(only four rhymes)
3	*abba abba*	*cde dec*	
4	*abab bccb*	*dea dae*	(highly unconventional sestet tied to octave)
5	*abba abba*	*cdc eed*	
6	*abba abba*	*cde dce*	
7	*abba baba*	*cdd ece*	
8	*abba abba*	*cde ecd*	
9	*abba abba*	*ccd eed*	(French or Marotique sestet)
10	*abba abba*	*cde edc*	
11	*abba acca*	*aca dcd*	(only four rhymes)
12	*abba abba*	*cde dce*	
13	*abba baab*	*cdc eed*	
14	*abba acac*	*dce ecd*	

The enterprising reader may trace the recurrences of rhyme patterns
from one sestet (or even tercet) to another (sonnets 1 and 7 are
identical, as they are to Wordsworth's "London, 1802": 5 and 13 are

[18]See John Fuller, *The Sonnet* (London: Methuen, 1972), pp. 2–4; Fuller notes that
of Petrarch's 317 sonnets, 116 are interlaced, 107 with alternative rhymes in the
sestets. On the archetypal forms, see Ernest Hatch Wilkins, *The Invention of the Sonnet
and Other Studies in Italian Literature* (Rome: Storia e Letteratura, 1959).

also identical). When one considers that on the one hand there are over fifty thousand possible rhyme schemes to draw from in this highly variable form, and on the other that the Italian sonnet is among the most formal and traditional of verse patternings, it is clear that Rossetti is constructing her sequence out of largely traditional Italian octaves and a controlled group of formally interrelated and variable sestets.[19]

It is as though the sequence is to be read as *in* a given form (Petrarchan sonnet sequence) and also as *against* that form. In the first quatrain, almost every sonnet (except sonnet 4) begins regularly. In the second quatrain there is more irregularity (5 sonnets), and finally in the sestet the form is almost straining against the convention, since not one of the two most common Petrarchan forms is used at all. Each sonnet seems to begin with some order, and then moves to test the limits of that order as it is conventionally expressed. The sequence acknowledges its genre while testing it by inventing more formal shapes for it to inhabit, deliberately inviting comparison with the tradition. And within the sequence, while the overall unity of form is maintained, each sonnet reflects on the forms of the other sonnets and invites comparison with them.

How this acknowledgement of form and the testing of it is mirrored in the texts of the sonnets is discussed later. For now, it is sufficient to observe that the sonnets set their argument and syntax within or against the sonnet form, using the variations in the *volta* and the concluding, often disquieting, unrhymed couplet. Rossetti's generally end-stopped lines maintain the regularity of each sonnet, while the occasional substitutions (or inversions) of iambic feet into trochees for emphasis, and the varying placement of the caesura, give variety to both rhythm and thought (as, for example, in sonnet 10). But other readers must be left to assess further these relations among form, meter, and syntax.[20]

---

[19]D. Thomas Ordeman, "How Many Rhyme Schemes Has the Sonnet?" *College English* 1 (1939): 171–73. None of these sonnets follows the pattern of the *Sonnets from the Portuguese* (*abba abba cdcdcd*); Meredith also uses a consistent rhyme scheme throughout his sequence (*abba cddc effe ghgh*); Dante Gabriel Rossetti uses some seventeen different patterns.

[20]See Alastair Fowler's chapter on "Sonnet Sequences" and their use of numerological and formal centering in his *Triumphal Forms: Structural Patterns in Elizabethan Poetry* (Cambridge: Cambridge University Press, 1970), pp. 174–97; and Roger Fowler, "Language and the Reader: Shakespeare's Sonnet 73," in *Style and Structure in Literature: Essays in the New Stylistics*, ed. Roger Fowler (Oxford: Blackwell, 1975), pp. 79–122.

The Epigraphs as Subtexts

A characteristic of Rossetti's sequence, following from the reference in the preface to Beatrice and Laura, is the use of two Italian epigraphs for each sonnet, the first from Dante and the second from Petrarch. William Michael Rossetti gives his own translations of these epigraphs (*PW*, pp. 462–63) without identifying their sources. A list of the sources follows.[21] William Michael Rossetti's translation is given for

[21]The line numbering for Dante follows the critical text of the Società Dantesca Italiana, *Le Opere di Dante,* ed. M. Barbi et al., 2d ed. (Florence: Società Dantesca Italiana, 1960), and the National Edition, *La Commedia,* ed. G. Petrocchi (Verona: Mondadori, 1966). The Italian quoted is the version given by Christina Rossetti, which does not follow the standard editions in a number of places with respect to elision and spelling. The Rossetti libraries contained copies of Dante edited by Cristoforo Landino (Florence, 1481), Aldus Manutius (Venice, 1515), Giovanni Berti (Venice, 1760), P. Baldassarre Lombardi (Rome, 1815–1817), Lord Vernon (London, 1858), and an edition issued in Brescia in 1870. The Rossettis also owned a parallel Italian-English text of the *Canzoniere* by Dante Gabriel Rossetti's godfather, Charles Lyell (London, 1835) and translations of the *Commedia* by Henry Francis Cary (London, 1850), James Ford (London, 1870), and Cayley, *Dante's Divine Comedy,* 4 vols. (London: Longman, Brown, Green, and Longmans, 1851–1855). Finally, the collections contained a number of editions in Italian and English of the *Vita nuova,* separate editions of the parts of the *Commedia,* and editions of poets of the age of Dante, such as those mentioned in the preface to Dante Gabriel Rossetti's *The Early Italian Poets* (London: Smith, Elder, 1861).

The numbering of Petrarch's poems follows the standard editions by Carducci (1889, 1957), Neri (1951), Contini (1964), and Zingarelli (1965). A useful translation is the literal rendering given in a line-for-line version in *Petrarch's Lyric Poems,* trans. and ed. Robert M. Durling (Cambridge: Harvard University Press, 1976). In standard collections the poems are numbered consecutively; in some others the 317 sonnets are numbered separately from the other poetic forms, each with its own numerical sequence (twenty-nine canzoni, nine sestine, seven ballate, four madrigali). Those numberings of the sonnets and other forms in separate sequences are given in parentheses following the standard poem number. The translation by Rossetti's friend, Charles Bagot Cayley (*The Sonnets and Stanzas of Petrarch* [London: Longmans, Green, 1879]), is the first complete translation of Petrarch's poems by "a single hand." Cayley's numbering follows the separate sequences for sonnets and other forms, and so is also that given in the parentheses. An earlier translation, *The Sonnets, Triumphs, and Other Poems of Petrarch* (London: Bohn, 1859), includes translations by several different authors; it was widely used, and divided the numbering at 266 (sonnet 227), calling those before 266 "Laura in Life" (*Laura in vita*), those after, with a separate numbering, "Laura in Death" (*Laura in morte*). Because the Italian for the first line is given for every poem in the Bohn text, it is an easy matter to locate poems in the standard editions. Modern scholars divide the poem before the canzone *I'vo pensando* (no. 264), based on the autograph MS. Vat. Lat. 3195.

each, together with Charles Bagot Cayley's translations of Dante (which Rossetti herself preferred in her own writing on Dante) as well as his translations of Petrarch (which she also knew). An asterisk * indicates that this passage and translation was quoted by Rossetti in her own writings on Dante. A dagger † indicates that the passage is quoted or referred to in Maria Francesca Rossetti's *Shadow of Dante*.

1   *Lo dì che han detto a' dolci amici addio.* [Dante, *Purg.* VIII. 3]
    The day that they have said adieu to their sweet friends. [WMR]
    . . . when they
    Since morn have said Adieu to darling friends; [CBC* †]
    Amor, con quanto sforzo oggi mi vinci! [Petrarch, 85 (64). 12]
    Love, with how great a stress dost thou vanquish me to-day! [WMR]
    Love, with what force thou dost me now o'erthrow; [CBC]

2   *Era già l'ora che volge il desio.* [Dante, *Purg.* VIII. 1]
    It was already the hour which turns back the desire. [WMR]
    It was that hour which thaws the heart [CBC* †]
    Ricorro al tempo ch' io vi vidi prima. [Petrarch, 20 (18). 3]
    I recur to the time when I first saw thee. [WMR]
    I've called to mind how I beheld you first [CBC]

3   *O ombre vane, fuor che ne l'aspetto!* [Dante, *Purg.* II. 79]
    Oh shades, empty save in semblance! [WMR]
    Ah shadows, that are but for sight inane! [CBC]
    Immaginata guida la conduce. [Petrarch, 277 (236). 9]
    An imaginary guide conducts her. [WMR]
    Now by a phantom guide it is controlled, [CBC]

4   *Poca favilla gran fiamma seconda.* [Dante, *Par.* I. 34]
    A small spark fosters a great flame. [WMR]
    Great fire may after little spark succeed; [CBC]
    Ogni altra cosa, ogni pensier va fore,
    E sol ivi con voi rimansi amore. [Petrarch, 72 (canzone 9). 44–45]
    Every other thing, every thought, goes off, and love alone remains there with you. [WMR]
    Take flight all thoughts and things that it contains,
    And therein Love alone with you remains. [CBC]

5   *Amor che a nulla amato amar perdona.* [Dante, *Inf.* V. 103]
    Love, who exempts no loved one from loving. [WMR]

98

Love, who from loving none beloved reprieves, [CBC†]
Amor m'addusse in sì gioiosa spene. [Petrarch, 56 (43). 11]
Love led me into such joyous hope. [WMR]
Love . . .
Required me into such sweet hopes to fall. [CBC]

6   *Or puoi la quantitate*
Comprender de l'amor che a te mi scalda. [Dante, *Purg.* XXI. 133–34]
Now canst thou comprehend the quantity of the love which glows in me
towards thee. [WMR]
"Now," said he, rising, "mayest thou rightly set
A value on the love with which I flame," [CBC†]
Non vo' che da tal nodo amor mi scioglia [Petrarch, 59 (ballata 6). 17]
I do not choose that Love should release me from such a tie. [WMR]
Me shall not Love release,
From such a knot, by pain or by decease. [CBC]

7   *Qui primavera sempre ed ogni frutto.* [Dante, *Purg.* XXVIII. 143]
Here always Spring and every fruit. [WMR]
Here spring was always, and each plant, [CBC†]
Ragionando con meco ed io con lui. [Petrarch, 35 (28). 14]
Conversing with me, and I with him. [WMR]
Love with me walks and talks, and with him I. [CBC]

8   *Come dicesse a Dio: D'altro non calme.* [Dante, *Purg.* VIII. 12]
As if he were to say to God, "I care for nought else." [WMR]
And breathe to God, "Nought reketh me, but thou." [CBC]
Spero trovar pietà non che perdono. [Petrarch, 1 (1). 8]
I hope to find pity, and not only pardon. [WMR]
I hope to miss not pardon—pity I mean. [CBC]

9   *O dignitosa coscienza e netta!* [Dante, *Purg.* III. 8]
O dignified and pure conscience! [WMR]
. . . by his conscience;
Ah! white and honorable! [CBC†]
Spirto più acceso di virtuti ardenti. [Petrarch, 283 (242). 3]
Spirit more lit with burning virtues. [WMR]
The soul, that warmest breath of virtue drew. [CBC]

10 *Con miglior corso e con migliore stella.* [Dante, *Par.* I. 40]
With better course and with better star. [WMR]

99

With better light, with better stars allied, [CBC* †]
La vita fugge e non s'arresta un' ora. [Petrarch, 272 (231). 1]
Life flees, and stays not an hour. [WMR]
Life flyeth, and will not a moment stay, [CBC]

11 *Vien dietro a me e lascia dir le genti.* [Dante, *Purg.* V. 13]
    Come after me, and leave folk to talk. [WMR]
    Let people talk, and thou behind me go; [CBC†]
    Contando i casi della vita nostra. [Petrarch, 285 (244). 12]
    Relating the casualties of our life. [WMR]
    Counting the chances that our life befall, [CBC]

12 *Amor, che ne la mente mi ragiona.* [Dante, *Purg.* II. 112 (also *Convivio* III.
    ii. 1 and *De Vulgari eloquentia* II. vi. 73)]
    Love, who speaks within my mind. [WMR]
    Love, that discoursing art within my soul, [CBC†]
    Amor vien nel bel viso di costei. [Petrarch, 13 (12). 2]
    Love comes in the beautiful face of this lady. [WMR]
    As Love amongst the ladies in your face
        Of loveliness appeareth [CBC]

13 *E drizzeremo gli occhi al Primo Amore.* [Dante, *Par.* XXXII. 142]
    And we will direct our eyes to the Primal Love. [WMR]
    And set we on the all-first Love our eyes; [CBC†]
    Ma trovo peso non da le mie braccia. [Petrarch, 20 (18). 5]
    But I find a burden to which my arms suffice not. [WMR]
    But for my arms this burden was too sore, [CBC]

14 *E la Sua Volontade è nostra pace.* [Dante, *Par.* III. 85]
    And His will is our peace. [WMR]
    In his good pleasure we have each his peace; [CBC†]
    Sol con questi pensier, con altre chiome. [Petrarch, 30 (sestina 2). 32]
    Only with these thoughts, with different locks. [WMR]
    Alone with these my thoughts, with altered hair, [CBC]

These epigraphs from Dante and Petrarch are an important means of engaging the whole poem with the tradition of the sonnet sequence, with its most famous ladies, and with the texts of Dante and Petrarch and the other "texts" that appear in them. Because Rossetti printed the epigraphs with ascriptions only to their authors and not to their source in a text, she is to a certain extent dissociating them from their context in the works from which they come. We cannot invade Rossetti's mind to learn her intentions or her reasons for this decision, or to discover why these texts rather than others were chosen. We are left with a variety of possible associations between the quoted lines and the poem that follows, and we can also pursue the contexts in Dante and Petrarch whereby these lines become sub-texts to the sequence. An intertextual dialogue is immediately initiated for the reader between the persona of the poem and the personae of Dante's and Petrarch's poems, an interchange quite distinct from the attribution of a source, or influence, or analogy.

These passages from Dante and Petrarch have received little attention, and even the three works on Rossetti that do address them raise problems. The effort to contextualize the quotations may be vitiated by relating them to suppositions about Rossetti's biography whereby the epigraphs become veiled allegory.[22] Or the lines and their contexts may be treated as a determinative source of implication having no structural or intertextual reverberations within the larger historical and literary framework of Dante's or Petrarch's works.[23] And when seen as "a context of allusion for Rossetti's love philosophy"[24] with links to the thought of the *dolce stil nuovo* of the Florentine Neoplatonists of Dante's circle, the epigraphs may be similarly constricted. None of these treatments considers the relation of the epigraphs to poetry or to other poetic texts.

Surprisingly, the Dante epigraphs are not drawn from the *Vita nuova*, which is in some ways the most obvious choice for Rossetti if she were "grounding" her poem in the sonnets and canzones that set out the course of Dante's awakening to new life through his love for Beatrice, and chronicle the course of his emotions after her death. The choice of the *Vita nuova* would also have appeared to be appropriate because it was so important to the Rossetti family: Dante Gabriel issued his translation in 1861, some twenty years before "*Monna Innominata*" was published, and his paintings and poetry manifest a continuing interest in the *Vita nuova*, as can be seen in the *First Anniversary of the Death of Beatrice* (1853), *Beata Beatrix* (1864–1870), and *Dante's Dream* (1871). And, in fact, Christina Rossetti's title does

---

[22]As Caldwell does; see "Christina Rossetti's '*Monna Innominata*,'" Chap. 2.
[23]Wion, "'Give Me the Lowest Place,'" pp. 65 ff.
[24]McCann, "Influence of the *Dolce Stil Nuovo*," p. 169; see also pp. 169–208.

come from one of the names for "Lady" (when used with a proper name) in the *Vita nuova*.[25] But all the Dante epigraphs are from the *Commedia*, and in the octave of sonnets (sonnets 1–8), the epigraphs of the first, second, and eighth sonnets are all from *Purgatorio* VIII (and the same passage of twelve lines), these epithetical references to the same canto both introducing and tying up the octave. In the entire octave of sonnets only two epigraphs are not from the *Purgatorio*, that of the poem ending the first quatrain of sonnets (sonnet 4), which comes from the first canto of the *Paradiso*, and the epigraph for the beginning of the second quatrain (sonnet 5), which is from the *Inferno*. The *Paradiso* passage speaks of a great fire coming from a little spark, a conventional way of speaking about passionate love, and the line from the *Inferno* contains the words of Francesca da Rimini whirling in the winds of passionate love. After the *volta* in the sequence in sonnet 9, there are three epigraphs from the *Paradiso* (sonnets 10, 13, 14), ending with a kind of paradisal couplet, the last being perhaps the most famous line from the entire *Commedia* (*E la Sua Volontade è nostra pace*, "and his will is our peace"). As the sestet of the sequence turns toward heaven, and possibly heavenly consolation, it is appropriate that more of the sonnets' epithets be from the *Paradiso*.

Most interesting, however, despite what appears to be an almost random citing of texts from the *Commedia* and notwithstanding their relation to the formal organization of the fourteen poems into a son-

[25]Dante, *Vita nuova*, sonnet 12 (*Io mi sentii svegliar dentro allo core*), where Dante sees Monna Vanna, the mistress of Guido Cavalcanti, coming toward him with Beatrice. In the introduction to *The Early Italian Poets*, Dante Gabriel Rossetti gives other hints pointing to Christina Rossetti's use of a female poet's act of writing love sonnets. He refers to a sonnet by "Guido Orlandi, written as though coming from a lady," and also to a lady named Nina, the love of Dante da Maiano, "herself, it is said, a poetess and not personally known to him" (p. 20). See also Salvatore Battaglia, *Grande Dizionario della lingua italiana* (Turin: Unione Tipografico (1961–), X, 809; s.v. "monna": "appelativo di rispetto, di onore, di cortesia preposto anticamente al nome di donne." Just after the publication of "*Monna Innominata*" Cayley refers to Christina Rossetti as "dolce monna" in a letter to her dated November 6, 1881 (*FL*, p. 101). For *innominata* see *Grande Dizionario*, VII, 42, citing Francesco da Buti (1324–1406), *Commento sopra la Divina Comedia*, 3 vols. (Pisa, 1858–1862): "Lo nostro autore finge come Beatrice si ritornò alla sedia sua, unde si mosse quando ella andò ne lo inferno, mossa dalla donna innominata e da Lucia" (III, 815): "Our author describes how Beatrice returned to her place, which she had left when she descended into Hell, urged by the unnamed lady and by Lucia." The reference is to *Inf.* II. 52 ff., and the "unnamed lady" is the Virgin Mary (*Donna gentil*), whose name is unspoken in Hell.

net, is the way in which the persona in each of the sonnets can be engaged intertextually with a variety of poets mentioned in the *Commedia* passages; most of these poets are themselves related intertextually to their own poems, or to other poets referred to in the same passages. Rossetti foregrounds the Dante passage at the head of each of the sonnets, and then decenters the passage away from the specificity of mere analogy to the experience in the poem.[26] The epigraphs' oblique references either involve a direct address by one of Dante's fellow poets or are spoken in the presence of those poets by Dante (or his persona) or allude to the invocation of the god of poetry. In order, these references are as follows: to Sordello (sonnets 1 and 2); Casella (3); invocation to Apollo (4); Guinizelli (5, echoed by Francesca); Statius (6); Matilda (7, referring to the poets of antiquity who sang of the golden age); Sordello again and the unknown penitent who sings to Dante Saint Ambrose's compline hymn (8); Virgil (9); the invocation to Apollo again, with the apostrophe to the sun (10); Virgil again (11); Casella again, quoting Dante's own canzone on love (12); and, finally in the last two poems, Saint Bernard as the Christian poet who begins the hymn that concludes the *Commedia* (13); and Piccarda (14), the sister of Dante's wife, who summarizes the poem in a passage that echoes Ephesians 2:15 and a phrase from Augustine's *Confessions* (XIII. 9), one of Rossetti's favorite texts (*In bona voluntate tua pax nobis est*, "In thy good pleasure is our peace," in Pusey's translation of 1838).

[26]Rossetti and her sister, Maria Francesca, had quoted all of these epigraphs or referred to them in their own commentaries on Dante's *Commedia*. Rossetti's two articles are "Dante, An English Classic," an introduction to Dante and an encomium of Cayley's translation, which she calls a "*tour de force*" and "a permanent contribution to our English classics" (p. 202); and, more important, "Dante, the Poet Illustrated Out of the Poem" in *Century Magazine* 28, 5 (February 1884): 566–73. Rossetti uses Cayley's translation, which she had known from the time she sent William Michael the manuscript on September 3, 1850 (*FL*, p. 15). She wrote to Edmund Gosse on January 30, 1883, asking to use Cayley's translation, which, she said, "I far prefer . . . [and] with which I am more familiar [than Longfellow's]" (quoted in Packer, *Christina Rossetti*, p. 359). In her article Rossetti praises Cayley's *terza rima*, for "with a master's hand he conveys to us the sense amid echoes of the familiar sound" (p. 567). Maria Francesca Rossetti's *Shadow of Dante* (London: Rivingtons, 1871) used the translation of the *Inferno* by William Michael Rossetti (1865) and the translations of Longfellow for the *Purgatorio* and *Paradiso* (1867). Dante's own intertextual treatment of poets in the *Commedia* is examined in Teodolinda Barolini, *Dante's Poets: Textuality and Truth in the "Comedy"* (Princeton: Princeton University Press, 1984).

The Dante epigraphs are subtexts that engage these personae and the invoked god of poetry intertextually on the subject and subjects of poetry. In almost every instance these epigraphs refer to recognition scenes in which Dante recognizes a poet or context, and the poet then disappears or fades into his craft, or the shadows, or a formula. One might think Rossetti was following a central convention in the love sequences, the activity of turning the entire love relationship into art, the eternizing of the beloved and the passion he or she inspired, to build, in Dante Gabriel's words, "a moment's monument."[27] But the convention is summoned forth only to be deconstructed, as reference after reference exploits the subject of poetry by having that subject disappear, and invokes the persona of a poet long dead for a fleeting colloquy before the shade passes again into the shadows. I shall consider the epigraphs more or less in order, diverging only to include those later in the sequence which are drawn from the same canto being considered.

In *Purgatorio* VII Sordello, the poet of the epigraph to sonnet 1, has explained to Dante that Mount Purgatory may not be climbed after sunset. In canto VIII, as night falls with its shadows, the preoccupied penitents sing their evening hymn at the hour in which, Dante says, "seafarers" recall old affection and farewells to dear friends (Dante's own exile would certainly be one allusion embedded in these lines). Rossetti's sonnets 1 and 2, on partings and the lost memory of a first meeting, are in ironic contrast to these Dantean references. Sonnet 8, concluding both the octave and the references to this canto (with Saint Ambrose's hymn, *te lucis ante terminum*, "To thee before the end of day"), relates the story of Esther and how she seductively used her beauty to save her people. Esther used earthly means for a divine purpose, unlike the preoccupied on earth who were too busy for heavenly concerns and forgot God. Sonnet 8, like sonnet 2, thus presents a reflection or memory collocation.

In *Purgatorio* II, Casella (referred to in the epigraph to sonnet 3) greets Dante, who tries to embrace him but ends up grasping only a shade. Dante repeats his gesture three times, each time failing to embrace the bodiless spirit.[28] Only then does Dante recognize his

[27]From the prefatory sonnet to *The House of Life* as it appeared in 1881. The poem was written in February of 1880 as a birthday gift to his mother. It echoes Shakespeare's Sonnet 55.

[28]To complicate the intertextuality, the commentators, such as Dorothy Sayers and Charles Singleton, note that in describing this thrice-attempted embrace Dante is imitating Virgil (*Aen.* VI. 700–702), who, in turn, is imitating Homer (*Od.* XI. 204–

fellow poet, and he asks Casella to sing a "song of love." Although
lacking bodily substance, Casella is very much present as a voice. And
the song the dead poet sings is one the living poet wrote, the canzone
from the *Convivio*, which is also the epigraph for Rossetti's sonnet 12.
Dante is entranced by Casella's singing the opening of his own poem,
until Cato, the moral guardian of Purgatory, interrupts Casella, recalling pilgrim and penitents to their purpose. Meanwhile the rapt Virgil
appears conscience-stricken for having paused in his journey to listen
to a love song (*Purg.* III. 8, where Dido comes to the reader's mind, is
the epigraph to sonnet 9). Thus in sonnet 3 the dream/waking or
shadow/substance motif is brought out; in sonnet 12 the alternate poet
(Casella singing Dante's canzone; Dante in Purgatory quoting himself
from the *Convivio*) is ambiguously set before us in the epigraph, while
in the sonnet the roles of the lover/poet persona are filled by another
person: "If there be any one can take my place." Sonnet 9, the *volta* of
the sequence, concludes the Casella reference just as Cato breaks off
the song with a call to moral purpose; similarly the "song" of Rossetti's
persona, of "all that was and all / That might have been," is canceled
with a phrase: "now can never be."

  I have commented briefly on the intertextuality of the epigraphs to
sonnets 1, 2, 8, 3, 12, 9 in that order to link the connected passages to
cantos in Dante, and also to see their relations to poets and poetry.
Sonnet 4 carries the first epigraph from the *Paradiso*, where Dante, in
the Earthly Paradise, has just concluded his invocation to Apollo, god
of poetry (*Par.* I. 34). He asks for inspiration for his third vision,
echoing James 3:5 (another intertextual decentering).[29] The invocation of the spirit of poetry for a greater vision is an inflated way of
describing the theme of sonnet 4, since in this sonnet the lady is the
poet who inspires the "loftier song," the small spark (*poca favilla*)
fostering the great flame (*gran fiamma*). In the epigraph to sonnet 10
this passage in *Paradiso* I is referred to again. This reference, however,
is to Dante's apostrophe to the sun, to the description of the propitious
moment in the stars when he enters paradise revealed as the realm of
light. So in the sonnet, by contrast, life on earth is wearisome, especially when set in ironic juxtaposition with "life reborn." Dante's

---

8). Barolini discusses the passage and cites relevant scholarship (*Dante's Poets*, pp.
31–40).

  [29]In her article "Dante, the Poet Illustrated Out of the Poem," Rossetti refers to
this invocation as "an invocation of the Spirit of Poetry" as she quotes its opening
lines from Cayley's translation (p. 567).

propitious moment is an echo of earlier subtexts, and gathers the lost moments of love into the "moment" of earthly time.

Sonnet 5 is introduced by the words of Francesca da Rimini,[30] but in the *Inferno* she herself is engaged in some intertextual play: she and Paolo de Malatesta were reading the romance of Lancelot, and that book and its author became the occasion of their love, sin, and death. Further, the book is described by Francesca as their "Galehalt," the name of the go-between between Lancelot and Guinevere. And Francesca is echoing Guido Guinizelli's canzone *Al cor gentil ripara sempre amore* ("Within the gentle heart Love shelters him," translated by Dante Gabriel Rossetti) in her three anaphoristic tercets. She begins *Amor, che al cor gentil ratto s'apprendre* ("Love which is quickly caught in gentle hearts," *Inf.* V. 100).[31] That line is followed by two further echoes, the first being Rossetti's epigraph (*Inf.* V. 103) and the second line 106, each beginning with *Amor*. Each of these lines expresses the conventional *dolce stil nuovo* sentiments of Guinizelli (his canzone is described as the "first great Italian lyric" in that style,[32] and it develops the flame/light motif appropriate to the *Inferno*). But the intervening lines in Dante are an erotic deconstruction of that idealistic style, an attack upon it, and an ecstatic outburst in favor of physical passion as, after each echo of the ideal, Francesca continues

[30]Maria Francesca Rossetti bore the Italianate form of her mother's name, Frances, an echo of Dante's Francesca, who represented a romantic ideal of the tragic lover. See *A Shadow of Dante*, where the episode is selected as one of the two most famous passages of the *Commedia* (p. 1), and where too the narrative is given in some detail (p. 68). Dante Gabriel painted only one episode from the *Inferno*, this episode, in his 1855 watercolor triptych *Paolo and Francesca da Rimini* (in the Tate Gallery), which shows, as Ruskin says, that "Rossetti has thoroughly understood the passage throughout" as referring to passionate love (Virginia Surtees, *The Paintings and Drawings of Dante Gabriel Rossetti [1828–1882]: A Catalogue Raisonné*, 2 vols. [Oxford: Clarendon Press, 1971], I, 36–39). The topic became popular through many reprints of Henry Cary's translation of Dante (1814 on) and also through Leigh Hunt's poem *The Story of Rimini* (1816; rev. ed., 1844). The Pre-Raphaelite sculptor, Alexander Munro, produced a version influenced by Rossetti's painting (see *Burlington Magazine* [November 1963], p. 510), and the scene figured in many other pictorial and musical representations (including at least twelve operas between 1828 and 1878).

[31]Guinizelli's line is also echoed and referred to in the eighth sonnet of Dante's *Vita nuova, Amore e cor gentil sono una cosa* ("Love and the gentle heart are the same thing"; trans. Dante Gabriel Rossetti); and in *Purg.* XXVI. 91 ff. Guido appears and Dante greets him as his father in poetry, in using the sweet and gracious rhymes of love (l. 99).

[32]Edmund Gardner, *Dante* (London: Dent, 1900), p. 43.

with references to the pleasures of the flesh in both love and vengeance. The epigraph to Rossetti's sonnet 5 suggests all these textual interrelationships and their attendant ambiguities. As a subtext itself, it calls into question the romantic and privileged place given to Francesca da Rimini by Rossetti's contemporaries. And, using an idealized *stil novista* echo from Guinizelli as its own subtext, it points to the *cor gentil* motif in the first line of Rossetti's sonnet: "O my heart's heart." That heart is then redirected from earthly service in an erotic sense to a divine service and vocation.

Sonnet 6 has as subtext the words of the second poetic interpreter in Purgatory (the first being Sordello). As Statius, the first-century Roman poet, is about to prostrate himself before Virgil, he speaks the quoted lines. Here, then, is one poet venerating another (as also happens in Rossetti's sequence). Sonnet 7's subtext is from the Matilda episode in the Earthly Paradise (picked up in the sonnet by "the flowering land"), in which she explains the nature of perpetual spring by referring to the classical poets' songs of the golden age.[33] The paradox of Matilda is that, as Maria Francesca Rossetti says, she is "the realization and development of the dream-Leah, and so the Christian type of the Active Life in the Paradise of Earth."[34] But she is caught in the perpetually static spring of the Earthly Paradise. The images of the canto reappear in the sonnet—the flowering land and the "dividing sea," which is seen as both the stream of the Earthly Paradise that separates Dante from Matilda (*Purg.* XXVIII. 22–23) and as the Hellespont separating Hero from Leander (*Purg.* XXVIII. 70–75). It is the latter image that emerges to control the course of sonnet 7, linking the death of Leander intertextually to the biblical storms that fall on the house built on a solid foundation (Matt. 7:24–27).

Just as Cato in *Purgatorio* II and III urged the pilgrims up Mount Purgatory and aroused Virgil's conscience, so Virgil in *Purgatorio* V rebukes and urges on Dante (sonnet 11). The important point for Rossetti in this passage is the literal "shadow of Dante," for, as a living person in Purgatory, Dante casts a shadow. (It is this passage which provides the title for Maria Francesca Rossetti's book). That shadow causes the spirits to gaze at Dante in wonder and to chatter among

---

[33]Around 1855 Dante Gabriel Rossetti did a study (now in the Ashmolean Museum) for a lost watercolor of Matilda gathering flowers (Surtees, *Paintings and Drawings of Dante Gabriel Rossetti*, I, 34).

[34]Maria Francesca Rossetti, *Shadow of Dante*, p. 185; see also *FD*, pp. 462–63.

themselves. Dante pauses and looks back, but Virgil, as poet-guide and shadow-spirit, urges Dante to follow on behind him, leaving the spirits to talk. (Dante is Orpheus to Virgil's Eurydice, the living following the shade.) In the sonnet that gossip is alluded to, but the real issue is not so much what the gossips say about the beloved as what the lover-poet says of herself as an Orpheus figure. The lover-poet, echoing Virgil ("Even let them prate"), rejects the gossips' prattle but also questions her own lover/beloved relationship, its Orpheus-Eurydice pattern of "parting hopeless here to meet again." We wonder whether the man has become a Eurydice-like shade.[35]

The two final sonnets have subtexts from the *Paradiso*. Just as the invocation to Apollo and the apostrophe to the sun open the *Paradiso* (see sonnets 4, 10), so the sonnet sequence moves to the threshold of its conclusion (sonnet 13) with a reference to Saint Bernard directing Dante's gaze into the center of the luminous mystic rose, to the true light of the Primal Love. The sonnets seem to be heading toward apotheosis of love, according to the subtexts and indeed according to the thirteenth sonnet itself. The lady's love for her lover, and his image in her mind, so hard to maintain throughout the painful partings of the sequence as a "sight most dim," are relinquished into "God's hand" for completion. But the closure is blunted, the vision turned aside, not in the last subtext (*Par.* III. 85, Piccarda's summary of the theology of the *Paradiso*, "and his will is our peace"), but in the last sonnet. *Paradiso* III opens with Dante's reference to his first love, Beatrice, and to Piccarda, the sister of Dante's wife. Dante married despite his spiritual commitment to Beatrice; so also Piccarda was forced to break her religious vow (her spiritual commitment) in order to marry. It is highly appropriate that Piccarda lifts Dante's sight by revealing to him the true spiritual ground for love beyond earthly passion. She concludes the canto by singing the *Ave Maria* to the supreme Christian muse and poet of the *Magnificat* (whom Bernard also appeals to as muse and mediator in his hymn of prayer and praise to the Virgin in *Paradiso* XXXIII), and as Piccarda sings, she literally vanishes into song, suggesting an ironic contrast to the ending of Rossetti's last sonnet: "Silence of love that cannot sing again." Thus

[35]The parting of Dante and Virgil in *Purgatorio* XXX. 49–51, echoing the Orpheus and Eurydice passage in Virgil's *Georgics* IV. 525–27, also uses a male Eurydice figure. Dante Gabriel Rossetti made a pencil drawing of "Orpheus and Eurydice" in 1875 (now in the British Museum) which shows the moment of Orpheus' backward glance and the fading away of Eurydice; see Surtees, *Paintings and Drawings of Dante Gabriel Rossetti*, I, 141.

both the first and final Dante epigraphs have subtexts of hymns from other poets and muses (Ambrose and the Virgin), and as Sordello and Piccarda sing, they disappear, like Rossetti's persona, leaving only their song to echo in the ear.

The Petrarch epigraphs can be dealt with more expeditiously, though we must leave the intertextuality of Petrarch and Dante largely untouched here. Eight of the Petrarch epigraphs come from poems that refer directly or obliquely to writing poetry (those for sonnets 2, 5, 7, 8, 9, 10, 13, 14). Furthermore, the epigraphs for the octave of sonnets (except for sonnet 3) all come from the first part of Petrarch's poem, "Laura in Life"; indeed, sonnet 8, concluding the octave, uses an epigraph from the first poem in the *Rime*, which serves there as an introduction. The *volta* sonnet, number 9, uses a subtext from the second part of Petrarch's poem, "Laura in Death," and sonnets 10 and 11 also use poems from the second section of Petrarch. The final three sonnets use epigraphs from earlier in the Petrarch poem: the epigraph for sonnet 12 offers a comparison between Laura and other ladies (parallel to the comparison in Rossetti's sonnet); that for sonnet 13 refers to the beauty of Laura as too "heavy" for the poet's arm, too high for his pen, arm, or intellect to rise to, just as Rossetti's persona trusts not in her "hand" but in "God's hand" for dealing with the conventional subject of the beloved's fame ("your fate"). The final sonnet, alluding to Petrarch's second sestina through the "hair" or "locks" reference (*chiome*), offers a kind of supra-textual commentary on the myth of Apollo and Daphne which underlies the subtext. This myth was a favorite of Petrarch, as it allowed full verbal play on the Laura-laurel image, the leaves of the poem, the garland or crown of the poet, the breeze (*l'aura*) and gold (*l'auro*), motifs all tied to the mythical figure of the god of poetry and his quest for his beloved nymph. In Rossetti's sonnet, the speaker refuses to "bind fresh roses" (not laurels) in her hair; she favors instead the common autumnal flowers growing with the wheat ready for harvest (Matt. 13:30). Since, as she says, "youth [is] gone and beauty gone" (a parallel to Petrarch's coming to death with white, frosty locks), she wonders "what doth remain?" In Petrarch what remains is inward fire; in Rossetti it is a muted version of God's will and our peace (Dante epigraph to sonnet 13), as with altered locks (Petrarch epigraph to sonnet 14) and longing heart she concludes the sequence and the song, fading into silence.[36]

---

[36]Petrarch, like Dante, was well known in the Rossetti household. Gabriele Rossetti refers to him in a number of his works. The Rossetti libraries contained various

Context: Interrogating the Tradition

In the sonnet dedicated to her mother which opens "A *Pageant*" *and Other Poems*, Rossetti writes that "sonnets are full of love." A better summary of the genre would be difficult to find. Yet according to convention, love is not so much the subject as the inspiration of a sonnet; a sonnet is the by-product of love, as emotion is turned into art. The artifact honors the beloved and endows the relationship with some objective status more permanent than fleeting emotion or even enduring affection. Rossetti's sonnet continues: "I have woven a wreath / Of rhymes wherewith to crown your honoured name." This description of her poetic act also fits the minimal action of "*Monna Innominata*," the writing of a sequence by an unknown poet to her male beloved, himself a poet.

Initially, then, "*Monna Innominata*" reverses the Italian and Eliz-abethan roles of the lover and the beloved. The tradition gives power to the dominant male poet to immortalize and possess in poetry the remote and passive female beloved, who, but for his art, would be unknown. Rossetti's sequence represents a radical reappraisal of that conventional notion. The female poet, the *monna innominata* herself, appropriates the traditional male role, and the lady, far from being passive and remote, asserts the power of the word in her art. But the power she exerts is a muted one: she neither explores nor immortalizes her beloved's qualities through the deployment of conceits, but em-phasizes, first, reciprocation rather than dominance, as the lovers are "happy equals" (sonnet 7) in a love whose effect is liberation (sonnet 5), and then transmission rather than possession, as the poet commits her beloved to a transcendent Word ("Book" in sonnet 7; "Love" in 8; "God's hand" in 13).

Further, most of the sonnets use a direct mode of address. "You" or "your" is used in the first lines of all the sonnets except 8 (which contains no direct address at all), 10 (which moves to direct address only in line 11), and 14 (no direct address). That is, all the poems except those ending the octave and the sestet of this sonnet of son-nets, directly address a "you." The personae of the "you" and the "I"

---

editions of Petrarch edited by: Lodovico Dolci (Vinegia, 1553; 1556); Allesandro Vellutello (Vinegia, 1560); and G. Baglioli, 2 vols. in 3 (Paris, 1821), as well as the Pallada edition (Florence, 1821). As Cayley's executor, Christina Rossetti continued to receive a small income from the sale of his books, which included *The Sonnets and Stanzas of Petrarch* (1879).

are kept remarkably distinct throughout the sequence. The "we-us" pronouns rarely join them: in dreams ("only in a dream we are at one," 3), in idealized future states (4, 7, 10), and in only one reference to the past (11). The "you" of direct address invites the reader to respond as the recipient of the address. The sequence is, in an important sense, written to us. We are at once the readers, the beloved, and the fellow poet. We do not merely overhear the agony and the supplication, we are the audience: we are entreated, we are absent, and we may also be silent. Indeed, we are the *muta persona*, the product of the text as the text creates both us and our role, and builds us into the moment's monument as critic and judge, as well as equal.

In a way an implied contest is being waged between the two poets, the persona and the *muta persona* (whether Love or the loved one or the reader or all these), a contest that from time to time surfaces as verbal sparring in a dialogue, or implied dialogue:

I loved you first   (4)

Trust me, I have not earned your dear rebuke   (6)

"Love me, for I love you"—and answer me,
"Love me, for I love you"   (7)

Many in aftertimes will say of you
"He loved her"—while of me what will they say?   (11)

But even the traditional device of the debate is put into question by the many rhetorical questions and conditional clauses placed strategically through the sequence in all but two sonnets, 9 and 10. (Rhetorical questions appear in sonnets 1, 4, 5, 7 [3 questions], 11, 13, 14 [2], and conditional "if" clauses in 2 [3 conditionals], 3, 6 [2], 8 [2], 12 [2], 13, 14.) While on the one hand the unity of each sonnet is synchronic, a unity of the "moment" of the sonnet and the experience it records, on the other hand it is in every instance rendered either conditional or interrogative. Each sonnet, in raising conditions and questions, points to a perceptual tension for the lady (what does she know as certainty?) and for us (what are we to believe?).

When we look further into the sequence and begin to ask the text about its own questions, a deeper level of indeterminacy emerges. What does the male beloved do? How does he react? In the Elizabethan sequences the tradition is reasonably clear about the role of the female beloved—she may remain remote, or grant a "grace," or require service to be performed, or cast a look, or even speak or die. But the "object" of Rossetti's lady is shadowy. He is never described; we know nothing of his hair, lips, teeth, eyes, or voice. Sonnet 13 questions the traditional exchange of hearts in which the lady gives hers—but does the man? In the seventh sonnet, does the man respond as the lady asks? The male beloved is the lurking "absence" at the center of the text, but an absence that is elaborated, refined, and embroidered upon and about by the sonnets' concerns and questions. And for us as readers, what response are we expected to give to all these rhetorical questions, and is our response the same one expected of the male beloved? It seems doubtful whether any expected response to these "second-level" questions we readers pose is even available; the questions in the text, however, are genuine and compelling, as well as rhetorical.

One central group of questions concerns poetry and the beloved. A key question for the whole sequence, and one that may help to identify the male beloved with the work of art, is that which concludes the first sonnet. It is a variant of the *ubi sunt* motif, but is no less poignant for its conventionality:

> Ah me, but where are now the songs I sang
> When life was sweet because you called them sweet?

The traditional answer to the *ubi sunt* question is "in the grave" (as in Villon's "Ballad of Dead Ladies," in Dante Gabriel Rossetti's translation of this *locus classicus*), but here no unambiguous answer is given. Nonetheless, the lady seems to suggest that it is the songs and their occasion which are lost and gone. But the one who is absent, and from whom parting is agony, is the male beloved, and here he too is identified with the lost songs. Were they another and sweeter love-sonnet sequence, called up by the spring days of passion ("when life was sweet") and then judged by the male beloved/poet to be sweet? Now, instead of the lost sequence we have this last sequence. So the answer to the sonnet's question might be, "here"—in this sequence are the songs I sing: this is the monument to fame in "powerful rhyme."

It is the notion of the poem as monument that is continually set against the tradition as both the sonnet form and its conventional content are interrogated throughout the sequence. In sonnet 4 the male poet is said to have excelled the sweetness of the lady in her "first" poems:

Questioning the Convention: "*Monna Innominata*"

> I loved you first: but afterwards your love
>   Outsoaring mine, sang such a loftier song
> As drowned the friendly cooings of my dove.
>   Which owes the other most?

Here the interplay moves between love and poetry, as love turns into "song," a Victorian metonymy for poem.[37] In sonnet 7 the central difficulty of the lovers' relationship is tossed back to the male poet as a problem for him to solve in *his* poetry; the lady, however, turns to the central love poem of the Bible, the Song of Songs (8:6), for her concluding lines, which thus again pick up the poem-song metaphor.

The song motif is continued in a more muted way throughout the rest of the sequence to its last diminuendo in the final lines that, while they revert to the opening, cast no more light on it:

> Youth gone and beauty gone, what doth remain?
>   The longing of a heart pent up forlorn,
>   A silent heart whose silence loves and longs;
>   The silence of a heart which sang its songs
> While youth and beauty made a summer morn,
> Silence of love that cannot sing again.

The sequence is done, in the sense that it is now completed, but it has not reached its conclusion by completing either the movement from diction into vision (implied in the epigraph to sonnet 13), or the movement from resignation into consolation (suggested in the second half of the sequence and epitomized in the Dante epigraph to sonnet 14). The poem ends with an expression of a much darker heart where art fades into silence. At that point nothing more can be said.

Rossetti's poem, however, deconstructs the tradition of the love-sonnet sequence even more radically than I have hitherto suggested. Rossetti sets out to subvert conventional signification. All the signs should point toward the reification of the late Victorian woman's place, to the conventional female lover's acceptance of a lowly position, her sublimation of forbidden passions into an otherworldly piety or into a long-suffering silence. But in this sequence the tradition of the Elizabethan lover-poet and the remote, ideal lady of love, and

---

[37]Cf. the opening lines of the first poem (after the dedicatory sonnet to her mother) in *A Pageant*, entitled "The Key-Note": "Where are the songs I used to know, / Where are the notes I used to sing?" (II, 59).

their counterparts, the Victorians caught in the lover-marriage-honor ideology, are set in collision. Again and again the Elizabethan tradition is challenged, and the challenge comes from the conflict between personal agony and sublimation, between passion and Christian morality.

The seeming unity of the text, so easy to explicate simplistically, is at variance with the agony of the persona. Even with the poet's efforts to externalize her passion into a religious renunciation of the lesser for the greater good, even with her appeal to an Absolute outside the poem, her conventional escape into poetry—a recognized quasi-theological device for the late-Romantic poet—offers no release into the transcendence of art or nature.[38] Poetry does not offer a better or a golden world here; it does not combine the expressive and the assertive modes of discourse; and the imagination is not the realm for which the poet's art or heart yearns.

The prevailing Victorian ideology of hierarchy and patriarchy, with its implications for those excluded from power (those not part of the hierarchy or the patriarchy, those at the bottom of the social scale, and almost all women), suggested an alternate route to a power that would not challenge it, namely deferment: submitting to suffering here and now while anticipating a spiritual power in a metaphysical hereafter. That prevailing ideology with its implications is challenged directly in sonnet 7 (in the lines on equality) and more obliquely elsewhere in the sequence through the motif of freedom. By emphasizing her equality with the beloved both in a professional or artistic role (as poet) and in sexual roles (she affirms their mutual love and reciprocal relationship), the female poet offers her critique of the Victorian ideology.[39] Although the poet is captured by the ideology—she

[38]See M. H. Abrams, *The Mirror and the Lamp* (New York: Norton, 1958), pp. 334–35: "Arnold's innovation . . . was to place on poetry, with this demonstrated power of achieving effects independently of assent, the tremendous responsibility of the functions once performed by the exploded dogmas of religion and religious philosophy." See also Derek Colville, *Victorian Poetry and the Romantic Religion* (Albany: State University of New York Press, 1970), pp. 58–64.

[39]That critique is apparently much at odds with Rossetti's comprehensive writings on the roles of women (in *LS* pp. 91–93; in *FD* pp. 312, 357, 400, 416, etc.; and in such poems as "Eve" and "A helpmeet for him"). These writings must be set against her strong response to Augusta Webster, the poet and suffragist:

Does it not appear as if the Bible was based upon an understood unalterable distinction between men and women, their position, duties, privileges? Not arrogating to myself but most earnestly desiring to attain to the character of a

cannot make her poem public and so lapses into silence; she suffers and is still—she can at the same time criticize. She writes her sequence, and her "agent," Christina Rossetti, publishes it for us. The critique progresses dialectically. In each sonnet contradictory and antithetical formulations—of the role of lover/beloved, poet/critic, and love/barrier to love—instead of resulting in the smooth suppression of difference into harmony, move into a new premise for the next sonnet, where the struggle continues, not for a higher goal of reconciliation, but simply for recognition.

The "*Monna Innominata*" sequence shares some characteristics with classic realist fiction.[40] It is built on or around a love-enigma (which is foreshadowed in the title), with hints in the preface of obstacles to the lovers' public expression of their love, obstacles dramatized by their infrequent meetings (referred to in sonnet 1). The sequence offers some promise that the reader might learn the "meaning" of the meetings and partings, the nature of the barrier between the lovers, or the course of their actual or "real" relationship: in realist fiction and in sonnets closure is conventionally offered through disclosure. But here

---

humble orthodox Xtian, so it does appear to me; not merely under the Old but also under the New Dispensation. The fact of the Priesthood being exclusively man's, leaves me in no doubt that the highest functions are not in this world open to both sexes: and if not all, then a selection must be made and a line drawn somewhere.—On the other hand if female rights are sure to be overborne for lack of female voting influence, then I confess I feel disposed to shoot ahead of my instructresses, and to assert that female M. P.'s are only right and reasonable. Also I take exceptions at the exclusion of married women from the suffrage,—for who so apt as Mothers—all previous arguments allowed for the moment—to protect the interests of themselves and of their offspring? I do think if anything ever does sweep away the barrier of sex, and make the female not a giantess or a heroine but at once and full grown a hero and giant, it is that mighty maternal love which makes little birds and little beasts as well as little women matches for very big adversaries.

Quoted in Mackenzie Bell, *Christina Rossetti: A Biographical and Critical Study* (London: Hurst and Blackett, 1898), pp. 111–12. See also the weighed assessment of Rossetti's attitude to women in Wion, " 'Give Me the Lowest Place,' " pp. 10–64.

[40]See the discussion of the relation of classic realist fiction to the interrogative text in Catherine Belsey, *Critical Practice* (London: Methuen, 1982), pp. 67–102. Belsey argues that "classic realism is characterized by *illusionism*, narrative which leads to *closure*, and a *hierarchy of discourses* which establishes the 'truth' of the story" (p. 70; italics in the original). Beginning in disorder (the result of "murder, war, a journey, or love"), the story moves to reestablish order, as in novels by Dickens, George Eliot, or Hardy.

the reader is granted no such revelation; disclosure is withheld. The story's plot does not unravel toward the end, the beloved is not identified, nothing in the lovers' relationship is made explicit, no closure to the sequence reveals implications. Instead the concealments become increasingly convoluted mysteries, the very mysteries invoked at the beginning of classic realist fiction and traditionally dispelled by the denouement.

I shall now examine the sequence as a whole to show how completely Rossetti's challenge to the convention is worked out in the individual sonnets of the sequence.

The Text: Challenging the Convention

The "*Monna Innominata*" sonnet sequence as a whole is structured in the form of a Petrarchan sonnet, with each of the fourteen sonnets functioning like one of its lines, their arguments like the traditional rhymes, supporting an overall interlocked pattern. The conventional sonnet subject, love, is explored throughout the sequence, together with subsidiary and interlaced themes of separation and loss, art, death, and God, six themes analogous to six rhymes. Over and over words for loss, parting, separation, and death, for love of the beloved and of God, for art and song, are interwoven through the sonnets, linking the themes by word echoes, variations, and reflections. Nor are these themes displayed randomly: a clear structural pattern emerges, pivoting on the traditional division of a sonnet into an octave that conventionally presents a problem and a sestet that offers a solution.

The first quatrain of the octave of sonnets presents the problem for passionate love when set against the loss of love within the dimension of time; the second quatrain describes that privation when it is extended beyond time in prayer to God for the beloved. In detail, the sequence moves from the grievous effect of partings on the lovers' passion and poetry (sonnet 1), to loss of the memory of the lovers' first meeting (2), to illusionistic dream-union (3), and to the separation caused by lovers' rivalry in both poetic art and love (4). Hence the quatrain begins and ends with themes of separation, which frame the memory and the dream. The second quatrain of sonnets places human separation within a larger spiritual dimension beyond time, in prayer and divine love. It begins with the unrestrained prayer of the lover (5) who, after being rebuked, would prefer losing the beloved rather than

God, if forced to choose between them. But she places her love, including the beloved himself, within the encompassing love of God (6). Then, in the balancing sonnet halfway through the sequence (7), she stresses equality and security of love, only to displace that theme with a poetic-military attack and an expression of a renewed fear of separation, a fear overcome only by the notion that love conquers death. At the end of the octave the lover moves to prayer for her beloved, using Esther's prayer as her model (8).

The *volta* of the sequence comes with sonnet 9, which opens the sestet: "all that was, and all / That might have been and now can never be." The sestet of sonnets first seems to suggest a solution in the lover-poet's dedication to service and faith in the final victory of love beyond time, but that solution is challenged as she commends her beloved to his own destiny and to God, while she repudiates poetry with an aching and longing heart.

The first tercet begins by acknowledging the loss described in the octave of sonnets but mitigates the conventional lover's despair at the loss of the beloved with muted hope leading through love to the grace of service (9). Sonnet 10 develops the motif of the race in which time, hope, life, and death are conquered by "life reborn," which annuls "loss and decay and death, and all is love." This more optimistic argument is challenged by others' gossip, by the lovers' hopeless separations on earth, and their uncertain future in heaven, though the beloved must testify to the fidelity of the lady's love at the Last Judgment (11).

In the final tercet, however, the mood darkens again, first with the possible replacement of the lover with another woman—and the lover's acquiescence in that possibility, knowing that the gift of her heart ensures her a place in any such relationship her beloved might have (12). Then the lover-poet commends her beloved to God in love and trust (13), and, with "youth gone, and beauty gone," she concludes the sequence by renouncing poetic art in an ultimate separation, lapsing into the silence of a longing heart "pent up forlorn" (14).

This pattern may be summarized rather arbitrarily, stating the main theme for each sonnet, together with an epithet and letter indicating a possible analogy to a Petrarchan sonnet's rhyme scheme:

1.	Impact of meetings and partings on love and art	SEPARATION	a
2.	Loss of memory of first meeting	LOSS OF MEMORY	b
3.	Illusionistic dream-vision	DREAM	b

117

4.	Separate rivalries in poetic art and love	SEPARATE RIVALRIES	a
5.	Prayer of lover for beloved	PRAYER	c
6.	Love of God, and of lover in God	LOVE IN GOD	d
7.	Equality and security of love, despite attack and separation: love conquers death	LOVE CONQUERS DEATH	d
8.	Esther's prayer as model for lover	PRAYER	c
9.	Loss, despair: muted hope through love to service	DEDICATION	e
10.	Race of time, hope, life, death: life reborn in love	LOSS CHANGED TO LOVE REBORN	d
11.	Gossip and hopeless partings; testimony of love at Last Judgment	LOSS CHANGED TO LOVE AFFIRMED	d
12.	Lover's place in beloved's heart, despite his love of another	COMMENDATION TO ANOTHER	f
13.	Lover commends the beloved to God in love and trust	COMMENDATION TO GOD	f
14.	Youth and beauty gone, longing and silence remain: final separation	VALEDICTION	e

Sonnet 1 develops the oxymoronic relationship of pleasure and pain connected with infrequent meetings and too frequent partings. The Elizabethan convention exploits a quite different notion, the absence of the beloved. This absence is the source of the poet's pain in the sonnets of Sidney (*Astrophel and Stella,* 87–89, 91–92, 106–8), Spenser (*Amoretti,* 52, 78, 87–89), and Shakespeare (57–58). Rossetti's sonnet, like those of the Elizabethans, is filled with temporal terms ("not yet," "then," "long," "before," "again," "while," "when") and one conventional image (the changing moon).[41] But while, for the sonneteers, time (which is the time of lovers' separation) comes to rest in waiting, memory, or death, the temporal terms of Rossetti's poet shift back and forth with no final resting place. The poet's one point of repose is in the synecdoche: "For one man is my world of all the men / This wide world holds." The beloved is the lady's metaphoric world, a static element contrasting with her vacillation and the image

[41]A few other traditional images appear in Rossetti's sequence: Cupid is possibly referred to once (sonnet 10), and nature appears in the cycles of time, the seasons, the sea (7), and in roses (14); but for Rossetti even the sky, traditionally compared to the beloved's eyes, acquires a religious connotation (heaven), and she uses no images of fire, ice, marble, or bronze. A number of conventional themes and conceits are reversed.

of the changing moon. The lovers' meetings are not the conventional consolation they should be, nor is parting Juliet's "sweet sorrow." Instead the lady waits and watches in the role of the mythological Hero waiting for her Leander. Her hope, the conventional solace of the lover in sonnet sequences, is changeable; and her art is dumb ("where are now the songs I sang?"), except that this new song chronicles this new pain.

The second sonnet challenges the convention of the lovers' first meeting, and the new dating of time from that event. That convention is determinative in the archetypal *Vita nuova* of Dante and is also celebrated in Petrarch's poem, especially in the sonnet that is the source of the epigraph (20), as well as in other sonnets (e.g., 13, 61, 96, 101, 175, and 196). Rossetti goes against the whole of this tradition in having her lady forget the circumstances of the first meeting— all the details are gone like "bygone snow," she says, again echoing Villon's refrain, "où sont les neiges d'antan?" The anaphoristic repetitions are almost a litany to invoke the past and condemn the lady's inattentiveness, while the repeated "re–" prefix summarizes that effort to grasp memory again ("remember," "unrecorded," "recollect," "recall"). The poem moves to its climax in line 12, contrasting appearance and reality in an antithesis: "It seemed to mean so little, meant so much." Petrarch was ashamed to capture the beauty of his lady in rhyme (*vostra bellezza in rima,* 20), and although he remembered his first sight of her, found his hand unable to write. Rossetti's poet, in contrast to yet another poet's rendering of a first meeting (Romeo's "If I profane with my unworthiest hand") cannot "recall that touch, / First touch of hand in hand."

The convention in sonnet 3 is sustained almost to the end, only to be challenged in the last line. The happy dream-vision is set out in the antitheses of dreaming/waking, blushing/waning, day/night, give/take, die/live. As long as her dream endures, the lady can meet her beloved without the fearful pang of parting (sonnet 1), and that is her wish, like that of Milton in his sonnet "Methought I saw my late espousèd saint / Brought to me like Alcestis from the grave." The aim of the conventional lover is to prolong the illusionistic dream, to avoid the realist awakening; Rossetti pursues that goal using in reverse order the terms of Hamlet's soliloquy: "to die, to sleep; / To sleep, perchance to dream." None of Rossetti's material is unconventional, but in the last line of the sonnet the entire courtly ethic collides with the biblical ethic. A central doctrine of the courtly tradition is the transforming power of love, which itself gives the lover a new life (*vita nuova*) and changes the dream-vision of the beloved into a reality that is absolutely unique, beyond compare; but Rossetti's lady escapes that traditional transformation with an allusion to one of the most fatalistic texts in the Bible, Ecclesiastes 1:9: "Though there be nothing new beneath the sun."

The implied background of sonnets 4 to 6 is a discussion between the lovers (the traditional form is the conceit of a debate) about priority in love and art (4), the comparative strength of their love (5), and the justification for the lady's apparently excessive love (6). Sonnet 4 presents a version of the conventional amorous and poetic contest: the inequality of the lovers' love is explored in the first half (seven lines) of the poem, but in the second half the poem turns (the *volta*) and balances the argument by affirming the lovers' equality. The rhyme scheme of the first quatrain (*abab*) underscores the rivalry, while in the next quatrain the beloved's "strong" love encloses that of the lady (*bccb*). Rivalry in terms of weights, measures, construing contests is then seen as wrong in both love and poetry; love is properly unifying and reciprocal, qualities reflected in the poem's enmeshed rhymes, internal rhymes, and echoic repetitions, chiasmus (l. 11), and parallelism between lines (ll. 9 and 12) and within them (l. 13):

> For verily love knows not "mine" or "thine;"
>   With separate "I" and "thou" free love has done,
>   For one is both and both are one in love:
> Rich love knows nought of "thine that is not mine;"
>   Both have the strength and both the length thereof,
>   Both of us, of the love which makes us one.

The notion that lovers should be so interpenetrated, far beyond the exchange of hearts, so as to cease rivalry, subverts the convention of the beloved as exalter, the lover as abased (queen/subject, mistress/slave, goddess/worshiper, saint/sinner, pride/humility, as in Petrarch, 21, 140, 154, 294, and 302). Instead, these equal lovers (already different from the conventional ones in that the Lady took the initiative both in love and in poetry) have, in the first four sonnets, progressed from separation into unity.

In sonnet 5 the theme of equality in sonnet 4 is renewed and given a new direction. Instead of building on the master-servant roles that dominate the convention (and dominated society—no less in Victorian than in Elizabethan England), the precatory predicates ("Keep,"

"Give," "Make," "Bless," "Perfect") ask that the beloved, traditionally the master or mistress of love, should become the obedient servant, not to the lover-poet, but to God, "To Him whose noble service setteth free" (an echo of the collect for peace at morning prayer in the *Book of Common Prayer*). The traditional service for the lady is here redirected to service for God and is thus transformed into perfect freedom. This service, the beloved's role, occupies the octave. After the *volta* (l. 9) the speaker's prayer shifts to her role, which she sees as that of an Eve figure, not after the Fall, but in a state of prelapsarian equality as helpmeet, loving her "Adam" into service by loving him "without stint." The Dante epigraph quoting Francesca da Rimini reminds us of another Eve figure who loved without stint, but an Eve after the Fall. The poem thus brings into collision two kinds of unstinted loving, dispassionate and passionate, especially ambiguous since no qualification is placed on the lady-poet's love for the man. As a result, the reader is left (as the beloved man himself might have been) with a triply unsettling feeling that the beloved is being prayed into God's service, that the lover is almost idolatrous in her love (despite the biblical and prayer book echoes), and that she is adopting an Eve role, always ambiguous, suggesting the societal and biblical convention of helpmeet-service.

One or more of these possibilities, or perhaps some other reason has, sonnet 6 leads us to assume, caused the Lady to be rebuked by her beloved ("your dear rebuke"). From the context it appears that the suggestion of idolatrous love is the most probable cause. Sonnet 6 carefully sets out the Lady's limits on her love, limits so much at variance with the unstinted love of sonnet 5. The lover devotes the octave to the assertion that her love for God is primary (had she to choose between her lover and God), and that her faithful eyes would not be averted from God by her lover—she would not look back longingly to him and so be lost (like Lot's wife gazing back at Sodom [Gen. 19:26], a neat variation on the Eurydice figure that will be referred to later in sonnet 11 and its Dante epigraph). In the sestet the persona moves from answering the rebuke to defending her position by an appeal to the expansiveness of love (the *volta* comes with "Yet") in the tradition of Donne's "Valediction: Forbidding Mourning." In the resolution (the last tercet, beginning with "Yea") the exclusivist convention that the lover have no rivals is deconstructed in the face of the Victorian emphasis on the summary of the law (Mark 12:29–31). The paradoxical conclusion is a more serious theological challenge to the beloved than the witty permission or excuse Spenser finds in the idea:

> So let us love, dear love, like as we ought:
> Love is the lesson which the Lord us taught.
>
> [*Amoretti*, 68]

The "balance" sonnet, number 7, balances two identical texts in the first two lines:

> "Love me, for I love you"—and answer me,
> "Love me, for I love you"—so shall we stand. . . .

The second line, of course, is psychologically different from the first, since the first conditions it as text; the intervening imperative "and answer me" makes a requirement of the beloved to which he might or might not wish to respond. All depends on his response, the "so" of the next phrase. Were he to so respond (we are not told he does), the balance of the "happy equals in the flowering land" can be realized. The octave explores the possible result of the beloved's acquiescence in a series of interconnected relationships to myth, text, and convention:

> . . . so shall we stand
> As happy equals in the flowering land
> Of love, that knows not a dividing sea.
> Love builds the house on rock and not on sand,
> Love laughs what while the winds rave desperately;
> And who hath found love's citadel unmanned?
> And who hath held in bonds love's liberty?

First the myth of Hero and Leander is introduced, to be rejected. Hero (whom Dante refers to in lines 71–74 of the same canto that provides the epigraph) is the conventional passive watcher for her actively swimming Leander, and the two together form an icon of tragic lovers separated by sea, circumstance, and death (cf. sonnet 1), a motif found throughout Elizabethan sequences.[42] But the lovers in

---

[42]See, for example, *Purg.* XXVIII. 70 ff.; the sonneteers: Barnabe Barnes, *Parthenophil and Parthenophe*, 44; Samuel Daniel, *Delia*, 41; Bartholomew Griffin, *Fidessa*, 13; William Smith, *Chloris*, 17, 25; and [anon.], *Zepheria*, 8. Narrative and other lyric

Rossetti's sonnet are not separated by a metaphorical Hellespont. Instead they stand secure "as happy equals" in love's landscape. The second quatrain replaces the dividing sea with the shifting sand, and the stance of the equal lovers with the image of their solidity—the house built on a rock. This house, however, is built not by a wise man, as in the biblical source (Matt. 7: 24–27), but by love. Greek myth and biblical parable are conflated, then questioned ("Love laughs [at] *what* [or with what words] while the winds rave desperately?" [italics added]). Is love seen as mocking Hero's mourning? Does love mock or praise the wise man with the solid house? What does love laugh at, and why does it laugh? Both texts, the biblical metaphor and the Greek myth, are put into question, since neither is given a privileged position as an authority.

The octave concludes with two further questions, both aimed at two sonnet-sequence conventions: the siege of love's citadel (conflated in Rossetti's sonnet with the house built on rock) and the lover's captivity by the love of his lady: he is held in the bonds of love, she remains free.[43] Surely we must suppose that the conventional answer to both questions is "no one"—no lover has ever found love's citadel undefended (for the lady is always chaste), and no lover, however bound, has ever been able to restrict his lady's, or "love's liberty." Even if the lover were able to penetrate love's citadel and capture love, love would still be free. But the convention demands the *unsuccessful* attack of the lover on the free citadel of the lady's heart, as well as the *successful* counterattack by the lady on the lover's heart, which is seized and bound while she continues to enjoy her freedom. The life of the lover is conventionally one of captivity, not freedom. Rossetti's questioning of the convention displaces these conceits from privileged

versions of the story include: Marlowe, *Hero and Leander*, with Chapman's continuation; Spenser in the *Hymn in Honour of Love*, 231, and various references in Shakespeare's comedies. Hero and Leander were popular Romantic and Victorian lovers too: see Keats, "Sonnet on a Picture of Hero and Leander" (1818); Leigh Hunt, "Hero and Leander" (1819); Thomas Hood, "Hero and Leander" (1827); Tennyson, "Hero to Leander" (1830); Thomas Moore, "Hero and Leander" (1840); Dante Gabriel Rossetti, "Hero's Lamp" (1881). W. J. M. Turner's oil of 1837, *The Parting of Hero and Leander—from the Greek of Musaeus* was also accompanied by his own verses in the catalogue.

[43]For the conceit of the citadel besieged, see Petrarch (274), Sidney (*Astrophel and Stella*, 12, 36), and Spenser (*Amoretti*, 14); for love's captivity in bonds and loss of liberty, see Petrarch (89), Sidney (2, 29), and Barnes (*Parthenophil and Parthenophe*, 65).

positions as clichés and leaves them uncentered. By reversing the conventional sex roles and by questioning the validity of the conceits, Rossetti undermines our expectations: we do not know whether the lady-poet's attack on the citadel of the male beloved is repelled by him or not, or even if she makes such an attack (possibly in this poem?); nor do we know who is captive in love's bonds, nor who is liberated by love.

The sestet of sonnet 7, which links the military imagery to the persona ("My heart's a coward tho' my words are brave"), begins by reviving from sonnet 1 the theme of seldom meeting and frequent parting of lovers (Hero and Leander again), not as a source of pain, as before, but as a "problem for your art." The motif of lovers' partings is tossed to the male beloved as a subject for his poetry. The final tercet turns on "still," another of these temporally or spatially ambiguous conjunctions that Rossetti uses to pivot a sonnet. At this point the speaker appeals to an external and privileged "signified" in the form of "his Book," not that of the male poet but that of the archetypal lover of the Hebrew Bible, Solomon. The lady quotes the Song of Songs (8:6), omitting the water imagery ("Many waters cannot quench love, neither can the floods drown it"), which would have linked the end of the sonnet too formally and conclusively with the earlier "dividing sea." Finally, the speaker introduces, quite unexpectedly, the notion of "jealousy," which, in the terms of the syllogism, love is able to conquer as easily as death. We are again left with unresolved questions: who is jealous, and of whom? The lady who finds comfort in the cited "Book"? Is the lady the object of another suitor's jealousy, or is the man jealous? Thus the balance of the poem, hinging on the opening lines with their identical phrases and the conditional protasis based on the "so" clause, and even the balance of the lovers as "happy equals," are effectively undermined in the sestet, first by the speaker's challenge to the beloved's craft and finally by the closing conundrum.

The eighth sonnet turns away from direct address to, in the first twelve lines, a description of a biblical event: Queen Esther's preparation to enter unbidden the preserve of King Ahasuerus to ask him to attend two banquets, at the second of which she will request him to repeal or modify Haman's edict ordering the annihilation of the Jews in Persia (Esther 3–9). Actually, however, the poem describes not so much an event or an action as a ceremonial occasion involving the risk of death. The poem's first conditional phrase is a direct quotation (Esther 4:16), but the next eleven lines gloss two verses from the Authorized Version: "Esther put on her royal apparel and stood in the inner court of the king's house: and the king sat upon his royal throne. . . . And it was so, when the king saw Esther the queen standing in the court, that she obtained favour in his sight" (Esther 5:1–2). This account is much expanded in the continuation of the Book of Esther in the Apocrypha (chap. 15), where Esther is described as "gloriously adorned" and carrying herself "daintily"; "ruddy through the perfection of her beauty . . . her countenance was cheerful and very amiable" (15:5). But entering the king's presence, she grew pale and fainted, whereupon the king "took her in his arms, till she came to herself again, and comforted her with loving words" (15:8).

The sonnet, however, ignores this drama and casts its various elements into one: the seductiveness of the beautiful lady setting out to entrap her victim (as in Daniel's *To Delia*, sonnet 14, and Spenser's *Amoretti*, 37). Rossetti's Esther is a kind of virtuous Dalila (see *Samson Agonistes*. 710 ff., "But who is this . . . bedecked, ornate, and gay?"). But while the beautiful temptress convention is treated erotically in the Elizabethan sonnets and destructively by Milton, Rossetti makes her temptress the instrument of divine will, the means of saving Israel, "her people's house" (cf. the solid "house on rock" in sonnet 7). The *volta* in the sonnet comes at the final tercet with an audacious comparison between Esther and the persona, who is to take her life in her hand, presumably in approaching her beloved, or so we are led to think at first as the lady prays "for my love to Love." We do not know whether the prayer is addressed to the mythological god of love, or to the loving biblical God, or whether "my love" refers to the lady's love for the beloved, or to the beloved himself. All that is clear is that the speaker is appealing to the power of Love beyond herself. In another sense, the life "so in my hand" might well be the poet's art, her art of poetry as prayer. This interpretation picks up the motif in the Petrarch epigraph, from the first sonnet of his *Rime*, where he asks for pity and pardon for his varied style (*vario stile*). Convention dictates that the poem immortalize the beloved (Daniel, *To Delia*, 37: "This may remain thy lasting monument"), but here the speaker prays that, just as Esther was able to eternize "her people's house" by means of her beauty adorned with her art, so she, through her poet's art, might be granted the eternizing of "my love." But the subject of the speaker's prayer, its content and goal, is never stated here (except that it is "for my love"). Further, even the prayer is conditional: "if I might."

The *volta* of the sequence comes with sonnet 9 and the "now" of the second line:

> Thinking of you, and all that was, and all
> That might have been and now can never be. . . .

That "now" is final and carries the consequence of "never" later in the line, whatever event "now" might refer to. For Dante and Petrarch the "now" events were the deaths of Beatrice and of Laura. Death, in fact, is addressed directly in the Petrarch sonnet from which the epigraph to Rossetti's sonnet comes, and the "now" is identified as an instant (*un momento*). In sonnet 267, which first announces Laura's death, the now (*omai*) is even clearer, and in the following *canzone* Petrarch laments what can never be, for he never hopes to see her more (*mai veder lei*, 268. l. 6). The barrier mentioned earlier in Rossetti's sequence, the "dividing sea" that caused the too brief meetings and too long partings, seems here to be elevated into something more final that excludes the possibilities of "might have been" as well as the actual "all that was." The effect on the lady is to make her feel "unworthy of the happier call," of her vocation to poetry, or to the married state, or to death, or to heaven, or to some elements of all four. The lament of the second quatrain, echoing the "alas" of Petrarch's sonnet 267 (*oimè*) in its repeated "woe is me . . . ah, woe is me!" turns to "his Book" for "comfort" (sonnet 7) in the sestet. In these last six lines, the poet pieces together a pattern of biblical echo and quotation which reveals that she still cherishes some hope and faith, because love endures.[44] The sonnet concludes with the task of love, the task of the poet, and the task of grace, that is, with the Beatrician task of giving guidance to the other poet. Here Rossetti challenges the convention of the dead lady as guide, for in her poem a living lady continues the task of eternizing the beloved in both the secular and theological senses, even though he remains unknown, a *dominus innominato*.

The octave of the tenth sonnet develops the metaphor of a race in which the runners are time, hope, life, and death, while faith "runs with each."[45] In the first tercet, the runners have grown weary and

---

[44]The biblical references are to Genesis 32:24; 2 Kings 20:2; Luke 5:5; 1 Corinthians 13; 2 Corinthians 12:15; Ephesians 6:24.

[45]Cf. Virgil, *Georgics: fugit irreparabile tempus* (III. 284); Ovid, *Amores: Dum loquor, hora fugit* (I. 11); Hebrews 12:1; Petrarch (37.17 ff.); Drayton, *Idea*, 61. The sestet, with some variants and dated 1870, was from a sonnet "By Way of Remembrance" ("I love you and you know it . . . "), and was printed in facsimile in William Michael Rossetti's *Some Reminiscences*, II, opposite p. 312, where he says that it was dedicated to C. B. Cayley (not noted in Crump, II, 373).

"when" love (a dove or Cupid?) folds his wings, then it is time, the speaker says, to "fall asleep, dear friend, in peace." Once more, we cannot be certain that it is the poet's love that, like life, has waned, but when it does, it is time for the poet to die. The apparently conventional final tercet states that after "a little while" "age and sorrow cease," as reborn life transmutes all into love; but whether that "little while" is the "now" of a permanent barrier to marriage, or the "then" of old age, or of the moment of death, we do not know. At any rate, this metamorphosis changes the eternizing function of the poem, which traditionally is the lady's only source of immortality, into an external, extra-poetical appeal to a divine act in the future. The lovers' temporal problems of the "now" and "never" of sonnet 9 have been projected in sonnet 10 into the "when" and "little while" of "life reborn," not in the materiality of a sonnet, but in a transcendent future.

In sonnet 11 both past and present are seen from the vantage of the future:

> Many in aftertimes will say of you
> "He loved her"—while of me what will they say?

That vantage, however, is not for sight but for sound. The poet's songs will not have informed others of her love, as her songs appear to be private (were his songs public, thus warranting the others' statement, "He loved her"?). Again the speaker refers to the pain of parting (as in sonnets 1 and 7) but refrains from appealing to the conventional solace of Dante and Petrarch, reunion in heaven, for "heaven is out of view." That comment is a serious questioning of the "all is love" assertion at the end of sonnet 10. The sestet, rising to a climax in this part of the sequence, but not mentioning anything about how "he loved her," becomes a charge to the beloved, grounded in the poet's exposed heart and on her love that he cannot modify, her love that has given him up (to marriage, or rather to death and God):

> Love that foregoes you but to claim anew
> Beyond this passage of the gate of death.

By these appeals the poet charges the beloved to make it plain at the Last Judgment how, contrary to the gossip of the opening lines (also suggested by the Dante epigraph), she loved: "My love of you was life and not a breath." She is declaring not only the word, the

127

words, the poem, or the art, but reality, truth, or life. Even if at the Last Judgment she says nothing of his love, he must assert hers. Her charge is an act of defiance carried to an extreme court, to the ultimate *terminus ad quem*, where, to reveal the truth about the quality of her love, she appeals, not to gossip (cf. Drayton, *Idea*, 24: "I hear some say, 'This man is not in love!'"), nor to the artifact (*Idea*, 24: "'Read but his Verse, and it will easily prove!'"), nor even to her own testimony, but to that of the beloved. Even the convention of the Final Judgment at which all are to give accounts of the quality of their own love is decentered, displaced into his evidence about her.

The twelfth sonnet questions at least three conventional sonnet-sequence themes: that of the jealous lover, the bridal-poetic crowning, and the exchange of hearts.[46] Thus, where we might expect the lady to be jealous of her replacement as lover or poet, she graciously yields her place to the one with "nobler grace" or "readier wit" or "sweeter face." Yet this conventional humility of the lady, still more typical of the sonneteer (as in Petrarch, 179), is governed by the conditional "if there be any one" that opens the sonnet. We do not know whether or not there is such a rival. The male beloved is even told to "conceive" and to understand that, were someone to replace her, the poet herself would be crowned while making another's bridal wreaths, through the exchange of hearts. The crowning with wreaths is seen also as an exchange of poetic gifts ("your riches make me rich") and laurels.[47]

In "*A Pageant*" *and Other Poems*, Rossetti, in the dedicatory sonnet to her mother ("Sonnets are full of love"), tied love, the wreath, and the poem together with the crown and honor:

> . . . because
> I love you, Mother, I have woven a wreath
> Of rhymes wherewith to crown your honoured name.

[46]For the jealous lover, see Petrarch (222); for the crowning, see Petrarch (23, 30, 34, 228, 263); for the exchange of hearts, see Shakespeare (Sonnets 22, 39, 40, 42, 48).

[47]In his laureate sermon delivered on the Capitoline Hill on Easter Day, 1341, Petrarch developed the idea of the laurel as a figure for poetry and immortality. See E. H. Wilkins, *Studies in the Life and Works of Petrarch* (Cambridge, Mass.: Medieval Academy of America, 1955), pp. 300–313. Gabriele Rossetti quotes Petrarch's sonnet 263 identifying the laurel as the honor of emperors and of poets, and also as the true lady (*Vera Donna*); see Rossetti, *Antipapal Spirit*, II, 88.

In sonnet 12, the poet's coronal of love and honor is to be woven into an epithalamium to celebrate the beloved's marriage to another woman. But the conception that in the nuptials the speaker is also crowned is tied to the "if there be any one" of the opening line, and so is put into doubt.

In the sestet the poet's concern with a possible rival on earth or in heaven is again set aside in favor of the exchange of hearts:

> But since the heart is yours that was mine own,
> Your pleasure is my pleasure, right my right,
> Your honourable freedom makes me free,
> And you companioned I am not alone.

A problem remains. We know the lady gave her heart—but did the man? Nothing is said of his feelings. The gift of her heart means she shares his pleasure, his rights, his freedom, and even his companion. Her audacious exploitation of the convention of the exchange of hearts leaves her neither spinster nor widow.[48]

The thirteenth sonnet raises the problem of trust with another opening conditional, "If I could trust mine own self with your fate." Whether the lady means as spouse, as judge, or as poet is not clear. Instead she commits the beloved's fate to "God's hand," echoing sonnet 8 ("If I might take my life so in my hand"). There follows a hymn in praise of God's providential care for creation in even the most humble cases (lily, sparrow); his vastness (he numbers the sand); his power (he weighs the winds and water); his otherness (to him the world is neither small nor great); and his omniscience, greatly surpassing in kind the lovers' concern with "weights and measures" in sonnet 4.[49] In the sestet, God's task of searching the heart (1 Chron. 28:9, Jer. 17:10, and elsewhere) is taken over by the lady, and in her heart she finds only love. She has cast off all her earlier roles—lover (5, 6), helpmeet (5), thinker with insight (6), perhaps even poet ("impotent to do")—and so, instead of returning a poetic subject to the man (7), she returns her poetic "subject" to God.

Having committed her beloved, the "you" in sonnet 13, back to God in the apparent ending of the outward-directed process of the

---

[48]Cf. Drayton, *Idea*, 11.

[49]The biblical echoes are from Isaiah 40:12 (also Job 28:25); Matthew 6:28–30; Matthew 10:29; Romans 8:29, and other related textual passages, such as Genesis 32:12; Psalm 139:18; and Revelation 20:8.

sequence, the lady/lover/poet has also committed her readers, the other "you" directly addressed in sonnet 13, back to God. In sonnet 14 it remains for her to assess her own inward state and to take a final leave both of the beloved and of us. Conventionally at the end of a sequence, the lover remains alone, resigned to enduring the changes of age and time as he waits for death and anticipates a reunion with the beloved in heaven. By contrast, Rossetti's poet has one remaining act she must accomplish, and in an unconventional envoi she bids adieu not only to her readers and to youth and beauty, but also to the lost, last song.

The theme of "youth gone, and beauty gone" (a final version of the *ubi sunt* question in sonnet 1) is repeated three times, in the first line of the octave, in line three, and in the first line of the sestet. The first instance is a conditional clause, the others are two rhetorical questions that merge into one: "what remains?" What remains is "the longing of a heart pent up" and the thrice-repeated silence: the silent heart "whose silence loves and longs," the silence of the poet whose song is sung, and the silence of the "love that cannot sing again." The silence of the completed sequence chimes in the mind's ear (like Piccarda)—an absent presence.

Rossetti's sequence ends by questioning the convention of acceptance and patient waiting with which it began; indeed, it challenges the traditional idea that the act of writing a sequence is a lover's self-justification (Daniel, *To Delia*, 55), as well as his effort to control the irresistible and fatal attraction of the lady. Rossetti's sequence seeks no such vindication or control, nor does it present itself as the inadequate monument to the beloved's conventionalized beauty (as in Henry Constable's *Diana*, "Last Sonnet," Eighth Decade, V). No description of the beloved is given at all; the conventional task of memorializing is dismissed. The now silent and longing heart had once, in summer days of youth and beauty, sung its "songs." Then, "life was sweet because [the beloved] called [those songs] sweet" (sonnet 1), but now that this final song, this sequence, is ended, the poet lapses into silence. Even poetic discourse, caught in the cycles of earthly mutability, cannot appeal to timeless realities; it is enmeshed in the time-ridden contradictions of a passion that endures without an enduring object. No verbal signifiers point behind the poem to either the beloved, or to the poet's relationship with him, as transcendental signifieds which confer meaning on the poem. The realist form of the sonnet sequence, conventionally the medium for narrating the progress of love, can, in Rossetti's poem, point to no unambiguous biography. The poetic art shared by lover and beloved is dumb; the reader's critical experience, once collaborative with the speaker in sustaining ambiguities, is disoriented and silenced too. Contrary to the convention, the lady sinks once more into the anonymity of the *monna innominata,* leaving her inner identity, her roles, and her relationship to her beloved enduring and beguiling puzzles to the reader.

DOLORES ROSENBLUM

Christina Rossetti
and Poetic Sequence

By any standards, Christina Rossetti had a long poetic career, extending over forty-six years, from the private publication of *Verses* in 1847, when she was seventeen, to the publication of a collection of her religious verse in 1893, a year before her death. By the end of her life she had written over eleven hundred poems and had published over nine hundred of them. Until Rebecca Crump's variorum edition, the only collected edition of her poetry was *The Poetical Works of Christina Georgina Rossetti, with Memoir and Notes*, published in 1904. This volume separates into groups first the longer poems, then the juvenilia (poems written between 1842 and 1847), followed by the "general" poems in chronological order. Poems for children and minor verse, followed by the Italian poems, make up the last two sections. Obviously, this arrangement does not give us a sense of Rossetti's careful sequencing of her poems in the original collections over which she exercised control. With Crump's edition, which reproduces the poems in the order in which they initially appeared, it is possible for the modern reader to appreciate the patterns of poems in sequence, some reflecting attractive shifts in tone, others revealing a deeper logical coherence.

Even a casual reading of Rossetti's poetry reveals striking thematic similarities from poem to poem, as if Rossetti were improvising variations on a small range of themes. In the "general," or secular, poems she writes most often of the absence, the progress, or the return of an emotional state linked to a typical change in situation: betrayal by a lover, for instance, or the premature death of a young woman. In the

132

religious poems similarities and repetitions are even more obvious: Rossetti writes more than one poem about Advent, more than one poem about the figure of the martyr and the Babylonian exile, more than one poem about the joys of Paradise; and it is not always clear how one lyric plea or praise differs significantly from another. Throughout Rossetti's work, then, we find clusters of poems related to each other both chronologically and thematically, poems that might also be plausibly related to actual experiences. We might say, that is, that these poems were written by a gifted and unusual-looking woman who had fantasies of being devastating and of meeting a man who would be her spiritual equal while stirring her physically—and was disappointed; or by a woman who wished to change and grow, to achieve recognition for her gifts, and who saw the unlikelihood of those wishes being fulfilled; or by a woman who, serious about poetry but also constrained by her sex to retain a certain amateur status, looked around for likely poetic situations and models, and found in her female precursors models for the aesthetic of renunciation, in the Christian scriptural tradition models for her foreshadowings, repetitions, and paradoxical assertions, and in her unchanging life the materials for the poetry of endurance.

But if the collected works reveal a poet writing under a compulsion to repeat, the original volumes reveal another kind of compulsion: the compulsion of the deliberate artist to select and arrange her work according to a plan that will best do justice to her intentions.[1] These arrangements go counter to chronology and undercut a literalistic biographical reading, suggesting instead, varieties of intertextual readings. By sequencing her poetry, Rossetti asserts her deliberateness as an artist and also the essential fictiveness of her art.

Rossetti's sequencing foregrounds certain themes and patterns so that poems echo each other not simply as parallels but as structural oppositions: a poem about presence echoes a poem about absence, a poem about deathly "sleep" echoes a poem about ghostly consciousness. By these arrangements Rossetti reinforces her characteristic po-

---

[1]In a most useful essay, David A. Kent has pointed out that the poems in Verses (1893) were arranged in eight sections that reflect Rossetti's own sense of a particular sequence. In the Poetical Works William Michael Rossetti arranged the selections from Verses in chronological order, thus disrupting the original order. Kent's argument that the sequential order takes precedence over the chronological order confirms my sense that chronological development is not an important criterion in assessing Rossetti's work. See David A. Kent, "Sequence and Meaning in Christina Rossetti's Verses (1893)," VP 17 (1979): 259–64.

etic strategies. We see how all her poems deal with beginnings and endings, but no middles, with the significant exception of the "threshold" states in which consciousness lingers; how seasonal change provokes meditation on mortality; how ballad narratives of betrayal and rivalry recast the situation of the lyric speaker to whom some catastrophe has always happened, and who steels herself to endure fragmentation and loss without giving up the desire for wholeness and transcendence; how an image that has been virtually emptied of meaning within the literary tradition—for example, the beautiful dead woman—can become reinvested with meaning as the inexhaustible Christian witness, watching out for her apocalyptic transfiguration in the world to come. Further, the formal devices of Rossetti's verse—the repetition of words and phrases within poems and from poem to poem, the simple, largely monosyllabic diction, the pervasive rhyming—both emphasize and are emphasized by this overall echoing. This thematic and formal repetitiveness, when viewed in the context of the sequencing, suggests that Rossetti is concerned less with poetic originality than with poetic inexhaustibility. She exploits an already exhausted mode and proves that for herself, as a woman poet, it is inexhaustible in the sense that the whole literary canon needs to be rewritten from the female point of view, even if in the same words, word for word. In what follows, I attempt to suggest how, through her sequencing, Rossetti develops what may be called a female myth that depends on a female aesthetic and a female revision of certain linguistic traditions.

I

Rossetti's first official volume, "Goblin Market" and Other Poems (1862), consists of fifty-four poems spanning the years from 1849 to 1860 and arranged without regard to chronology. Forty-five of the poems are secular, and sixteen devotional. The title poem stands at the head. Elsewhere, I have shown how this poem is not only central to all of Rossetti's work but is also deeply related to her other poems.[2] While it belongs to the Victorian literature of the fantastic, it is uniquely powerful in its effects, and lends itself easily to parabolic if not allegorical readings. It is a narrative, more particularly a verse

[2]Dolores Rosenblum, Christina Rossetti: The Poetry of Endurance (Carbondale: Southern Illinois University Press, 1986).

fable, of what befalls two sister-selves, Laura and Lizzie, one of whom succumbs to goblin temptations while the other stands fast and saves her sister through a sacrificial act. More than almost any other Rossetti poem, with the exception perhaps of "A Birthday" (I, 36–37), it is characterized by the dense fabular texture associated with Pre-Raphaelite poetry. Goblin Market (I, 11–26) is followed by fifty-three shorter poems, most of them first-person lyrics, but some third-person lyric statements and dialogues—between self and self, self and God. The group also includes the long narrative dream-vision, "From house to home" (I, 82–88; 1858), and a number of ballad narratives derived from Percy through Scott. Interspersed are some landscape or seasonal poems, all of which are strongly stylized and moralized. Looking more closely at the sequencing in this volume, we see at once how Rossetti's thematic repetitions are rich in structural variety, and how structural variants compose thematic wholes.

The title poem is followed by "In the round tower at Jhansi, June 8, 1857" (I, 26), a brief narrative of heroic renunciation in the final moments before the death of a British colonial officer and his wife. Rossetti confesses in a note that the narrative is not strictly accurate but that she nevertheless chooses to include it. The high drama of the poem makes it an obvious Victorian crowd-pleaser, a bracing shock after the incantations of Goblin Market. But it is also a telescopic version of the former poem, the juxtaposition of the two implying that heroic renunciation has many forms, that the passion for self-sacrifice transcends time, place, gender, and even genre. From this perspective, even scale is significant, for while the small but timeless world of the sisters is extended and speeded up—by the narrative form itself—the larger time-bound world of the colonial officer and his wife is reduced to a brief cameo. It is possible to conclude, therefore, that the female domestic sphere is as "epic" as the world of heroic action, and that within the world of heroic action the space between husband and wife is where the significant heroism takes place.

The next poem in the volume continues the sequencing by extending or varying the theme of renunciation in a lyric valediction. "Dream-Land" (I, 27), the first poem Rossetti published in The Germ, introduces her prototypical figure of heroic endurance: the insensible dead woman who "sleeps" until the end of time. The structural variant of this figure is the subject of the next lyric, "At Home" (I, 28), written nine years later (1858), in which the dead woman is as transparent as the dead woman of "Dream-Land" is opaque. Although both women are poised in a transitional or liminal state, the ghost in "At

Home" is represented as fully conscious, lingering forlornly, acutely aware of her exclusion from ongoing life. Taken together, then, these two poems, along with *Goblin Market* and "In the round tower at Jhansi, June 8, 1857," compose a structural schema; one poem mirrors another and inverts states of being: small world/large world, sisters/husband and wife, life/death, unconscious/conscious. What is going on is a kind of poetic undoing, saying and unsaying, making two opposites mean the same, or, in the Freudian sense, saying one thing and meaning another. In "At Home" we are, in effect, taken through the mirror to the other side, into the consciousness of a woman who can desire but not will, a version of the Laura of *Goblin Market* who "dies" and lingers in a mesmerized state of unachieved desire.

What appears to be different, then, turns out to be really the same, for "sameness" is an important constituent of Rossetti's female myth. We see this equivalence in the fifth poem, "A Triad" (I, 29), which sums up the kinds of death-in-love a woman might encounter: one woman "falls" to her death, the second pines away for lack of love, while the third grows fat and "soulless" in married love. The different women are all the same, and none of the alternatives is preferable to any other. All point to an impasse that is suddenly resolved by the next poem, "Love from the north" (I, 29–30), which offers a solution to unconsummated desire and unachieved identity: a strong lover from the "north," not unlike bridegroom death, bursts into the church and bears the bride away from her weak groom. One could go on reading the volume in this way, as itself a whole poem, but this kind of analysis is basically a new critical exercise to be practiced with a light touch, while at the same time we take Rossetti's own practices seriously, recognizing that Rossetti's sequencing is her way of telling the truth, and, like Emily Dickinson, telling it "slant."[3]

The highlights of the rest of *"Goblin Market" and Other Poems* include "A pause of thought" (I, 51–52; 1848) in which the speaker represents herself as the tenacious and obsessed watcher who "looked for that which is not, nor can be," who cannot give up her compulsion to repeat: "Thou knowest the chase useless, and again / Turnest to follow it" (ll. 19–20). What is striking here is the way in which Rossetti, in her concern to trace the shape of obsessive desire, refrains from naming the object, which remains "that which," or "it." What is equally striking is that the poem immediately preceding, "May" (I, 51), written in 1855, seven years later, is a clear structural comple-

---

[3]*The Poems of Emily Dickinson*, ed. Thomas H. Johnson, 3 vols. (Cambridge: Harvard University Press, Belknap Press, 1955), II, 792 (no. 1129).

ment to the earlier poem. It is a typical post-crisis poem, in which the loss has always already occurred, and the object is again unnamed: "I cannot tell you what it was; / But this I know: it did but pass. . . . / And left me old, and cold, and grey" (ll. 9–13). Taken together, the two poems reveal that it does not matter whether something has been lost or never gained, that the speaker's stance in both situations is essentially the same, and that to persist is to endure. No particular biographical event is needed to account for this condition—no unrequited love, that is. Rather this is a "typical" situation in Rossetti's poetry, and one that reflects a more general social and cultural situation: "it" has always happened to women, "it" being the loss that signifies their exclusion from full power over their lives.

The loss is explored further in two significant poems: "Shut Out" (I, 56–57; 1856), in which the speaker narrates her exclusion from her own garden of the self, and "Dead before death" (I, 59; 1854), in which the crisis has left the subject entombed within herself, the "living" correlative of the "dead" woman who persists as consciousness. "Dead before death" is preceded by one of Rossetti's most famous poems, "Song" ("When I am dead, my dearest"; I, 58), a resigned valediction that renders an imaginative flexibility that persists after death. This sequencing thus highlights the rigidity of the dead-before-death woman. In their powerlessness, women in life are cold corpses or statues; like Emily Brontë's prisoned souls, they are freed by death. Or, rather, imagined death frees the imagination.

The whole secular sequence of the Goblin Market volume ends with a vivid parable, "Up-Hill" (I, 65–66; 1858), which breaks free of the stasis of the cycle of desire, as the soul's "up-hill" and linear progress toward night, rest, and death is asserted as the only possible movement. "Up-Hill" is preceded, however, by a fairly long dramatic monologue, "The convent threshold" (I, 61–65; 1858), which conflates the ballad heroine and the lyric speaker, and gathers up the themes of betrayal, loss, renunciation, and endurance. The poem stresses the liminal state—here, literally the threshold—in which the speaker is half-turned, like the speaker of "When I am dead," both to go and to stay, lingering on the edge where desire and renunciation meet. If life is a living death, and death a renewed life, if "it" has always happened, or is about to happen, and if to be a woman is always to endure the same fate, then the threshold may be particularly suited as a female vantage point. Ever more about to be, Rossetti's threshold woman sits poised between mutually exclusive—and often equally impossible—alternatives.

The remaining sixteen poems in the Goblin Market volume are

designated as "devotional," the first seven being "'The love of Christ which passeth knowledge'" (I, 66–67; 1858), "'A bruised reed shall he not break'" (I, 67–68; 1852), "A better resurrection" (I, 68; 1857), "Advent" (I, 68–70; 1858), "The three enemies" (I, 70–72; 1851), "One Certainty" (I, 72; 1849), "Christian and Jew. A Dialogue" (I, 72–74; 1858). Again the seeming arbitrariness of sequencing yields meaning. In these poems, even more than in the secular poems, the variety in forms is apparent: the initimate colloquy between speaker and Christ in "'The love of Christ,'" "'A bruised reed,'" and "A better resurrection"; the dramatic dialogue in "The three enemies" and "Christian and Jew"; the exhortatory lyric in "Advent"; the sonnet form of "One Certainty." The variety underscores the improvisatory effect; these poems are all different ways of saying the same thing. That improvisation, which reduces to and heightens female "sameness" and female powerlessness, is the primary intent of the sequencing in this and other volumes: Rossetti elaborates secular themes as religious ones and thus establishes a religious ground for the representation of the female dilemma. Christ in "'The love of Christ,'" for instance, is a model for female desire, suffering, and endurance—and, I would argue, vice versa; time, which is always at an end or not yet begun for the female persona, is telescoped into beginning and ending in "Advent"; the inadequacy of mortal life and its transience, which is the ground for a particularly female experience of ephemerality, is adumbrated in "One Certainty"; and, finally, the joys of paradise, which create a realm of "insatiate" pleasure that might be appropriated by the woman who has been shut out of her garden, are litanized in "Advent" and "Christian and Jew."

Of the remaining nine devotional pieces, the two most significant are "Symbols," (I, 75–76; 1849) an early poem that provides in cameo a vision of the dispossession from the self-garden, and "From house to home" (I, 82–88), an extended dream-vision composed about five months before *Goblin Market,* and a larger-scale version of the crucial exile. "From house to home" describes in detail an Edenic garden that is destroyed by the departure of a mysterious companion-lover. The speaker's anguished and fruitless search for him ends in a dream-vision of a suffering female figure who treads on thorns and drinks the bitter cup, whereupon she is assumed into paradise and reunited with her lover. Taking into account the order of composition, we can easily see how the earlier poem is a precursor of *Goblin Market,* and how both poems derive from the same materials. In the tradition of dream-visions, "From house to home" is markedly allegorical, didactic, and transparent. The Edenic garden is clearly the garden of the self and of erotic abundance; the departure of the angelic companion represents anything and everything that makes it impossible for the female self to stay in the garden; the suffering dream-woman who bleeds and weeps is the female poet and heroine who embraces her exile and welcomes her stigmata as signs of her eventual transfiguration. At the end the speaker renounces the garden and house of self-fulfillment and announces her will to endure in exile, as the woman clothed in white: "my soul shall walk in white, / Cast down but not destroyed" (ll. 203–4).

This poem shows us quite clearly, then, how the aesthetic of renunciation is formulated and the poetry of endurance achieved. The speaker of the poem—or rather her dream-vision self—is not unlike both Laura and Lizzie in *Goblin Market;* like Laura, she inhabits the garden, experiences its devastation, and embarks on a fruitless search; like Lizzie, she suffers, endures, and "saves" by self-sacrifice. The later poem, however, is far more opaque and impersonal, and, in its more complex fictiveness, a more mature version of the process set forth in "From house to home."

But there are several structural differences between the two which justify Rossetti's choice to place the earlier poem toward the end of the volume, making it serve as a commentary on or even a resolution of the issues raised in *Goblin Market.* The differences involve will and choice. While Laura is tempted by and chooses fruits she has been warned against, the dreamer in "From house to home" is cast out of her garden, which seems unequivocally benign, for no good reason, except that it is, as the end of the poem tells us, simply illusory. While Laura is awakened from spiritual "death" by the self-sacrificing sister who provides the fiery antidote, the dreamer is restored by a fortifying vison of apocalyptic transfiguration as well as of suffering. While the fabular Laura is restored to an idyllic sisterly community, the "real" dreamer—that is, the confessional "I"—is reconciled to her exile not so much by an undoing of error as by a growth of consciousness, a vision of sublimity which justifies her renunciation and makes possible her endurance. In this sense, "From house to home" is the "later" poem, the poem that lays down the program for the course of the rest of Rossetti's poetry.

II

"The Prince's Progress" and Other Poems, Rossetti's second volume, published in 1866, follows the patterning of *"Goblin Market" and*

Other Poems by opening with a narrative poem, an "epic" that Dante Gabriel wanted Rossetti to write (I, 95–110). This quest narrative is peculiarly blocked, as stubborn, in its way, as Rossetti herself was in resisting her brother's prescriptions. Neither the questing prince nor the repining bride have much energy, and the nature of the prince's temptations is mechanical and derivative. What the poem seems to be about is, again, the threshold state: the prince lingering in the moment—"Loth to stay, yet to leave her slack, / He half turned away, then he quite turned back:" (ll. 85–86)—the princess lingering between life and death. Her condition is similar to the trancelike state of the dead women in other lyrics and, like some of those states, involves perpetual recurrence: "The long hours go and come and go, / The bride she sleepeth, waketh, sleepeth" (ll. 3–4). Time, that is, passes eventlessly. The arrival of the prince is crucially belated, allowing the princess to carry out her project of dying and transcending him. Here the Bloomian concept of poetic belatedness seems particularly applicable, because the poem is so deeply embedded in the context of Dante Gabriel's and Christina's struggle over its composition.[4] The prince may represent Rossetti's sense of her own belatedness, in relation not only to her brother-poet but also to the entire literary tradition. He may also represent, however, Dante Gabriel himself. In this reading, Rossetti the poet discards Dante Gabriel's project as belated, while, in the persona of the princess, she accomplishes her poetic aims: to mark the time of the waiting or transition, and to transcend her "death" within literary tradition by dying in order to escape her traditional role. By exaggerating the symbolic function of the female in male art, the female poet escapes the masculine project into projects of her own.

With a few exceptions, the poems in the *Prince's Progress* volume range in date from 1861 to 1865, when Rossetti was in her early thirties and obviously experiencing a creative flowering. The range of subjects and forms is roughly the same as that of the *Goblin Market* volume, except that the *Prince's Progress* volume contains fewer short ballad-narratives and a greater variety of longer narrative poems, including "Maiden-Song" (I, 110–16), a pastoral tale, and "'The iniquity of the fathers upon the children'" (I, 164–78), an attempt at realistic narrative with social import which bears a resemblance to Tennyson's *Maud* and "Locksley Hall." "Maiden-Song"'s sequential

[4]Harold Bloom, *The Anxiety of Influence* (New York: Oxford University Press, 1973).

140

position, right after *The Prince's Progress*, is particularly significant, since it is a poem about different orders of "singing" and about the Orphic creativity of female art. In contrast to *The Prince's Progress* and its preoccupation with belatedness, this poem celebrates aptness and timeliness, as three sisters "sing" themselves appropriate mates. Margaret, the oldest and most powerful, not only sings herself home a kingly mate, but also sings a whole magical world into creation: "So Margaret . . . / Sang free birds out of the sky, / Beasts along the earth, / Sang up fishes of the deep— / All breathing things that move" (ll. 210–15).

In general, the *Prince's Progress* volume contains more poems about "singing" and the nature of art, as well as more poems involving active renunciation, than does the *Goblin Market* volume, and Rossetti seems to be linking the issues more explicitly, making renunciation the typical subject of her art, both in its rejection of complex metaphor and sensuous imagery and in its deliberate negations. A particularly meaningful sequence involving strong negations includes the early poem "A Portrait" (I, 122; 1847–1850), "Dream-Love" (I, 123–24; 1854), "Twice" (I, 124–26; 1864), and "Songs in a cornfield" (I, 126–29; 1864).

"A Portrait" is an assertion of radical renunciation and equally radical restitution and transfiguration. The poem consists of two sonnets, the first of which sums up the character of a woman who gave up beauty, hope, joy, even "her own self," and "hated all for love of Jesus Christ." The second sonnet, a cameo of her deathbed, goes through to the other side of the mirror, to the realm where the dying woman is Bride, dove, fruitful vine. These transformations occur at the very moment that her friends are kneeling by her deathbed: while they sorrow she is at peace. The following poem, "Dream-Love," belongs to a group of "masques" involving the figure of Love. Not unlike the dying woman in "A Portrait" or the repining princess, the figure of Love is completely rapt and unperturbable, sleeping and dreaming of some ultimate perfection of his pleasure. The only resolution is to "close the curtains / Of branched evergreen" (ll. 57–58) which cannot change. "Love," like the dying woman, has renounced the impoverished world of desire for another world of consummation: for the woman, the consummation involves splendid transfiguration, for "Love," perfect sameness. Again, one poem reinforces the other; one provides a reading of the other. The poem immediately following "Dream-Love," however, makes a sharp break with lotos-land atmospherics. In "Twice" a lyric speaker recalls a moment of crisis, when

141

she offered her heart to a lover who rejected it as "unripe" (l. 13). She now offers her "broken heart" (l. 27) to her God, who is to "refine" (l. 37) it with fire. Here then is another poem about renunciation that ends in transfiguration: the speaker finally becomes that which she is and offers "All that I have . . . / All that I am" (ll. 45–46). The poem that begins as a love lament ends with a celebration of self.

"Songs in a cornfield," the poem immediately following "Twice," can be read as a pendant to "Maiden Song" in that it too deals with singing and mating. And, like "Dream-Love," it moves towards a consummation that involves the perfection of emptiness or absence. This perfect lack is at once the opposite of transfiguration and its perfect form. Three of the reapers in the cornfield sing, while the fourth, Marian, cannot, because her sweetheart is mysteriously "away" (l. 8). When, at the end, Marian does sing, her song is a lament for the dead—in fact, an interrogation of the dead. What feeds her song is loss and death. Here there is no celebration or affirmation, but rather another female "escape" similar to that of the repining princess: the song ends and the singer vanishes.

Although there are several other meaningful sequences in the volume, of chief interest is the final secular poem, " 'The iniquity of the fathers upon the children,' " a long narrative and one of the few poems in which Rossetti takes up a specific women's issue. It is also a pivotal poem in that it confronts the issue of what is and is not canonical in art, specifically in Rossetti's art, and thus comments on the "belatedness" of The Prince's Progress. Further, the theme of rejection and renunciation is made to serve an assertion of selfhood, while the whole issue of social exclusion, renunciation, and the integrity of self is qualified and clarified by the religious poem that follows it, "Despised and rejected" (I, 178–80), a commentary on Christ's isolation. The title of the poem in the first edition of 1866 was "Under the rose," the English rendering of the Latin sub rosa, which means secretly or illicitly. Rossetti is thus ironically qualifying the symbol of womanhood—the rose—and linking it with the fall or fate of women, for this poem tells the story of an illegitimate child, a consequence of male seduction, and of the mother, who, fearing the judgment of a patriarchal society, rejects her daughter. At the end of the poem the heroine (the daughter and narrator) has experienced a renunciation that refines and defines a self: she stands "nameless," a free spirit, undefined except by the limits of mortality. The illegitimate daughter, then, is the "answer" to the repining princess: the only power for women resides outside the framework of patriarchy.

The *Prince's Progress* volume concludes with nine devotional poems. The first of these is "Despised and rejected," the poem immediately following "'The iniquity of the fathers upon the children.'" "Despised and rejected" was written in 1864, one year before "'The iniquity of the fathers.'" It reveals the kind of model of endurance that Rossetti was able to develop in her religious poems and then to "apply" to typical problems of female identity. Like the poem preceding it, "Despised and rejected" is about hardness of heart, isolation, and rejection. The speaker at the end of "'The iniquity of the fathers,'" having fused her outcast social condition with her secret identity, becomes a social and moral isolate who is inwardly secure in her election. "Despised and rejected," by its place in the sequence, forecasts what might happen to this singular soul should it reject everything but its own community. As the inner drama unfolds, Christ the outcast, the "female" Christ, knocks at the speaker's "door" (l. 6), and through the night continues to exhort the despairing soul: "'Open to Me'" (l. 39) and "'Rise, let Me in'" (l. 41). Cut off from the human community, the soul entombed in self rejects her only authentic community—the suffering, bleeding Christ. She awakes to bloody footprints and "on my door / The mark of blood for evermore" (ll. 57–58). This poem in effect replays the agon of "The convent threshold," which is also marked by threshold bloodstains, and recasts the struggle of self with self against an unholy love as a struggle between the self and Christ against holy love. Rejection and renunciation are common to all three poems. Their linkage creates a moral framework in which the social suffering of the outcast female is illuminated, as through a stained-glass window, by the suffering of the unheeded Christ, and the stoicism of renunciation is colored by the urgency of such suffering.

This reframing of "female" suffering continues in the sequencing that follows. "Long Barren" (I, 180) and "If Only" (I, 181) are passionate declarations of the true triumph in renunciation, manifested in the inversion of temporal values and the rewording of standard tropes. In "Long Barren" the speaker beseeches the God who hung "upon a barren tree" (l. 1) to strengthen her so that her barrenness may end, and in a litany based on the Song of Solomon, intermingled with her *own* language, she brings forth her own literary fruit:

> Thou Rose of Sharon, Cedar of broad roots,
> Vine of sweet fruits,
>   Thou Lily of the vale with fadeless leaf,

Of thousands Chief,
Feed Thou my feeble shoots.
[ll. 11–15]

In the two succeeding poems she represents herself as impatient for the flowering transformation, chastised by a God who requires her to live on, against her "nature," but who accepts her as she *is: "I love thee here or there, / I will accept thy broken heart, lie still"* ("Dost thou not care?" ll. 7–8; I, 181).

Two slightly longer poems follow these colloquies, the 1863 "Martyr's Song" (I, 182–84) and the 1856 "After this the judgment" (I, 184–86), both eschatological visions. In the former, the martyrs encounter first the community of saints, then their own "Welcoming angels" (l. 21), and finally Christ; this vision gives them the strength to endure the pain of death. The earlier poem is a more personal vision in which the speaker complains of her "lack" (l. 9) and envisions the apocalyptic moment when "all time's mighty works and wonders are / Consumed as in a moment" (ll. 48–49), and she is totally exposed before God. These eschatological visions are followed by a return to the timeless yet commemorative moment in "Good Friday" (I, 186–87). In this poem the speaker represents herself as a stone, a variant of the monumental woman dead before death, and, in a powerful typological analogy, beseeches Christ to break down her rigidity: "Greater than Moses, turn and look once more / And smite a rock" (ll. 15–16). The volume ends with the infamous—from the feminist perspective—"The lowest place" (I, 187) in which Rossetti's request for the lowest place suggests, in secular terms, the utmost self-abnegation. When "translated" into the idiom in which "the last shall be first," however, this becomes a daring request, the presumption of which has to be qualified by "or if for me / That lowest place too high, make one more low" (ll. 5–6). In the religious context the lowest place in heaven is infinitely higher than the highest place on earth, for that lowest place is still breathtakingly close to the throne of heaven.

The whole volume, then, can be seen as a "progress," not of the prince, but of the female—and Christian—soul, who at the beginning disappears behind a scrim of "poetically" colored language—the choric song that invokes a poppied sleep—and at the end reappears, self-possessed, surrounded by the choirs of heaven, and bathed in the white light that shines through the transparency of the religious language. The progress can also be regarded as that of the poet, of course, moving from the exhausted idiom of a tradition that idealizes and denatures the female to the inexhaustible idiom of a tradition in which a "female" Christ provides the model for recasting female identity.

III

In 1875 Rossetti published an edition combining the *Goblin Market* volume with the *Prince's Progress* volume. She rearranged the original poems, omitting five entirely, and incorporating thirty-seven new poems. In this collection Rossetti pays even less attention to chronology and appears to make more obvious matches in sequencing. Thus *Goblin Market* is followed, predictably and obviously, by *The Prince's Progress:* both are title poems, and the domestic allegory contrasts with the quest romance. But each comments on the other in a way that is less obvious, for while the domestic allegory is bold in its confrontations and insistent in its closure, the quest romance is a triumph of evasion and escape. *The Prince's Progress* is followed, as in the original volume, with "Maiden Song," which here again appears as a re-envisioning and empowering of the repining princess. "Maiden Song" is followed by the two poems that follow "In the round tower at Jhansi, June 8, 1857" in the *Goblin Market* volume, "Dream-Land" and "After Death." It seems likely that Rossetti placed these poems third and fourth in the original sequence, fourth and fifth here, because they effectively introduce the themes of renunciation and alienation. A significant omission, however, is the poem that follows these two in the original volume, "A Triad," the poem that expresses extreme skepticism about the heterosexual relation, and groups the fallen woman with the virgin and the matron. Instead, in the 1875 edition "At Home" is followed by a more conventional thematic choice, another ghost poem, this time "The poor ghost" (I, 120–21) from the *Prince's Progress* volume. The poems immediately following this one are "Grown and flown" (I, 158–59), the thirty-third poem in *The Prince's Progress,* which details the failure of love, and "A farm walk" (I, 159–61), Rossetti's tribute to a beautiful milkmaid, a "wayside posy" (l. 68) whose destiny is to become a "cosy" (l. 66) wife— and inaccessible to the speaker. This vision of health is followed by a vision of morbidity, the renunciatory dying woman of "A Portrait" (I, 122) from the beginning of the *Prince's Progress* volume. In this later volume, then, it would seem that Rossetti backs off from some of the powerful suggestions created by the structural echoes in the original sequences, arranging poems by the more obvious criteria of thematic similarity and contrast in pace.

The exclusions and additions remain interesting, however, and occasional rearrangements seem to heighten the informative content of sequences. For instance, the twentieth and twenty-first poems are the added "Once for all" (I, 193) and "Enrica, 1865" (I, 193–94), both significant poems in the Rossetti canon. "Once for all" uses the image of a patch of snow unmelted by the summer sun to convey a chilling perception of limitation, while "Enrica, 1865" celebrates an Italian woman's warmth and generosity, "She summer-like and we like snow" (l. 8). The following poem, the childlike "A Chill" (I, 161–62), repeats the idea of longing for a generative warmth from the perspective of an exclusionary coldness. One can see, then, how Rossetti makes each poem serve the other: nature's intransigence suggests another kind of intransigence, that of the Englishwomen who are cold, but "Deep at our deepest, strong and free" (l. 24), while the persistence of desire is imaged as longing for maternal warmth.

Another significant poem, "Memory" (I, 147–48), from the *Prince's Progress* volume, is here preceded by a poem of the same year and originally in the *Goblin Market* volume: "Fata Morgana" (I, 49–50), which, like "Memory," deals with false hopes. "Memory" is here followed by the added "'They desire a better country'" (I, 195–96), which readjusts the perspective of the former by presenting a speaker who is not stalled by brooding memory, but rather accepts her past joyfully and goes forward to the "unknown land" (l. 15) that is paradoxically her home from exile. Rossetti's additions and rearrangements can thus be seen to readjust and reframe her female myth so that it becomes increasingly comprehensive and increasingly oriented toward a "progress" that involves translation not only to another realm of being but to another realm of language.

IV

This "progress" is evident in Rossetti's third volume of new poems, "*A Pageant*" *and Other Poems*, published in 1881. This volume was incorporated in the 1890 collected edition, which included the first two volumes, as "the second series." Since the 1875 edition of the first two volumes was already stereotyped, Rossetti could make additions only to "*A Pageant*" *and Other Poems* when she came to prepare the

1890 collected edition. In my comments on sequencing in the original
Pageant volume, I shall also deal with the additions to the collected
edition as they occur. In general, the additions are obviously thematic, and they reinforce the preexisting sequence rather than disturb it.

The original *Pageant* volume is itself more "set" than the earlier
volumes. In this volume Rossetti can be seen moving toward a more
overtly didactic mode, asserting more firmly her stoical acceptance of
loss and lack of fulfillment within the context of the paradoxes of
Christian orthodoxy, in which loss is translated into its exact opposite. Unlike the other two volumes, it contains no representations
of threshold states; rather, it emphasizes decisions and conclusions and
the feeling states that accompany them. But these feeling states are
relatively impersonal; more than ever Rossetti seems concerned with
making an "example" of herself. The persona in the poems is both a
part of the grim pageant of the world and its only witness who can
endure and testify to the concluding transformation of loss into gain.

The lead poem, "The Key-Note" (II, 59–60), sets the tone of the
whole volume as Rossetti goes about reevaluating her aesthetic. The
songs she used to sing are all forgotten now that it is "the Winter of
my year" (l. 8); her role from now on will be like the robin's—to
create one warm space by his song and by his "ruddy" (l. 12) breast.
Whether or not the robin's breast and the "ruddy jewels" (l. 11) of
winter bushes suggest the blood of the poet, the theme of the volume
is clear: in the world of mutability only one stance is possible—self-
sacrificing renunciation coupled with the capacity to endure until the
apocalyptic end.

Even the title poem, *The Months: A Pageant* (II, 60–74), which
suggests a lighter vein and is actually written as a pageant, with roles
for children as months and animals, shows Rossetti exploiting her
characteristic concerns and strategies. Here Rossetti was able to create
a literary product that had considerable mass appeal: it is both light
and serious, both spectacular and didactic. The parade of seasons
enacts the passage of time and invokes the theme of vanity, as successive months "startle" or anticipate each other, and, inevitably,
"fly" (l. 101), thus providing an edifying display that both accedes to
and triumphs over mutability.

The poems that follow *The Months* and lead up to Rossetti's important sonnet sequence "Monna Innominata" (II, 86–93), by their titles
alone show the direction of Rossetti's thoughts: "Mirrors of life and
death" (II, 75–79), "Birchington Churchyard" (II, 167), "A ballad of
boding" (II, 79–85), "Yet a little while" (II, 85). The fourth poem in

the volume, however, bears less overt resemblance to the others, both in its generosity and its assertion of some kind of continuing pleasure. "Italia, io ti saluto!" (II, 74–75) dates from 1865 and therefore can be paired with Rossetti's other "Italian" poem of the period, "Enrica, 1865." While presenting a thematic contrast to the poems that follow and precede it, "Italia io ti saluto!" still belongs to the poetry of renunciation and endurance that characterizes this volume. The speaker renounces that country "half my own," (l. 6) and turns to "that bleak North / Whence I came forth" (ll. 8–9). Henceforth hers is the landscape, as well as the season, of destitution, less dangerous than the fertile south. Her only action will be the decisive turn, with a solace in memory triggered by seasonal return, for when the swallows turn southward again, the "sweet name" (l. 15) (of Italy) may come again to her mouth. Rossetti, we see again, enacts and elaborates the renunciation that both mandates and makes possible the poetry of endurance. She will keep on writing poetry that illustrates how memory and repetition—poetry's repetition—make it possible to endure, and to keep on writing poetry.

With the "Monna Innominata" series, Rossetti claims to innovate, to tell the same old story from a new perspective, that of the unnamed lady who herself is a poet, sharing her beloved's talent. But in terms of the body of Rossetti's work, and in particular the context of this volume, "Monna Innominata" is a virtuoso set of variations on a recurring theme. As I have dealt with this series in greater depth elsewhere, here I shall only say that it is the apotheosis of Rossetti's great theme of renunciation and endurance, and a culmination of her poetic project, which is to retell the woman's story by incorporating it into the "new" story of Christian scripture.[5] At the end of her thwarted courtship, Rossetti's speaker is precisely she who remains enduring until the next life, when love shall be subsumed into Love.

The titles of the poems that follow "Monna Innominata" read like a catalogue of last things: "One sea-side grave" (II, 167), "Tempus Fugit" (II, 94–95), "Till To-morrow" (II, 101), "Death-Watches" (II, 101–2), "Touching 'Never'" (II, 102), "Memento Mori" (II, 111–12). Although there are divergences into lighter strains with such poems as "Golden Glories" (II, 95), "Johnny" (II, 95–97), and "Brother Bruin" (II, 168–69), the tone is predominantly somber, with poems such as "An October garden" (II, 116) and "Summer is ended" (II, 116–17) continuing the seasonal identification established in

---

[5]See Rosenblum, *Christina Rossetti.*

"The Key-Note." One of the notable additions in the 1890 volume is "'A helpmeet for him'" (II, 169), in which Rossetti asserts without qualification that "Woman was made for man's delight" (l. 1) and that "Meek compliances veil her might" (l. 6). While affirming the orthodoxies that disempower women, Rossetti seems also to suggest that women are strong even when they appear weak and that they choose to mask their power. But in this volume Rossetti also affirms a woman's unmasked power, a power that derives from a woman's "minimalness," her intransigent refusal to participate in the metaphors of courtly love, for instance. The heroine of Rossetti's last ballad, "Brandons Both" (II, 102–5), which is framed by several short poems dealing with general mutability, is a spirited woman who spurns the lover who has rejected her and who asserts her valorization of the "thorny rose" (l. 57) of self. To a certain extent, Rossetti can be considered as offering a counterbalance both to aesthetic decadence and to the bathetic excesses of some of her female contemporaries. Whereas decadent poetry feasts on the richness of decline, Rossetti's poetry offers a kind of linguistic minimalism that is based in part on her refusal to assent to female "natural" decline, even if this refusal means foregoing the sumptuousness that attends the peak of the cycle, the rich, full-blown rose, for instance.

This perspective is manifest in a further sequence. The 1878 poem "An October garden" (II, 116), asserts the value of the "last rosebud" (l. 3), much as "Brandons Both" asserts the value of "the thorny rose" precisely because it is a last and least thing, the remainder that outlives even as it declines. The poem following, "Summer is ended" (II, 116), emphasizes the rose as a symbol of mutability—"To think that this meaningless thing was ever a rose" (l. 1)—and immutability both, as an end that is irreversible, "An end locked fast, / Bent we cannot re-bend." The harshness of this vision is echoed in the next poem, "Passing and glassing" (II, 117), in which the rose is specifically designated as a symbol of female decline and female powerlessness, a part of the nature that is "woman's looking-glass" (l. 2). Individually, these three poems present variations on a theme, yet, taken as a group, they express a contradiction: the rose is both valuable and valueless, an ephemeral phenomenon and a lasting emblem. By the time we reach "Passing and glassing," however, the rose is no longer singular, but one thing of many, and female "vanity" has been re-inscribed as the fate of all things. In this sense, *A Pageant" and Other Poems* is a pivotal work in which Rossetti achieves firmer closure and firmer self-possession. From now on she will write almost exclusively of a world that is a passing show and a breeder of death, in which partings only prefigure the final separation—between soul and body, heaven and earth—and in which the vigilant witness has set her face toward the new Jerusalem. This world is marked by deep divisions and grim constancies: "Never on this side of the grave" begins "A life's parallels" (II, 105), the poem that follows "Brandons Both," while the closing lines assert eternal recurrence as the speaker endures, "Faint yet pursuing, faint yet still pursuing / Ever" (ll. 11–12).

Two more poems from the volume's secular series in the *Pageant* volume illustrate the art of Rossetti's sequencing. These are "Soeur Louise de la Miséricorde (1674)" (II, 119–20; b.1882) and "An 'immurata' sister" (II, 120–21), written some years earlier, in about 1865. While the nun in the later poem has wasted her spiritual patrimony on vain "desire" (l. 2) and now only longs for her spiritual home, the nun in the earlier poem, denouncing the futile search for meaning in an "empty" (l. 22) world, links that futility directly to woman's condition: "Men work and think, but women feel; / And so (for I'm a woman, I) / And so I should be glad to die" (ll. 5–7). It is evident that Rossetti places this poem after the "later" "Soeur Louise" because of psychological and doctrinal shifts: the later poem is prelude to the earlier one because Soeur Louise is still "in progress." Her "heart" is still being refined by fire, while the "immurata" sister has passed the liminal stage and is ready for her soul's ascent in fire to its flaming source. This transposition of the two poems from their chronological order provides further justification both for respecting Rossetti's arrangement above chronology and for disturbing that arrangement according to Rossetti's own organizing principles, which seem to suggest a cycle that revolves upon itself while still advancing to an "end," the refining by fire that would render her poetry fully transparent. For Rossetti herself rearranges by her later interpolations. In the collected edition of 1890 Rossetti interpolated between the two "nun" poems an 1881 poem, "Today's Burden" (II, 171), an elaboration of the biblical text, "Arise, depart, for this is not your rest." "Today's Burden" presents "unrest" as a cosmic condition, an entropic movement toward death. It suggests that the spiritual turbulence that besets the nuns is both vain and necessary, and that their immurement is by no means an escape into "rest" or peace of soul. Further, this insertion significantly qualifies the perspective of "An 'immurata' sister" on male endeavors, for under the eye of eternity their activities are as futile as those of women: "These have no rest who sit and dream and sigh"—repining women, cloistered nuns; "Nor have those rest who wrestle and who fall"—the men who work and think. Thus in the *Pageant* volume one nun's voice complements the other's, and in the *Collected Poems* of 1890 both those voices are complemented by the essentially prophetic voice of "Today's Burden."

The remaining nineteen titles in *"A Pageant" and Other Poems* belong to the devotional category, and most were written between 1865 and 1882. They include the extraordinary "The thread of life" (II, 122–23), in which Rossetti asserts her strong sense of self-continuity; the longer dream-vision, "An old-world thicket" (II, 123–28), which represents a dark night of the soul followed by a redeeming pastoral vision; and Rossetti's other sonnet sequence, "Later Life" (II, 138–50), a string of devotional poems that compose in essence Rossetti's apologia, her appraisal of the value of life and her commentary on how one must live. All are similar to the extent that they are strongly dogmatic, asserting orthodox beliefs on the brevity and sinfullness of life and the compensations of life after death. The shorter lyrics include an Easter sequence, and the *Collected Poems* adds a Christmas sequence. Of the 1890 additions to this section, perhaps the most striking is "Mary Magdalene and the other Mary" (II, 177), a brief and simple lyric that identifies the "Marys" as those who weep and keep vigil, Rossetti's own actual and fictive role. For the rest, they demonstrate Rossetti's versatility as well as her single-mindedness. She is at home with any religious subject, whether it is the descent from the cross, or the homecoming of all saints, or the fervor of the martyr, or a particularly resonant text, for example, " 'Love is strong as death' " (II, 164).

V

The only other volume over which Rossetti had control was *Verses* 1893, compiled from three previous volumes of religious prose and poetry published by the Society for the Promotion of Christian Knowledge. It is evident that Rossetti turned increasingly to the composition of religious poetry after 1870, after she turned forty, that is, and after the onset of her debilitating Graves's disease. The reasons are obvious. As a middle-aged poet she could not appropriately go on writing about youthful themes: early death, disappointment in love, or the kind of florid renunciation that characterizes "The convent threshold" (I, 61–65), for instance. Both as lyric poet and as woman poet she could hardly adopt the role of Victorian sage. But as witness rather than prophet she would go on to write prolifically in the mode she had already established in the religious verse she wrote and published in the sixties: the lyrics in which she decries the world's vanities and dramatizes an intimate relation with God.

She had also laid the ground-plan for continuing in the vein of the secular lyrics: the renunciation that was once motivated by an imagined critical event now became a "free" choice, both a way of asserting singularity and a kind of spiritual insurance, guaranteeing her the coveted lowest place. Now she could go on writing poems in which the renunciatory act is part of a continuing inner drama: the speaker chooses again and again what she always chose. Further, having exhausted a literary tradition that, as I have pointed out, is already exhausted—although it needed to be rewritten, word for word, supplying the woman's part—Rossetti turned to a tradition that is generically inexhaustible. The language of scripture and liturgy can be repeated endlessly, for, as often as it is said, it is renewed. Prayers and praises are inexhaustible in that the suppliant cannot say the same thing often enough, nor can she say too much: there is no possibility of redundancy. There is a sense, also, in which devotional language is language that has been emptied out: it consists of sacred words and sacred names, but their meaning is less important than their utterance. Further, any word or name becomes sacred in the performative speech act that constitutes prayer. But most important for Rossetti, the religious tradition allowed her to efface herself in a particularly meaningful way, to become simply one of the catholic community of souls, living and dead. This community erases hierarchical and patriarchal distinctions, and, in practical terms, Rossetti's concentration on religious poetry made it possible for her to reach a far wider audience. It also allowed her—and this must be stressed—to achieve a relatedness, both human and divine, that transcended the alienation she experienced, self from self, self from other, and alienation built into the tradition of loss, absence, and fragmentation which fed her art. Such relatedness is not easily sustained; it needs to be constantly reasserted and reestablished, as the lyric speaker does in bringing to bear her "whole" and "true" self, however flawed. In so doing, she achieves integration as well as reciprocity, for God "sees" and accepts this "true" self, indeed calls it forth. Rather than dramatizing the static assumption of roles, masks, and poses, these poems consistently enact a relation.

The element of choice that characterizes Rossetti's religious verse both thematically and formally has an important modifying effect on the issue of chronology. It becomes clear that in reference to the religious poetry, chronology and "development" are almost irrelevant. This irrelevance is evident in the way in which Rossetti chose to publish her religious poetry. First, she embedded the bulk of it within her exhortatory prose, and then, for *Verses*, she arranged the poems in sequences within larger groupings that completely ignore chronology. The chronology is restored by William Michael Rossetti in the *Poetical Works*, in that the larger divisions are rearranged chronologically, while the sequences within the divisions are maintained. Thus, for instance, a grouping entitled "Songs for strangers and pilgrims," which Rossetti places last in *Verses*, is first in the *Collected Poems*, because it contains only thirty-two out of seventy-one poems from the latest date, b. 1893, while the majority range in date from 1853 to b. 1886. On the other hand, the grouping entitled "Out of the deep have I called unto Thee, o Lord," which leads off *Verses*, is comparatively late chronologically.

The sequence "Christ our All in all" (II, 188–211) is a division that is fairly representative of Rossetti's mature and continuing concerns, for most of its poems date from her later period, although a few were written during the fifties and seventies. In this sequence we recognize the following thematic constants: the self as flawed and "trembling" (l. 9) ("'The ransomed of the Lord'"; II, 188–89), as an unmoved stone ("'An exceeding bitter cry'"; II, 189–90), as "marred" and "withered" ("O Lord, when Thou didst call me"; II, 190), as fearful ("Lord, I am here"; II, 194–95), as impoverished ("Me and my gift"; II, 197), and as allied to Christ in its lack and its desire—"The cup I drink, He drank of long before; / He felt the unuttered anguish which I dread; / He hungered Who the hungry thousands fed" ("'Surely He hath borne our griefs'"; II, 203). All these themes are present in the secular poems: the unmoved stone-soul is a variant of the stone-woman who inhabits the secular poems; the "marred" and "withered" self is an outgrowth of the repining maiden who waits in vain for her fulfillment in love, and also of the self who is exiled without cause, "shut out" from the garden and cultivating her barren lot, as well as the poet who chooses the withered garland of the aesthetic of renunciation; and the thirsty and hungry soul is a version of the insatiate Laura in *Goblin Market*, and of the woman who, in so many of the secular poems, simply wants *more*. All these essential themes are redefined by the new context, however. The speaker of the lyrics in "Christ our All in all" has an intimate and often reciprocal relation with Christ, who first and foremost accepts her as she is—even as the faint-hearted soul Rossetti wrote of in the early "'A bruised reed shall he not break'" (I, 67–68; June 13, 1852). Like that poem, many of the poems in this grouping consist of a colloquy between the speaker and Christ, a direct exchange involving question and answer, problem and resolution. Even though the relation with Christ may at times be difficult, Christ is essentially "sweetness" to the soul that is all bitterness ("Lord Jesu"; II, 198–99), and the inexhaustible source that the speaker, seeking, finds, "and finding seek Thee still" ("Darkness and light"; II, 204). These themes and images, then, are some of those which Rossetti explores from her early to her late religious verse, and which often bear either a homologous or a paradoxical relation to the themes and images of the secular poems.

More clearly than any other groupings in Rossetti's work, the groupings in *Verses* represent deliberate sequences. Taking up the sequence at any point in "Christ our All in all," for example, we can see how Rossetti manipulates certain common tropes, using a method that is deeply rooted in the associative patterning of religious forms: prayers, litanies, biblical commentary, meditations. The fourteenth poem of "Christ our All in all," for instance, begins with Christ's new order, His "New Creatures" (II, 195), a designation that immediately leads Rossetti to antithesis: where they are all different, he is the "Same." This designation, however, calls up the inevitable rhyme and the distinguishing mark, the "Name." This name is not the ineffable Jahweh, but that which cannot be repeated too often, the name of the intimate, knowing Jesus, who is only a handclasp away: "We know Thy wounded Hands: and Thou does know / Our praying hands." We need not shrink, then, from "newness," because the Name that marks the difference is also the Name that marks sameness: "Our King of old and still our Self-same King." The next lyric takes up the power of the Name as contrasted with the metonymic epithets, "'King of kings, and Lord of lords,'" (II, 195), which are fit for saints and seraphs to utter. But for the ordinary mortal it is the Name of Jesus that signifies the fulfillment of the promise, "Man's life and resurrection from the grave."

The next brief poem, however, as if in contradiction, searches out "new" names, the metaphors of the New Testament: the Name like incense, that sweetens our names before God and is God's promise, his last word, his "Amen" and his "Yea." If he is the end of names, then what can we call him? The answer is anything and everything: we can name him Shepherd, Door, Life, Truth, Way—according to the words of the New Testament—because he *is* everything, because words are *not*, in this sense, metaphors. Having established the grounds for such specificity—all names and each name—Rossetti puts next a poem entitled "'The good shepherd'" (II, 196), one of the most resonant nominations of the New Testament, derived from the parable that stresses individual uniqueness: the one hundredth sheep that is lost is more dear to Christ than the ninety-nine that are saved. In this lyric Rossetti uses the cadences of secular pastoral complaint to emphasize the "catholicity" of the biblical trope and the power of the Name to recall and renew all names, even the names of literary artifice: "O Shepherd with the bleeding Feet, / Good Shepherd with the pleading Voice, / What seekest Thou from hill to hill?" This four-poem sequence, then, moves through a series of names that mark both sameness and difference, and which derive their richness of association from both biblical and literary traditions—or, rather, interweave those traditions in a single name. Rossetti follows out a train of associations which is almost "free," in that rhymes call up meanings that call up other rhymes and meanings and which circle round—as, in psychoanalysis, associations circle round—to underlying obsessions and fixations (the new is the same old thing), and simultaneously break through to new grounds of feeling.

But having examined the sequences within sequences, the Chinese boxes of Rossetti's religious verse especially, we must return to the larger question of the shape of Rossetti's career, in particular to the obvious fact that after 1870—that is, in the second half of her life and career—Rossetti primarily wrote religious poetry and her secular output correspondingly diminished. As I have attempted to show, however, the vision of art, life, and individual identity is essentially the same in both "canons." Moreover, Rossetti's deliberate sequencing within separate volumes sets up a variety of echoes and cross-references that encourage us to read individual poems as commentary on one another, and the religious poems as a whole as commentary on or elaboration of the secular poems, and vice versa. Rossetti's "sameness" and her turning from secular to religious poetry are not symptoms of creative weakness. Rather, the religious poetry reveals an inexhaustible exfoliation of poetic language: Rossetti's barren tree and withered leaves are transformed into something like stylized Byzantine trees with gilt leaves. But this stylization is in no way an attenuation, for in the process of transformation Rossetti is able to shift from a vision of the female self as passive and helpless, fading away like the vanity of vanities, forever deserted, untouched, unknown, to a vision of a self whose "female" weaknesses are strengths, and who can convert "masculine" evasion—a turning away and a passing by—into a direct, intimate, and reciprocal imaginative relation: "Thou Face to face with me, and Eye to eye" (II, 185).

Part Two

ROSSETTI: WOMAN ARTIST AND PROSE WRITER

BETTY S. FLOWERS

The Kingly Self:
Rossetti as Woman Artist

One difficulty modern readers tend to have with Christina Rossetti's poetry is that it does not easily respond to the kind of reading we are used to giving most short lyric poems. We tend to read poetry the way the Romantics taught us to. For the generation of poets immediately preceding Rossetti, poets were the "unacknowledged legislators of the world." Psychologists and critics dealing with the creative personality also tend to be influenced by Romantic notions of the individual, pitted as rebellious hero against all the inhibiting cultural, social, and religious values of his society. Otto Rank, for example, in his fascinating study of the artistic personality, argues that "personal creativity is anti-religious in the sense that it is always subservient to the individual desire for immortality in the creative personality and not to the collective glorification of the creator of the world."[1]

Rossetti, artist though she was, saw the source of immortality not in art, but in obedience. She accepted the notion that women were inherently inferior artists, and she attempted to live up to the highest Victorian ideals of what it meant to be a devout Christian. Rossetti's poetry embodies the conflict between artistic creativity and the ideal of obedience which, for women, included the injunction to "keep silent." Rossetti does not, therefore, fit the aesthetic model of the artist producing art for art's sake alone. While Rossetti is not primarily an aesthete, those critics who concentrate on the explication of her

[1]Otto Rank, *Art and Artist: Creative Urge and Personality Development* (1932); trans. Charles Francis Atkinson (New York: Knopf, 1943), pp. 16–17.

159

secular lyrics are right to point out that her poems deserve more than a biographically reductive reading. In this essay I hope to pay full attention to the form of her work while neither ignoring her own view of her work as the product of a religious woman nor dismissing the sources of much of the work, which lie outside merely aesthetic concerns.[2]

Readings of Rossetti's poetry which ignore the implications of the biographical context tend to emphasize the secular poems, relegating the religious poems to a later, less interesting stage of Rossetti's career. When the religious poems are overlooked, however, Rossetti appears to be much more of a Pre-Raphaelite than she really was. In spite of her close alliance with personalities in the movement and her honorary title as "queen of the Pre-Raphaelites," the bulk of her work reflects Tractarian rather than Pre-Raphaelite concerns.[3] While Dante Gabriel was moving from the stark image of the thin-faced virgin (modeled after Christina) in white on a white bed to the massive fleshly shoulders, undulating necks, and blood-red lips of his richly clad Venuses, Christina was chiseling her spare verse as a kind of model of the way a woman might shape her life in obedient service to her Lord. In a sense, she stayed in the ascetic virgin's room of Dante Gabriel's painting, her poetry growing toward more control and conciseness even as his painting moved toward more elaboration and lusciousness. In spirit at least she owes much more to the model of her Anglican nun sister, Maria, than to her Pre-Raphaelite artist brother, Dante Gabriel.

---

[2]Some advances have been made toward the kind of fruitful criticism in which close readings of Rossetti's texts are informed by wide knowledge of her biography and of what it meant to be a woman in Victorian England. Both Jerome J. McGann ("Christina Rossetti's Poems: A New Edition and a Revaluation," VS 23 [1980]: 237–54) and Dolores Rosenblum ("Christina Rossetti: The Inward Pose," in *Shakespeare's Sisters*, ed. Sandra Gilbert and Susan Gubar [Bloomington: Indiana University Press, 1979], pp. 82–98), for example, have taken Rossetti as a female artist into account when looking at her poetry. Using Simone de Beauvoir's and John Berger's discussions of woman as object, Rosenblum explores Rossetti's use of the relation between seer and seen, the witness and the model, the watcher and the watched. In "Christina Rossetti's Religious Poetry: Watching, Looking, Keeping Vigil," VP 20 (1982): 46–47, Rosenblum says that "the myth of suffering for art's sake—Promethean, egoistic, male—is overlaid by the myth of suffering for its own sake—Christian, selfless, female."

[3]This argument is discussed further in G. B. Tennyson, *VDP*, pp. 133, 187, 198–203, 204–13, and *passim*. Jerome J. McGann points out the importance of seeing Rossetti's poetry as religious even when it is not specifically devotional ("The Religious Poetry of Christina Rossetti," *Critical Inquiry* 10 [1983]:127–44).

Rossetti often felt her own work to be inferior to her brother's. This feeling arose not from a careful comparison of her poetry with Dante Gabriel's but from a kind of a priori assumption that, as the male in the family, he was of course the better poet. In a letter to Dante Gabriel (April 1870), she said, "Here is a great discovery, 'Women are not Men,' and you must not expect me to possess a tithe of your capacities, though I humbly—or proudly—lay claim to family-likeness" (*FL*, p. 31). In this opinion, Rossetti was echoing the Victorian assumption that females made inferior artists and, conversely, that a woman who pursued art would damage her femininity. Woman's intellect was held to be inferior because so much vital energy was taken by her generative processes. Although he admired Rossetti's work, Gerard Manley Hopkins insisted that the "most essential quality" for an artist was "masterly execution: it is a kind of male gift and especially marks off men from women, the begetting of one's thought on paper, on verse, on whatever the matter is. . . . The male quality is the creative gift."[4] Rossetti agreed, not only because the Bible pictured woman as the weaker vessel but because the processes of her own logical mind led her to radical and unacceptable conclusions when she thought about equality for women. In response to a leaflet written by the poet Augusta Webster and printed by the Women's Suffrage Society, Rossetti said:

Does it not appear as if the Bible was based upon an understood unalterable distinction between men and women, their position, duties, privileges? Not arrogating to myself but most earnestly desiring to attain to the character of a humble orthodox Xtian, so it does appear to me; not merely under the Old but also under the New Dispensation. The fact of the Priesthood being exclusively man's, leaves me in no doubt that the highest functions are not in this world open to both sexes: and if not all, then a selection must be made and a line drawn somewhere. —On the other hand if female rights are sure to be overborne for lack of female voting influence, then I confess I feel disposed to shoot ahead of my instructresses, and to assert that female M.P.'s are only right and reasonable. Also I take exceptions at the exclusion of married women from the suffrage,—for who so apt as Mothers—all previous arguments allowed for the moment—to protect the interests of themselves and of their offspring? I do think if anything ever does sweep away

[4]Gerard Manley Hopkins and Richard Watson Dixon, *The Correspondence of Gerard Manley Hopkins and Richard Watson Dixon*, ed. Claude Collier Abbott (London: Oxford University Press, 1935), p. 133.

the barrier of sex, and make the female not a giantess or a heroine but at once and full grown a hero and giant, it is that mighty maternal love which makes little birds and little beasts as well as little women matches for very big adversaries.[5]

Meanwhile, however, the barrier of sex still stood. Rossetti was acutely aware that males were favored, whether as artists or simply as the brothers in the family. In her short story "The Waves of This Troublesome World" the widow teaches her daughter Jane "her business, calls her her right hand and little forewoman, yet feels perhaps a secret preference for Harry, so like his grandfather."[6] Although evidence for Nesca Robb's assertion that Rossetti's imagination often dwelt on murder, especially fratricide,[7] is somewhat hard to find, the female speaker in at least one Rossetti poem wishes she were a man:

> It's a weary life, it is, she said:—
> Doubly blank in a woman's lot:
> I wish and I wish I were a man:
> Or, better than any being, were not:
> ["From the antique"; PW, p. 312]

Whereas Dante Gabriel was given the money and time to train his artistic talents, Christina was sent off to work as a governess—a job at which she failed. "I myself feel like an escaped Governess," she wrote Swinburne, "for had I only learnt my lessons properly at the proper age I too might have taught some one something,—and doubtless I should have had to do so."[8]

Rossetti was keenly aware of the time taken up in the household duties women were expected to perform. In *Time Flies* she talks about occupations, which spring from within and are the outcome of will, and interruptions, which arrive from without. A modern woman artist, giving advice to readers, might be expected to describe ways in which interruptions can be minimized, but Rossetti, as a Victorian woman artist, points out to her readers that "the occupation may be

[5]Quoted in Mackenzie Bell, *Christina Rossetti: A Biographical and Critical Study* (London: Hurst and Blackett, 1898), pp. 111–12.

[6]Christina Rossetti, *Commonplace, a Tale of Today: and Other Short Stories* (Boston: Roberts, 1870), p. 328.

[7]Nesca Robb, *Four in Exile* (London and New York: Hutchinson, 1945), p. 113.

[8]Quoted in Lona Mosk Packer, "Swinburne and Christina Rossetti: Atheist and Anglican," *University of Toronto Quarterly* 33 (October 1963): 39.

wilful, while the interruption must be Providential" (*TF*, p. 161). As one of the most popular Victorian books of advice for women states, a woman "has no business to be so far absorbed in any purely intellectual pursuit, as not to know when water is boiling over on the fire."[9] Since woman's work was never done, the only excused absence from household occupations was illness. Many women artists—Rossetti and Elizabeth Barrett among them—spent a great deal of time in sickbeds with undiagnosed illnesses. Florence Nightingale complained that "women never have half an hour in all their lives (excepting before or after anybody is up in the house) that they can call their own, without fear of offending or of hurting some one. . . . A married woman was heard to wish that she could break a limb that she might have a little time to herself."[10] To be a devout woman meant to sacrifice the self, to give oneself in service to others. The Victorian ideal woman exactly matched the Victorian ideal of the obedient Christian—dutiful, self-sacrificing, always attuned to the needs and wishes of others. To fail to be a good woman was to fail to be a good Christian, and so the failure was all that much more to be avoided. Thus a woman who let the water boil over because she was preoccupied with intellectual pursuits was ultimately risking much more than the censure of her husband.

The uneasy relationship between woman as artist and woman as devout Christian is seen most clearly in Rossetti's preoccupation with the theme of obedience. "Whatever else may be deduced from the opening chapters of *Genesis*," says Rossetti in *Letter and Spirit*, "their injunction of obedience is plainly written; of unqualified obedience, of obedience on pain of death" (*LS*, pp. 18–19). As Rossetti put it early in *The Face of the Deep*, "Obedience is the key of knowledge, not knowledge of obedience" (*FD*, p. 10). Later in the book, Rossetti interjects a prayer that refers explicitly to the relation between the first woman and the sin that led to death for all humankind: "O God All-Wise, let us not be as our mother Eve who thought to hanker after good knowledge denied, when in truth she hankered after evil knowledge kept back" (*FD*, p. 16).

The book in which this prayer appears is one of six lengthy devotional works that Rossetti wrote and published under the auspices of

[9]Sarah Ellis, *The Mothers of England*, in *The Prose Works*, 2 vols. (New York: Langley, 1844), I, 101.
[10]Florence Nightingale, *Cassandra* (1852; rpt. Westbury: Feminist Press, 1979), p. 34.

the Society for Promoting Christian Knowledge. The close study of Scripture was one form of intellectual work which women were encouraged to undertake. They were, however, to study "to obey" rather than to question. Rossetti instructed her readers that studying the Apocalypse "should promote holy fear, unflinching obedience, patient progress and patient waiting, unhesitating trust, conformity to the Perfect Will," and that "so long as these are aimed at, to sit down ignorant and even to rise up equally ignorant may along with these virtues help forward humility" (FD, p. 266). By far the largest number of prayers in Rossetti's devotional book *Annus Domini: A Prayer for Each Day of the Year, Founded on a Text of Holy Scripture* are pleas for "obedience," for the subduing of will, and for humility. Also common are prayers "to fear and love Thee," for fear led to obedience at times when mere love might not. Not surprisingly then, one of Rossetti's suggested designs for Frederic Shields's decoration of the chapel at Eaton Hall was "*Obedience* Proverbs xxiii. 26. Youthful figure kneeling, elevating and offering a flaming and smoking censer, of heart-shape, golden and set with rubies."[11] The verse alluded to reads: "My son, give me thine heart, and let thine eyes observe my ways," followed by, "For a whore is a deep ditch; and a strange woman is a narrow pit."

Given this emphasis on the virtue of obedience, artistic self-expression becomes a hazardous undertaking. William Michael Rossetti pointed out in his *Memoir* that Rossetti "certainly felt that to write anything for publication is to incur a great spiritual responsibility" (PW, p. lxvii). Spiritual responsibility meant that the welling up of images and emotions which characterized the Romantic notion of poetic creation had to be strictly controlled. "How shall a heart preserve its purity," asked Rossetti, "if once the rein be given to imagination, if vivid pictures be conjured up, and stormy or melting emotions indulged?"[12] Even originality was suspect, as Rossetti makes clear in *Called to be Saints*: "No graver slur could attach to my book than would be a reputation for prevalent originality" (CS, p. xvii). Whenever any conflict arose between what might be required of Rossetti as an artist and what she perceived to be required of her as a Christian, she chose obedience to God. When Dante Gabriel chided her for spending so much time on the books she wrote for the Society for Promoting Christian Knowledge, she answered, "I don't think harm

[11]Quoted in Bell, *Christina Rossetti*, p. 121.

[12]Quoted in Lona Mosk Packer, *Christina Rossetti* (Berkeley: University of California Press, 1963), p. 145.

will accrue from my S.P.C.K. books, even to my standing: if it did, I should still be glad to throw my grain of dust into the religious scale" (*FL*, p. 92). Even the autobiographical novella *Maude* shows the development of the female artist as consisting of a growing awareness of the vanity of writing culminating in the death of the young writer. As Sandra Gilbert and Susan Gubar, among others, have noted, "the moral of this story is that the Maude in Christina Rossetti—the ambitious, competitive, self-absorbed and self-assertive poet—must die, and be replaced by either the wife, the nun, or, most likely, the kindly useful spinster."[13]

It could be argued that the conventions of Rossetti's religion contributed to what many have seen as defects in her poetry: limited subject matter, conventional forms, an ascetic turning away from this world. But while her religious ideals as a Victorian woman may have narrowed the possibilities of her artistic life, it was her religion that enabled her to break free enough of the conventions of Victorian womanhood to write at all. While her religious faith created a barrier between herself and the wider world that her agnostic brothers inhabited, it also enabled her to establish a position outside the Victorian conventions of romantic love and marriage, a position from which she criticized those conventions in subtle but effective ways. The ideal of the obedient Christian paralleled that of the obedient Victorian wife—except that the master in one case was a human being and in the other Christ himself. Rossetti's poetry clearly speaks of the advantages of aligning oneself with Christ rather than with an earthly husband. For example, many of Rossetti's poems explore what she saw as the great danger that the cult of Victorian love and marriage posed to the souls of women. Any earthly master, whether husband or brother as head of the household, could come between a woman and her love of God. Rossetti felt that it was much safer to love and serve a brother, whom God had chosen, than to assume the duties of marriage in relation to an object chosen simply by the fallible human will: "A wife's paramount duty is indeed to her husband, superseding all other human obligations: yet to assume this duty, free-will has first stepped in with its liability to err; in this connexion woman has to reap as she has sown, be the crop what it may: while in the filial relation all is safe and flawless, for all is of Divine ordaining" (*LS*, p. 43).

Her Christian heritage gave Rossetti an alternative to marriage on

[13]Sandra M. Gilbert and Susan Gubar, *The Madwoman in the Attic: The Woman Writer and the Nineteenth-Century Literary Imagination* (New Haven: Yale University Press, 1979), p. 552.

which to model her life as a woman. Like her sister Maria, she was very much influenced by the revival of medieval ideals of the contemplative life. In commenting on the twenty-seventh canto of Dante's *Purgatorio*, Maria wrote, "Leah is the symbol of the Active Life; Rachel of the Contemplative, which is the more perfect."[14] Christina too saw Leah and Rachel as "figures of the Active and Contemplative Lives" (*FD*, p. 462). In the New Testament (Luke 10:38–42), Christ himself is shown choosing the contemplative Mary, seated at his feet and listening to him as a teacher, over the more housewifely Martha, "careful and troubled about many things," among them the fact that she is slaving in the kitchen while Mary sits at the feet of the Master. "Mary hath chosen that good part," said Jesus, a sentiment many of Rossetti's poems embody. Not that all women were destined to be Marys rather than Marthas: "Our study of Martha and Mary (St. Luke x.38–42) assures us that the former was not wrong in the main, the latter setting an example to be followed cautiously because (we flatter ourselves) not applicable to all persons" (*LS*, p. 28). Christ validates the life of Mary, pointing also to that afterlife which Rossetti reminds the reader of, a life in which the lowest shall be made highest—and perhaps, following the logic so clearly displayed in her answer to the suffrage pamphlet, a life in which women and women artists trade places with their more successful brothers.

Given such a hope for the future, many of Rossetti's poems double as prayers addressed to Christ, who functions not only as the final cause of the poems, the superior, heavenly lover, but also as the efficient cause, her muse, the one who "bids me sing" ("The thread of life"; II, 123). The speaker of a great deal of her poetry is the inferior woman, who is at the same time the humble Christian. Both Christian and woman strive to be forgiven for their failings, to be accepted by the Lord and Master in their lives, to please him. The woman (Christian) in these poems is in the position of a younger sister in relation to an older sister, or a child in relation to a parent, or the traditional wife in relation to her husband: an inferior who must please the superior. And there is only one way to please—obedience.

Because Rossetti's poems were shaped not simply in relation to an ideal of art but in relation to the ideal of a self, it is misleading to read them simply as aesthetic objects. On the other hand, it is also mislead-

[14]Maria Francesca Rossetti, *A Shadow of Dante* (London: Rivingtons, 1871), p. 181.

ing to overemphasize Rossetti's personal biography because her concerns, both in her poems and in her life, are not focused on herself as a
particular Victorian woman artist, but on the inner life of a representative Christian absorbed in the heavenly future and not the earthly
present. Thus the mode of Rossetti's poetry is not so much confessional
as what could be called "redemptive." A characteristic Rossetti poem
does not lay bare personal concerns of the speaker which the reader
overhears any more than it is designed as a thing made of words to be
contemplated for the sake of aesthetic pleasure. Rossetti's goal lies
outside the text of the poems, in a kind of witnessing to a specific form
of self-making. In this process words function "as Goads and as Nails"
(FD, p. 322) or as "stepping stones[s], or curb[s], or tool[s]" ("Of each
sad word"; II, 310). Rossetti's implied reader is the "female" in us
(whether the reader be male or female), the chastened Eve or sinful
Christian. Rossetti's poetry enacts the process by which the "woman"
learns obedience, the process through which the Laura within can be
saved from the goblin market of the world by the Christ-like self-
sacrifice of a Lizzie, and through which an artistic, rebellious Christina
can become a holy Maria.

This shaping of the self from rebellious Eve into obedient, contemplative Mary, is clearly seen in the dualistic structure of many of
Rossetti's poems. Theo Dombrowski and other critics have pointed
out that this characteristic dualism is manifested in, for example, her
titles ("Life and death" [I, 155] or "To-day and to-morrow" [PW, pp.
339–40]), her use of word pairs and of two opposing characters, and
her use of dialogue.[15] Dolores Rosenblum, too, notes that "doubleness
becomes a structural principle" in Rossetti's verse: "her poetry is organized around distinctions so relentlessly absolute that the syntactic
relation between opposed entities is as important as the semantic
signification of the individual words."[16] Although this dualistic structure does set up "opposed entities," it also creates a parallelism in
which slight echoes undermine the "relentlessly absolute" distinctions
suggested by the content of the poem. In "Twice" (I, 124–26), for
example, the first three stanzas, which describe the speaker's past-
tense relationship with the earthly lover, are mirrored by the second
three stanzas, which depict her present-tense relationship with God.
While the lover rejects the speaker's heart, God is expected to accept

[15]Theo Dombrowski, "Dualism in the Poetry of Christina Rossetti," VP 14 (1976):
70–76.
[16]Rosenblum, "Christina Rossetti: The Inward Pose," p. 82.

it—or so conventional Christian theology would lead us to think. But the parallel structure of the poem, which makes the contrast between the rejecting earthly lover and an accepting God so clear, also allows other, more ambivalent elements to come into focus.

The lover of the first three stanzas gives the speaker a "friendly smile" (l. 10) while examining her heart, yet he ultimately rejects it. In the second half of the poem the speaker addresses God: "Smile Thou and I shall sing"; but although we expect this smile to lead to acceptance, the line that follows this plea leaves us with some doubt about the conditions under which the speaker's heart might be judged acceptable:

> Smile Thou and I shall sing,
> But shall not question much.
> [ll. 47–48]

The judgment of the lover has left the speaker broken-hearted and unsmiling. Perhaps more significantly, she has learned not to question, a lesson she carries into her relationship with God. By the end of the poem, the speaker has asked God to judge her heart "contemned of a man" (l. 33), but has not heard his judgment. The parallel structure of the poem, designed in part to illustrate the difference between giving one's heart to an earthly lover and giving one's heart to God, also suggests that there might be ominous similarities, and that, like the lover, God might judge her heart "unripe" (l. 13) and not smile upon her. The title "Twice," in this context, makes us wonder how much of what has happened in the first three stanzas will happen again, in the judgment for which the speaker is waiting at the end of the poem.

A poem in which the second section so clearly parallels the first calls attention to differences as well as to similarities. In such a context even minor changes take on significance. For example, the second line of the first three stanzas is set off by parentheses: "(O my love, O my love)"; the parallel line in the second three stanzas, however, is not enclosed in parentheses: "O my God, O my God." Since in the second half of the poem the speaker is addressing God, the exclamation seems in keeping with the dramatic situation. But the parenthetical exclamation in the first half emphasizes the immediacy of feeling which persists in the present for a lover whom the speaker has claimed no longer holds her heart. The events of the first three stanzas are described in the past tense but in the second person, as if the ghost of the lover were still present to speak to. While the narrative of the poem may depict a transferring of loyalty from the lover to God, the parallel structure of the poem reminds us of the continuing presence of the past, shaping the present, and of the ways in which our experiences with humans shape our experiences with the Divine. Unlike religious mystics, Rossetti never reported any immediate or transcendent experience with her God. Her lifelong relationship with God was based on faith, and while her faith led her to compare poems in which religious life is presented as preferable to secular life, the speaker's relationship with God and her understanding of him are colored by the disappointments experienced in those earthy love relationships ostensibly set up as "opposites" to the heavenly one. The heaven-earth opposition in many of Rossetti's poems is thus undercut not only by the parallelism inherent in the dualistic structures but also by the narrative voice. Although the narrative voice inevitably moves to the side of heaven, it has, meanwhile, presented earth's temptations—and sometimes very persuasively. What has appeared fair in the beginning of the poem is shown to harbor a hidden flaw—a vulnerability to time, and therefore to death. This "worm" spoils the object of our desire, but not our desire for the object in its unflawed state. Rossetti's poems are shaped, not to remove our desire for the object, but to train our understanding to look for that object in a future heaven rather than in this death-corrupted earth.

When we see the narrator as a woman, the dualism assumes a new emphasis. While the woman narrator can do nothing about fading beauty, for example, or about time, she can choose to bend her own will before time bends her. This theme of submission to time is common in religious poetry, but in the context of the many poems by Rossetti in which the female speaker first laments her fading beauty and then anticipates the happier future that awaits her in heaven, it assumes a new dimension. If we read the following argument as a work written by a female narrator, the opposition it dramatizes is not simply that of heaven versus earth but of one way of living as a woman versus another, with a plea to the male not to value the beautiful but earthly woman over the saint. Like a man looking at a beautiful woman, man regarding the beauties of earth is "befooled" because he does not take time into account.

> What is she while time is time,
>   O Man?—
> In a perpetual prime

Beauty and youth she hath;
And her footpath
Breeds flowers thro' dancing hours
    Since time began.

While time lengthens what is she,
    O Saint?—
Nought: yea, all men shall see
How she is nought at all,
When her death-pall
Of fire ends their desire
    And brands her taint.

Ah, poor Man, befooled and slow
    And faint!
Ah, poorest Man, if so
Thou turn thy back on bliss
And choose amiss!
For thou art choosing now:
    Sinner,—or Saint.
        ["What is this above thy head,"
        ll. 15–35; II, 261–62]

Rossetti's poetry reflects not simple dualism but a tension between the insufficient present and the future that is yet to be. A poem such as "'Luscious and sorrowful'" (II, 93), for example, asserts a difference between now and what is to come "in the land of home"; and yet, as this difference is being asserted, the rhymes, rhythms, and images of the poem keep heaven and earth inextricably bound together:

Beautiful, tender, wasting away for sorrow;
Thus today; and how shall it be with thee tomorrow?
    Beautiful, tender—what else?
        A hope tells.

Beautiful, tender, keeping the jubilee
In the land of home together, past death and sea;
    No more change or death, no more
        Salt sea-shore.

                    [II, 93]

170

Like so much of Rossetti's poetry, this poem is simple and straight-forward, yet close examination reveals the multiple cross-meanings that Rossetti's strict formal constructions lead to. At first glance, the poem exhibits Rossetti's characteristic heaven-earth dualism. But it contains, in addition to the present time of today's sorrow and the future time of heaven, a third vantage point, at which the narrative voice questions: "what else? / A hope tells." "Beautiful, tender" is repeated in connection with all three perspectives. The point of questioning, while in the continuing present, differs in quality from it; the continuing present is a present *condition*, a containing background, while the pivot point is a present *moment*, a decision point. The decision point, that pivot point from which many of Rossetti's narrators speak, links today with tomorrow even while the narrator asserts opposition. Rhyme, too, connects the wasting of today with the keeping of tomorrow, for the opening couplets of each stanza link opposites by revealing their physical similarity: "sorrow" with "tomorrow," "jubilee" with "death and sea." Even the final assertion that there shall be "no more change or death, no more" is followed by the rhyming "salt sea-shore."

In spite of the assertions to the contrary, the bitter, liminal space of the seashore seems to have the last word in "Luscious and sorrowful," because it *is* the last word and because the combination of noun-based adjective ("salt") and concrete noun ("sea-shore") is found nowhere else in the poem. "Home," "death," and "sea" are large abstractions when compared with the "salt sea-shore." The series of three-syllable words—"beautiful," "tomorrow," "jubilee," "together"—is followed by the two monosyllabic closing lines, which express hope in negative terms: no more change, death, or salt seashore. The sorrow with which the poem begins and which "tomorrow" seems to promise to end is evoked vividly by "salt," an adjective with the impact of a noun, so that by association (salt/tears/sorrow) the poem circles back to its beginning. The final effect is not so much one of dualism as of doubling, as in a mirrored reflection. We face toward the future in order to leave the sorrows of the present, but our vision of the future is a reflection of the present (death, change) accompanied by the assertion "no more"—"no more change or death, no more / Salt sea-shore." Effects such as these in the construction of the poem make the explicit message of duality far more complex than it at first appears to be. While the speaker of the poem may be a "Mary" working to redeem the "Eve" within us, persuading us at the point of choice to look forward to heaven and to leave earth behind, the poem itself does not allow us to leave earth behind so easily. Like God, the poet has created an earthly structure that points toward a future that can be conceived only in terms of itself. The poem bodies forth the tension inherent in the structure of things in which God's earth, while being made for us to give up, also seems to call us in godly ways through the vision of perfection we imagine on the other side of death—earth without time's flaws.

Thus in a profound way we cannot fully give up the earth. Earth remains in Rossetti's vision of heaven; and words, even when used as stepping stones, cannot lead directly to that which they cannot embody. The tree of the knowledge of good and evil, of heaven and earth, lives in the center of our earthly garden, and disobedience seems to be in the nature of things human, including speech. The woman poet who uses words, even while speaking of heaven, comes nearer to disobedience than she would have through silence. "Let the woman learn in silence," said Paul (1 Tim. 2:11–14), a stricture Rossetti took seriously even as she disobeyed it.

Rossetti as artist was acutely conscious of what her religion demanded of her as a woman and what she sacrificed—and was unwilling to sacrifice—for it. When charged with deliberately refraining from making her verse as good as she could, she responded ironically, "Perhaps as devout self-denial?"[17] The image of the ideal female as one who was self-effacing, humble, and silent was not entirely attractive to Rossetti even when it appeared as the object of the greatest love poetry. In her introductory comments to "*Monna Innominata,*" Rossetti admits that she finds Dante's silent Beatrice and Petrarch's silent Laura "resplendent with charms, but (at least, to my apprehension) scant of attractiveness" (II, 86). "*Monna Innominata*" is designed as the speech of the beloved woman to fill the void of silence. Interestingly, the woman speaker, while declaring her love for her beloved, even her willingness to die for him, also reminds him that she loves "God the most; / Would lose not Him, but you, must one be lost" (II, 89). While Elizabeth Barrett Browning's *Sonnets from the Portuguese* ask "How do I love thee? Let me count the ways,"[18] Rossetti's "sonnet of sonnets" charts not only her feelings for the beloved but also the ways in which she is willing to give him up for God. And in

---

[17]Quoted in Packer, *Christina Rossetti*, p. 387.

[18]Sonnet 43, in *The Complete Poetical Works of Elizabeth Barrett Browning*, ed. Harriet Waters Preston (Cambridge, Mass.: Riverside Press, 1900), p. 223.

the fourteenth and last sonnet, the lady who has spoken for herself throughout the poem concludes that, all having been given up, only silence remains:

> Youth gone and beauty gone, what doth remain?
> The longing of a heart pent up forlorn,
>   A silent heart whose silence loves and longs;
>   The silence of a heart which sang its songs
> While youth and beauty made a summer morn,
> Silence of love that cannot sing again.
>
> [II, 93]

Yet between the silence of celebrated ladies and this silence the artist has given us fourteen sonnets—the movement toward silence is itself a form of rebellion against silence.

Rossetti's interplay of the themes of song and silence is characteristic of her struggle as a religious Victorian woman poet. In the universal drama of choice between heaven and earth, Rossetti presents her role as something of a poetic messenger. Surely this is one reason she so often depicts herself as a bird, singing a song between heaven and earth, and, like the robin in winter, reminding us of better times to come. It is significant that her "first formulated ambition was to write a really fine hymn."[19] Hymns are characterized by repetition and strict form and are intended to be understood by members of a congregation singing together. Similarly, Rossetti's poems are built on patterns of repetition and depend on close attention to small variations in an otherwise strict form. And they are intended to be read as prayers are read, as the internal dialogue of the reader with God. The reader does not read them from the outside as the expression of genius, but internalizes them, makes the prayers his or, more appropriately, her own. The hymnlike quality of the third section of "The thread of life," for example, is immediately apparent:

> Therefore myself is that one only thing
> I hold to use or waste, to keep or give;
>
>   . . . . .
>
> And this myself as king unto my King
> I give, to Him Who gave Himself for me;

[19]Elisabeth L. Cary, The Rossettis (New York: Putnam's Sons, 1907), p. 270.

Who gives Himself to me, and bids me sing
A sweet new song of His redeemed set free;
He bids me sing: O Death, where is thy sting?
And sing: O grave, where is thy victory?

[II, 123]

In these lines, as in so much of Rossetti's poetry, the familiar Christian sentiments may blind us to the way in which the poem functions as a model of Rossetti's practice as a female artist. "*Monna Innominata*" is the song of a woman who denies herself to an earthly lover so that she might give herself to Christ, who "gave Himself" to her and continually "gives Himself" anew. "The thread of life" illustrates what this relationship might mean to the female artist.[20] In describing her relation to her heavenly beloved, the speaker presents herself not as queen but "as king unto my King," so that even though the relationship follows the model of inferior to superior, the speaker has a relatively higher position (king) than a woman who gives herself simply as female (queen) to an earthly male (king). The words "king unto my King" echo Rossetti's response to the Women's Suffrage Society leaflet, for they "sweep away the barrier of sex, and make the female not a giantess or a heroine but at once and full grown a hero and giant"—or, in this case, not a queen but a king; not a poetess but a poet.

In relation to man, woman is represented as the silent inferior. But in relation to Christ, the woman speaker asserts her role as singer. In much of Rossetti's poetry, Christ as Muse bids the woman sing of victory over death, of victory over earthly time that destroys feminine beauty and romantic relationships. Written in the face of the biblical injunction to women to keep silent and the Victorian insistence on female inferiority, Rossetti's poetry offers itself as an act of obedience—but obedience to a Muse who calls forth the woman artist's kingly self and bids her sing.

[20]Lona Mosk Packer, in "The Protestant Existentialism of Christina Rossetti," *Notes and Queries* n. s. 6 (June 1959): 213–15, also discusses this poem in terms of the relation between religious commitment and poetic productivity. Packer, however, emphasizes self-abnegation as a way of receiving "as a divine gift the freshening through faith of the poetic impulse" (p. 215) rather than the female artist's relation to Christ as Muse.

DIANE D'AMICO

Eve, Mary, and Mary Magdalene:
Christina Rossetti's Feminine Triptych

In *The Face of the Deep,* Christina Rossetti's devotional commentary on the Apocalypse, there is a passage in which Eve, the Virgin Mary, and Mary Magdalene appear in a sort of feminine triptych:

> Eve exhibits one extreme of feminine character, the Blessed Virgin the opposite extreme. Eve parleyed with a devil: holy Mary "was troubled" at the salutation of an Angel. Eve sought knowledge: Mary instruction. Eve aimed at self-indulgence: Mary at self-oblation. Eve, by disbelief and disobedience, brought sin to the birth: Mary, by faith and submission, Righteousness.
>
> And yet, even as at the foot of the Cross, St. Mary Magdalene, out of whom went seven devils, stood beside the "lily among thorns," the Mother of sorrows: so (I humbly hope and trust) amongst all saints of all time will stand before the Throne, Eve the beloved first Mother of us all. Who that has loved and revered her own immediate dear mother, will not echo the hope? [*FD,* pp. 310–11]

These three women, both as individual saints and as representative figures, characterize the limits and possibilities Rossetti sees as particularly feminine: Eve, the disobedient daughter who broke God's law, hankering after possibilities denied, and Mary, the obedient daughter who graciously submitted to God's will. Yet Mary, the mother of God, and Mary Magdalene, the sinner, stood together at the Crucifixion. Therefore the disobedience that had cost Eve Eden need not cost her heaven. Although all Eve's daughters, Rossetti and her beloved moth-

175

er included, have to bear the burden of Eve's sin, they can hope: one might follow the example of Mary's obedience, and, when failing, follow Magdalene's example of repentance. When this world and its time end, repentance and forgiveness will bring sinner and saint together as equals before God.

When Eve appears in Rossetti's poetry and prose, whether as a major or minor figure, she is consistently portrayed as inherently weaker than Adam. Even before the fall she was intellectually weaker; therefore her mind was easily swayed by the subtle snake. Succumbing to her own foolish curiosity, she "diverted her mind . . . from God" and thus disobeyed divine will (LS, p. 18). Rossetti's reading of Genesis led her to conclude that "curiosity [was] a feminine weak point inviting temptation, and doubly likely to facilitate a fall when to indulge it woman affects independence" (FD, p. 520). In other words, Eve should not have wandered off alone, away from Adam. Eve was made from Adam's side to be his helpmeet,[1] and thus were all Eve's daughters to be seen. In her sonnet sequence "Monna Innominata," Rossetti has her unnamed lady state simply, "Woman is the helpmeet made for man," and so she will love "without stint and all [she] can" (II, 89, 88). The speaker of a later poem entitled "'A helpmeet for him'" tells woman that her purpose is to serve man, to be "his shadow by day, his moon by night" (II, 169). Furthermore, if Eve is Adam's helper, then it follows that he is her lord and her dearest "treasure." Exiled from Eden, Eve still has "yet the accustomed hand for leading, / Yet the accustomed heart for love" ("An After-Thought"; PW, p. 318). She is "propped upon his strength" (II, 144).

This representation seems rather traditional: woman as curious and frail and as subordinate to man. These characteristics, however, represent only one side of Rossetti's Eve: although it is through Eve's foolish choice that sin enters the world, repeatedly in both Rossetti's poetry and prose, Eve appears as a sympathetic figure. In the poem "An After-Thought," we see her as "saddened Eve with sleepless eyes"; if

[1]My thanks to Mrs. Harold Rossetti for providing me with a copy of Christina Rossetti's manuscript notes on the book of Genesis. Rossetti made these notes (approximately two pages in length) expecting to write a volume of devotional prose on the subject. As yet these notes have not been published.

In the note for Genesis 2:22, Rossetti makes a typological association between Eve, built from Adam's side, and the Church, built from the side of Christ. This association suggests that Rossetti accepted the predominant view that Eve was created from Adam's rib as opposed to the view that Eve and Adam were created by God in his image at the same time, as described in Genesis 1: 27.

she was "supremely happy once," she is now "supremely broken-hearted." Moreover, she remains, despite her sin, our "fair first mother" (PW, p. 318). In Rossetti's work Eve is a significant maternal figure, more so than Blessed Mary, the Virgin Mother. Furthermore, in her role as our mother she is not an amoral Mother Nature, but a very human individual who grieves over her sin. And it is as grieving mother that Rossetti portrays Eve most movingly. In the poem simply entitled "Eve" (I, 156–58), the first woman appears, not in any of the traditional poses—Eve listening to the snake or Eve offering Adam the forbidden fruit—but mournfully weeping beside the body of Abel. She mourns not only because one son has killed another but because she feels responsible:

> "I, Eve, sad mother
> Of all who must live,
> I, not another,
> Plucked bitterest fruit to give
> My friend, husband, lover;—
> O wanton eyes, run over;
> Who but I should grieve?—
> Cain hath slain his brother:
> Of all who must die mother,
> Miserable Eve!"
>
> [ll. 26–35]

Her anguish is underscored by the responsibility she bears and accepts; she knows it is she who let sin and death into the world.

That we as readers are to sympathize with Eve is suggested first by the implication that her intentions were innocent (she plucked forbidden fruit "to give" some to Adam, perhaps to share what she thought was good fortune wrongfully denied, not to tempt and destroy him), and second by the image of all nature mourning with her: the mouse, cattle, the eagle, larks, bees, the raven, the conies all pause in their daily habits, each in its way "sympathetical" and "answering grief by grief." The only exception is, of course, the snake, who appears in the concluding lines:

> Only the serpent in the dust
> Wriggling and crawling,
> Grinned an evil grin and thrust
> His tongue out with its fork.
>
> [ll. 67–70]

177

The poem ends with our attention on the snake as the source of evil, the villain responsible for all this grief. Therefore, although it was Eve through whom evil entered the world, she herself is not a personification of evil. Eve's sin does not make her demonic; she is exiled from Eden but not from the Paradise to come.

Although Rossetti does follow the interpretation of Genesis that sees Adam sinning because of his love for Eve (he "deemed poison sweet for her sweet sake" [II, 144]), she does not accept the view of Eve that often accompanies this interpretation. In Rossetti's work, Eve may appear as Adam's "lost bride," but she is never an evil seductress.[2] In Rossetti's mind both Adam and Eve sinned, and we humans need not "attempt to settle which (if either) committed the greater sin" (LS, p. 56). Moreover, it is not our place as fallible human beings to make such judgments: "Some have opined that a woman's wickedness even exceeds that of a man; as Jezebel stirred up Ahab, and Herodias outstripped Herod on feet swift to shed blood. But this point must stand over for decision to the Judgment of that Only Judge to whom each and all of us will one day stand or fall" (FD, p. 400).

When the biblical record left enough room for Rossetti to offer an interpretation in Eve's favor, she did so. Repeatedly, she stresses the fact that Eve was deceived by Satan. She did not intend to let sin into the world. But Satan was a master of "guile," and she was "cajoled" (TF, p. 237). When he offered her the fruit, she was innocent, and when she offered the forbidden fruit to Adam, her motives were innocent still. The most striking example of this sympathetic view of Eve appears in Letter and Spirit as part of Rossetti's commentary on the first commandment. Although lengthy, the passage is important enough to quote in full:

> It is in no degree at variance with the Sacred Record to picture to ourselves Eve, that first and typical woman, as indulging quite innocently sundry refined tastes and aspirations, a castle-building spirit (if so it may be called), a feminine boldness and directness of aim combined with a no less feminine guessiness as to means. Her very virtues may

[2]Rossetti's note on Genesis 2:22 includes the following reference to Eve: "Also consider His [Christ's] parallel with Adam casting in his lot with his lost bride." Rossetti's sympathetic portrayal of Eve becomes all the more striking when we compare it to the depiction of Eve as seductress found repeatedly in Western culture. On Eve as she has been presented in Western theology and art, see John A. Phillips, Eve: The History of an Idea (San Francisco: Harper & Row, 1984).

178

have opened the door to temptation. By birthright gracious and accessible, she lends an ear to all petitions from all petitioners. She desires to instruct ignorance, to rectify misapprehension: "unto the pure all things are pure," and she never suspects even the serpent. Possibly a trace of blameless infirmity transpires in the wording of her answer, "*lest* ye die," for God had said to the man ". . . in the day that thou eatest thereof thou *shalt surely* die:" but such tenderness of spirit seems even lovely in the great first mother of mankind; or it may be that Adam had modified the form, if it devolved on him to declare the tremendous fact to his second self. Adam and Eve reached their goal, the Fall, by different routes. With Eve the serpent discussed a question of conduct, and talked her over to his own side: with Adam, so far as appears, he might have argued the point for ever and gained no vantage; but already he had secured an ally weightier than a score of arguments. Eve may not have argued at all: she offered Adam a share of her own good fortune, and having hold of her husband's heart, turned it in her hand as the rivers of water. Eve preferred various prospects to God's Will: Adam seems to have preferred one person to God: Eve diverted her "mind" and Adam his "heart" from God Almighty. Both courses led to one common result, that is, to one common ruin (Gen. iii). [*LS*, pp. 17–18]

What is especially significant about Rossetti's interpretation of this first human sin is that she does not present it in sexual terms. For Rossetti, Genesis was primarily a warning against disobedience, not lust: "Whatever else may be deduced from the opening chapters of Genesis, their injunction of obedience is plainly written; of unqualified obedience, of obedience on pain of death" (*LS*, p. 19). Although Rossetti did follow those who saw in Adam and Eve's disobedience a breaking of all God's commandments ("Adam by one sin broke the whole law: offending in one point he became guilty of all" [*TF*, p. 243]), she did not specifically equate forbidden fruit with sex. Eve ate the fruit because she wanted to "become like God" (*FD*, p. 249). Such a desire is prideful, not lustful. Secondly, Adam diverted his heart from God not because of lust, but because of love, a misguided and earthly love perhaps, but love nonetheless:

> Did Adam love his Eve from first to last?
> I think so; as we love who works us ill,
> And wounds us to the quick, yet loves us still.
> [II, 144–45]

179

Although Rossetti did not see Eve as a demon, or even as more wicked than Adam, the Bible proved to her that in this world men and women had different roles assigned them by God. When Augusta Webster wrote to her, urging her to join the women's suffrage movement, Rossetti replied: "Does it not appear as if the Bible was based upon an understood unalterable distinction between men and women, their position, duties, privileges? Not arrogating to myself but most earnestly desiring to attain to the character of a humble orthodox Xtian, so it does appear to me; not merely under the Old but also under the New Dispensation."[3] Although Rossetti was willing to assert the creative power of her own "Poet Mind" when she disagreed with her brother Dante Gabriel,[4] and proud that in her will she could leave her brother William Michael enough money to pay him back for twenty years of financial support (FL, p. 155), she was not in favor of women getting the vote. Her position can be explained at least in part by her reading of Genesis: women were from the beginning of creation assigned a certain place in this world, subordinate in some respects to that of man, and to seek a higher place was to do as Eve had done "when she postponed obedience to knowledge" (SF, p. 142). A major theme in both Rossetti's prose and poetry is the necessity of achieving humility, of accepting the "lowest place" (I, 187). For all women this meant serving as the left hand in a right-handed society, and for the wife it meant being subordinate to the husband. In fact, dependency upon an individual man might be part of woman's special burden, part of her punishment: "Eve, the representative woman, received as part of her sentence 'desire': the assigned object of her desire being such that satisfaction must depend not on herself but on one stronger than she, who might grant or might deny" (FD, p. 312).

Despite her acceptance of "woman's place," however, Rossetti did not overlook the possibility that such acceptance might bring difficulty and pain: "A wife's paramount duty is indeed to her husband, superseding all other human obligations: yet to assume this duty, freewill first stepped in with its liability to err; in this connexion woman has to reap as she has sown, be the crop what it may: while in the filial relation all is safe and flawless, for all is of Divine ordaining" (LS, p. 43). In other words, it was safer, perhaps even better, to stay a daugh-

---

[3]Quoted in Mackenzie Bell, *Christina Rossetti: A Biographical and Critical Study* (London: Hurst and Blackett, 1898), pp. 111–12.

[4]*Three Rossettis: Unpublished Letters to and from Dante Gabriel, Christina, William,* ed. Janet Camp Troxell (Cambridge: Harvard University Press, 1937), p. 43.

ter than to become a wife, for if a woman married the "wrong" man, then she most likely would suffer more than her husband. Indeed, Rossetti seemed to feel that in relationships between men and women, women are far more likely to be hurt: "Society may be personified as a human figure whose right hand is man, whose left woman; in one sense equal, in another sense unequal. The right hand is labourer, acquirer, achiever: the left hand helps, but has little independence, and is more apt at carrying than at executing. The right hand runs the risks, fights the battles: the left hand abides in comparative quiet and safety; except (a material exception) that in the *mutual* relationship of the twain it is in some ways far more liable to undergo than to inflict hurt, to be cut (for instance) than to cut" (FD, p. 410). Even in the case of Adam and Eve, Rossetti did not overlook the verse in Genesis (13:12) in which Adam seems quite willing to let Eve take all the blame: "The meanness as well as the heinousness of sin is illustrated in Adam's apparent effort to shelter himself at the expense of Eve" (LS, p. 84). Rossetti stresses this point again in *The Face of the Deep* when, after quoting from Psalm 118 and Psalm 146, both of which tell us to trust in God, not man, she adds her own warning: "Adam seems not to have found one word to plead for Eve in the terrible hour of judgment" (p. 418).

Although Rossetti considers the married and the unmarried life to be in "gracious harmony," she sees the life of the married woman, especially her spiritual life, as much less satisfying than that of the unmarried woman, for the wife must approach God indirectly through her husband: "She sees not face to face, but as it were in a glass darkly. Every thing, and more than all every person, and most of all the one best beloved person, becomes her mirror wherein she beholds Christ and her shrine wherein she serves Him" (LS, p. 92). But "she whose heart is virginal . . . beholds the King in His beauty; wherefore she forgets, by comparison, her own people and her father's house. Her Maker is her Husband, endowing her with a name better than of sons and of daughters." The unmarried woman gives all to God and loses herself in him: "She contemplates Him, and abhors herself in dust and ashes. She contemplates Him, and forgets herself in Him. . . . The air she breathes is too rare and keen for grosser persons; they mark the clouds which involve her feet, but discern not those early and late sunbeams which turn her mists to rainbows and kindle her veiled head to a golden glory" (LS, pp. 91–92). Certainly, such a spiritual life seems more fulfilling than that of the wife who must see "in a glass darkly."

Furthermore, it is important to notice that the center of Rossetti's description of the unmarried woman is an image of weakness made strong. She may abhor herself in dust and ashes, but at the same time her feet are in the clouds and she radiates a golden glory. Adam's love, the husband's earthly love, might be a comfort or a prop for a woman to lean on in this life, but ultimately it was Christ's redeeming love that would transform her. Eve, the grieving mother who brought death and sin to her children, would become the virtuous woman of the book of Proverbs because of Christ's sacrifice:

> Hail, Eve and Adam, source of death and shame!
> New life has sprung from death, and Jesu's Name
> Clothes you with fame.
>
> Hail Adam, and hail Eve! your children rise
> And call you blessed, in their glad surmise
> Of Paradise.
>
> ["That Eden of earth's sunrise
> cannot vie," ll. 16–21; II, 220]

And while on earth, each woman, whether married or not, could find in loving God an answer to Eve's special burden of desire: "Many women attain their heart's desire: many attain it not. Yet are these latter no losers if they exchange desire for aspiration, the corruptible for the incorruptible" (*FD*, p. 312).

One woman who had made such an exchange was the Blessed Virgin Mary. In fact, Rossetti associated the life of the unmarried woman with that of the Blessed Mary: "If she [the unmarried woman] rejoices, it is on the spiritual heights, with Blessed Mary magnifying the Lord" (*LS*, p. 92). Rossetti accepted the doctrine of Mary's perpetual virginity, but it was not Mary as Virgin Mother that attracted Rossetti's interest. Mary's virgin motherhood was "a marvel," yet that marvel would never have occurred if she had not first obeyed God's will: "Yet never had she gone on in pursuit of all mysteries and knowledge if she had not first answered in simple obedience: 'Behold the handmaid of the Lord; be it unto me according to thy word'" (*FD*, pp. 12–13). It was Mary's humility, not her virginity, that drew Rossetti to her. By presenting Mary as the humble daughter of God and not stressing her virgin motherhood, Rossetti was, in a sense, keeping Mary from the pedestal many others had placed her upon, but significantly she was keeping her within reach.[5] Mary as a virgin mother, no woman could emulate; Mary as obedient daughter of God, all could.

Rossetti did agree with those who regarded Mary as special because she "bore the Saviour of all mankind": we should, Rossetti said, cherish [her] in grateful memory" and also "aspire to honour" her (TF, p. 236). But Rossetti drew a clear distinction between honor and worship: "Mary is a shut gate, not a gate of access: Christ is our open door" (CS, p. 181). In Rossetti's opposition to the worship of Mary, we find an indication of why she would never have considered changing her faith, "going over to Rome," as many of her fellow Tractarians did. According to William Sharp, a family friend, although Rossetti "had much sympathy for the Church of Rome . . . the rock which she took to be a beacon of wreck was Mariolatry. This at all times seemed to her the most cardinal error of Roman Catholicism."[6] In his memoir of his sister, William Michael assures his readers that, although Rossetti was not "hostile" to Catholicism, she was "firmly opposed to anything savouring of Mariolatry" (PW, p. lii). Rossetti herself makes this point clear when she opposes having favorite saints: "Favouritism is quite possible, but is highly objectionable in our love of saints" (TF, p. 16).

Rossetti's strong opposition to anything "savouring" of Mariolatry seems to have influenced both the poetry and prose she wrote to honor the Virgin. Quite often a poem that at first seems to focus on Mary actually places a greater emphasis on Christ. In Called to be Saints, the poem Rossetti includes in her chapter on the Annunciation depicts Mary as "a rose, who bore the Rose." She is pure as a lily, but Christ far surpasses her:

> Lily herself, she bore the one
> Fair Lily; sweeter, whiter, far
> Than she or others are:
> ["Herself a rose, who bore
> the rose," ll. 6–8; II, 238]

Mary is "gracious," but Christ is "essential Grace" (p. 193). In Time Flies, in Rossetti's entry for December 8, The Feast of the Conception

[5]For a thorough study of the Virgin Mary, see Marina Warner, Alone of All Her Sex: The Myth and Cult of the Virgin Mary (New York: Knopf, 1976).

[6]William Sharp, "Some Reminiscences of Christina Rossetti," Atlantic Monthly 75 (June 1895): 745.

of the Blessed Virgin Mary, she again emphasizes that God is the source of all holiness: "She whom God sanctified is holy. . . . Her gifts are His gifts to her, her graces His graces in her" (p. 236). In such passages and poems Rossetti seems to be keeping her poetic imagination in check lest she encourage Mariolatry. The clearest example of such restraint is the poem "The Feast of the Annunciation" (II, 238) which begins "Wherto shall we liken this Blessed Mary Virgin?" Rossetti then offers several possibilities, only to decide such names belong to Christ: "Lily we might call her, but Christ alone is white; / Rose delicious, but that Jesus is the one Delight." Finally she simply encourages us to copy the angel Gabriel:

> "Blessed among women, highly favoured," thus
> Glorious Gabriel hailed her, teaching words to us:
> Whom devoutly copying we too cry "All hail!"
> Echoing on the music of glorious Gabriel.
>
> [ll. 7–10]

Never does Rossetti encourage us to place the creature, even if she is the mother of Jesus, before the Creator. Even when it comes to Mary's ideal humility, Rossetti does not overlook the two instances when Christ had to instruct his mother: "Taking humility as our subject: He taught His blessed Mother once and again by check (St. John ii. 4; St. Mark iii. 31–35)" (SF, p. 321). Perhaps Rossetti found some comfort in the fact that even Mary, the handmaiden of the Lord, occasionally had to be reminded to be humble.

There is ample evidence that choosing the lowest place was not easy for Rossetti, despite her devout faith. Indeed, to her mind, suffering was inextricably woven into the process of becoming humble: "All these instances [biblical lessons in humility] taken together illustrate not the necessity merely of our acquiring humility, but the painfulness of the process whereby it must be acquired" (SF, p. 322). In Rossetti's later years many of her contemporaries saw her as a Victorian saint: quiet and reclusive, patient and humble. She herself was by middle age content with her "assigned" place: "Please do not say 'The grapes are sour!' beautiful, delightful, noble, memorable, as is the world you [William Michael] and yours frequent,—I yet am well content in my shady crevice; which crevice enjoys the unique advantage of being to my certain knowledge the place assigned me" (FL, p. 168). Yet such acceptance had not come easily. At times she had yearned to play a more active part in a brighter world:

> When it seems (as sometimes through revulsion of feeling and urgency of Satan it may seem) that our yoke is uneasy and our burden unbearable, because our life is pared down and subdued and repressed to an intolerable level: and so in one moment every instinct of our whole self revolts against our lot, and we loathe this day of quietness and sitting still, and writhe under a sudden sense of all we have irrecoverably foregone . . . then the Seraphim of Isaiah's vision making music in our memory revive hope in our heart. [CS, p. 435].

Before she came to "trust and submit" to the limits God imposed on human knowledge, she had longed to know much more "than the melancholy world doth know, / Things beyond all lore."[7] As a mature woman she insisted that when young she had been the "ill-tempered one of the family."[8] Even after the temper had long been under control and she had accepted her quiet place, she still saw herself as a sinner trusting in God's mercy: "Not that I arrogate to myself so blessed an end [the shady rest of Paradise]: but God's Mercy to sinners is infinite" (FL, p. 166). With this her self-image, a sinner turning to God, Rossetti naturally found comfort in the image of Mary Magdalene and the Virgin Mary standing together before the Cross.

Rossetti's interest in the life of Mary Magdalene began early. At age fifteen she wrote a five-stanza poem entitled simply "Mary Magdalene" (PW, p. 89). It depicts the scene in Luke 7: 36–50 in which an unnamed sinner, considered to be Magdalene, enters the home of Simon the Pharisee to anoint Christ with oil. Rossetti follows the biblical text in that Mary Magdalene is presented as a repentant sinner, kneeling at Christ's feet and washing them with her tears and hair. Also, the last line of the poem, "Loved much and was forgiven," clearly echoes Christ's response to Simon, "Wherefore I say unto thee, Her sins which are many, are forgiven; for she loved much" (Luke 7:47). Similarly, Rossetti follows the traditional interpretation of this biblical story by describing Magdalene as a beautiful, young woman, renouncing "her jewels / And her rich attire." Rossetti, how-

---

[7] Quoted in Ellen Proctor, A Brief Memoir of Christina Georgina Rossetti (London: SPCK, 1896), p. 30.
[8] Sharp, "Some Reminiscences," p. 740.

ever, departs from tradition in that she does not clearly associate Magdalene with prostitution.[9] When Rossetti refers to Magdalene's sin, it is in very general terms: "the great transgression, / The sin of the other time." In her rich attire and jewels Magdalene is an image of a worldly woman but not necessarily a prostitute.

Although such an interpretation does not depart radically from the biblical text (for nowhere in the Bible is Magdalene's sin ever named), it varies considerably from the traditional interpretation, which stresses the carnal nature of her sin. In Rossetti's own Victorian England, "Magdalene" was a synonym for a reformed prostitute, and in the 1860s Rossetti herself took part in the social movement to "reclaim fallen women" by working at St. Mary Magdalene's on Highgate Hill, a church institution described by William Michael Rossetti as a home "for the reclamation and protection of women leading a vicious life" (FL, p. 26). Therefore the association of Magdalene with sexual sin was, in a sense, readily available for Rossetti to employ in her prose and poetry, yet even in her mature devotional works she does not do so. The most specific reference Rossetti ever makes to Magdalene's past is to allude to Luke 8:2, a text that identifies Magdalene as one of the women Christ "healed of evil spirits." Thus, in Rossetti's work, Mary Magdalene is not so much a penitent whore representing fallen women but a penitent sinner representing all humankind. Moreover, it is not so much the nature of a specific sin that interests Rossetti as the possibility of redemption.

Rossetti's entry in *Time Flies* for July 22, Mary Magdalene's feast day, begins with Magdalene's life after she chose God:

> A record of this Saint is a record of love. She ministered to the Lord of her substance, she stood by the Cross, she sat over against the Sepulchre, she sought Christ in the empty grave, and found Him and was found of Him in the contiguous garden.
>
> Yet this is that same Mary Magdalene out of whom aforetime He had cast seven devils.
>
> Nevertheless, the golden cord of love we are contemplating did all along continue unbroken in its chief strand: for before she loved Him, He loved her. [pp. 139–40]

---

[9]For further discussion of Mary Magdalene as the penitent whore, see Warner, *Alone of All Her Sex*, pp. 224–35. Rossetti's portrayal of Magdalene as repentant sinner, not penitent whore, is in keeping with her nonsexual view of Eve's fall, and is perhaps, at least in part, a consequence of that view.

It is the transforming power of divine love that draws Rossetti to the story of Mary Magdalene: because of Christ's unwavering love and a human choice to return that love, a woman once possessed by demons became a bride of Christ. When Magdalene appears to the repentant sinner in "Divine and human pleading" (to upbraid him for invoking her aid rather than turning directly to God), Rossetti refers to her as a "vision of the blest." Light literally shines from her:

> Her footsteps shone upon the stars,
>   Her robe was spotless white;
> Her breast was radiant with the Cross,
>   Her head with living light.[10]
>
> [ll. 21–24]

When Rossetti describes the moment when Magdalene and the Risen Christ meet, she compares Magdalene to the beloved in the Song of Songs: "On the first day of the week while it was yet dark St. Mary Magdalene sought the sepulchre, and outlingered all other lovers of Jesus save angels only; with whom she held high converse, being as it were the very bride of the Song of Songs (v. 9, 10): 'What is thy Beloved more than another beloved, O thou fairest among women? . . . My Beloved is white and ruddy, the chiefest among ten thousand.' And none but she out of whom went seven devils was the first to behold our risen Saviour" (SF, pp. 231–32).

For Rossetti, the image of the Risen Christ and Mary Magdalene together in the garden outside the sepulcher represented the moment when each soul called by Christ will joyously recognize him, the moment in "the beatified life" when one would finally see face to face: "When Christ shall call each happy, heavenly soul by name, as once He called 'Mary' in an earthly garden, then each will perceive herself to be that which He calls her; and will no more question her own designation than did those primitive creatures whom the first Adam named in the inferior Paradise" (FD, p. 73). In expectation of this second birth, each human being should emulate Mary Magdalene:

---

[10]Gwynneth Hatton, An Edition of the Unpublished Poems of Christina Rossetti with a Critical Introduction and Interpretative Notes to All the Posthumous Poems (B. Litt. thesis, St. Hilda's College, Oxford, 1955), p. 35. William Michael Rossetti did not choose to include "Divine and human pleading" in the Poetical Works, and as yet it has not appeared in Crump's variorum edition. Christina Rossetti included a version of this poem in her privately printed volume Verses (1847).

"Grant us ever to be . . . as St. Mary Magdalene in the garden when lo! the Unknown was Thyself"; "Make us as Mary when she turned and said Rabboni" (*FD*, p. 317, p. 515). This moment of recognition is the spiritual consummation for which the soul longs, a consummation made possible, despite mankind's fall, by human penitence and divine love.

When discussing the Holy Innocents, Rossetti suggests that anyone who lives much beyond early childhood loses the state of innocence, but "blessedness" is still within reach through penitence, for through penitence one recovers purity. And, Rossetti reasons that such purity must be recovered if one is to be saved: "Penitence *must*, on pain of ultimate rejection, recover purity and guilelessness" (*FD*, p. 354). Yet immediately after this rather firm declaration, which has a note of warning about it, Rossetti placed a poem that serves to balance the warning with the assurance that God does work wondrous things:

> Can peach renew lost bloom,
> Or violet lost perfume,
> Or sullied snow turn white as overnight?
> Man cannot compass it, yet never fear:
> The leper Naaman
> Shows what God will and can;
> God Who worked there is working here;
> Wherefore let shame, not gloom, betinge thy brow,
> God Who worked then is working now.
>
> ["'Go in peace'"; II, 321]

Because Rossetti's faith in the transforming power of divine love was so strong, her image of Magdalene, once a sinner possessed by demons, as a bride of Christ was neither incongruous nor inappropriate. Most likely this faith contributed to Rossetti's ability to resist the Victorian tendency to see a woman once stained by sin, especially sexual sin, as forever fallen, with no future except exile or death.[11]

Rossetti wrote several poems that focus on the figure of the fallen woman, such as "Songs in a cornfield" (I, 126–29), "An Apple-Gathering" (I, 43–44), "Margery" (*PW*, pp. 360–61), "Cousin Kate" (I, 31–32), and "From sunset to star rise" (I, 191–92). Rossetti's

---

[11]For an analysis of the figure of the fallen woman in Victorian literature, see Nina Auerbach, *Woman and the Demon: The Life of a Victorian Myth* (Cambridge: Harvard University Press, 1982), especially the chapter "The Rise of the Fallen Woman."

attitude toward these women who have, certainly by society's standards, loved unwisely, is sympathetic and even compassionate, as in "Margery":

> Yet this I say and I maintain:
>   Were I the man she's fretting for,
>   I should my very self abhor
> If I could leave her to her pain,
> Uncomforted to tears and pain.
>
> [ll. 51–55]

Although the individual woman must bear the burden of her sin, Rossetti reminds us that she is not alone, for all human beings have sinned:

> It was her own fault? so it was.
>   If every own fault found us out,
>   Dogged us and snared us round-about,
> What comfort should we take because
> Not half our due we thus wrung out?[12]
>
> ["Margery," ll. 31–35]

In these poems on the fallen woman the woman is shown fretting away ("Margery"), loitering in the cold dew ("An Apple-Gathering"), howling in dust ("Cousin Kate"), and weeping in sorrow ("Songs in a cornfield"). But Rossetti does not imply such suffering is proper punishment and that therefore the woman should stay in her barren spot, without comfort and hope.

For example, in the opening lines of "From sunset to star rise," a

[12]It is interesting that Rossetti later used this stanza, having revised it slightly (changing the opening question from "It was her own fault?" to "The sinner's own fault?"), for the first stanza of an untitled poem that appears as the full entry for July 21 in *Time Flies*, the day before Mary Magdalene's feast day. The second and concluding stanza of this untitled poem underscores Rossetti's opinion that we should not abandon sinners, for we all share in their guilt:

> Clearly his own fault. Yet I think
>   My fault in part, who did not pray,
>   But lagged, and would not lead the way.
> I, haply, proved his missing link.
> God help us both to mend and pray.
>
> [TF, p. 139]

sonnet perhaps directly linked to Rossetti's charity work at St. Mary Magdalene's,[13] the sinner warns others, her summer friends, to leave her:

> Go from me, summer friends, and tarry not:
> I am no summer friend, but wintry cold,
> A silly sheep benighted from the fold,
> A sluggard with a thorn-choked garden plot.

The reference to "silly sheep" immediately recalls Matthew 18:12, the biblical text that depicts Christ as the Good Shepherd seeking the one lost sheep. Thus we can infer that although summer friends may abandon the speaker, Christ will not. Her second warning, "Take counsel, sever from my lot your lot," in which she describes herself as "athirst and hungering on a barren spot," echoes the voice we hear in the Psalms, the voice of one longing for God: "My soul thirsteth for thee, my flesh longeth for thee in a dry and thirsty land, where no water is" (Ps. 63:1). Finally, in the imagery the speaker uses to describe her sin, "I have hedged me with a thorny hedge," there is a slight echo of Hosea 2:6: "Therefore, behold I will hedge up thy way with thorns, and make a wall, that she shall not find her paths." This thorny hedge is to keep the children of Israel who have turned to other gods, and thus "played the harlot," cut off from those false gods. Thus, as Rossetti interprets Hosea 2:6–7, a thorny hedge can become a blessing: "Hosea shows us that our heavenly Father most willingly turns our curse into a blessing, making of thorns not a scourge but our safeguard" (SF, pp. 98–99). Furthermore, in the same chapter of Hosea, God promises that someday he will make Israel his bride. Rossetti believed that God had already sent Christ, "an innocent loving lamb" through "the thorny hedge / Into the thorny thistly world" to make this "marriage" possible ("Bird or beast?"; I, 155–56). Therefore, although the woman in "From sunset to star rise" lives alone in her "thorn-choked garden," we should not see her as exiled

---

[13]In the *Poetical Works* (p. 485), William Michael Rossetti provides an editorial note to this poem stating, in part: "In the note-book containing the MS. of the sonnet I find a pencil note, 'House of Charity,' written against the title. The House of Charity was, I think, an Institution at Highgate for reclaiming 'fallen' women." There is also some evidence, however, to suggest that "House of Charity" refers not to the London Diocesan Penitentiary at Highgate but to The House of St. Barnabas in Soho, a refuge for both men and women in need of shelter.

beyond God's love, and if she is not beyond God's love, her fellow human beings have no reason to abandon her. Each human being has only to turn to Christ with "tears and love," as Mary Magdalene did, to become his bride (FD, p. 434).

Although Rossetti concluded from her reading of Genesis that woman must be more passive and submissive than man, she did not deny any woman her humanity or spirituality, no matter the number or the nature of her sins. Furthermore, although Genesis told her of Eve's weakness and shame, Revelation told her of woman's ultimate strength and glory. In the Apocalyptic figure of the "woman clothed with the sun" (Rev. 12:1), Rossetti found hope for all Eve's daughters:

> I trust there is no harm in my considering that her sun-clothing indicates how in that heaven where St. John in vision beheld her, she will be made equal with men and angels; arrayed in all human virtues, and decked with all communicable Divine graces: whilst the moon under her feet portends that her sometime infirmity of purpose and changeableness of mood have, by preventing, assisting, final grace, become immutable; she has done all and stands; from the lowest place she has gone up higher. [FD, p. 310]

In this exalted figure, Rossetti saw "weakness made strong and shame swallowed up in celestial glory" (FD, p. 309). Ultimately, by following Mary Magdalene's example of penitence and love, Eve might stand with the Virgin Mary before the throne of God, and if Eve, then any daughter of Eve as well.[14]

[14]It is noteworthy that Rossetti's reading of the biblical scene in which Mary Magdalene and the Virgin stand together before the Cross as a sign of hope that Eve will one day stand with Mary before the Throne (FD, p. 310) is also part of her commentary on Revelation 12:1. In her commentary there is a pattern of association that links Eve's weakness and shame to the image of the "woman clothed with the sun," in which we see "weakness made strong and shame swallowed up in celestial glory" (FD, p. 309). It is as if Rossetti cannot see Eve's fall without also seeing her possible redemption: the image of Eve as fallen woman contains within itself its opposite, the image of the woman clothed with the sun.

ANTONY H. HARRISON

Eighteen Early Letters
by Christina Rossetti

Among the treasures for students of Pre-Raphaelitism in the Troxell
Collection at Princeton University Library are typescripts of eighteen
unpublished letters by Christina Rossetti introduced by a four-page
preface in the hand of her brother William Michael. William's preface
explains his purpose in wishing to edit and publish these letters written to him between 1845 and 1854, in many respects the most event-
ful period of Christina Rossetti's life. The autograph date of this collection is July 1898, six months after the publication of Mackenzie
Bell's life of Christina Rossetti. Bell's biography, according to
William, presents a somewhat distorted image of his sister's epistolary
talents. William explains

> When Mr. Mackenzie Bell's book came out, early in 1898, scant justice
> was done by critics to her aptitude as a letter-writer. Several re-
> views . . . pronounced that she had no aptitude at all in that line, or
> next to none. Now to me it appears that some of her letters, published
> in that book, are the reverse of despicable. I speak here more especially
> of letters addressed to persons not of her own family: while, as regards
> those to members of the family, it is to be observed (but the reviewers
> were not bound to divine it) that only letters of very minor scope and

I am grateful to Princeton University Library (Troxell Collection, Box 2) and to
Yale University Library for permission to quote from unpublished letters by Christina
Rossetti.

192

significance were placed in Mr. Bell's hands. These came to him—all of them, I think—from myself; and were actually only such unimportant notes as I keep by me, not to be included in the general bulk of correspondence that I receive, but to be given away to any one who likes to ask for an autograph. I am far from saying that Christina was pre-eminent or exceptionally gifted as a letter-writer: but, writing letters as she did without any wish or pretense of putting into them profound reflections or criticisms, or vivid descriptions, she had (I conceive) a light and graceful touch, and telling turns of expression, along with much that revealed an earnest affectionate nature, replete with sweetness, and by no means destitute of playfulness. [Troxell Collection, MS., p. 3]

As a corrective, William wished to publish these eighteen letters, which Bell had not known of before 1898. They are indeed of enormous interest to students of Christina Rossetti because they reflect—perhaps more than any other single group of her letters—Rossetti's sense of her own artistic vocation, her engagement with all matters concerning the Pre-Raphaelite Brotherhood, her intelligence, wit, vitality, and resiliency.

But William never succeeded in finding a publisher for his slender volume. In his preface to the 1908 edition of his sister's *Family Letters*, however, he does perplexingly allude to this group of letters: "The correspondence in my collection, belonging to the earlier period of Christina's life, is rather scanty," he explains, "owing to the fact that eighteen of her letters, of dates ranging from 1845–1854, are now the property of her sympathetic biographer Mr. Mackenzie Bell, and are thus not at my disposal."

A lengthy correspondence between William Michael Rossetti and Bell (also in the Troxell Collection) reveals that William, unable to find a publisher for his proposed volume of early letters with explanatory notes, agreed to sell them in 1899 to Bell through his agent, Morris Colles, the founder and managing director of the Authors' Syndicate. In 1907, however, undertaking to edit his sister's *Family Letters*, William applied to Bell for permission to include this early correspondence, but Bell refused, at first amicably, later insistently. Bell intended to produce a revised, fifth edition of his biography of Christina Rossetti (which had gone through four editions in 1898), and surmised that its foremost attraction would be the inclusion of these important but previously unknown letters. Bell never did publish a revised edition,[1] of course, and the contents of these letters have remained largely unpublished until now.[2]

Had William Michael Rossetti's projected volume of his sister's early letters been printed, readers would have found in them an extended self-portrait of the thoroughly engaging Christina Rossetti who beams from the first twenty-five pages of the *Family Letters*. William Michael apparently selected for his proposed volume these particular eighteen letters from his sister's correspondence with him because they were of deeper and more enduring interest than the "scanty" ones that appear in the 1908 volume, but they reveal the same personality that emerges from the published letters, as well as the writer's preoccupation with a number of the same subjects. The variety of topics mentioned or dwelt on is similarly broad; the pace leisurely; the tone intimately familiar, sometimes confessional. These unpublished letters, however, do demonstrate more fully than Rossetti's published correspondence her self-concept, especially in their implicit revelations about her sense of vocation as a writer. They also contain useful notes and commentary on some of her reading during the period, along with often playful and intriguing remarks on members and projects of the Pre-Raphaelite Brotherhood. They include intriguing commentaries on nature and animal life, as well as allusions to Rossetti's changing relationship to her fiancé, James Collinson. They illustrate, both playfully and earnestly, the family's and her own financial worries.

But for some readers the collection's greatest appeal might be its revelation of Rossetti's manifestly eager desire to participate fully in life—in family affairs, in creative and artistic projects, and in the life of nature. As all students of Rossetti's work know, this desire very significantly diminished after her illnesses of the late 1860s and early 1870s, when excursions into the world outside her home became increasingly "formidable." Although flashes of her youthful playfulness, humor, and resiliency do decidedly appear in the later correspondence, as well as in her poems and prose works, the dependable animation of her early letters and poems is disappointingly missing. Examining selected passages from the early unpublished letters to her brother, we can find a

[1]See R. W. Crump, *Christina Rossetti: A Reference Guide* (Boston: G. K. Hall, 1976), p. 44.

[2]Brief passages from several of these letters are quoted by Lona Mosk Packer in *Christina Rossetti* (Berkeley: University of California Press, 1963), pp. 66, 76; and by Georgina Battiscombe in *Christina Rossetti: A Divided Life* (New York: Holt, Rinehart and Winston, 1981), pp. 52, 54, 74.

good deal that we want to know about Christina Rossetti between the ages of fourteen and twenty-three.

During the first five of the eight and one-half years represented by these letters, Rossetti was searching for a clear social and vocational status, largely through her creative efforts, through her relations with the Pre-Raphaelite Brotherhood, and through her prospective marriage. Finally, in 1851, with her father in ill health, Rossetti and her mother resignedly joined forces and made the decision to open a small day school in London. In 1853 Rossetti and her mother, caring for the invalid Gabriele Rossetti, moved the school to Frome, where they operated under the auspices of the Anglo-Catholic Reverend W. J. E. Bennett, who had been given the living there by the Rossettis' close friend, Lady Bath. Before these last three difficult years, however, Rossetti was quietly working out the future directions of her life, as well as a system of active social, moral, intellectual, and literary values that would sustain those directions. Her correspondence with William Michael took place for the most part when she was visiting friends, and it reveals her cautiously exuberant personality. Her most striking quality during the entire period in which these letters were written is a paradoxical combination of diffidence, self-confident strength, and playfulness. In her energetic, sometimes rambling, but always self-conscious letters, she is anxious to forge a self-concept and to project an image of someone at once engaging, endearing, competent, and modestly ambitious.

As early as September 17, 1845, for instance, while visiting the Reads, where her sister Maria was working as a governess, Rossetti writes facetiously—despite ill health—that "all sorts of accomplishments have showered down upon your talented sister. I have commenced initiation into the mysteries of backgammon: I have coursed gallantly. (N. B. I have ridden Jack once, on which memorable occasion he walked, except once when he trotted till I was wild with terror.)" As remarks in later letters further illustrate, through a veil of self-deprecation and self-effacement, Rossetti is quite seriously concerned with "accomplishments." In the early 1850s she studies sketching and painting under Ford Madox Brown, and for the previous five years she has been constantly at work upon her poems and stories. As early as 1846 she is also attempting woodcuts for what William describes as "a scrapbook which my brother and I were getting up." Dante Gabriel Rossetti, however, seems to have been unreceptive to her work. Rossetti writes to William on August 11: "Finding that Gabriel receives my woody gleanings with such scorn . . . I question whether your Scrap Book is worthy of any more of my benefactions; however, I need not decide just at present, as, in any case, I have nothing to send."

Rossetti's pride in her productions, as well as her assumptions of their moral rectitude, is unmistakable in remarks to William Michael Rossetti the following year (on August 10, 1847), just after her privately printed *Verses* had been sent "by way of compliment, to the Reverend Mr. Bray, a Devonshire clergyman who was the second husband of a cousin" of her mother. As William reports, "Mr. Bray had some pretensions of his own—very meagre ones—as a poet; and he had sent in acknowledgement some lines of verse—I suppose, in a philandering semi-amatory vein." Rossetti's response to these "unwelcome" poetic overtures is uncharacteristically vitriolic:

> Though I cannot tell you the extent of my contempt for Mr. Bray's equivocal compliments, inasmuch as it is illimitable; nor define it, it being indescribable; I can at least inform you that Mamma fully shares it. I will give you an extract from one of Maria's letters to me on the subject of these verses. For the sake of the writer's spirit, pray excuse the vanity of the transcriber. "As to your enclosure" (the poem) "I can only say I am provoked that any one who could write such stuff, equally below the dignity of a man and a clergyman, should ever have had anything half as nice as your poems to write about. I return the lines with disgusted thanks, and adequate astonishment."

As if to efface the ardor of her own prefatory remarks here, however, Rossetti concludes her letter to William on a facetiously mystical note: "I have a vision of you before my eyes; very quiet, inoffensive, and comfortless . . . [P]robably you will never reach this point of my letter, by reason of having fallen asleep."

Two years later Rossetti is writing verses prolifically. Her playful competitiveness in the poetic lists appears in her continuing *bouts-rimés* contests with her brothers.[3] On September 24, 1849, she sends a new sonnet and fourteen rhymes "for your especial torment." She determines to "select rhymes from one of my own sonnets . . . [i]n the certainty that you cannot possibly equal that work of art."[4]

---

[3]On the manuscript verses that resulted from such contests, see R. W. Crump, "Eighteen Moments' Monuments: Christina Rossetti's *Bout Rimés* Sonnets in the Troxell Collection," *Princeton Library Chronicle* 33 (Spring 1972): 210–29.

[4]The "new sonnet" appears in *PW*, p. 422. My later quotation from *Goblin Market* is from Crump I, 20.

Rossetti's own works of art had already seen print: her *Verses* appeared in 1847 from her grandfather Polidori's private press, and the *Athenaeum* had published two of her poems ("Death's chill between" and "Heart's chill between") in 1848. And her eager interest in the success of *The Germ* in December of this year and the following January is, of course, due in part to her own appearances in its pages under the pseudonymn (invented by Dante Gabriel) of Ellen Alleyn. Two of the eighteen letters repeatedly recur to matters concerning the short-lived P. R. B. magazine. On January 18 Rossetti writes William, "your next *Germ* promises well, but I fear a little heavy. Mr. Brown's article rather alarms me." Thirteen days later, after alluding to a sonnet and two poems by William Bell Scott which appeared in the second issue of *The Germ*, she observes sympathetically, "Your editorial troubles are indeed commencing; was there not also some difficulty as to the timely appearance of this month's No. ? Do not think *The Germ* fails to interest me: indeed the forthcoming number is continually in my thoughts." And in a long letter of January 31, she encourages William to publish his *Plain Story* ["Mrs. Holmes Grey"]: "For the credit of the Magazine let it appear soon." Such flattery serves as a prelude to asking whether William considers "it particularly judicious to bring out [in the next issue] the only two things of mine which" had appeared in the *Athenaeum*. She concludes with a delightful fantasy which is at once self-inflating and self-deprecatory:

> Do you know, I seriously urge on your consideration the increase of prose and decrease of poetry in the *Germ*, the present state of things strikes me as most alarming. Should all other articles fail, boldly publish my letters; they would doubtless produce an immense sensation. By hinting that I occupy a high situation in B——ch——m P——l——e, being in fact no other than the celebrated lady ———, and by substituting initials and asterisks for all names, and adding a few titles, my correspondence might have quite a success. . . .

In a similar vein is a letter written three and one-half years later. Despising the life of a teacher and straining to be optimistic about the family's financial prospects, Rossetti announces to William (on August 13, 1853) that she has "conceived a first-rate scheme for rebuilding the shattered fortunes of our house." By indulging in facetiously hyperbolic speculation about the future publication of her short story "Nick" (then in circulation but not finally published until 1870 in *Commonplace, and Other Short Stories*), she displaces fears that the drudgery of making a living will undermine her future as a poet.

ANTONY H. HARRISON

Hannay (l'ami de la maison) forwards Nick (in Addey's absence) to
Addey's man of business; accompanying the work by my portrait. Man
of business (a susceptible individual of great discernment) risks the loss
of his situation by immediately forwarding me a cheque for £20, and sets
his subs to work on an elegant edition of Nick. Addey returns; is first
furious; but, seeing the portrait, and with a first-rate business head
perceiving at a glance its capabilities, has it engraved, prefixed to Nick,
and advertised all over the civilized world. The book spreads like wild-
fire. Addey at the end of 2 months, struck by a late remorse, and having
an eye to future contingencies, sends me a second cheque for £200; on
which we subsist for a while. At the publication of the 20th edition Mrs
Addey (a mild person of few words) expires; charging her husband to do
me justice. He promises with one suppressed sob. Next day a third
cheque for £2000 reaches me. This I divide; assigning half to Maria for
her dowry, and handing the rest to Mamma. I then collapse. Exeunt
Omnes.

Throughout these years the Rossetti family fortunes, as well as
Rossetti's own artistic and marital prospects, are deeply tied to those of
the P. R. B. She eventually commemorates the dissolution of such ties
in her well-known "remarkable doggrel [sic] on the P. R. B.," as she
calls it. She sends the earliest version of this poem to William in a
letter of September 19, 1853, congratulating him "heartily" on his
"riz," a promotion he had received at Somerset House:

> The two Rossettis (brothers they)
> And Holman Hunt and John Millais,
> With Stephens chivalrous and bland
> And Woolner in a distant land,
> In these six men I awestruck see
> Embodied the great P. R. B.
> D. G. Rossetti offered two
> Good pictures to the public view:
> Unnumbered ones great John Millais,
> And Holman more than I can say.
> X   X   X   X   X
> William Rossetti calm and solemn
> Cuts up his brethren by the column.

Not surprisingly Rossetti does not mention James Collinson, not only
because the memories of her engagement to him would perhaps still

198

have been painful two years after the affair's conclusion but also because she has remarkably little to say about Collinson, even at the height of their relationship.

The first mention of matters connected with her engagement appears in a letter she writes William on April 28, 1849, while visiting her mother's old friends, the Marshes, in Clapham. Thomas Woolner has apparently asked to see some of her poems, a request she agrees to, but, realizing that some of these works about disappointed love might prove embarrassing under the present circumstances, she adds this proviso: "Only I must beg that you will not fix upon any [poems] which the most imaginative person could construe into love personals [;] you will feel how more than ever intolerable it would *now* be to have my verses regarded as outpourings of a wounded spirit; and that something like this has been the case I have too good reason to know."[5] Rossetti's final statement is both intriguing and prescient, suggesting that she had already been the victim of unjustified biographical readings of her poetry and indicating her awareness that she would be similarly vulnerable to such readings in the future. In the same letter she tells William, "Yesterday I heard from Collinson. He mentions having received another of your nice letters; and regrets that he cannot give as much pleasure as he receives from the correspondence."

In subsequent letters her allusions to Collinson are brief. She indirectly makes clear her interest in Collinson's painting by her studies in early 1850 of the legends of Saint Elizabeth of Hungary, a result of Collinson's decision to do a painting on the subject. In January she tries to account for her detailed interest in Elizabeth, explaining to William, "Lady Bath was discussing *The Saint's Tragedy* [by Charles Kingsley] the other night, and she has lent me a very interesting Life of St. Elizabeth by Montalembert. Does not the Poem and its notes give you the idea that the Saint was a *little* woman?" She then quotes two long passages in French from Montalembert, the first mistakenly, but the second to her point, finally confiding to William, "I still have to explain my motive for copying all this: if [Collinson's] painting from St. Elizabeth's life is ever executed, all details may be useful." That Rossetti's own renunciatory poem on the subject was not written for two and one-half years, well after her break with Collinson, is significant: her own amatory and poetic values become increasingly reified after this crisis.

[5]Battiscombe quotes this passage in *Christina Rossetti*, p. 54.

In a letter written four days before her remarks about Saint Elizabeth (January 14, 1850), Rossetti begins to reveal renewed anxieties about the status of her relationship with Collinson. She thanks William for his "kindness in the selection of news" he forwards to her at Longleat, while she is staying with her Aunt Charlotte Polidori at Lady Bath's estate. But she adds the instruction, "In your letter pray never forget the one thing that *does* interest me." Here, as in the postscript of her next letter to William, she is doubtless concerned about James Collinson's renewed religious waverings.[6]

Her anxieties are unmistakable in this letter of January 18, as she continues to probe the issue and asks for news from James's brother, Charles, whom she had grown quite fond of during a visit to the Collinsons in the spring of 1849. She pleads, "If you are so charitable as to write again will you tell me whether C[harles] C[ollinson] has written?" Finally, in a tone of consternation, she appends this postscript to a letter of the 25th: "C. C.'s silence astonishes me. Perhaps he wishes the acquaintance to cease." Indeed, all acquaintance with the Collinsons did end shortly afterward, when Collinson—as a result of the broken engagement—resigned from the P. R. B. and joined the Jesuit community at Stonyhurst as a lay brother.

In these letters Rossetti is far more chatty about other members of the P. R. B. and about P. R. B. affairs in general than about her fiancé. She once comments on the quality of William Bell Scott's poetry and several times inquires after the health of both Scott and his wife. She is also deeply interested in the fortunes of William Holman Hunt and Thomas Woolner. In a letter of July 30, 1852, as the P. R. B. was disbanding, she is delighted at Hunt's success with *The Hireling Shepherd,* while frankly revealing her attachment to Woolner, who had recently left England to seek his fortune in Australia:

> I am heartily glad of Hunt's success; and, if you like to tell him so (with the information that I will paint a picture on considerably lower terms, if he would kindly name this to his patrons), you are at liberty to do so. Another feeling of yours in which I cordially sympathize is regret at Woolner's departure for the diggings; poor fellow, I hope he will come back safe and well, and not estranged from his old friends, by any amount of gold. Pray let me see his remarkable first drawing: it must be curious and interesting to the eye of affection, even if not artistically meritorious.

[6]See Battiscombe, *Christina Rossetti,* pp. 54–57.

On a similar note in a letter of December 3, 1853, Rossetti inquires of William whether or not Hunt's "devout picture," *The Light of the World,* will still be on exhibition in London when she and her mother are in town. With Hunt now about to leave for Palestine to paint *The Finding of the Saviour in the Temple* and *The Scapegoat,* Rossetti thoughtfully adds, "Mamma and I share in our degree your sorrow for the loss of Mr. Hunt. If you see him and do not forget, pray remember us to him with all good wishes for his prosperous journey and (*entre nous* much more) for his safe and not so very distant return." She concludes with a curious statement reverting to *The Light of the World:* "I suppose the £300 for his picture are particularly appropos." Presumably Hunt needed the cash for his travels, but this statement additionally reflects what would seem to many readers an uncharacteristic concern with money in these letters.

Part of Rossetti's interest in her fiancé's brother, Charles Collinson, appears to result, for example, from his being "reckoned a good man of business" by contrast with James, whose financial prospects in late 1849 seemed especially dreary. Further, on July 30, 1852, a year before her fancifully mercenary remarks about her short story "Nick," she suggests to William, again sardonically, that, to revive the fortunes of *The Germ,* he forward it to their entrepreneurial acquaintance, Knight: "Might it not prove a profitable *spec?* . . .—he might dilute it into quite a library of *Half-Hours* with the best authors." In a more serious vein, writing from Frome on December 3, 1853, just before her remarks on Hunt's upcoming departure for the Holy Land, she congratulates William on his association as critic with the newly established journal *The Artist,* edited by Thomas Delf:

I am glad the *Artist* has hatched at last, and hope it in its turn will lay golden eggs; you remember it was a goose did so before and what goose has done goose may do. I wish I could get into the *Delphic* connexion, and receive my two thirds. Do you think there would be any possibility of such a thing? I have plenty of time down here, and can work hard on occasion; if any opening occurs, please recollect me.

At this period Rossetti is, of course, deeply oppressed by her less than fulfilling work as a teacher. Nearly three months later, about to abandon the project of her school, she begins a letter to William with a paragraph that wittily demonstrates her continuing facetious interest in the residual fortunes of the P. R. B. and *The Germ.*

Is the "A. C. Tupper," who I see in last week's Athenaeum has been elected an Associate Archaeologian, our old friend Alic? This apparition is the staple commodity of my letter; pray deign it an answer. Considerable was my surprise thereat—perhaps however reflexion shows that he looked archaeological or at least by no means anti-arch etc. Well, admitting A. C. T. to be the genuine article, could he not foist the defunct *Germ* on his astonished co-archaeologians as a unique relic of British virtu? He would thus *rinfrank* his brother and illustrate ourselves. To render the work more valuable we might each affix an arbitrary mark of no assigned period, thus giving food to many a discussion in which Alic would be rewarded by shining supreme as decipherer and interpreter. Should you like to suggest this in the influential quarter and thereby gain the thanks of many big-wigs, the scheme is at your service.

Significantly, all but three of the letters in William Michael Rossetti's projected volume of Christina's correspondence are, like this one, written during periods of crisis. In these eight years she is perplexed, frustrated, angered, or desolated by crises related to her sense of artistic vocation, her marital prospects, the vicissitudes of the P. R. B., her own or her father's deteriorating health, and her family's financial situation. Yet, the letters themselves demonstrate the ways in which, as a passive observer of events and as someone largely at the mercy of decisions made by others, Rossetti is able to sustain her vitality, her wit and good humor, her ambition, and her sensitivity. Almost never does she allude to her religious faith as a prop and stay, as she very often does in her later letters (although this conspicuous omission may be deliberate, a tacit acknowledgement of William's agnosticism). She does, however, find diversion in her reading and in observations of nature.

In the very first letter of the series she remarks upon her restricted ventures into Ariosto: "I am sorry to say that, not having brought with me [to the Read's] a list of the prohibited passages, I have hardly been able to read any of Ariosto. What little I have seen, however, seems very fine, and makes me greatly regret my omission." She has, nonetheless, apparently compensated for this lack with the other great Italians:

Of Tasso I have perused several portions, and do not believe that Ariosto or any one else can surpass him. Happy the poet who has only equalled his beauties. What can be more exquisite or sublime than

Clarinda's combat with Tancred, and her death; than the parting of Rinaldo and Armida; than the final battle; than Armida's attempt to kill herself, and subsequent meeting with Rinaldo; than the combat and death of Argante? I have also read a little of Dante's *Inferno*, a very small portion of Petrarca, and sundry short productions of Tasso. His *Lodi di Amore* are most beautiful.

Given her Italian lineage, these writers are, of course, obligatory for Rossetti, as she indicates in one of her mature essays on Dante,[7] but they are also a significant influence on the stylistic and prosodic texture of her verse, as well as on the mythologies of erotic and spiritual love embedded in her most important poems.

In 1847 Rossetti read Bulwer's *Pelham* and was "somewhat disappointed" in it. "It is certainly very clever, but appears to me wanting in interest," she explains. In September 1849, she mentions reading the last number of *Pendennis* with limited satisfaction; and following her brothers' lead four months later, she studies Poe's newly published *Annabel Lee,* which she insists, "I do not like." Her own interpretation of the poem does not survive, but after a corroborative response from William, she confesses, "I do not cease to congratulate myself on your taking my view of Poe's poem. If no one agreed in my interpretation, its extreme strangeness would give it the appearance of having emanated from a maniac; as it is, I will abide by my version of the Story of *Annabel Lee.*" That same January of 1850 Rossetti was also reading Kingsley's *The Saint's Tragedy* and Montalembert's life of Saint Elizabeth, while Lady Bath at Longleat was serving as her "initiator into [the] unexplored mysteries" of Goldsmith's *Deserted Village* and *Traveller.* Six months later, Rossetti reports that she does "not much like" the *Legend of Montrose.* This report, coming on the heels of her break with Collinson and her own physical and psychological collapse, is the last we hear of Rossetti's reading in these letters. After her recovery, by the summer of 1852, she has become preoccupied with her work as a governess and then with teaching.

The beauties and curiosities of nature divert Rossetti less consistently than does her reading. She writes of nature only in the letters of the early 1850s, when she is under enormous stress, and she does not find its attractions renovating. During her stay with Lady Bath in January of 1850 she twice turns her attention from her reading and

[7]Christina Rossetti, "Dante: The Poet Illustrated Out of the Poem," *Century Magazine* 28, n.s. 5 (February 1884): 566–67.

writing, her engagement, and the affairs of the P. R. B., to brief but telling commentaries on the countryside around Longleat. Curiously, she discovers no poetic inspiration in it:

> The other day I met a splendid frog. He was of [sic] a sort of *sere yellow* spotted with black, and very large. Were you in this lovely country, you could hardly fail to gush poetry; with me the case is altogether different. The trees, the deer, the scenery, and indeed everything here, seems to influence me but little, with two exceptions, the cold, and the frog. The cold can never fail to interest a well brought-up Englishwoman; and the frog possesses every claim on my sympathy. He appeared to be leading a calm and secluded life.

Eleven days later she similarly laments the inadequacy of her intercourse with "the out-of-door beauties of this place," but this time blames a cough and expects soon to make up for past neglect. "Somewhere in the grounds here," she confesses to William, "there are some splendid ivy-overgrown trees which would delight you; but my acquaintance with [them] is very limited; I think I have not stirred out since Sunday. As however my cough is very much less, perhaps I may before long be allowed to run wild."

Typically, animal life possesses more potential to amuse, enrich, and inspire Rossetti than do "out-of-door beauties," as her earlier remarks on the frog—along with many of her poems—make clear. Once again at Longleat in July 1851, she insists that "even" William "might be somewhat entertained" by the household's monkeys: "One of their best feats is Peter's standing up on the top of the stick to which he is fastened. Jack yesterday favored us by arranging his whiskers as anyone else might his shirt collar. They are not beautiful certainly, but have intelligent expressions." One is tempted to see these monkeys as prototypes of Rossetti's goblin men, "Cat-like and rat-like, / Ratel- and wombat-like," who are "Full of airs and graces" (*Goblin Market*, ll. 340–41, 337).

Nearly two years later, on April 22, 1853, without such lively companions to lighten the weight of her teaching duties at Frome, Rossetti occasionally turns to nature for its beauty, as well as for its potential as material for her now frequent attempts at sketching and painting. She forwards to William two portraits of her mother. Dissatisfied with these, she writes in an at first humorous, but then earnest and solemn tone, "Perhaps the noble enclosures will not buoy you up with hopes of my future greatness. Well, at worst I shall not be the first person who has failed." Yet her following remarks reveal a typical determination to persevere: "We have discovered some beautiful country hereabouts; abundance of green slopes and gentle declivities; no boldness or grandeur, but plenty of peaceful beauty. The wild flowers are charming; perhaps, if incapable of aught higher, I may try my hand at primroses."

Though Rossetti here shows no great expectations of her talents or the art that they generate, the temperament revealed in this letter is one of buoyancy and resiliency in the face of adverse circumstances, the single dominant feature of this intriguing group of letters from sister to brother during a crucial period in all the Rossettis' lives. From the perspective of early 1854, the date of the last letter in this series, the preceding half-decade doubtless seemed heavily weighted with failure and with lost potential. The dissolution of the school at Frome was only the last in a sequence of disappointments which began with Rossetti's broken engagement to Collinson and included the demise of *The Germ* and then of the P. R. B., the deterioration of her father's health, the collapse of the family's finances, and the periodic collapse of her own health. Despite these misfortunes, however, Rossetti inevitably regains her strength and good humor, especially in her aspirations to become a recognized poet.

Five months after sending the final letter of this series to William Michael Rossetti, Christina wrote to William Edmonston Aytoun, the satirist of Spasmodicism and contributing editor of *Blackwood's*. Describing herself as an "unknown and unpublished" writer, a "nameless rhymester," she solicits the publication of six new poems, explaining,

I hope I shall not be misunderstood as guilty of egotism or foolish vanity, when I say that my love for what is good in the works of others teaches one that there is something above the despicable in mine; that poetry is with me, not a mechanism, but an impulse and a reality; and that I know my aims in writing to be pure, and directed to that which is true and right. I do not blush to confess that . . . it would afford me some gratification to place my productions before others, and ascertain how far what I do is expressive of mere individualism, and how far it is capable of approving itself to the general sense. It would be a personal favour to me if you would look into the enclosed with an eye not inevitably to the waste paper basket, and a further obligation if, whatever be the result, you would vouchsafe me a few words as to the fate of the verse. I am quite conscious that volunt[ary]eer contributors have no right to expect this of an editor; I ask it simply as a courtesy. It is mortifying to have done something sincerely, offer it in a good faith; and be treated as a 'non avenue.'[8]

Blackwood's took none of Rossetti's poems, and indeed for the next seven years she was able to publish only one poem and one short story. Yet this self-confident letter to Aytoun formalized a commitment implied in a passage near the conclusion of the last of her eighteen unpublished letters to William. This letter was written on February 23, 1854, just after William's promotion at Somerset House and the Rossettis' decision to abandon the school at Frome and reestablish "co-tenancy" with William in the house at 45 Upper Albany Street, where Christina Rossetti lived for the next thirteen years. Relieved, but also sensitive to this new failure in her life, as she and her mother prepare to return to London, Rossetti concludes her last letter to William on a poignant and prescient note of irony: "Today Mamma has realized £5/0 sterling by the sale of some books; they were works of such a character that we had agreed, if their fortunate purchaser would not give anything for them, he might have them for carrying them away. An honourable prospect for authors. Perhaps if ever I realize a publisher, my arguments may yet be treated as of some weight." Whether or not William perceived the fact in preparing his small edition of his sister's letters, the final thrust of this letter is symmetrical with the opening of the first one in his series: both are concerned with worldly accomplishments, the last especially with her sense of vocation as a professional writer. But Rossetti's tone has significantly altered. In 1845, with potentially the richest years of her life still before her, she could indulge in playful self-deprecation. In 1854, with nearly nine years of various disappointments behind her, she can generate only limited irony to qualify aspirations to genuine achievement that are more earnest than skeptical.

[8]Mary F. Sandars quotes this letter in a slightly different form in The Life of Christina Rossetti (London: Hutchinson, [1930]), pp. 85–86. The autograph manuscript of the letter is in the Yale University Library.

Appendix

The following list provides the dates for the eighteen letters in William Michael Rossetti's prospective volume of Christina Rossetti's early letters.

1. 17 September, 1845
2. 11 August, 1846
3. 10 August, 1847
4. 28 April, 1849
5. 24 September, 1849
6. 14 January, 1850
7. 18 January, 1850
8. 25 January, 1850
9. 31 January, 1850
10. 21 July, 1851
11. 30 July, 1852
12. 22 April, 1853
13. 4 July, 1853
14. 13 August, 1853
15. 19 September, 1853
16. 3 October, 1853
17. 3 December, 1853
18. 23 February, 1854

Roderick McGillis

Simple Surfaces:
Christina Rossetti's Work for Children

In almost everything Christina Rossetti wrote for young readers we
hear an authorial voice strong in ambiguity, whispering secrets beneath what Jerome J. McGann calls "those deceptively simple poetic
surfaces."[1] As we allow our minds to play upon the surfaces, what
appears straightforward becomes richly complex, so much so that
meaning often becomes of doubtful certainty and of less importance
than the simple surfaces themselves. We look less for meaning in this
work than for the subtleties of form and language. In other words,
Rossetti's work for children treats its readers to an experience of the
high morality of art, thus offering them the opportunity for freeplay,
for participation in imaginative understanding. The function of fantasy in works such as Goblin Market (1862), Sing-Song (1872), and
Speaking Likenesses (1874) is to deconstruct allegoric and didactic
meaning; the characteristic psychological tension in Victorian fantasy, the pull of both duty and desire, is evident in Rossetti's work, but
its implications go beyond simple dichotomy. It posits a reader capable
of comprehending and accepting this uncertain world as a schoolhouse
where we prepare for a certain world yet to come.

Rossetti's works for children include Maude: Prose and Verse, written in 1850, but not published until 1897, three years after her death.

[1] Jerome J. McGann, "Christina Rossetti's Poems: A New Edition and a Revaluation," VS 23 (1980): 240. In a more recent article on Christina Rossetti, McGann
writes: "Her poetry does not get worked up at the surface" ("The Religious Poetry of
Christina Rossetti," Critical Inquiry 10 [1983]: 130). These articles will hereafter be
cited in the text as VS and Critical Inquiry with the relevant page numbers.

208

Maude's story lacks the vibrancy of Rossetti's other works for children, and it has not reached the audience Rossetti had in mind. *Goblin Market*, *Sing-Song*, and *Speaking Likenesses* are much more successful works for children. *Goblin Market* and *Sing-Song* continue to appear in children's lists. *Speaking Likenesses* has not received the same approval as the two earlier works, but it deserves attention because of its intricate form. In the following discussion I examine the three works in the chronological order in which they appeared to show that Rossetti's interest in language and form does not alter radically from work to work.

Criticism has had less to say about *Sing-Song* and *Speaking Likenesses* than about *Goblin Market* (I, 11–26), for reasons that are not difficult to imagine. Rossetti did not, in fact, write *Goblin Market* for children, and therefore the poem invites the attention of a mature reader; *Goblin Market* manifestly contains the theme of sexual frustration, a sure hook for academic readers; and finally the poem satisfies the critic's desire to allegorize. As McGann has noted, despite Rossetti's claim that *Goblin Market* is not an allegory, readers refuse to take her at her word (*VS*, p. 240). Even a sympathetic reader, Rossetti's brother William Michael, reports in one sentence his sister's repeated assertion that, as he puts it, the poem "is not a moral apologue consistently carried out in detail," and in the next asserts: "I find at times that people do not see the central point of the story, such as the authoress intended it: and she has expressed it too, but perhaps not with due emphasis" (*PW*, p. 459). Critics have proposed various allegoric interpretations for *Goblin Market*: Christian, sexual, psychological, social, artistic, subversive.[2] Most critics are not as candid as A. A.

[2]According to Georgina Battiscombe, "the religious interpretation of *Goblin Market* is much nearer to her own way of thought than the sexual one" (Georgina Battiscombe, *Christina Rossetti: A Divided Life* [New York: Holt, Rinehart and Winston, 1981], p. 107). For Christian readings of the poem, see Alan Barr, "Sensuality Survived: Christina Rossetti's *Goblin Market*," *English Miscellany* 28–29 (1979–1980): 279–80; and McGann, "Christina Rossetti's Poems," *VS*, p. 247. Sexual readings include those of Maureen Duffy, *The Erotic World of Faery* (New York: Avon, 1980), pp. 319–22; and Stephen Prickett, *Victorian Fantasy* (Bloomington: Indiana University Press, 1979), pp. 103–6. For a psychological reading, see Ellen Golub, "Untying Goblin Apron Strings: A Psychoanalytic Reading of *Goblin Market*," *Literature and Psychology* 25 (1975): 158–65. See also Winston Weathers, "Christina Rossetti: The Sisterhood of Self," *VP* 3 (1965): 81–89. McGann's article "Christina Rossetti's Poems" contains a brilliant commentary on *Goblin Market* as social criticism (pp. 247–54). A. A. DeVitis, in "*Goblin Market*: Fairy Tale and Reality," *Journal of Popular Culture* 1 (1967): 418–26, reads the poem as an allegory of "the conflict in

DeVitis, who sees "the essential meaning of the poem" revealed by "an interpretation of the symbolism and an appreciation of the imagery" (pp. 420, 422). If other readers are not as forthright as DeVitis, they nonetheless imply they have grasped the poem's "essential meaning."

Even when a reading formally deconstructs the poem's stated meaning, we are not left in doubt as to its real meaning. Jeanie Watson, in the most recent essay on *Goblin Market*, analyzes Rossetti's use of the "interplay between moral tale and fairy tale that allows [the poem] to be utterly subversive and yet ultimately moral" (p. 61). In this poem "the immoral moral triumphs," and the reader learns that "maidens have the right to buy the fruit of Goblin Market" (pp. 78, 75). In short, Watson allegorizes the poem as a Romantic text that calls for "perception and participation in whole vision" (p. 73). *Goblin Market* becomes, in effect, a sequel to *The Book of Thel*, only in Rossetti's poem the female does not retreat from experience. In Watson's reading, Lizzie and Laura repudiate the "fruits of knowledge," but the reader remains unconvinced that they are right in doing so: "Laura and Lizzie are saved to their damnation, and we and Christina Rossetti know it, even if they do not" (p. 73). Reading this interpretation, I find it difficult to understand the "discomfort" the ending of the poem communicates, since Rossetti (apparently) and Watson had no difficulty accepting the subversion of the poem's ostensible moral.

But Laura and Lizzie are manifestly not "saved to their damnation." Not only does Laura come through her experience young and refreshed, but years later she tells her children the story of her relations with goblin men. Questions come to mind, among them: who are the men Laura and Lizzie marry? and why does Laura, not Lizzie, become a story-teller? But answers are as stubbornly irretrievable (or perhaps irrelevant) as the questions are insistent. The poem's subversive power derives from its refusal to offer pat morals of any sort; it refuses allegory. When Watson says the two sisters are saved only to be damned, she bases her argument on the idea that Laura and Lizzie accept convention and mouth familiar Victorian pieties regarding sisterly love and the avoidance of experience. In this view Laura, after tasting

---

the creative personality" (p. 425). Jeanie Watson sees *Goblin Market* as "an extremely subversive poem" ("'Men Sell Not Such in Any Town': Christina Rossetti's Goblin Fruit of Fairy Tale," *Children's Literature* 12 [1984]: 61–77). References to these works will hereafter be given in the text.

the fruits of experience and later falling into a trance, awakes renewed; apparently she has retreated to innocence.

The result of Laura's long night of senselessness certainly gives the impression of a return to innocence:

> Laura awoke as from a dream,
> Laughed in the innocent old way,
> Hugged Lizzie but not twice or thrice;
> Her gleaming locks showed not one thread of grey,
> Her breath was sweet as May
> And light danced in her eyes.
>
> [ll. 537–42]

Laura's awakening is reminiscent of the scene in the *Odyssey* in which Odysseus' sailors return to human form after Odysseus has overpowered Circe. Transformed, the sailors "not only became men again but looked younger and much handsomer and taller than before."[3] Their experience has proved efficacious; they seem rejuvenated. We understand the sailors' fall into bestiality as transitional. If their renewal is a renewal of innocence, however, it is closer to what in Blake's terms is organized innocence than to unorganized innocence. Laura's trial is similarly renovating. She wakes "as from a dream." Her experience is perhaps as inevitable as dreaming, for it is a mental or psychological event. When she laughs in the "innocent old way," we can hear (helped by the emphasis on "old way") an ambiguity. She laughs in the *manner* of her former innocence; she laughs in an innocent, yet aged, wise, old way. Laura, however, is not so much renewed as she is transfigured: her hair "gleams" and light dances in her eyes.

Transfiguration, of course, is not simply transformation; Rossetti's values are not Homer's. Laura's awakening has Christian import. She rises in the early morning as

> early reapers plodded to the place
> Of golden sheaves,
> And dew-wet grass
> Bowed in the morning winds so brisk to pass,
> And new buds with new day
> Opened of cup-like lilies on the stream
>
> [ll. 531–36]

[3]Homer, *The Odyssey*, trans. E. V. Rieu (Harmondsworth: Penguin, 1972), p. 166.

The language here resonates with biblical echoes. In Psalm 126, for example, the Lord turns "the captivity of Zion" and fills the Israelites' "mouth . . . with laughter, and [their] tongue with singing"; they "were like them that dream." Similarly, on a fresh harvest morning, Laura wakes from her dream to laugh. The psalm tells us that he who "goeth forth and weepeth, bearing precious seed, shall doubtless come again with rejoicing, bringing his sheaves with him." And Isaiah 18:4 tells us that the Lord's dwelling place is "like a cloud of dew in the heat of harvest." Finally, the lilies, as Dante Gabriel Rossetti's *The Girlhood of Mary Virgin* (1849) and *Ecce Ancilla Domini!* (1850) remind us, represent purity and virginity. The "golden sheaves," "new buds," "new day," and "cup-like lilies" in *Goblin Market* suggest not only harvest but also revelation, the uncovering of a better world. Rossetti's description, then, suggests a spiritual awakening, an awakening of almost apocalyptic import. The revelation that has come to Laura has come after her soul's sleep. The soul's sleep, as McGann points out, is a "peculiar millenarian and Anabaptist doctrine," and "the single most important enabling principle in Rossetti's poetry" (*Critical Inquiry*, pp. 134, 135). The soul's sleep is a "waiting time" between death and judgment, a time during which the soul can dream of or catch glimpses of paradise. In *Goblin Market* Laura experiences the soul's sleep after receiving the "fiery antidote" (l. 559) from Lizzie. We do not know what passed in her mind during that long night, but we do know Laura was "past" both pleasure and anguish. "Is it death or is it life?" asks the mysterious narrator. Whichever state it is, the result is "life out of death" (ll. 522–25). The life Laura returns to on the harvest morning brings her marriage and children; more important, she becomes a storyteller.

We might recall that after eating the goblin fruit Laura becomes silent: "She said not one word in her heart's sore ache" (l. 261). She lies awake "silent till Lizzie slept," and then she rises to weep and gnash her teeth "for baulked desire" (ll. 265, 267). For days, she watches "in sullen silence of exceeding pain" (l. 271). The goblin men have effectively silenced Laura; in accepting their fruit she has lost her voice. In this world men are the rhymers, the speakers, the storytellers, the merchants. Before Lizzie starts out to meet the goblin men on their own terms, with a "silver penny in her purse," she remembers Jeanie

> Who should have been a bride;
> But who for joys brides hope to have
> Fell sick and died

In her gay prime,
In earliest Winter time,
With the first glazing rime,
With the first snow-fall of crisp Winter time.
[ll. 313–19]

It is not too much to imagine that the goblins' "sugar-baited words" (l. 234), their glazing rhymes, silenced Jeanie because she, like Laura, paid the goblin price: "a golden curl" (l. 125). Lizzie refuses this price and tosses her penny to the goblins. Taking part in the market place as an equal, Lizzie confounds the goblins:

They began to scratch their pates,
No longer wagging, purring,
But visibly demurring,
Grunting and snarling.
[ll. 390–93]

They then buffet and batter her until her resistance wearies them. Flinging back her penny and kicking their fruits, the goblins disappear into the ground, into the brook, or into the air. They are incorporated into three of the four elements.

The fourth element—fire—remains for Laura. She receives the "fiery antidote" (l. 559) from Lizzie, and this brings her release from the goblin bondage and its accompanying release of language. Bondage to goblin men is replaced by maternal bonding. Laura and Lizzie are bound up in their children, their "mother-hearts beset with fears" (l. 546). The word "beset" suggests not only that fears assail them from all sides but also that the fears brace those hearts with maternal care. For Laura this care includes telling the story of her experience with the goblin men; she repeats her history in words and transforms this history into fiction, into fairy tale. She gathers "the [not "her"] little ones" about her and tells them "of her early prime" (ll. 548–49). She would tell of

Those pleasant days long gone
Of not-returning time:
Would talk about the haunted glen,
The wicked, quaint fruit-merchant men,
Their fruit like honey to the throat
But poison in the blood . . .
[ll. 550–55]

213

It is notable that Laura recalls her past experiences as "pleasant," a strange adjective in light of her listlessness and frustration after she ate the goblin fruit. But in the form of narrative those experiences *are* pleasant. And what Laura is now capable of seeing is the worth of her early fall from innocence. She now perceives the nature of the goblins' wickedness: their perversion of language.

Laura not only calls the goblins "wicked," she also calls them "quaint," which indicates the goblins are strange in appearance, as indeed they are. But "quaint" also refers to their cleverness with language; they are quaint orators, cunningly reversing what we know: "One parrot-voiced and jolly / Cried 'Pretty Goblin' still for 'Pretty Polly'" (ll. 112–13). One of them speaks in "tones as smooth as honey" (l. 108), a metaphor that appears again in Laura's narrative when she describes the goblin fruits as "honey to the throat / But poison in the blood" (ll. 554–55). This line echoes Revelation 10:8–10, in which an angel commands John to take the "little book" that the angel holds and to "eat it up," and, John says, "it was in my mouth sweet as honey: as soon as I had eaten it, my belly was bitter." In other words, Laura's experience is revelatory; she has become a seer and sayer free of the earthbound goblins who would silence her and confine her to a sterile natural cycle.[4] Yet without the goblins, without the nameless bitterness, she would not be free to speak.

We might conjecture that Laura, speaking as she does to an audience of children, chooses the fairy tale as her form of utterance. As many commentators have pointed out, *Goblin Market* is a fairy tale. Alan Barr compares the poem to "Snow White," in which the beautiful girl who eats a poisoned apple can be revived from her deadly sleep only by a prince (p. 281). Dorothy Mermin speaks of Rossetti's story as "a transformation of a traditional fairy tale," but, unlike Snow White (whom Mermin does not mention), Laura is not "cured" by a prince; her cure comes when she "ceases to want him." According to Mermin, Lizzie, who not only brings the antidote to Laura but who also "*is* the antidote," is the "folktale heroine," since she outwits the goblins, "getting their treasure without paying their price."[5]

---

[4]Although something of an overstatement, Robert Pattison's remark that Rossetti has a "morbid concept of nature" is acute. The goblins, one could argue, represent the Blakean sense of nature as a veil or as that which binds. See Pattison's *The Child Figure in English Literature* (Athens, Ga.: University of Georgia Press, 1978), p. 144. Alan Barr speaks of the "hurtfulness of Nature" in Rossetti's poems. See Barr, "Sensuality Survived," p. 269.

[5]Dorothy Mermin, "Heroic Sisterhood in *Goblin Market*," *VP* 21 (1983): 110, 111, 112.

That Rosetti has the fairy tale tradition in mind is hardly questionable, and that she is aware of the fairy tales' understanding of female identity and the demands made upon it by a patriarchal society (especially as presented by the Brothers Grimm) seems just as clear. In many of the tales females are robbed of their identity and pushed to the edge of hysteria by male attitudes and male tyranny (see, for example, "The Rabbit's Bride" or "Fred and Kate"). In *Goblin Market* Laura speaks of stealing from the goblins: "Good Folk, I have no coin, / To take were to purloin" (ll. 116–17). Ironically, it is the goblins who "purloin"; they steal Laura's identity—her voice, her lock of golden hair, her maidenhood. The goblins do not show "all good fidelity";[6] truly they do not sell such fruit in any town, since once paid with that which is most precious, they depart. In actuality, because of Lizzie's efforts, the goblins do not accomplish the theft of Laura's identity. Lizzie and Laura are perhaps "two sides of a single individual" (Barr, p. 273), and, after Lizzie's successful confrontation with the goblins, Laura's identity is restored.

If there is one fairy tale from which *Goblin Market* derives, it surely must be "The Robber Bridegroom." In this story a father offers his younger daughter in marriage to a stranger, despite the fact that his daughter does not love him "as a bride ought to love her bridegroom."[7] The girl visits her prospective husband only to learn that he is the leader of a band of robbers. An old woman in the robber's house warns her that her "wedding can only be with Death." Hiding behind a large cask, the girl witnesses a gruesome scene: the robber with his henchmen returns with another young girl "that had been ensnared like the bride." The robbers kill the young girl. One tries to remove a ring from one of the dead girl's fingers (in some translations he chops off the finger), and the ring flips behind the cask. The robbers soon fall asleep; the girl escapes. When the bridegroom comes for his bride, a feast is set and the guests tell stories. When the bride's turn comes she tells of her "dream" in which she describes the events she had witnessed in the robber's house. She tells her tale carefully, building up to the moment when she reveals the ring. The bridegroom and his gang of thieves are executed. In this story the murdered young girl,

---

[6] See Titus 2:10, "Not purloining, but showing all good Fidelity: that they may adorn the doctrine of God our Saviour in all things." This passage may be the source for Rossetti's use of the word "purloin."

[7] *Grimm's Fairy Tales* (Harmondsworth: Puffin, 1972), pp. 244–47. This text reprints tales from the Edgar Taylor translation of 1823, *German Popular Stories translated from the Kinder-und Hausmarchen by MM Grimm*.

like Jeanie in *Goblin Market,* illustrates the fate of the female who accepts male domination. The old woman, whose role is like Lizzie's but without the implications of Christian sacrifice, assists the bride in avoiding the usual female fate. The bride becomes master of her fate.

McGann points out that "personal independence" is one of Rossetti's "central subjects," and to the extent that Laura and Lizzie are free of the goblin menace, they become independent (*VS,* p. 246). Apparently, however, the two girls do not (as Mermin suggests Laura does) cease to desire a male. Whom they marry remains a mystery, but it is certain that they become "wives / With children of their own." Marriage is in keeping with the biblical overtones of the poem and in Rossetti's poetry often represents "wholeness, sanity, and integration" (Weathers, p. 84). We might recall "Snow White" or especially "Sleeping Beauty," in which the marriage signals a renewal of the kingdom, a recovery of the land. Or we might recall "The Frog Prince," in which, paradoxically, the ugliness of sex, when rejected, is transformed into the lineaments of gratified desire. Perhaps Rossetti (in *Goblin Market* at least) is not so much "ambivalent about the sensual joys of this world" (Barr, p. 268) as she is aware of the fairy tale attitudes to marriage and to male-female relationships generally. Perhaps she goes farther and plays with the form. McGann speaks of *Goblin Market* as exhibiting "the disarming formal appearance of a children's fairy story" (*VS,* p. 251).

It is true, I think, that *Goblin Market* troubles the reader through its formal as well as its thematic ambiguities. The poem teases us out of thought; it plays with our reactions and expectations; it shifts our understanding of language. It might not be too much to say that the poem is about its own form, its language. Like the fairy tale, *Goblin Market* foregrounds design and language. The opening announces this formal interest:

> Morning and evening
> Maids heard the goblins cry:
> "Come buy our orchard fruits,
> Come buy, come buy:
> Apples and quinces,
> Lemons and oranges,
> Plump unpecked cherries,
> Melons and raspberries,
> Bloom-down-cheeked peaches,
> Swart-headed mulberries,

> Wild free-born cranberries,
> Crab-apples, dewberries,
> Pine-apples, blackberries,
> Apricots, strawberries;—
> All ripe together
> In summer weather . . .
>
> [ll. 1–16]

And the catalogue continues for fifteen more lines. These lines establish, as Barr says, "the obvious tone of wonder and fairy-tale like fantasy" and also a "strongly commercial aspect of the language" (Barr, p. 273). What Barr does not point out is that fairy tale language and commercial language are opposites, just as morning and evening are opposites.[8] The reader immediately learns to be wary of goblin language; goblins are hawkers, double talkers. Why, for example, need they say "orchard fruits" rather than simply "fruits" (the third line would then scan the same as the fourth line)? What the goblins are selling is language; they take a familiar patterning of language in children's literature—the list or catalogue—and charm Laura with it ("Their offers should not charm us"). They "suck" her in, although it is she who "sucked until her lips were sore" (l. 136).

The verbal stream at the beginning of the poem is, of course, a lie. Instead of freeing language and releasing passion, the goblin words fix, enclose, suspend, and exhaust those who listen to them with eager curiosity. The thirty-one-line opening bark of the goblins begins and ends with the exhortation to "come buy." In all, there are only six different rhymes in this passage. The rhyme on "buy" ("cry," "fly," "by," "try," and "eye") sounds at the beginning, middle, and end of the passage, effectively enclosing and fixing it. Further, the most frequently repeated rhyme, on "berries," clogs these lines. The goblins sound sweet "cooing all together" (l. 78); they sound "kind and full of loves" (l. 79), but their sound is deceiving, cloying. Tucked into the middle of this list of fruits is the familiar *carpe diem* warning: "Morns that pass by, / Fair eves that fly" (ll. 17–18). Here is the nub of the goblins' argument: come buy before it is too late. But the roll call of fruits from apples to citrons mutes this hint of change and decay. The catalogue fills the mind with the fullness of nature, yet it, like innocence, can deceive. Nursery rhyme and fairy tale unlock the word

---

[8]See Theo Dombroski, "Dualism in the Poetry of Christina Rossetti," *VP* 14 (1976): 70–76.

hoard and play with language; the goblins' list purports to do the same, while in truth it is merely a huckster's cry. The language the goblins sell betrays the sense of community that fairy tales and nursery rhymes promote. Laura restores this sense of community at the end when she gathers the little ones about her and bids "them cling together" (l. 561). The final words of the poem, Laura's words, are often thought to be overly didactic, but they speak of brotherhood—or, in this case, sisterhood—of the importance of friendship and community. The poem has shown, through its similes, through its repetition, through its verbal echoes, that "sister" is as much figurative as actual.

Finally, then, *Goblin Market* is a poem of figuration. Its surface dazzles with similes (there are forty in all), accented rhythms, and intricate rhymes. Its verbal ingenuity turns a "kernel-stone" (l. 281) into a "carnal" stone and the act of sucking becomes a draining of the self, a shrinking into the self. Clearly, it is not by eating but by being eaten that one comes closest to the soul of another. Clearly, it is by perceiving nature as figuring a higher reality and not as a reality in itself that we free ourselves from the tyranny of material things. Laura's mistake is in accepting the goblin fruit as literal; she buys from the goblins a language without polysemy. The result is a craving for more and more, a carnality that cannot be satisfied, at least not until Lizzie returns home and offers herself to her sister: "Laura, make much of me" (l. 472). And the reader must make much of *Goblin Market*. Language is untrustworthy when we fail to make enough from it. The fall from innocence is a verbal fall as much as anything else, and if children are not to experience language only as the hectoring babble of the market place they must be prepared at an early age to appreciate the play inherent in it.

This emphasis on the imaginative possibilities of language informs Rossetti's first published work for children, *Sing-Song*. *Sing-Song* is a book of nursery rhymes, as the subtitle informs us, but these rhymes are acutely aware of the verbal world children live in, and they encourage children to enjoy the play of language. Some rhymes are obviously playful:

> A city plum is not a plum;
> A dumb-bell is no bell, though dumb;
> A party rat is not a rat;
> A sailor's cat is not a cat;
> A soldier's frog is not a frog;
> A captain's log is not a log.

[II, 21]

That words are not so much referential as they are metaphoric is clear. A city plum is and is not a plum, but a plum, whether city or otherwise, *is* dumb. Words in poetic discourse move in the direction of sound play and their semantic meanings loosen. A frog may sit on a log, although a soldier's frog more appropriately sits on a shoulder. And it has nothing whatever to do with a captain's log. A captain's log, although not a log, is probably made from one. In Saussurian terms the signifiers are not at one with the signifieds; instead, Rossetti's rhyme points out how in poetic discourse metaphor detaches us from the one-dimensional relationship between word and concept. In other words, poetic language need not refer to a direct reality. The purpose of "A city plum is not a plum" is not, as R. Loring Taylor suggests, to give information or to teach children "basic skills."[9] As Anthony Easthope says,

> The language of a poem may aim for transparency but this does not make a poem referential. Transparency, a certain relation of signifier and signified, is not the same thing as reference, which is a relation between signified and reality . . . in all discourse the signifier precedes the signified and no discourse is by nature transparent. But this fact does not preclude there being a discourse which gives knowledge by referring to a reality. It does mean that discourse providing such knowledge depends upon the reader being positioned so as to read the discourse as transparent and treat it as referential. On this basis the study of poetry can give knowledge of poetry by referring to it accurately.[10]

The poems in *Sing-Song* (at least a great many of them) give pleasure in the way all nursery songs give pleasure, through their rhyme, their rhythms, and their metaphors; they teach children to understand, and to have fun with, the play of language. In these poems, as in *Goblin Market*, Rossetti emphasizes sound, repetition, and the heavily accentual line. Meaning emerges from the reader's engaging the poem as discourse, that is, as a form of communication that differs from statement. Any prose statement we might produce from our reading of Rossetti's poems derives from formal elements. Take for example this poem:

"Kookoorookoo! kookoorookoo!"
Crows the cock before the morn;

9R. Loring Taylor, Preface to the Garland edition of *Sing-Song, Speaking Likenesses, Goblin Market* (New York: Garland Publishing, 1976), p. xii. Page references to this preface will hereafter be given in the text.
10Anthony Easthope, *Poetry as Discourse* (London: Methuen, 1983), p. 17.

"Kikirikee! kikirikee!"
Roses in the east are born.

"Kookoorookoo! kookoorookoo!"
Early birds begin their singing;
"Kikirikee! kikirikee!:
The day, the day, the day is springing.

[II, 20]

More obviously than other poems in the book, this poem derives from nursery rhymes such as "Cock-a-doddle doo! My dame has lost her shoe", "Titty cum tawtay," and "Bow, wow, wow." The voice that speaks the poem produces two sound words that are similar yet opposite. The consonants are the same, but the vowel sounds differ. In the first stanza this pattern raises the question: if cocks crow "kookoorookoo," then who or what cries "kikirikee"? The second stanza might indicate that early birds sing "kikirikee," but the semicolon at the end of the second line (in both stanzas) works against this reading. If we allow the semicolon to divide each stanza in half, then the "kikirikee" is a general sound communicating the energy and life of the new day. The last line with its three repetitions of "day" reinforces this sense of vitality. So too do the alliteration and assonance: "crows cock before morn kee east roses born."

The word "springing" not only supports the energetic bounce of the poem's rhythm and the liveliness of the new morn, it also suggests springtime and that pastoral freshness so pervasive in Sing-Song. A hint of this quality is perhaps evident in the roses that have their birth in the east. Rossetti delicately shades her meaning so that pastoral freshness is inseparable from spiritual celebration. Georgina Battiscombe notes that Sing-Song contains "no mention of God, or of the Christian stories so familiar to Victorian children, or indeed, of religion in any form" (p. 144). Yet angels, the Maker, heaven, faith, hope, love—all these appear in Sing-Song. An aura of spirituality is apparent both in this poem and throughout Sing-Song. We begin to suspect there is a spiritual meaning in the line "Roses in the east are born," especially when we consider that roses and other flowers appear as figures in at least fifteen poems in the volume. The poem, then, is a celebration of birth, a new morning, spiritual vitality, and natural harmony. The "kookoorookoo" and "kikirikee" do not belong exclusively to specific birds, and the speaker of the poem is not a specific individual. This verse, like all nursery rhymes, is a collective song, only here the song is a collective hymn of praise to a world that reflects the divine.

But this reading presents only half the story. "Kookoorookoo, kookoorookoo" is but one poem of many in this volume. We experience Sing-Song as we experience Blake's Songs of Innocence and Experience, [11] as a coherent text; and, Battiscombe points out, "even in these childlike verses for and about children Christina cannot forget the great central themes of her poetry, love, death, and parting" (p. 144). In other words, there is a dark side to the pastoral innocence of Sing-Song. The reader learns that spring blossoms and youth are frail and that today and tomorrow are brief; in one poem the poet exhorts three children not to "wait for roses" (II, 26) and so lose the day. We might recall the opposition of vowel sounds in "kookoorookoo" and "kiki-rikee." Add to this the opposition (in the same poem) of bird and flower, active verb and passive verb in the first stanza, and we might catch a hint of deeper, unstated opposites: east and morning imply west and evening, birth leads to death, and what springs up must come down.

One of the best-known poems in Sing-Song reflects the presence of the divine. "Who has seen the wind" gives simple, yet intense, expression to the numinous:

> Who has seen the wind?
> Neither I nor you:
> But when the leaves hang trembling
> The wind is passing thro'.
>
> Who has seen the wind?
> Neither you nor I:
> But when the trees bow down their heads
> The wind is passing by.
>
> [II. 42]

The movement from three to two to four to three stress lines in the first stanza accurately suggests the passing wind, and the half stress on

[11] As Taylor points out, critics have called Sing-Song "a Blakean paean to childhood joy and innocence" (p. ix). Dante Gabriel Rossetti describes the book as "alternating between mere babyism and a sort of Blakish wisdom and tenderness" (Letters of Dante Gabriel Rossetti, ed. Oswald Doughty and J. R. Wahl, 4 vols. [Oxford: Clarendon Press, 1965–1967], II, 797). See also Dorothy Margaret Stuart, Christina Rossetti (London: Macmillan, 1930), p. 85; and Annie E. Moore, Literature Old and New for Children (Cambridge, Mass.: Houghton Mifflin Co., 1934), p. 298.

"hang" effectively modulates the breeze. Line three of the second stanza has five stresses to convey the strength of the wind that bends the branches. The sense of the wind as *inspiritus*, the breath of the divine, comes through in the word "trembling"; the leaves that tremble express awe. Reverence is in the line: "But when the trees bow down their heads." And the two words "thro'" and "by" convey the spiritual power to penetrate or to brush by. In other poems, too, Rossetti uses the wind as an image of divine immanence and power both to emphasize the pastoral harmony of her world and to show the darker side of pastoral innocence. "O wind, where have you been" and "O wind, why do you never rest" depict sweetness and restlessness. In "The wind has such a rainy sound," wind and sea combine to present an evocation of death.

It is fair to say, however, that joy dominates here and throughout *Sing-Song*. Even when their theme is clearly death and parting, the poems express an element of joy:

> "Goodbye in fear, goodbye in sorrow,
>   Goodbye, and all in vain,
> Never to meet again, my dear—'
>   Never to part again."
> "Goodbye today, goodbye tomorrow,
>   Goodbye till earth shall wane,
> Never to meet again, my dear—"
>   Never to part again."
>
> [II, 49]

Two voices speak. One voice, that which speaks the first three lines of each quatrain, is melancholy and negative. The second voice, however, transforms the first speaker's negative into a positive. Like the child in Wordsworth's "We Are Seven," the second speaker does not accept discontinuity. In its verbal repetition and its complicated interlocking rhymes, the poem centers on form; the two quatrains draw together. Although the implication here is not exactly that "death is the bringer of joy" (Battiscombe, p. 76), in *Sing-Song* as a whole Rossetti presents death as a positive aspect of life. In part, she accomplishes this transformation by identifying death as one point in a larger pattern, and as a natural event. A child may die, but the child is a rose: "I have but one rose in the world, / And my one rose stands a-drooping" (II, 39). Ships may go down, but they do so like apples in the orchard tumbling from their tree. A baby dies making father and mother sigh; flowers also "bloom to die" and they ask not why: they accept the way of things, especially since "if all were sun and never rain, / There'd be no rainbow still" (II, 24). Finally, death is soul's sleep: "Our little baby fell asleep, / And may not wake again / For days and days, and weeks and weeks" (II, 20). But the poem assures us he will "wake again." Death sends a child's soul "home to Paradise" and leaves his "body waiting here" (II, 22).

Throughout *Sing-Song* death is an imaginative idea, not a sign of closure. In other words, just as Rossetti's poems delight in word play and intricacy of form and allusion, her notion of death is equally fertile and equally at variance with discontinuity and finality. Rossetti's concern with death and attention to poetic form is perhaps best summarized in the volume's final poem:

Lie a-bed,
Sleepy head,
Shut up eyes, bo-peep;
Till daybreak
Never wake:—
Baby, sleep.

[II, 51]

Taylor finds an "alarming ambiguity" in this lullaby, and he also finds "disconcerting" a "tendency to equate sleep with death" in *Sing-Song* generally (p. xi). The sleep that is death, however, is Rossetti's depiction of the soul's sleep, that comforting time of preparation and waiting for a grand new morning. In "Lie a-bed" the masculine rhymes and strong end-stops at the third and last lines signal finality, closure, death. But the two halves of the little poem are hooked together with the rhyme of "bo-peep" and "sleep." "Bo-peep" reminds us we are in the world of nursery rhyme where rhyme is strongly musical; the words have a nonreferential significance and power. If we catch a somber note here, as Taylor does, if we allow our minds to play on the meaning of "wake" and consider its two senses—emerging from sleep and watching over the body of a dead person—we might also consider the wake of the poem as the track it leaves behind, the residue in the mind. We might hear that coupling of "peep" and "sleep," an aural connection that suggests a seeing in sleep. During the soul's sleep we catch glimpses of the greater reality to come; we peep into the future. During our nightly dreams we peep into our unconscious. This little lullaby allows us a peep into the mystery of sleep both in its nightly and in its premillenarian aspects. This baby will not sleep the sleep of death, but this baby may or may not sleep until the next morning or the final morning. The sense of closure in all lullabies is premature, since there is always more to come, more to sing.

Sing-Song contains many themes: death, mother love, pastoral delicacy, desire, class divisions, suffering, the importance of family, love, and fantasy. There are lessons in arithmetic, time, money, and color. Even in these teaching poems we can discern play with closure and its opposite. The poem explaining time, for example, begins with the smallest unit of clock time: "How many seconds in a minute? / Sixty, and no more in it." The sense of closure is blunt: "and no more in it." Time circumscribes experience; we have twenty-four hours in a day "for work and play," and the almanac "makes clear" there are twelve months in a year. Yet time cannot circumscribe experience, as the poem's final couplet makes clear: "How many ages in time? / No one knows the rhyme" (II, 30). "Time" and "rhyme"—the two words are united and remind us that neither completes anything. Rhyme is part of a poem's time, its musical beat, but it has nothing to do with measurable clock or seasonal time. Rhyme is as timeless as language and sound. Time, on the other hand, is rhymeless in the sense that it cannot be packaged in a couplet, since "no one knows the rhyme"; paradoxically, time and rhyme perform this coupling which the poem says is impossible.

Sing-Song, like *Goblin Market,* is less concerend with allegory or didacticism than it is with intensity of both form and language. Rossetti chooses her forms—fairy tale and nursery rhyme—carefully. These forms foregound play, repetition, song, and language. What Douglas Kneale says in the context of Wordsworth's *Prelude* applies here: "The question of what a text is 'about' . . . shifts from a concern with historical or referential meaning to a concern with rhetorical or semiological foregrounding."[12] This concern is nowhere more apparent than in Rossetti's last book for children, *Speaking Likenesses,* the only prose work Rossetti published for children. *Speaking Likenesses* is a fantasy consisting of three stories held together by the framing device of an aunt who tells the stories to five sisters while they sew, draw, or darn. The first story, by far the longest, tells of little Flora's eighth birthday and the dream she has during the afternoon. The second story tells of a girl named Edith who attempts vainly to

[12]Douglas Kneale, "The Rhetoric of Imagination in *The Prelude,*" *Ariel* 15 (1984): 112.

boil a kettle. The last story takes place on Christmas Eve, and it concerns the night journey of Maggie to the country house of a doctor. The first and third stories contain frightening and disturbing images and action. This is probably why the *Times Literary Supplement* called *Speaking Likenesses* "a peculiarly revolting book" (May 29, 1959, p. xi). Taylor too finds the stories in *Speaking Likenesses* self-defeating and "unclear"; rather than a children's book Rossetti has written "a sad and sometimes bitter parable of a lonely lady" (pp. xvi, xviii). But in this book too Rossetti's concerns are playful. Her narrator, for example, is a source of fun, and we should be careful not to conclude that this "aunt" speaks for Christina Rossetti. True, the narrator's "didactic stance permeates the book" (Taylor, p. xiv), but the children who are her audience manage to undercut her didacticism.

Clara, Jane, Laura, Ella, and Maude continually interrupt the narrator's storytelling. They comment on the oddness of a name, they ask for clarification, or they point out improbable assertions. The cumulative effect is to point out the difference between the irritable, presumptuous, and matter-of-fact aunt from the curious children who are receptive to fancy and wonder. For example, when, in the first of the three stories, the narrator describes the sunny afternoon of Flora's birthday, she remarks that "bell flowers rang without clappers."[13] Before she can complete her sentence, Maude interrupts to ask whether bell flowers can ring without clappers. The narrator shrugs the question off with the reply: "Well, not exactly, Maude: but you're coming to much more wonderful matters!" (p. 15). In other words, don't ask difficult questions and attend to the rest of my story.

Yet the narrator's attitude to storytelling is rather strange: she urges her listeners to occupy themselves with sewing, painting, or darning while they listen. When Jane and Laura appear to become engrossed in the fantastic room with animated furniture, the narrator admonishes them not to "*quite* forget the pocket handkerchiefs you sat down to hem" (p. 21). Sitting down to hear a story is apparently too idle an occupation for this aunt. Like many other writers for children in the nineteenth century, Rossetti, through her narrator, expresses a distrust of fantasy, of make-believe, of story for its own sake. When Jane asks whether the furniture that arranges itself flat against the walls also flattens itself across the door, her aunt answers briskly: "Why, yes, I suppose it may have done so, Jane. . . . At any rate, as this is all

[13]References to *Speaking Likenesses* are to the Garland edition cited in note 10 above, and specific page references will hereafter be given in the text.

make-believe, I say No. Attention!" (p. 27). At one point in the third story the narrator interrupts herself to ask the children if they know what would happen to the heroine of her story (a girl named Maggie) if she were to sleep out in the cold winter weather. This interruption allows the narrator to speak of death.

This is the last interruption that occurs. The book ends without a return to its narrative frame. Each of the first two stories ends abruptly, followed, apparently a day later, by a conversation between the children and their aunt concerning the next story. What are we to assume at the end of the third story? That there is no next day? The disjunction between the opening, where the narrator tells the "dear little girls" (p. 1) to gather round her, and the end, where Maggie and her Granny go quietly to bed, is clear. The book begins with a call to story, and it ends within the world of story. What matters is story, not the narrator's lessons on acoustics or her warning that one should never put an empty kettle on a fire. The children's interruptions show their interest in and engagement with the stories; they ask for details when their aunt appears insufficiently clear or niggardly with detail. In short, they ask with Laura, "And please, Aunt, be wonderful" (p. 71).

Just as the narrative frame draws attention to the act of storytell-ing—to the notion that details impede linearity of plot, to the fact that the reading experience involves the interruption of narrative—the stories themselves draw attention to form, to the play of allusion, to impediments to linearity. The second story, the account of Edith's failure to boil a kettle, can serve as an illustration for them all. Edith and the kettle are "spending one warm afternoon together in a wood" (p. 50), which has, "by some freak," one vine that grows among the beech trees and silver birches and that "dangled bunches of pale purple grapes among its leaves and twisted tendrils" (p. 51). Just where the vine grows a party is to take place, and Edith decides to take the kettle there and light the fire to boil it. First, however, she eyes the grapes and longs to grasp a cluster. Then she turns her attention to the fire; she fails with her six matches to start the fire, and her helpers, various animals, also fail. Just before the project is brought to an end by the arrival of Nurse, a fox bustles up, brushes the dust from Edith's frock, attempts in vain to reach the grapes and then trots away mutter-ing "they must be sour" (p. 68). The allusion is clearly to Aesop. If we look for a moral in this story of Edith and the kettle, Aesop's famous fable provides one. The fox does not worry about not reaching the grapes; Edith is in "despair" (p. 69) and sits down to cry: some people blame circumstances when they fail through their own incapacity, while others take disappointment with indifference. Edith, however, does neither. Rossetti inverts Aesop's moral.

Yet to point such a moral contrast is to ignore the story's more obvious nonsense. While Rossetti inverts Aesop's fable, her story does not suggest a more acute moral. She simply plays with the form of fable. The fox trots into the scene and out again, and what he signals is first the unexpected and then "fable." The fable's primary function is fun, and as several versions of Aesop indicate (most notably the 1692 translation by Roger L'Estrange), the moral explanation simply refuses to satisfy, or in some cases even to apply. Indeed, Rossetti's whole story is free association, made up as the aunt speaks (she states at the beginning that she does not know the story of the frog who couldn't boil the kettle but that she will try to tell it anyway). What ultimately matters in her story is this frog, the toad whose father lived in a stone, and the other animals who try to help so ineffectually. In short, behind *Speaking Likenesses* lies an impulse to the condition of Lewis Carroll. Rossetti wrote to her brother Dante Gabriel that *Speaking Likenesses* was "merely a Christmas trifle, would-be in the *Alice* style" (*FL*, p. 44). Most readers have found the book a pale shade of *Alice*, yet the two works do have certain similarities: the atmosphere of dream, fantastic creatures and talking animals, animated objects, the uncovering of desire, and the nakedness of fear.

The first story in *Speaking Likenesses*, that of eight-year-old Flora and her birthday party, presents the clearest parallel to Carroll's own "Alice style." Flora, who is irritated at the manner in which her birthday party is passing and not interested in listening to a story, falls asleep and dreams about another birthday party where furniture comes to life and the children's bodies consist of hooks, angles, or slime. These quaint children in Flora's dream, the boys Hooks, Angles, and Quills, and the girls Sticky, Slime, and Queen, play two games: "Hunt the Pincushion" and "Self-help." The nightmare quality some readers perceive in *Alice's Adventures in Wonderland* is also evident in Rossetti's story in these two games that reveal a deep fear of sexual violence and a disturbing disrespect for humanity. The first game treats human beings as objects, things without feeling or dignity; it reverses the fairy tale convention of imagining inanimate objects as human. This mis-imagining is Rossetti's point. In Carroll's first *Alice* book inanimate objects such as mallets and balls become hedgehogs and flamingos. The Queen of Hearts presides over a lively game in which there are no rules and no ill consequences. "Hunt the Pincushion," however, reverses this situation. The hunt is no longer an innocent search for an object; it is a bloodsport. Rossetti clarifies the sexual implications of the game and draws attention to its nastier aspects. Through her representation of this game, as well as the second game, "Self-help," Rossetti provides a criticism of her culture. In modern terms, this is a feminist criticism. Players of "Hunt the Pincushion" select "the smallest and weakest player (if possible let her be fat: a hump is best of all)," and they "chase her round and round the room" (p. 33). The pincushion is female. In "Self-help" the "boys were players, the girls were played" (p. 36), and in describing this game, Rossetti satirizes the whole notion of self-help, made popular in the mid-century by Samuel Smiles's *Self-Help* (1859). The unpleasant implications for females in Smiles's assertion that "energy of will may be defined to be the very central power of character in a man"[14] are uncovered in Rossetti's imagined game. In Flora's dream "self-help" comes to mean a male helping himself at the expense of the female.

Most readers of *Speaking Likenesses* will be brought up short by Rossetti's descriptions of these games. Plot and linearity are irrelevant. Satire and innuendo halt—or should halt—the reader. Rossetti herself indicates the proper response by having her narrator interrupt the narrative to say, "Don't look shocked, dear Ella, at my choice of words . . ." (p. 36). What these shocking words are we can only suppose, but since the description of "Self-help" that immediately precedes this interruption is harmless enough, we can imagine Ella (and the other girls) registering a growing amazement as the story proceeds. Certainly, the description of "Hunt the Pincushion" contains shocking words:

> Quills with every quill erect tilted against her, and needed not a pin: but Angles whose corners almost cut her, Hooks who caught and slit her frock, Slime who slid against her and passed her, Sticky who rubbed off on her neck and plump bare arms, the scowling Queen, and the whole laughing scolding pushing troop, all wielded longest sharpest pins, and all by turns overtook her. [p. 34]

The passage that follows, in which the narrator reflects on the effect of the game upon the "stickers," combines colloquial expression ("cutting corners") with tautology ("pricking quills, catching hooks") and alliterative effect ("particular personal pangs"). In short, the narrator

---

[14]Quoted in Walter E. Houghton, *The Victorian Frame of Mind* (New Haven: Yale University Press, 1970), p. 117.

directs our attention to vocabulary and to stylistic effects, and in so doing she impedes the narrative. The story is not the thing; words become things.

Christina Rossetti's work for children, then, is difficult only in the sense that the reader who expects simple narrative or clear didacticism will be surprised. The three works I have discussed do appear conventionally didactic and traditionally narrative in impulse (*Sing-Song*'s traditional quality is in its nursery rhyme simplicity). Yet they are also disturbing and confusing. What appears straightforward is, upon reflection, askew. The reader confronts nursery rhyme and fairy tale in a new guise, and so discovers Rossetti's conscious playing with form and traditional themes. Even the shortest rhyme in *Sing-Song* is an exercise in stylistics: "Motherless baby and babyless mother, / Bring them together to love one another" (II, 50). The first line is an example of antimetabole, a repetition of words (here with morphological change) in reverse order. The second line overcomes the first in that the negative "less" gives way to the positive "to" (together, to love). Opposites come together in this rhyme, opposites that are not, in fact, so opposite to begin with. The disturbing fact of death, the uncertainty of life—these are defeated by the stronger sense of continuity: the continuing mystery of mother love, of human relationships, and of a language strong enough to communicate these mysteries.

Because children's literature generally appears simple, unconcerned in its content with the complexities and vagaries of human emotion, thought, and psychology, it has attracted little critical scrutiny. Because serious literary commentary has never allowed children's literature a canonical status, it has remained outside the great tradition. Rossetti's *Goblin Market*, however, has been embraced by critics and anthologists as a children's poem precisely because it invites the kind of literary debate they are hard-pressed to generate from works more forthrightly presented as children's literature—even though *Goblin Market* finds its formal impetus in the same tradition that informs the more obviously childlike *Sing-Song* and *Speaking Likenesses*: the tradition of fable, fairy tale, and nursery rhyme. These forms derive their power from ellipsis and symbol and freedom from the contingencies that govern realistic and referential forms of literature. By using these forms, Rossetti—like many other women writers of the Victorian period who wrote for children—was able to voice her desires and her feminine concerns at once openly and secretly. Thus a child can read these works for the adventures of plot and language; an adult may look for the edifying lessons in behavior that will benefit a child; and the

careful reader will discern the desire of a passionate woman who wanted to express her identity as a woman and to create an art that was
truly personal and yet truly representative of humanity's possibilities.
Clearly, if we have eyes to see and ears to hear, the deceptively simple
surfaces of Rossetti's art reveal secret delights and imaginative truth.

P. G. Stanwood

Christina Rossetti's
Devotional Prose

Almost all Christina Rossetti's prose works are "devotional" in one particular sense of that term, for they seek to define and increase religious knowledge by informing and instructing the Christian worshiper. Rossetti wrote these books during the last twenty years of her life. The first was *Annus Domini: A Prayer for Each Day of the Year, Founded on a Text of Holy Scripture* (1874), followed by *Seek and Find: A Double Series of Short Studies of the Benedicite* (1879), *Called to be Saints: The Minor Festivals Devotionally Studied* (1881), *Letter and Spirit: Notes on the Commandments* (1883), *Time Flies: A Reading Diary* (1885), and *The Face of the Deep: A Devotional Commentary on the Apocalypse* (1892). This is a substantial volume of work, but still of minor significance when set beside the poetry. Poetry was to Rossetti always the primary and most natural concern of her life; she began to write in the 1840s, at age eleven or twelve, and continued almost to the end of her life in 1894. She also continued to write poetry at the same time as the prose, even interspersing it with appropriately devotional poems. One may feel tempted to say, indeed, that the best features of some of the prose works are these poetical interpolations.

But the prose works have an integrity, a solemnity, and a thoughtfulness characteristic of much of Rossetti's best writing, although sometimes they also convey a sense of dutifulness, as if their author felt conscience-bound to write them. I intend to discuss the imagination that shaped these books, the historical context within which they were written, and also their interest to readers of the poetry. Because these books are so little known—and now very difficult to obtain—I will briefly describe the contents of each one, and, in doing so, I will begin to explore some of the major issues I have just identified.

Annus Domini (Oxford: James Parker), the first of Rossetti's devotional prose works, was published in 1874 with a brief commendatory preface by the Reverend Canon H. W. Burrows, Vicar of Christ Church, Albany Street, where Rossetti was for many years a parishioner. This little book contains 366 collects, one for each day of the year. Each collect begins with a scriptural text, opening with Genesis 3:15, and continuing with various texts from both Old and New Testaments; the last collect is founded on Revelation 23:16. The principle of selection is roughly clear, for Rossetti evidently favored texts of a prophetic nature, such as Isaiah 32:1, "Behold, a King shall reign in Righteousness," or the numerous texts from Revelation; or else she chose New Testament texts that specifically touch the mystery of the Incarnation, such as "The Light shineth in darkness; and the darkness comprehended it not" (John 1:5). It is noteworthy that forty collects are based on texts from Isaiah, and forty-two on the Apocalypse; another thirty-two come from the Gospel of John, and a further sixty-four from the Psalms, many of which can be easily related to Christian sensibility and worship, as, for example, Psalm 43:4: "Then will I go unto the Altar of God, unto God my Exceeding Joy: yea, upon thy harp will I praise Thee, O God my God." Hebrews is another important source (31), as are 1 and 2 Peter (14) and 1 John (10).

A typical collect can be illustrated by no. 198, on John 1:14: "We beheld His Glory, the Glory as of the Only Begotten of the Father":

O Lord Jesus Christ, the Only Begotten of the Father, lift up our hearts, I entreat Thee, that with Cherubim and Seraphim, with Angels and Archangels, with Saints who labour and Saints who rest, we may love, worship and adore Thee in the Mystery of the Ever Blessed Trinity.

The text becomes the occasion of the beginning of the collect, with an invocation always to Christ—not, as in the *Book of Common Prayer*, to God the Father. The invocation is followed by an entreaty in the first person "I," a statement of the general intention, and a final gathering up of the imprecation in terms of all mankind. Canon Burrows was right to describe these prayers in his preface as "valuable in themselves from their fervour, reverence, and overflowing charity, and [for] . . . the use which should be made of Holy Scripture in our devotions. Each little Prayer may be considered as the result of a meditation, and as an example of the way in which that exercise should issue in worship." He noted also that the book could be used properly only "as supplementary to other devotions," the purpose that their author surely intended.

Rossetti was thinking of a daily prayer that would help people concentrate their thoughts around a meditation on the Incarnate God, the Word made flesh. She also provided for the whole book a calendar-index of the major seasons of the church year from Advent and Christmas through Easter and Trinity, assigning appropriate collects to the different times and including separate sections for Saints' Days, Feasts of the Blessed Virgin, Saint Michael and All Angels, Ember Weeks, and Rogation Days. The small format of the book, which measures 9.0 cm. x 12.0 cm. (printed in foolscap 8°), with marginal rules on every page and an ornamental cross at each corner of the rule, and neatly bound in limp, dark red buckram (stamped with double sets of black rules), seems to be declaring itself a suitable accompaniment to the *Book of Common Prayer*. Rossetti's first devotional book fits nicely into the series that her publisher James Parker was bringing out as the Oxford Editions of Devotional Works. Among the books on his list are Lancelot Andrewes's *Devotions*, Archbishop Laud's *Private Devotions*, Jeremy Taylor's *Holy Living* and *Holy Dying*. Although very different from any of them, *Annus Domini* deserves a place in this worthy company of seventeenth-century manuals, written by some of those who were most representative of the "golden age" of Anglican devotion.

Rossetti's five other works of devotional prose were published with similar elegance: the physical object complements the content itself, reinforces it, helps the reader to move into a specially shaped, aesthetically pleasing religious world. The Society for Promoting Christian Knowledge (SPCK) became her "religious" publisher, beginning with *Seek and Find*, which appeared in 1879, five years after *Annus Domini*. The book is carefully and handsomely produced, though it is not quite so elaborate as the volumes that would follow it. Rossetti's brother Dante Gabriel protested over so much and such committed religious publication, but she objected that "I don't think harm will accrue to me from my SPCK books, even to my standing: if it did, I should still be glad to throw my grain of dust into the religious scale."[1]

---

[1]Quoted by Lona Mosk Packer, *Christina Rossetti* (Berkeley: University of California Press, 1963), p. 329. Packer also quotes (pp. 329–32) a number of interesting passages from Rossetti's unpublished notes on Genesis and Exodus, which she may have been writing at the same time as *Seek and Find*.

The Benedicite, which Rossetti intends to elucidate in *Seek and Find,* is one of the alternative canticles appointed to be said or sung in the office of morning prayer in the *Book of Common Prayer.* It is known also as the "Song of the Three Children," that is, of Ananiah, Azariah, and Mishael, whom Nebuchadnezzar threw into the fiery furnace because they had refused to bow down and worship before his golden statue. This canticle, an apocryphal addition to the Book of Daniel (inserted between 3:23 and 3:24), is a long poem of exaltation and blessing of God's works—the heavens, the waters, the sun and moon, dews and frosts, whales, fowl and beasts, "children of men," and more. In composing her "double series" of studies, Rossetti sets out all the separate objects of praise in a first series that she considers in terms of "creation," drawing together many scriptural passages that could be relevant. Then, in the second series of studies on the "redemption," she gathers other scriptural texts around the same subjects as before. The result is a kind of "harmony" of the Benedicite, with its "Praise-givers" as, on the one hand, the creatures of God, and, on the other, the servants of God, the one side prefiguring the other, but both expressing, with different emphasis or direction, the glory of God.

Little about *Seek and Find* is original, apart from its ingenious structure and the telling arrangement of the biblical texts. Only occasionally does Rossetti allow herself to speak or comment about any of the divisions in the Benedicite and, when she does so, it is usually in rather vague terms. But in one instance, in the "first series," she muses about the stars, and provides us a rare glimpse of her intellectual leanings:

> There is something awe-striking, over-whelming, in contemplation of the stars. Their number, magnitudes, distances, orbits, we know not: any multitude our unaided eyes discern is but an instalment of that vaster multitude which the telescope reveals. . . . Knowledge runs apace: and our globe which once seemed large is now but a small planet among planets, while not one of our group of planets is large as compared with its central sun; and the sun itself may be no more than a sub-centre, it and all its system coursing but as satellites and sub-satellites around a general centre; and this again,—what of this? Is even this remote centre truly central, or is it no more than yet another sub-centre revolving around some point of overruling attraction, and swaying with it the harmonious encircling dance of its attendant worlds? [pp. 35–36]

These comments reveal Rossetti's interest in the new astronomy, which was undergoing dramatic changes during the last half of the nineteenth century, especially in its conceptions of stellar structure and evolution.

Rossetti's fascination with the magnitude of the created world (and sometimes also with its minuteness) is manifested throughout her writings. Her journey to the Continent with her mother and brother William Michael in 1861 (and again in 1865), and in particular the sight of the Alps, made a strong impression that deepened with succeeding years. *Time Flies* (1885) contains numerous references to the Italian and Swiss part of her journey; the mountains fill her with sadness as well as sober excitement:

> Their mass and loftiness dwarf all physical magnitudes familiar to most eyes, except the low-lying vastness of the ocean and the boundless overarching sky. They touch and pass through those clouds which limit our vision. . . .
>
> Well, saddened and probably weary, I ended one delightful day's journey in Switzerland; and passed indoors, losing sight for a moment of the mountains.
>
> Then from a window I faced them again. And, lo! the evening flush had turned snow to a rose, "and sorrow and sadness fled away." [entry for June 10]

The observation of mountains in the earlier *Seek and Find* is similarly evocative:

> Mountains bestow, valleys receive: snowy heights form a water-shed for the low-lying fertility which engarlands their base. Moreover they bestow necessaries not in mere naked sufficiency, but in forms which make hill-streams and waterfalls rank among the beauty-spots of this beautiful world: such streams descend with murmur, tumult and thunder, in crystal expanses, in ripples, leaps and eddies, in darkness and light, in clearness and whiteness, and foam and foam-bow. [pp. 91–92]

In this description, Rossetti reveals something of her imaginative life, whereas in the description of stars she revealed a certain intellectual predisposition. But for the most part *Seek and Find* lacks such moments, for its essential aim is to present a scriptural gloss or interpretation of a well-known canticle.

The next devotional book Rossetti wrote allowed her greater scope for more personal statements. *Called to be Saints*, published in the same year as "*A Pageant*"*and Other Poems* (1881), was in fact completed five years earlier.[2] In some respects the book is a straightforward, that is, scriptural, account of the apostolic saints remembered in the *Book of Common Prayer*, and of its solemn days set aside for the Holy Innocents, the Presentation or Purification, the Annunciation, Saint Michael and All Angels, and All Saints. Starting with Saint Andrew (November 30), Rossetti sets out all the scriptural references to the saint, then provides "Biographical Additions" gathered from such traditional stories and legends as would have been available to her in Alban Butler's *Lives of the . . . Saints* (1756–1759, and frequently reprinted) or S. Baring-Gould's *Lives* (1872).[3] There follows a prayer appropriate to the character of the saint—for Saint Andrew, this is a prayer for "Large-Heartedness"—evidently of Rossetti's own composition; afterward comes "a memorial" in which scriptural passages about the saint are distributed in one column, with the Psalms appointed for the feast in parallel columns. To each saint, the author assigns a stone and a flower (for Saint Andrew, the jasper and the daisy).

"The Key to my Book" helps clarify this curious arrangement:

Those verses in the Book of Revelation [21:19–20] which name the twelve apostolic foundation stones of New Jerusalem, when set against the Calendar naturally assign the jasper to St. Andrew; and thence progressing in a regular order throughout, the amethyst at last to St. Jude: according to which arrangement, in default of any clue to the contrary, I have written concerning them. [p. xiv]

Rossetti's choice of flowers is even more arbitrary, for there is no catalogue similar to that of the stones:

[2]Rossetti offered the book to Alexander Macmillan in a letter of November 4, 1876: "I have by me a completed work, a sort of devotional reading-book for the red-letter Saints' Days, which of course is longing to see the light & which I shall be glad if you will consent to look at." The letter is quoted by Packer, *Christina Rossetti*, p. 328.

[3]Rossetti acknowledges Baring-Gould as the source of her "black letter Feasts" in *Time Flies* (entry for March 1). His *Lives of the Saints* (London: John Hodges, 1872–1889), which finally filled seventeen volumes, was being published even as Christina wrote. My references to *Time Flies* are by entry, rather than by page, and thus they apply to any of the several editions of the book.

But precious things of the earth and of the deep are for those who are gorgeously apparelled and live delicately and are in kings' courts. I think the Gospel records more lessons drawn by our Master from a seed or a plant than from a pearl. So I will, as it were, gather simples and try to spell out their lessons: I will adorn the shrines of Christ's friends with flowers, and plant a garden round their hallowed graves. [pp. xv–xvi][4]

The most interesting portions of *Called to be Saints* are its "additions": hagiographical, petrographical, botanical. Rossetti is most effective when she writes meditatively about the saints and their festivals, about the stones she assigns to the twelve apostles, and about the single-flower gardens she plants for each one of them, but much else seems mechanically ordered, as if with the help of a large memory or a good concordance.

The section on Saint Michael and All Angels is especially full, and includes much scripture but also much of Rossetti's distinctive prose.[5]

[4]Immediately following this explanation, Rossetti refers to Thomas Fuller, *The Worthies of England* (1662), who writes of flowers in his description of Norwich (under "Natural Commodities"): "In the morning when it groweth up, [the flower] is a lecture of Divine Providence. In the evening, when it is cut down withered, it is a lecture of human mortality." (Rossetti misquotes "withered" as "and withereth.") Fuller is writing of the reputation of flowers in the city, which was advanced by the Dutch who brought many "pleasurable curiosities" with them (*Worthies of England*, ed. John Freeman [New York: Barnes & Noble, 1952], p. 419). Rossetti probably consulted one of the nineteenth-century editions (1811, 1840). Fuller's *Church History of Britain* (1655) also went through several nineteenth-century editions, including J. S. Brewer's edition of 1845. Victorian interest in Fuller is further manifested in J. E. Bailey's *Life* (1874) and his edition of the *Sermons* in two volumes (1891).

[5]The epigraph of the book, which appears on a third separate leaf, following the title page and the dedication, is from Richard Hooker, *Of the Laws of Ecclesiastical Polity* (1597), V.71.11, the chapter of "Exceptions against our keeping of other festival days besides the Sabbath." Hooker is defending the keeping of saints' days against the objections of the protestant reformers; he concludes by saying that "to celebrate these religious and sacred days is to spend the flower of our time happily." What follows is quoted in *Called to be Saints*: "They are the splendour and outward dignity of our religion, forcible witnesses of ancient truth, provocations to the exercise of all piety, shadows of our endless felicity in heaven, on earth everlasting records and memorials, wherein they that [Hooker writes "which"] cannot be drawn to hearken unto that we teach, may only by looking upon that we do, in a manner read whatsoever we believe." Rossetti is quoting from John Keble's edition (1836, 1841, etc.). Packer (*Christina Rossetti*, p. 328) thinks that "the sonority and stately rhythms of the rhetorical prose of the great Anglican divines resound in her sentence-paragraphs," implying Hooker's particular importance in shaping Rossetti's prose style. This is a loose judgment that would be difficult, perhaps impossible, to prove.

237

One interesting passage describes the desolate life, with the antidote offered by the seraphic vision (Isaiah 6:1–8):

> When it seems (as sometimes through revulsion of feeling and urgency of Satan it may seem) that our yoke is uneasy and our burden unbearable, because our life is pared down and subdued and repressed to an intolerable level: and so in one moment every instinct of our whole self revolts against our lot, and we loathe this day of quietness and of sitting still, and writhe under a sudden sense of all we have irrecoverably foregone, of the right hand, or foot, or eye cast from us, of the halting-ness and maimedness of our entrance (if enter we do at last) into life, — then the Seraphim of Isaiah's vision making music in our memory revive hope in our heart.
>
> For at the sound of their mighty cry of full-flooding adoration, the very posts of the door moved and the house was filled with smoke. No lack there, nothing subdued there; no bridle, no curb, no self-sacrifice: outburst of sympathy, fulness of joy, pleasures for evermore, likeness that satisfieth; beauty for ashes, oil of joy for mourning, the garment of praise for the spirit of heaviness; things new out of God's treasure-house, —things old also, please God. . . . [pp. 435–36][6]

The contrast of the dull spirit with the vision of joy in its fullness provides a happy example of Rossetti's prose style. The circumstances of deprivation, described abstractly yet in plaintive detail, are nicely presented within the controlling view of praise and worship. A similar kind of genius touches the curious description of the flower assigned to Saint Michael and All Angels—flowerless flowers, the ferns, especially bracken and maidenhair. Through close observation, we may realize tender meanings: fronds have much to teach us, "for if instead of merely plucking a well-developed frond we sever its thick stalk in a smooth slant, the surface thus disclosed exhibits markings which (more or less) resemble the figure of the imperial spread eagle, the outline shifting according to the angle of the cut. Which leads us to a thought of wings out of sight, and angels unawares" (p. 449).

[6]Georgina Battiscombe quotes most of this passage in her biographical study, *Christina Rossetti: A Divided Life* (New York: Holt, Rinehart and Winston, 1981), p. 169, but for the purpose of demonstrating her point that Rossetti "knew moments of inward rebellion against the limitations and sameness of her life in a dull London house with only three old ladies for company." Such a reading takes a limited vision of Rossetti's artistic ability; surely this passage shows above all Rossetti's creative and imaginative power as a writer.

Called to be Saints is one of the most attractively printed of Rossetti's books. Every page is set out by rules (an ornamental device in each corner), with running headlines and section titles in gothic type. There are ornamental, engraved initial letters at the beginning of each sub-section, accompanied by engraved illustrations of each flower (or plant). The paper is an antique white, and the whole book is bound in dark blue, fine-ribbed buckram; the title is stamped in gold on the spine. Such care for the physical appearance of the book is, of course, typical of much Tractarian publishing, and all Rossetti's books, beginning, as we have seen, with *Annus Domini,* received devoted attention.

Letter and Spirit appeared only two years after its predecessor, using the same rules and devices on each page and the same type. It is clear upon opening this book that one is, as it were, entering a devotional work, as if George Herbert's admonition in *The Temple* (1633) had been given literal translation:

> Avoid, Profanenesse; come not here:
> Nothing but holy, pure, and cleare,
> Or that which groneth to be so,
> May at his perill further go.[7]

This little book on the commandments, like all the companion volumes Rossetti wrote, communicates a certain spare chastity, a purity of intention, a sense of duty and calling. Like the other devotional books, this one also depends upon another book or writing, which it intends to elucidate or support. Possibly more than the others, *Letter and Spirit* strikes a chord for charity, which is part of one's continuing duty. The two great commandments—and in them lies the spirit of the Old Testament letter of Mosaic code—lead to this knowledge: "Thou shalt love the Lord thy God with all thy heart, and with all thy soul, and with all thy mind, and with all thy strength. . . . Thou shalt love thy neighbour as thyself."

If we approach the book "in charity," we may better recognize both its strengths and its failings. The latter lie in the easily formulated and superficially considered theological statements, the former in Rossetti's kind and affectionate wish "to throw [her] grain of dust" into sustaining the devotional life of the ordinary faithful Christian. We

[7]*The Works of George Herbert*, ed. F. E. Hutchinson (1941; rpt. Oxford: Clarendon Press, 1959), "Superliminare," ll. 5–8.

can learn little from Rossetti's discussion of the Trinity: "A self-surrendering awe-struck reverence is all that beseems us in contemplating this Mystery of Mysteries, the Trinity in Unity" (p. 12), for this statement describes a devotional, not an intellectual understanding of doctrine. Rossetti similarly says we must be faithful to the Church and to "the Catholic religion" (Rossetti's inverted quotation marks), which teaches the unity and trinity of the Godhead:

> It seems that to grasp, hold fast, adore the Catholic Mystery leads up to man's obligation to grasp, hold fast, adore the Christian Mystery; rather than this to the other. What is Catholic underlies what is Christian: on the Catholic basis alone can the Christian structure be raised; even while to raise the superstructure on that foundation is the bounden duty of every soul within reach of the full Divine Revelation. [pp. 8–9]

The appeal to charity is more helpful:

> Party feeling, whether called religious zeal or national antagonism or political creed, becomes simple malice and is simply devilish when it leads us not only to condemn opponents . . . but to wish that they may really be as unworthy as history or rumour makes them, to court and hug and blaze abroad every tittle of evidence which tells against them, to turn a dull ear and lukewarm heart to everything which tells in their favour. "Charity . . . rejoiceth not in iniquity, but rejoiceth in the truth." It is a solemn thing to write history. [pp. 157–58]

William Michael Rossetti recalls in the *Memoir* of his sister that she lived above all by the precept, "Judge not, that ye be not judged." Her life was one of charity, long-suffering, and ready affection for everyone. William Michael's judgment that her faith was pure and absolute is clearly reflected in such a work as *Letter and Spirit:* "To learn that something in the Christian faith was credible *because it was reasonable,* or because it rested upon some historic evidence of fact, went against her. . . . 'My faith is faith; it is not evolved out of argumentation, nor does it seek the aid of that.'"[8] This last remark might well be the epigraph or motto for all Rossetti's devotional prose.

Letter and Spirit is somewhat awkwardly organized, for it attempts both to show how the Ten Commandments of the old law are reflected in the two commandments of the new covenant and to display

[8]See *PW*, pp. liv, lxvii.

the different commandments in relation to one another. The text contains numerous reminders of these divisions and branches; nonetheless, it leaves the impression of a peculiar and unnecessary confusion of parts without headings or obvious breaks—an unusual feature, not characteristic of the other devotional works. Another quality unique to *Letter and Spirit* is its use of "characters," such as (and notably) The Idler and The Money-grubber, both egregious transgressors of the fourth commandment, "that thou keep holy the Sabbath-day." The Idler is "the last man to draw an unswerving line of sacred demarcation around the seventh day. His mind is lax; his habits are unstable as water, dribbling out in this direction, overflowing in that, running short somewhere." The Money-grubber is also grossly indolent, but he repudiates Sunday for different reasons:

> If importunate decency transports our Money-grubber into his pew on Sunday morning, then before his mental eyes ledgers and their kin flaunt themselves, where neighbours only discern Bibles, Prayer-books, Hymn-books, on the desk. His bales of goods, cattle, hay-ricks, would be no more out of place in Church than is he himself; his money-bag would occupy a seat as worthily; they would put full as much heart into their attendance, and full as much spirituality. [p. 180]

In these portraits, Rossetti follows the tradition going back to the Greek writer Theophrastus and continuing in such English authors as Sir Thomas Overbury, John Earle, and Thomas Fuller, especially in his *Holy and Profane State* (1642), which Rossetti may have read (we know she was reading Fuller's *Worthies* because she alludes to it in *Called to be Saints*).[9] But the English writer Rossetti's characters first bring to mind is William Law. In *A Serious Call to a Devout and Holy Life* (1728, and frequently reprinted), Law not only draws notable "characters," such as the tradesman Calidus who is too busy to keep the Sabbath, but he also writes with an uncompromising and austere view of religion, filled nevertheless with charity and honest devotion. Of "imaginary conversations," I can fancy few more amiable than one between William Law and Christina Rossetti.

Rossetti's next prose work followed soon after her "notes" on the commandments. In 1885 she published *Time Flies*, descriptively subtitled "A Reading Diary." For this volume, SPCK provided an especially handsome format using heavy, laid hand-made paper with

[9]See note 4, above.

uneven deckle edges. The book has much in common with *Called to be Saints*, physically resembling it in size and binding. As for content, the earlier book concentrates on the prayer book saints, whereas the later one describes not only these saints but many others, especially martyrs of the Church and such British saints as Alban, David, and Chad. Thus every day of the year has an entry, and all the prayer book feasts are mentioned, as are many minor saints' days. Rossetti provides no commemoration for some days, however; rather she includes a poem or writes a meditation, occasionally related to the season of the year. *Time Flies*, like *Called to be Saints*, contains numerous personal observations, but it comes closer to being a book of commonplaces, thus reminding us of its diary-like composition.

Reading *Time Flies*, we seem to overhear Rossetti's speech, and since this book brings us so close to her attitudes and views, it enables us to fill out her portrait. The portrait is of a somber, sensible person, moved by the infinite and unremitting sadness of life, who is alternately touched by grief and quiet joy. The full entry for November 7, written about her sister Maria, who had died in November 1876, shows these bittersweet qualities well:

> One of the dearest and most saintly persons I ever knew, in foresight of her own approaching funeral, saw nothing attractive in the "hood and hatband" style toward which I evinced some old-fashioned leaning. "Why make everything as hopeless looking as possible?" she argued.
>
> And at a moment which was sad only for us who lost her, all turned out in harmony with her holy hope and joy.
>
> Flowers covered her, loving mourners followed her, hymns were sung at her grave, the November day brightened, and the sun (I vividly remember) made a miniature rainbow in my eyelashes.
>
> I have often thought of that rainbow since.
>
> May all who love enjoy cheerful little rainbows at the funerals of their beloved ones. [10]

In another entry (September 4), Rossetti writes again of human affection: we love others without wanting them to be different, and we readily overlook blemishes. Yet when one whom we have loved dies, the faults become memorable, even growing in beauty and helping

---

[10]See Battiscombe, *Christina Rossetti*, p. 169. The copy of the first edition of *Time Flies* at the University of Texas contains the author's marginal notes identifying persons and places mentioned in the text.

"our 'vale of misery' [turn] to a perennial well of very sweet and refreshing water."

We are not likely to forget such sensitively felt passages as these, no more than we can ignore the particular kind of religious devotion that shaped Rossetti's life. Rossetti was an Anglican in the High Church tradition, and much of her writing reflects the depth of her belief. One need hardly know more about her biography than that she was above all else an inheritor of Tractarianism in the supreme flowering of the Oxford Movement. Consequently, she saw the Church of England as a true and historical part (some would say "branch") of Catholic Christendom. She can speak naturally, without really being smug or arrogant, of "our venerable Anglican Mother Church" (entry for June 28), and write:

> Great is our privilege as members of the English Church, in that we are not commanded, or invited, or in any way encouraged to assert what contradicts history, or to override facts by pious beliefs, or in any form to hold "the thing that is not."
>
> When we reflect on points susceptible of improvement in our beloved Mother Church, it is well to betake ourselves to prayer; well also to give thanks for her grace of sincerity . . . [March 18]

This comment comes in her commemoration of Saint Edward, King of the West Saxons, who might have been martyred (the Anglican calendar is quite proper in its silence on this point).

Rossetti's interest in the natural environment is especially apparent in her devotional prose, but nowhere so clearly as in *Time Flies*. Rossetti saw the natural world as emblematic of God's Incarnational presence: "To him 'that hath ears to hear,' any good creature of God may convey a message" (March 31). Thus she observes the significance of a millipede, jackdaws and starlings, a four-leaf clover, frogs, a tame robin, a spider in its web. Her observation of a water rat, or possibly "a water-haunting bird," illustrates how she sees nature and interprets it:

> One day long ago I sat in a certain garden by a certain ornamental water . . . so long and so quietly that a wild garden creature or two made its appearance. . . . I was absorbed that afternoon in anxious thought, yet the slight incident pleased me. If by chance people noticed me they may have thought how dull and blank I must be feeling: and partly they would have been right, but partly wrong.

243

Many . . . whom we pity as even wretched, may in reality, as I was at that moment, be conscious of some small secret fount of pleasure: a bubble, perhaps, yet lit by a dancing rainbow.

I hope so and I think so: for we and all creatures alike are in God's hand, and God loves us. [April 10]

Everything in nature can teach the love of God and his presence. Rossetti recalls her first experience of death when, in early childhood, she found a dead mouse in the grounds of a cottage. In sympathy, she buried the mouse in a mossy spot. Remembering the place, she went back a day or two later and, moving the moss away, discovered a black insect: "I fled in horror, and for long years ensuing I never mentioned this ghastly adventure to anyone." The initial sympathy, and the horror of decay, were both childish reactions, she now understands: "Contemplating death from a wider and wiser view-point, I would fain reverse the order of those feelings: dwelling less and less on the mere physical disgust, while more and more on the rest and safety; on the perfect peace of death, please God" (March 4).

In order to read Rossetti's many accounts of martyrdom and saintly deaths appropriately, one must appreciate in them the spirit of an intense Incarnationalism, in which the Word made flesh discourses with those who can speak and hear. Saint Richard (April 3) edifies us in his death: having collapsed when hearing Mass, he later spoke gently from his deathbed, "I was glad when they said unto me, We will go into the house of the Lord." Saint Boniface (or Winfrid) is an English martyr who had "from early childhood . . . set his heart on piety and the service of God"; when he was about to be executed, he placed under his head a volume of the Gospels, on which he stretched forth his neck for the blow of the executioner. Although Rossetti borrows from various sources, particularly in writing her martyrologies—*Time Flies* is after all "a reading diary"—she shapes these materials to accord with her own design. This design emphasizes her Incarnational orientation, her High Church devotion to sacramental worship with its encouragement of a lively sense of God at work in all creation.[11]

---

[11]G. B. Tennyson cogently describes Rossetti as "the true inheritor of the Tractarian devotional mode in poetry" (*VDP*, p. 198), thus reinforcing Raymond Chapman's view of Rossetti as a full product of the Oxford Movement: see Chapman's *Faith and Revolt: Studies in the Literary Influence of the Oxford Movement* (London: Weidenfeld and Nicolson, 1970), especially the chapter "Uphill All the Way." Rossetti

The last of Rossetti's devotional prose works is also the longest. *The Face of the Deep* (1892) contains more than 500 pages of close commentary on the Apocalypse. But it is not so much a commentary as a loosely connected and free-ranging discussion of many topics and ideas that concerned Rossetti. The entire Book of Revelation is set out a verse at a time; for each verse, Rossetti provides some discussion, often extended, at other times rather abbreviated, depending on her inclination. But if one is hoping to discover a theological or analytical exegesis of Revelation, this is not the work in which to find it. Rossetti more than once apologizes for what she is doing, because she hopes no one will misunderstand her purpose: "What I write professes to be a *surface* study [Rossetti's italics] of an unfathomable depth: if it incites any to dive deeper than I attain to, it will so far have accomplished a worthy work. My suggestions do not necessarily amount to beliefs; they may be no more than tentative thoughts compatible with acknowledged ignorance" (p. 365). The book is a difficult one to read consecutively from beginning to end, for it seems to make no progress, and it develops by a loose association of ideas.

In the discussion of Revelation 8:2, "And I saw the seven angels which stood before God; and to them were given seven trumpets," Rossetti sees first Jericho and its destruction, then the ark of the Lord placed before Jericho; she then remembers that Christ is "our true and sole Ark of Safety" and that he has promised to be with his Church even to the end of the world. Christ's promise of salvation to his Church and to his people reminds us that we are to worship him regularly; thus the Sabbath day should be kept holy and undefiled, for it "ranks amongst venerable and immutable Divine institutions, dating back to unfallen man in the Garden of Eden" (p. 243). This observation gives Rossetti the chance to comment on contemporary worship, which is desultory and mean:

Already in England . . . the signs of the times are ominous: Sunday is being diverted by some to business, by others to pleasure; Church congregations are often meagre, and so services are chilled. Our solemn

---

collected her devotional poetry, nearly all of which had appeared in the prose works, in *Verses* (1893). William Michael Rossetti included all this verse in his edition of the poetry in 1904, but he distributed it among a rather confusing set of headings; even so, it is obvious that much of the poetry is either narrowly "devotional" or generally religious. What has been said about the Tractarian temper of Rossetti's poetry applies almost equally well to her prose.

feasts languish, and our fasts where are they? . . . So Joshua and his host when summoned to storm Jericho day after day for seven days, must amongst those days have kept one unexampled Sabbath, if not in the letter yet in the spirit. [pp. 243–44]

Thus we return to Jericho, but not before a string of more or less related ideas are laid before us.[12]

The Face of the Deep is a patchwork of scriptural citations, meditations, admonitions, studies of spiritual climate, and self-criticism—of almost everything except the proposed subject, the Apocalypse itself. In *The Face of the Deep*, Rossetti is engaged in a self-study similar to that of "holy George Herbert," to whom she makes one notable reference: the concluding line of "Miserie." In this poem Herbert has been complaining of man's foolishness, his imperfection, and consequently his loss of Paradise; but whom he has really meant to criticize is, as he says in the final line, "My God, I mean my self." Rossetti's self-study, though less subtle than Herbert's, is more explicit; she prays that "God grant us . . . self-knowledge and humility" (p. 226).

Self-knowledge, charity, avoidance of judgment of others, and energetic and ceaseless instruction characterize Rossetti's devotional prose, and evidently her own personality. Her attraction to these qualities is at work in the "commentary" on the Apocalypse, as in the studies of the Benedicite and of the commandments. But there is another, complementary, aspect of the prose works, illustrated most obviously in the book of collects, the consideration of the festivals, and the diary of daily reflections. And that aspect is the impossible desire to prepare oneself to know something of the incomprehensible mystery of God. The attitude is familiar in the Anglo-Catholicism that Rossetti practiced: God cannot really be known except as he wishes to reveal himself; and to find him, one must exercise patience and prayer, and everywhere in the created world look thoughtfully. Patience, indeed! In her prefatory note to *The Face of the Deep*, Rossetti tells us that patience is the lesson in the Book of Revelation: "I seek and hope to find Patience in this Book of awful import.

---

[12]Packer writes that Rossetti first knew the Bible, and particularly the Book of Revelation, from childhood, when her mother read it to her (*Christina Rossetti*, p. 5). Another favorite of Frances Rossetti was Jeremy Taylor, whose *Holy Living* and *Holy Dying* must have touched a sympathetic listener in Christina Rossetti. Taylor's manuals possess that kind of systematic austerity and orderly, sometimes elevated devotion that underlies so much of Rossetti's own work. She alludes approvingly to Taylor, though in passing, in *Time Flies* (entry for August 19).

Patience, at the least: and along with that grace whatever treasures beside God may vouchsafe me."

Perhaps this last work in fact combines dutiful, regulated study and its waiting on patience with the happiness of fulfillment, or at least the joy of expectation, which may, after all, be the greatest gift of sacramental understanding and faith in the Incarnation. As the commentary in *The Face of the Deep* demonstrates, Revelation 8:4 ("And the smoke of the incense, which came with the prayers of the saints, ascended up before God out of the angel's hand") offers an especially rich text for someone such as Christina Rossetti, whose affections always wanted, but did not need to be stirred, except as she so determined. Rossetti observes that

> the incense and smoke of the incense should kindle us to utmost adoration and love, by thus setting before us Christ Who for our sakes made Himself once for all a whole Burnt Offering, an Offering and a sweet-smelling Savour to the Glory of God the Father; and Who in the Blessed Sacrament of His Body and Blood having left to His Church a perpetual Memorial of His sole sufficient Sacrifice, receives us and our petitions into the "secret place" of that Presence and sets us in heavenly places with His own Self. [p. 245]

PART THREE

ROSSETTI: PREDECESSORS
AND CONTEMPORARIES

DAVID A. KENT

"By thought, word, and deed": George Herbert and Christina Rossetti

When W. David Shaw in a 1981 review identified Christina Rossetti as "the George Herbert among Victorian Anglicans," he was reiterating an established critical assumption.[1] About the time of her death in 1894, when her reputation stood highest, she was called "the sister" of Herbert by Edmund Gosse and "the poetic inheritor" of Herbert and other seventeenth-century devotional poets by William Sharp.[2] Her massive collection of religious lyrics, *Verses* (1893), even prompted some enthusiastic reviewers to rank her "higher" than Herbert or any of her predecessors in the expression of "religious senti-ment." This kinship with Herbert had actually been noted by the reviewer of her first published volume of verse, "*Goblin Market*" *and Other Poems* (1862), who observed "the manner of Herbert" in some of her devotional lyrics.[3] Surprisingly, despite the frequent association

[1]W. David Shaw, review of G. B. Tennyson's *Victorian Devotional Poetry: The Tractarian Mode, VS* 24 (1981): 85.

[2]Edmund Gosse, "Christina Rossetti," in *Critical Kit-Kats* (New York: Dodd, Mead, 1896), p. 156; William Sharp, "Some Reminiscences of Christina Rossetti," *Atlantic Monthly* 75 (June 1895): 748.

[3]For Rossetti's possibly "higher" status than Herbert, see W. Robertson Nicoll, "Christina Rossetti," review of Mackenzie Bell's *Christina Rossetti: A Biographical and Critical Study, Bookman* 7 (March 1898): 74; the phrase "religious sentiment" is part of a passage praising Rossetti's religious poetry in the anonymous "Christina Georgina Rossetti," *Dial* 18, no. 206 (January 16, 1895): 38; the "manner of Herbert" is noted by an anonymous reviewer in "Miss Rossetti's Goblin Market," *Eclectic Review*, n.s. 2

250

of Rossetti's devotional poetry with Herbert's, there has been little analysis of their literary interrelations. Following Rossetti's death and the gradual decline in her reputation, biographers and critics—with two exceptions—have remained satisfied with noting possible parallels with Herbert or commenting briefly on superficial similarities.[4] Mary Sandars's tentative remark is all too typical: "we feel that had George Herbert not existed, some of Christina Rossetti's poems would not have been composed in their present form."[5] If the nature of Rossetti's indebtedness to Herbert can be more precisely delineated, it will help to clarify her own distinctive achievement in devotional poetry.

Any study of influences on Rossetti, however, must first acknowledge special difficulties. Her brother, William Michael Rossetti, put it succinctly in his *Reminiscences:* "Christina Rossetti has passed away; personally known to few, understood by still fewer, silent to almost all."[6] Her reserved manner and reclusive habits of life seriously hamper any examination of her work or account of her life. Since she was, as she told Katherine Hinkson, "'tenacious of [her] obscurity,'" her letters published to date contain few Keatsian self-revelations.[7] Usually they report matters of health, weather, and visitors, and only occasionally mention circumstances of publication (normally to her other brother, Dante Gabriel Rossetti) or the subjects of her reading and reflection. When Herbert Gilchrist wanted to retrieve letters his mother Anne had sent to the poet, William Michael Rossetti had to return disappointing news and described his sister as follows: "She is one of those persons who (unlike myself) wd. bury letters, & personal

---

(June 1862): 494. For other comments linking Rossetti and Herbert, see James Ashcroft Noble, "Christina Rossetti," *Literary Opinion,* n.s. 6 (December 1891): 157; and Mackenzie Bell, *Christina Rossetti: A Biographical and Critical Study* (London: Hurst and Blackett, 1898), pp. 243, 254.

[4]The exceptions are Molly Mahood, "Two Anglican Poets," in *Poetry and Humanism* (New Haven: Yale University Press, 1950), pp. 22–53; and Conrad Festa, "Studies in Christina Rossetti's 'Goblin Market' and Other Poems" (diss., University of South Carolina, 1969).

[5]Mary F. Sandars, *The Life of Christina Rossetti* (London: Hutchinson, [1930]), p. 277. See also Eleanor Walter Thomas, *Christina Georgina Rossetti* (New York: Columbia University Press, 1931), p. 167.

[6]William Michael Rossetti, *Some Reminiscences of William Michael Rossetti,* 2 vols. (London: Brown, Langham, 1906), II, 315.

[7]Letter of September 14, 1893, as quoted in Lona Mosk Packer, *Christina Rossetti* (Berkeley: University of California Press, 1963), p. 394.

documents or details generally, in oblivion: she herself for instance, as a rule, destroys as soon as answered all letters that she receives.[8]

What glimpses Rossetti's letters give of literary activity suggest a continuing round of reading and writing. She was, of course, scrupulously guarded about what she allowed herself to read and on the whole probably read less than other members of her family.[9] Mackenzie Bell remembered that the two bookcases in her Torrington Square home (where after 1876 she lived with her mother and two elderly aunts) contained many "religious and devotional" works.[10] Among these, no doubt, were the writings of such Anglican theologians as Richard Hooker, Thomas Fuller, Lancelot Andrewes, and Jeremy Taylor, to all of whom she alludes in her own work.[11] Rossetti's lack of privacy throughout her working life only accentuated her withdrawn, reticent nature. When we consider her living arrangements together with her undeserved reputation for "indolence," we can only be astonished at a life whose industriousness has been grossly underestimated.[12] The story of her writing on a washstand as she stood in the small bedroom at the rear of the house is one of those literary anecdotes which misleads more than it informs.[13]

Rossetti's resolute guarding of her privacy extends to her acknowledgments of debt to other poets. She does write a poem "On Keats," and there is a short imitation of Blake's "The Lamb" in *The Face of the Deep* (p. 44). Generally, though, she rarely mentions other poets. An observation Bell makes is therefore pertinent to this discussion: "Seldom in her books did she quote the verses of other poets. Probably this was because, in her case, it was so easy to write verse. But was there

[8]Letter of July 4, 1886 in *Letters of William Michael Rossetti to Anne Gilchrist and Her Son Herbert Gilchrist*, ed. Clarence Gohdes and Paull Franklin Baum (1934; rpt. New York: AMS Press, 1968), p. 172. See also *FL*, pp. 169 and 212.

[9]Bell, *Christina Rossetti*, p. 14. A standard reading list of devotional works associated with Rossetti is given by, for example, Eugene Mason, "Two Christian Poets," in *A Book of Preferences in Literature* (London: John G. Wilson, 1915), p. 120. And yet, even in *FL* (e.g., pp. 150 and 174), we find references to her reading Sara Coleridge and Marlborough's memoirs, authors that suggest more extensive reading than she has been credited with.

[10]Bell, *Christina Rossetti*, p. 148.

[11]Fuller, for example, is quoted in *CS*, p. xvi, while Andrewes is quoted in *TF*, p. 259.

[12]Ralph H. Bellas describes Rossetti as having "an inclination towards indolence" in *Christina Rossetti* (Boston: Twayne, 1977), p. 42.

[13]*Three Rossettis: Unpublished Letters to and from Dante Gabriel, Christina, William*, ed. Janet Camp Troxell (Cambridge: Harvard University Press, 1937), p. 138.

another reason? It is a somewhat interesting field of speculation."[14] Bell does not pursue his "speculation" on the subject, but that the poet did preserve an aura of secrecy about her work is clearly suggested by an aside to her brother William Michael in a letter of July 21, 1879: "At last I can indulge you with a gleam of light on some of those mysterious literary avocations at which you have occasionally caught me——" (*FL*, pp. 79–80).

I would suggest that this kind of secrecy was partly Rossetti's way of trying to preserve a world independent of her family members and partly a way of helping depersonalize poetry which, as she saw from the reactions to her brother Dante Gabriel's love poems, was vulnerable to reductive biographical interpretation.[15] Furthermore, her secrecy was a way of veiling indebtedness and thereby enhancing the originality of her own poetry. As a signal of poetic genius, originality in style or manner may be one of the more dubious legacies of Romanticism, but Rossetti was conscious of its importance. There is evidence, for example, that her revision of poems sometimes eliminated obvious echoes of earlier poets.[16] She certainly concerned herself with the public response to her publications and read reviews assiduously.[17] The review of "*Goblin Market*" *and Other Poems* mentioned earlier would therefore not have escaped her attention. This review included the comment that the "influence of Tennyson" is "suspected" but "of positive discipleship and imitation," there is happily "no trace." Although the rather ambivalent commentator goes on to praise the "originality" of Rossetti's poetry, he does point out that "'The love of Christ which passeth knowledge'" (quoted in the review) has evidently been written "in the manner of Herbert."[18] More alarming to Rossetti may have been comments in a review of the American edition of the same volume four years later. Here her debt to Herbert is

[14]Bell, *Christina Rossetti*, pp. 298–99.
[15]See her early remarks (April 28, 1849) quoted by Georgina Battiscombe, *Christina Rossetti: A Divided Life* (New York: Holt, Rinehart and Winston, 1981), p. 54. For Dante Gabriel, see *Letters of Dante Gabriel Rossetti*, ed. Oswald Doughty and J. R. Wahl (Oxford: Clarendon Press, 1965–1967), 4 vols. II, 821; IV, 1857 and 1896. On Rossetti's elimination of personal feelings in her poems, see the comments of G. M. Hatton as quoted in *The Rossetti-Macmillan Letters*, ed. Lona Mosk Packer (Berkeley: University of California Press, 1963), p. 107, n. 1.
[16]For the removal of an echo of Coleridge in "The convent threshold," see Packer, *Christina Rossetti*, p. 129.
[17]See, for example, *FL*, p. 27, pp. 43–44, 122.
[18]"Miss Rossetti's Goblin Market," pp. 493, 494.

again cited but this time in a gesture of back-handed praise: "In them [her "devotional pieces"] she seems to us more imitative, less to be writing from the fulness of her own mind and heart than in the other poems. Many of them would have been worthy of Herbert if Herbert had done them."[19]

Rossetti's concern with appearing merely derivative of her greatest predecessor in devotional poetry may thus explain the dearth of overt references to him in her writings. That she was, on the whole, sensitive to possible charges of unacknowledged borrowing emerges in her introduction to *Called to be Saints:*

> My occasional linguistic statements are given at second-hand, as are most of the authorities I cite whether by name or anonymously. No graver slur could attach to my book than would be a reputation for prevalent originality: and I hope my here, once for all, acknowledging how deeply and widely I am indebted to the spoken or written words of many, will be accepted as sheltering me equally from charges of rashness and of plagiarism. [p. xvii]

Here the embarrassed self-defense, the protesting disavowal of originality (though this is a volume of religious prose), the touch of impatience, and the long-delayed mention of plagiarism all seem to suggest her awareness of what W. Jackson Bate has called "the burden of the past."[20] Rossetti was caught between betraying marks of her poetic apprenticeship (in which Herbert figures centrally) and her desire to succeed both with a reading public who valued singularity and with critics, such as H. B. Forman, who encouraged poets "to throw off conventionality and assert originality in form and style."[21] Rossetti's dilemma does not affect her particular debt to Herbert or the pragmatic strategy of secrecy she adopted to overcome it. But, when added to her natural reticence, her suppression of references makes it much more difficult for critics to substantiate Herbert's influence objectively.

In 1835, just five years after Rossetti's birth, the Rev. R. Cattermole compiled a two-volume anthology entitled *Sacred Poetry of the*

---

[19]"Miss Rossetti's Poems," *Nation* 3, no. 55 (July 19, 1866): 48.

[20]W. Jackson Bate, *The Burden of the Past and the English Poet* (London: Chatto & Windus, 1971), p. vii.

[21]H. B. Forman, "Criticisms on Contemporaries, No. VI, The Rossettis—part I," *Tinsley's Magazine* 5 (1869): 66.

Seventeenth Century, in which Herbert's lyrics are prominent. Cattermole laments that Herbert is presently "known to few besides the
curious literary enquirer," but his selection is intended to reintroduce
Herbert to the English public.[22] Almost as testimony to such renewed
interest, William Pickering's edition of Herbert's complete writings
(the first such edition) appeared immediately afterward to mark the
poet's official reappearance after a century of obscurity.[23] Other
important editions appeared in the nineteenth century (e.g., that by
Rev. Robert A. Wilmott for Routledge and George Gilfillan's edition
of the *Poetical Works* for J. Nichol in Edinburgh), not to mention the
increasing number of selections or editions of *The Temple* published in
the last thirty years of the century. But it was the Pickering edition
that found its way into the Rossetti household. Each of the two volumes, one of prose and one of poetry, bears Christina Rossetti's sig-
nature and volume I (the prose) is dated December 5, 1848, her
eighteenth birthday.[24]

Among Rossetti's contemporaries, Herbert received unequal treatment. The Tractarian poet Isaac Williams, for example, dedicated a
poem to "Meek Herbert" in *The Cathedral*, a work whose structure was
itself partly inspired by *The Temple*.[25] Elizabeth Barrett Browning,
however, barely mentioned Herbert in her rapid survey of English
poets in *The Greek Christian Poets and the English Poets*, and he apparently made little mark on either Robert Browning or Tennyson.[26] On
the other hand, John Ruskin, well-known to the Rossettis, found
much "solace" and "wisdom" in Herbert and ranked him as one of his

[22]*Sacred Poetry of the Seventeenth Century*, ed. Rev. R. Cattermole (1835; rpt. New
York: Burt Franklin, 1969), p. 229. There are some useful nineteenth-century references to Herbert in Joseph E. Duncan, *The Revival of Metaphysical Poetry: The History
of a Style, 1800 to the Present* (1959; rpt. New York: Octagon, 1969); see, for example,
pp. 43–45.

[23]*The Works of George Herbert in Prose and Verse*, 2 vols. (London: William Pickering, 1835, 1836). I have used Pickering's third edition (1846) and hereafter refer to it
in the text as Pickering, volume number, and page number.

[24]Mahood, "Two Anglican Poets," p. 309, n. 11. Rossetti may later have encoun-
tered *The Poetical Works of George Herbert* (London: James Nisbet, 1857), since
several of the illustrations in this volume were by a family friend, the artist John R.
Clayton. On Clayton, see Bell, *Christina Rossetti*, pp. 179–80.

[25]Isaac Williams, *The Cathedral, or the Catholic and Apostolic Church in England*
(Oxford: John Henry Parker, 1843), pp. 192–93 and "Advertisement," p. v.

[26]Elizabeth Barrett Browning, *The Greek Christian Poets and the English Poets* (London: Chapman & Hall, 1863), p. 146.

favorite poets.[27] And William Dyce's painting, *George Herbert at Bemerton*, exhibited at the Royal Academy in 1861, reveals the kind of idealization of Herbert possible for an artist influenced by both Pre-Raphaelitism and Tractarianism.[28] One Victorian assessment of Herbert which provides an interesting perspective is that of George Mac-Donald (a writer Rossetti knew) in *England's Antiphon*, a history cum anthology of English religious verse with Robert White's drawing of Herbert on the title page.[29] The "motions" of Herbert's muse may be as "grotesque" as Donne's, in MacDonald's view, but Herbert "is always a gentleman": "We could not bear to part with his most fantastic oddities, they are so interpenetrated with his genius as well as his art" (MacDonald, pp. 114, 183). Like MacDonald, most writers acquainted with Herbert were prepared to forgive him his "oddities" (MacDonald, p. 187) and "quaintness" for the sake of the inspired "intensity" of his poetry.[30] It was Coleridge who believed that Herbert's "quaintness" had "blinded modern readers to the great general merit of his poems" (Pickering II, 384). It may be no coincidence that Rossetti's critics have often cited "quaintness" as one of the central qualities she shares with Herbert.[31]

While Coleridge confessed to having been initially amused by Herbert's "quaintness," he later came to read *The Temple* for the "substantial comfort" it provided.[32] In his "Notes on the Temple and Syn-

[27]See John L. Idol, "George Herbert and John Ruskin," *George Herbert Journal* 4 (1980): 13, 14; and George P. Landow, *The Aesthetic and Critical Theories of John Ruskin* (Princeton: Princeton University Press, 1971), p. 363.

[28]William Dyce (1806–1864) was a leader of the High Church movement, composed church music, and painted frescoes in All Saints' Church, Margaret Street; these factors make it likely that Rossetti knew of him. The picture in question is most conveniently reproduced in Timothy Hilton, *The Pre-Raphaelites* (New York: Harry N. Abrams, 1970), p. 131. Joe K. Law has discussed the significance of Dyce's picture in "William Dyce's *George Herbert at Bemerton*," *Journal of Pre-Raphaelite Studies* 3 (1982): 45–55. See also the major study by Marcia Pointon, *William Dyce 1806–1864: A Critical Biography* (Oxford: Clarendon Press, 1979), pp. 175–76.

[29]George MacDonald, *England's Antiphon* (London: Macmillan, [1868]). Hereafter cited in the text as MacDonald and page number. I am grateful to Roderick McGillis for alerting me to MacDonald's book. For Rossetti's knowledge of MacDonald, see Bell, *Christina Rossetti*, p. 121.

[30]*The Treasury of Sacred Song: Selected from the English Lyrical Poetry of Four Centuries*, ed. Francis T. Palgrave (Oxford: Clarendon Press, 1890), p. 333 (notes).

[31]See, for example, Thomas, *Christina Georgina Rossetti*, p. 129; and Sandars, *Life of Christina Rossetti*, p. 54.

[32]*The Collected Letters of Samuel Taylor Coleridge*, 6 vols., ed. Earl Leslie Griggs (Oxford: Clarendon Press, 1959), IV, 893.

agogue" he states the qualifications of the ideal reader of Herbert. Such a reader should be "both a zealous and an orthodox, both a devout and a devotional, Christian," and "a child of the Church" who finds the "forms and ordinances [of the Church] aids of religion, not sources of formality" (Pickering II, 379). Rossetti was just such a reader. Unlike the majority of her contemporaries, she read Herbert not only as an important master for her poetic apprenticeship—as her manner, style, and techniques reveal—but also as an act of Christian devotion. She valued the powerful example of holiness he embodied and what his dedication to the calling of Christian poet implied and taught her. I would argue that his influence on her was seminal and formative and that there are grounds for agreeing with Conrad Festa's contention that "her poetry, and most especially her devotional poetry, owes more to him than to any other single poet.[33]

Rossetti's mother introduced her to Herbert's poetry at an early age. When she was about thirteen, Rossetti copied out Herbert's "Vertue" as the first entry in a commonplace book that Frances Rossetti kept for her pupils and then subsequently for her children.[34] The young poet later wrote her own imitation of Herbert's poem and included "Charity" among the verses privately printed by her grandfather, Gaetano Polidori, in 1847. In a manuscript note to "Charity" she declares her debt to Herbert with a forthrightness that in retrospect can only be called uncharacteristic: "'The foregoing verses are imitated from that beautiful little poem *Virtue* by George Herbert'" (*PW*, p. 465). I say uncharacteristic since, with one exception, this reference to Herbert is her only explicit allusion to his influence on her in the entire body of her work. If we examine "Charity" (*PW*, p. 84) in the light of its model, we see that Rossetti's debt to Herbert is, as we might expect, first of all a matter of poetic technique.[35]

[33]Festa, "Christina Rossetti's 'Goblin Market,'" p. 190.

[34]Battiscombe, *Christina Rossetti*, pp. 22–23. As Battiscombe notes, p. 22, Rossetti read *The Sacred Harp* (Dublin: W. F. Wakeman, 1834) at about fourteen years of age, but this anthology of religious lyrics contains only one of Herbert's poems, "Sweet Peace," pp. 105–6. The book had been given to William Rossetti by Reverend T. W. Paule in 1837, and it came to Christina Rossetti in 1844.

[35]If Rossetti did not receive the Pickering edition until 1848, she could have known "Vertue" from part 1, chapter 5 of Izaak Walton's *Compleat Angler*, another book in the family library. My information about such books comes from W. E. Fredeman's introduction to *Books from the Libraries of Christina, Dante Gabriel, and William Michael Rossetti* (London: Bertram Rota, 1973), catalogue no. 180. I am grateful to William Whitla for showing me this catalogue and the one in note 70 below.

Besides its remarkable precociousness, Rossetti's imitation is interesting for the modifications she introduces into the structure of the original. In Herbert's four four-line stanzas three major images ("Sweet day," "Sweet rose," and "Sweet spring") are used to illustrate the theme of worldy transience; only "a sweet and vertuous soul" in the final stanza (virtue furnishing the decisive power) is said to survive material destruction. The key number in "Vertue" is four (consider the catalogue of four adjectives in the first line, the four-word refrain in the opening three stanzas, the iambic tetrameter rhythm, and the four four-line stanzas). The key number in "Charity," however, is three. Three images in Rossetti's poem embody transience, the sun and two flowers (Herbert's rose plus the myrtle), and these images help exemplify the speaker's encounter with death. The flowers in the first stanza last but a day, and the "Summer sun" in the second stanza is just as short-lived. In the third and final stanza a new Pauline triad of personifications is invoked and said to embody permanent values: "All, all, save Love alone, shall die; / For Faith and Hope shall merge together / In Charity." The greater stress Rossetti places on the number three in structural terms is entirely appropriate to the trinitarian overtones she intends to suggest. She has nevertheless made her poem very rhythmically similar to Herbert's; both poems are written in iambic tetrameter with important interventions by trochaic and spondaic feet. "Charity" has more instances of enjambement which seem to speed up reading, but this impression is misleading because both poems have an equal proportion of caesuras, terminal commas, and full stops.

Herbert's attention to symmetry and numerical balance in "Vertue" characterizes many other poems in The Temple, and reading these others would have reinforced for Rossetti what she had already absorbed. The formal equivalence between number and structural elements is most marked in poems such as "Trinitie Sunday" or "The Call," both more or less based on patterns of three. Such concern with symmetry is part of Herbert's effort to imitate and recreate the divine orderliness, beauty, and significant detail of creation. Rossetti is equally careful of formal balance in her verse and presumably for the same reasons. The trinitarian structure of "Charity," for example, recurs in the three-part development of theme in "None with Him" (PW, pp. 238–39) and "Weary in well-doing" (I, 182), both composed in 1864. Typically, the first two stanzas state contrary propositions (thesis, antithesis), and the third provides some kind of resolution (synthesis). Although there is no evidence that Herbert directly inspired either poem, or even "A better resurrection" (I, 68) of 1857, the structural design of all three poems was based on what Rossetti learned from Herbert about the apt congruence of form and meaning in devotional poetry.

In dedicating all his skill with language to God, Herbert bequeathed to later poets lyrics of considerable freedom and inventiveness that yet conformed to the concomitant restrictions imposed by faith and doctrine. In addition to symmetry and balance, where appropriate, Herbert also exploits lyric shape and syntax to match form with meaning. For example, the circularity of "Sinnes round," in which the first line is also the last line and the last line of each stanza (again, there are three stanzas) is the first line of the next, formally suggests the vicious "ring" of sin which is the poem's subject. An even more elaborate kind of patterned repetition occurs in "A Wreath," where the words in the second half of a line are repeated in the first half of the next line so that the whole twelve lines of the lyric are intricately knit together. Rossetti's "If love is not worth loving" (II, 305–6) is a less complex variant of the same technique in which alliteration and repetition of the central terms provide the weaving effect. Similarly, in "All heaven is blazing yet" (II, 317) Rossetti repeats different forms of "will" and "choose" to stress her uncompromising dedication to Christ. One of Rossetti's favorite poetic forms displays her appreciation for formal significance through the elements of balance, symmetry, and repetition. She uses the roundel more than any other set form, except the sonnet. The roundel consists of three stanzas, the first and third with four lines each, the central stanza with three lines. The form also features the three-fold repetition of the opening phrase in the fourth and then again the final line. The roundel thus formally lends itself to a didactic intention and, by its circular and repetitive features, also fosters a sense of inevitability—the inevitability Rossetti thought appropriate to human powerlessness before providential will. Her frequent use of the roundel gives her devotional poetry much of its ceremonial and liturgical flavor.[36] "Lord, grant us grace to rest upon Thy word" (II, 260) is an especially effective example, since the repeated phrase itself constitutes an independent prayer.

Herbert's contraction of line length, as in the last line of each stanza of "Vertue," becomes especially significant in such poems as "Easter Wings," whose form has become completely emblematic.

[36]On this point I differ with Mahood, who thinks Rossetti's use of the roundel "gives a false and manufactured air to many of . . . [her] devotional poems" ("Two Anglican Poets," p. 47).

DAVID A. KENT

Rossetti borrows this technique to some degree in her brilliant brief lyric "Ash Wednesday" (II, 221–22). The final line in both stanzas in this confessional poem suddenly contracts in imitation of the poet's felt impotence to articulate first her guilt and then her gratitude. Here is the first stanza:

> My God, my God, have mercy on my sin,
> For it is great; and if I should begin
> To tell it all, the day would be too small
> To tell it in.

More important than the masterly management of rhythm and allusion here (including the poem's probable echoes of Herbert's "Praise [II]") is the fact that the contraction of the final line has become formally equivalent to an act of contrition. What the poet finally offers God, then, is a deferral from speech, the assumption of a posture of listening, of silently waiting upon the Word.[37]

A related technique, isolating a phrase at the end of a stanza (as in Herbert's "Gratefulnesse"), is a means of stressing certain words. If the phrase is repeated (as in his "Unkindnesse"), it becomes a refrain and the poet can exploit its different implications as the context shifts with each additional stanza. Rossetti's "'It is finished'" (II, 154–55) illustrates her use of this technique. These are the opening two stanzas:

> Dear Lord, let me recount to Thee
> Some of the great things Thou hast done
> For me, even me
> Thy little one.

[37]Herbert takes the form and meaning congruence even further in "Nature" and in "Deniall": "Then was my heart broken, as was my verse." It should also be noted that Rossetti exploits typographical space rather in the manner of a Herbert emblem poem when she positions "Amor Mundi" (I, 213–14) and "Up-Hill" (I, 65–66) one after the other in her "Goblin Market," "The Prince's Progress," and Other Poems (London: Macmillan, 1875). With its short lines (and its clipped rhythms), "Up-Hill" represents the "narrow" way to life; in contrast, "Amor Mundi," with its long lines, slippery participles, and bouncing rhythms, represents the "broad" way to destruction (Matt. 7:13–14). That these two poems are deliberately paired is persuasively argued by Eugene J. Brzenk, "'Up-Hill' and 'Down-' by Christina Rossetti," VP 10 (1972): 367–71.

> It was not I that cared for Thee,—
> But Thou didst set Thy heart upon
>   Me, even me
>   Thy little one.

The repetition of "Thy little one" throughout the poem opens up all the implications of meaning in the phrase and also becomes a testimony to God's faithful love for all human beings. Herbert's "Grace" and "Home" both feature petitionary prayers as refrains.

The artful use of rhyme is yet another aspect of technique which signals the poet's effort to offer all the resources of his craft to God's glory. Herbert's "Paradise," for example, features five stanzas (of three lines each) in which the rhyme word is semantically altered in each line while the harmony of the rhyme is maintained. One letter falls away from the beginning of each rhyme word, and yet the poet miraculously discloses new meanings in his godly anatomy of words. Here is the first stanza:

> I blesse thee, Lord, because I grow
> Among thy trees, which in a row
> To thee both fruit and order ow.

A similar dedication of technical virtuosity is evident in Rossetti's "'Can I know it?'—'Nay.'—" (II, 302–3), in which twenty-eight consecutive lines rhyme with the "a" sound; or in "Passing away, saith the World" ("Old and new year ditties," l. 3; I, 89–90), in which two stanzas of nine lines each maintain the "a" rhyme throughout. Specific evidence that Rossetti borrowed this device from Herbert appears in the final stanza of her poem "This near-at-hand land breeds pain by measure" (II, 267–68):

> Come, where all balm is garnered to ease you;
> Come, where all beauty is spread out to please you;
>   Come, gaze upon Jesu.
>
>   [ll. 31–33]

The rhyme was obviously suggested by Herbert's reconstruction of the name "JESU" (in the poem of the same name) into "I ease you." A similar debt seems behind Rossetti's frequent playing upon the rhyme of mine and thine, which one critic has described as "the central rhetorical *topos* of Herbert's poetry" and most clearly exploited in his "Clasping of hands."[38] In this complex poem Herbert demonstrates the complicated nature of his relationship with God by manipulating these two key words. Rossetti's less involved use of the rhyme appears in "Because Thy Love has sought me" (II, 208), as the first stanza illustrates:

> Because Thy Love hath sought me,
>   All mine is Thine and Thine is mine:
> Because Thy Blood hath bought me,
>   I will not be mine own but Thine.

Rossetti echoes the same rhyme in many other poems (e.g., "'Half Dead'" [II, 321] and "Lord Jesus, who would think that I am Thine?" [II, 191]).[39] Although Rossetti never sang Herbert's lyrics as hymns in church, she evidently appreciated the musicality of his verse.[40] His influence on her manipulation of rhyme, meter, and devices of sound (such as assonance) certainly provides a new context for Ruskin's well-known complaint about Rossetti's "irregular measure" and for one reviewer's criticism of "some newfangled shape or shapelessness" in her poetry.[41] As we have seen, George MacDonald was more receptive to the "flow and ebb" (MacDonald, p. 182) of line length, the exploitation of rhyme, the complicated symmetry, and the "music" (MacDonald, p. 174) of Herbert's verse—many of the very elements

[38]William V. Nestrick, "'Mine and Thine' in *The Temple*," in *"Too Rich to Clothe the Sunne": Essays on George Herbert*, ed. Claude J. Summers and Ted-Larry Pebworth (Pittsburgh: University of Pittsburgh Press, 1980), p. 115. For an additional example of Rossetti's playing with orthography, see *FD*, p. 448.

[39]See *FD*, pp. 181–82, 183. Rossetti seems to imitate the single rhymed stanzas of Herbert's "Trinitie Sunday" in her "The three enemies" (I, 70–72), except at much greater length.

[40]On Herbert's poetry being set to music in the later Victorian period, see *A Dictionary of Hymnody*, ed. John Julian (1907; rpt. New York: Dover, 1957), 2 vols., I, 512. On Rossetti's youthful ambition to write hymns, see Sharp, "Some Reminiscences," p. 739. On her poems being set to music by others, see Packer, *Rossetti-Macmillan Letters*, p. 35, and *Rossetti Papers 1862 to 1870*, comp. William Michael Rossetti (1903; rpt. New York: AMS Press, 1970), p. 338.

[41]Ruskin's comment is quoted by Battiscombe, *Christina Rossetti*, p. 99; the review is quoted by Jerome Bump, "Hopkins, Christina Rossetti, and Pre-Raphaelitism," *VN*, no. 57 (Spring 1980):6. Rossetti's close friend, Charles Bagot Cayley, was also interested in metrical experimentation. See his *Psalms in Metre* (London: Longman, Green, Longman, and Roberts, 1860), preface, p. xiv.

of poetic technique, in fact, which Rossetti was helping to bring to prominence again in English poetry.[42]

Besides the early manuscript note to "Charity," Rossetti's only other explicit reference to Herbert appears in her late prose work, *The Face of the Deep*:

> We talk of the unrighteous hating the righteous: do they hate because they are unrighteous, or are they unrighteous because they hate? If at all the latter, I fear there are so-called and self-called righteous people who will scarcely if at all be saved.
>
> 'My God, I mean myself,' said holy George Herbert. God grant us a like self-knowledge and humility. [p. 226]

These remarks form part of Rossetti's commentary on Revelation 7:3: "Saying, Hurt not the earth, neither the sea, nor the trees, till we have sealed the servants of our God in their foreheads." Herbert comes spontaneously to Rossetti's mind as one of the "righteous servants" of God—one of the "rare saints," "Heirs of salvation," and "fearless, self-evident Christians" whom she praises elsewhere in this same section (pp. 225, 227). Herbert's exemplary Christian character was evidently as powerful an influence on Rossetti as was his mastery of poetic technique. Her quotation here ("My God, I mean my self") is from *The Temple*, the final line of Herbert's "Miserie." Herbert's sudden admission follows a lengthy, somewhat abstract meditation on man's sinfulness and inability to praise God because sin "hath fool'd him." From the perspective of the whole poem, the reader can see that Herbert has been deliberately avoiding his own guilt and sin and hiding behind an attitude of cynical realism. His closing confession, however, prepares the way for a poetry of authentic praise. Having confessed further in "Jordan (II)," "I sought out quaint words, and trim invention," Herbert is then astonished by God's merciful and immediate responsiveness, described in "Prayer (II)." For Rossetti, this short sequence of poems from "Miserie" to "Prayer (II)" would have been but one demonstration of Herbert's "self-knowledge and humility" and further testimony to his "holy" character.

The phrase Rossetti uses to describe Herbert—"holy George Herbert"—is something of an invariable formula in accounts of Herbert

---

[42]See MacDonald's discussion of "Aaron," pp. 181–82, and his remarks on Herbert's music, pp. 174–75. On poetry as music, see Bump, "Hopkins, Christina Rossetti, and Pre-Raphaelitism," p. 3.

she would have read. It may derive from Walton's biography ("that great example of holiness"), from his *Compleat Angler* ("that holy poet, Mr. George Herbert" in chapter 1, or "holy George Herbert" in chapter 5), or from Barnabas Oley's sketch ("The Holy George Herbert"), since all these materials were available in Pickering's edition.[43] Herbert's status as a Christian saint (Walton says, "Thus he lived, thus he died like a Saint" [Pickering I, 90]) would have helped inspire Rossetti's own life of moral and aesthetic discipline.

Rossetti, too, was eventually described as "a great saint" by Edmund Gosse, "one of the saintliest of women" by William Sharp, and a "nun-like and saintly woman" by Ford Madox Brown.[44] Those who see her life of self-denial as the futile effort "to frustrate deliberately the experiences she naturally desired"[45] do not understand the nature of her commitment or acknowledge the strain of asceticism in Christian tradition—an asceticism as central to Herbert as it was to someone such as Thomas Wilson, whose devotional manual, *Sacra Privata*, was part of the Rossetti family library.[46] Whether we ascribe the two poets' asceticism to psychological or physiological causes (their close relationships with their mothers, their similarly frail health), we should recognize that both poets believed themselves to be serving God "in holiness" (Luke 1:74–75).[47] Herbert's description of the ideal country parson would have confirmed and strengthened the inclinations and principles about holiness of life that Rossetti was also imbibing from Anglo-Catholicism.[48] The priest's circumspect manner, his plain clothing, food, and furniture, and his imitation of

[43]These quotations can be found at Pickering I, 93, 95, 96, and 141. Even Isaac Williams picks up the phrase in part; see *The Cathedral*, p. 75.

[44]Gosse, "Christina Rossetti," p. 162; Sharp, "Some Reminiscences," p. 736; Ford Madox Hueffer, "Christina Rossetti," *Fortnightly Review* 95 (March 1911): 429.

[45]Bellas, *Christina Rossetti*, p. 46.

[46]See, for example, the prayer for "the graces of mortification and self-denial" in Right Rev. Thomas Wilson, *Sacra Privata* (New York: D. Appleton, 1844), p. 37; see also pp. 118, 119ff., and 125. Compare Herbert's comment in *The Country Parson*, chaps. 2 and 3, and Oley's description in Pickering I, 120.

[47]On Herbert's health, see Walton in Pickering I, 32. Rossetti's frequent "invaliding" is well known (*Letters of William Michael Rossetti to Anne Gilchrist*, ed. Gohdes and Baum, p. 112). For a catalogue of ills affecting her in 1871–1872, see *The Diary of W. M. Rossetti 1870–1873*, ed. Odette Bornand (Oxford: Clarendon Press, 1977), pp. 60, 127, 179, 187, 190, 198.

[48]High Church elements in Herbert's *The Country Parson* are noted by Leah Sinanoglou Marcus, "George Herbert and the Anglican Plain Style" in *"Too Rich to Clothe the Sunne,"* ed. Summers and Pebworth, pp. 184, 187. On personal holiness as an aim of Tractarianism, see Mahood, "Two Anglican Poets," p. 52.

Christ's charity, mercy, and humility (*The Country Parson*, chapters 9, 3, and 10; also Pickering I, 36) all have their counterparts in Rossetti's life and stated ideals. The "Quaker-like simplicity of her dress,"[49] her plain diet and frugality, her dedication to various charitable works, and her faithful nursing of family members all suggest how Herbert's example may have aided her in pursuing Christian ideals of living. She would have understood "holy George Herbert" to be part of the communion of saints to which she aspired, and she would have seen herself as his "spiritual descendant" (*FD*, p. 210). In "earnestly desiring to attain to the character of a humble orthodox Xtian [*sic*]," as she told Augusta Webster, she would have seen Herbert's life as another text, like his poems, to be read and studied.[50] After all, as she notes in *The Face of the Deep*, "The saints are God's epistle known and read of all men" (p. 129).

The Christian values shared by Rossetti and Herbert also inspired a common dedication to a style and poetic of "plain intention" ("Jordan [II]"). Rossetti's practice implicitly endorses Herbert's claim in "A True Hymne" that nothing is too "slight" or small when given in prayer or praise to God. The controlled simplicity of "An Easter carol" (II, 155–56) and the restraint of the six-line petitionary lyric "Lord, make me pure" (II, 254) are translations of Christian humility into an austere poetic style characterized by brevity and monosyllables. There is, Rossetti says in *Letter and Spirit*, "no difference between the testimony of words and of conduct" (p. 149). Both poets understand language as a form of conduct that is to be strictly governed by Christian values. Herbert's distrust of artifice ("Jordan [II]"), or at least of its abuse, may be behind Rossetti's remarks in *The Face of the Deep* which advise the reader to beware of "enchantments," "the rapture of poetry," and the "glamour of eloquence" (p. 399). Elsewhere, she seems to go beyond Herbert in berating mere "cleverness in matters poetic" and outlawing puns as "a frivolous crew likely to misbehave unless kept within strict bounds" (*FL*, p. 183; *TF*, p. 26).[51]

[49]See Sharp, "Some Reminiscences," p. 742. On Rossetti's prescriptions for diet and dress, see *LS*, pp. 120–23. On her charitable works, see Battiscombe, *Christina Rossetti*, p. 94; and Bell, *Christina Rossetti*, pp. 36, 54.

[50]Quoted by Bell, *Christina Rossetti*, pp. 111–12.

[51]Her serious punning is evident in this line from "A death of a first-born" (*PW*, p. 282): "Stoop to console us, Christ, sole consolation." With respect to Rossetti's poetic restraint, Dolores Rosenblum observes that this quality also "saves" her poetry "from the sentimental excesses of some of her female contemporaries and predecessors" ("Christina Rossetti's Religious Poetry: Watching, Looking, Keeping Vigil," *VP* 20 [1982]: 35).

DAVID A. KENT

A major criterion of acceptable devotional poetry is, for Herbert, sincerity of heart: "when the soul unto the lines accords" ("A True Hymne"). Another poetic manifestation of this particular Christian value is the profound sense of intimacy generated by Herbert's lyrics. It was, above all, this personal "expression of feeling as it flows from individual conditions," "the analysis of his own moods," and his focusing upon "the peculiar love and grief in the heart of George Herbert" which so impressed Rossetti's contemporary, George Mac-Donald (p. 192). The open confession of feeling in such poems as "Affliction (I)" or "Repentance" puts the reader in the position of overhearing the poet's colloquy with God. Although the majority of Rossetti's poems reveal a public, liturgical, and representative character, the strengths we discover in some of her devotional poems are closely connected with this very freedom to articulate the most private of thoughts and feelings. Herbert's practice in *The Temple,* his record of spiritual conflict, legitimized such expressiveness. It is difficult to account for the reluctance of many readers to grant that a considerable number of Rossetti's poems also "dispute and grieve," as Herbert says in "Submission". Whether admitting her inability to respond to God's suffering ("Good Friday"; I, 186–87), confessing her sense of futility and self-loathing ("'For thine own sake, o my God'"; II, 150–51), or strenuously arguing with God about the justice of his ways ("Have I not striven, my God"; II, 205), Rossetti's poetry can often match Herbert's in vigor and rebelliousness. In this respect her work is distinctive among the religious poets who were her contemporaries. For example, the "Thoughts in Verse" (part of the subtitle of *The Christian Year*) of John Keble's poetry are very different from the many poems of personal engagement composed by Rossetti.[52] In them she sees life as a "battle-ground" (II, 273) and her pilgrimage as her "rugged way to heaven" (I, 89); like Herbert, she too struggles to discipline her "restive heart" (II, 299), laments her weaknesses ("Who shall deliver me?"; I, 226–27), and seeks God's mercy on her "faults and follies" (II, 187). In her quest to be made "holier" (*PW,* p. 188), Rossetti knew as well as Herbert the "painfulness of the process" by which humility "must be acquired" (*SF,* p. 322). In this struggle she knew that "self" was the "deadliest of all our enemies" (*FD,* p. 103). Her

[52]Keble, in fact, seems to refer to his poems in *The Christian Year* (London: Griffith, Farran, Okeden & Welsh, 1827) as "'attempts at hymns'"; quoted from a letter to John Davison in Brian W. Martin, *John Keble: Priest, Professor, and Poet* (London: Croom Helm, 1976), p. 31.

266

own "self-knowledge" and sense of individual responsibility appear clearly in the following remarks that draw upon Herbert's central metaphor: "There is one temple whereof I am custodian and votaress; of its services, devotions, worship, I alone shall have to render an account" (*FD*, p. 287).

Herbert's commitment to Christ, united with the exercise of his artistic talents, must have represented for Rossetti the ideal wedding of life and value with consummate expression in literary art. As a passage in *Time Flies* indicates,[53] Rossetti would have approved of Milton's notion that the poet's life should itself be a good poem.[54] Among her contemporaries, only the painter Frederic Shields seemed to have achieved that union of Christian principle and artistic vocation which Herbert so completely exemplified. Rossetti told Mackenzie Bell that sacred themes were "part of his [Shields's] life in a way that I have never known them to be of any other artist."[55] The sense of vocation that brought Herbert to the priesthood and to Christian poetry is made clear in his advice about vocation in *The Country Parson*: "All are either to have a Calling, or prepare for it." Individuals must "examine with care, and advice, what they are fittest for, and to prepare for that with all diligence" (chapter 33).

Rossetti also had a powerful sense of calling to God's service and at one point even speaks of her "several vocations" (*FD*, p. 326). Though too young to go to the Crimea as a nurse, she faithfully served her family in what Florence Nightingale describes as "an art of charity"; nursing, Nightingale also maintains, is a "calling" that demands "a religious and devoted woman."[56] Rossetti, seeing herself as an "'escaped governess'" (as she wrote to Swinburne in 1884),[57] put her teaching gifts to use in the role of devotional writer to which she increasingly committed herself. Whereas Herbert allowed Ferrar to

---

[53]"Scrupulous Christians need special self-sifting. They too often resemble translations of the letter in defiance of the spirit: their good poem has become unpoetical" (p. 2).

[54]According to Milton, the true poet "ought him selfe to bee a true Poem, that is, a composition and patterne of the best and honourablest things" (John Milton, *An Apology for Smectymnuus*, in *The Works of John Milton*, gen. ed., Frank Allen, 20 vols. [New York: Columbia University Press, 1931], III, 303).

[55]Bell, *Christina Rossetti*, p. 152.

[56]Florence Nightingale, *Notes on Nursing: What It Is, and What It Is Not* (1859; rpt. Philadelphia: J. B. Lippincott Co., n.d.), pp. 75 and 70. This book was also in the Rossetti family library.

[57]Quoted in Battiscombe, *Christina Rossetti*, p. 29.

judge whether his writings would benefit "any dejected poor Soul" (Pickering I, 84) or someone "who a sermon flies" ("Perirrhan-terium"), Rossetti believed that "some grade of pastoral work de-volves" (*TF*, p. 123) on every Christian. Writing is a form of testi-monial witness, as the following statement from *The Face of the Deep* implies (p. 199): "Some Christians are called to become literal Evan-gelists, and every Christian is at the least a minor missionary." Poetry is thus the "gift" of graceful inspiration, a talent she "must use and improve" (*FD*, p. 431).[58] Her best description of the Christian's voca-tion, stated in terms of the priesthood of all believers, appears in *The Face of the Deep*. According to Rossetti, the Christian's multiple re-sponsibilities include self-rule, edifying "our brethren," the "priestly function of intercession, offering up prayers and thanks for all men," and lastly the oblation of self "in will and in deed as His reasonable and lively sacrifice" (p. 16). All these duties find expression in her devotional poetry and prose.

The phrase "self-oblation" (p. 16) indicates another important theme or posture that it is likely Rossetti adopted from Herbert. The synecdochical offering of one's heart to God is a recurrent gesture in the work of both poets. In "The Dedication" Herbert offers back the "first fruits" of his art to the God who originally bestowed them. "The Altar," "Love (II)," "Obedience," "Providence," and "An Offering" all contain offerings of the "gifts" ("An Offering") of poetic ex-pression back to God. One of Rossetti's best-known poems, still a popular Anglican hymn, follows Herbert's example. In "A Christmas carol" (I, 216–17) the speaker's (and the world's) spiritual desolation is figured by the "bleak mid-winter" landscape into which Christ was (and is) born, their unresponsive spirit imaged by emblematic detail: "Earth stood hard as iron, / Water like a stone" (ll. 3–4). In the final stanza, once the wonders of Christ's birth have been recited and have brought renewal to both speaker and world, the poet faces the problem of appropriately responding to God's love. She speaks of giving her heart, that is, the allegiance of her whole being, and yet her gift is equally and simultaneously the poem she has written.[59] In such poems of "self-oblation" Rossetti displays the "self-knowledge" for which she praises Herbert. She is aware that "we proffer half a heart while life is strong" and that God is especially responsive to the contrition of "a broken heart" (II, 300). She knows the paradoxical truth of "the kept

---

[58]On poetry as a gift, see Bell, *Christina Rossetti*, p. 88, where he quotes from Rossetti's letter to Rev. W. Garrett Horder (May 20, 1885). See also *FD*, p. 514.
[59]See also "Me and my gift" (II, 197).

we lose, the offered we retain / Or find again" (II, 210), and therefore she offers her heart, be it "heavy" (II, 305), "tired" (II, 316), or "closed" (II, 240). She can confess to being unable to respond to the liturgical imperative, " 'Lift up your hearts' " (II, 311), and still recognize that her good intentions will be generously accepted: "Accept a faltering will to give, / Itself Thy gift" (II, 257). Both Rossetti and Herbert know the impossibility of matching God's own sacrificial love (their utter incapacity to yield appropriate praise), but both nevertheless "simply offer whatever they have" (FD, p. 63). As God's instrument, each depends completely on God. And so, in "Deniall," Herbert prays: "O cheer and tune my heartlesse breast." And Rossetti can echo him in this prayer: "Tune me, O Lord, into one harmony / With Thee" (II, 255).

I have argued elsewhere that Rossetti's major collection of religious lyrics, Verses (1893), needs to be read in the sequence of sections which she designed for it, not according to the chronological principle of her brother William Michael's ordering in the Poetical Works of 1904.[60] Rossetti was acquainted with any number of collections of religious lyrics organized by liturgical sequence (Lyra Eucharistica), the events of Christ's life (Lyra Messianica), the ordering of the Bible itself (The Poets' Bible), and the chronology of the Church year (Keble's The Christian Year), or simply by theme (The Illustrated Book of Sacred Poetry).[61] Except for The Christian Year, though, each of these collections is simply an anthology of various writers. The Temple, on the other hand, illustrates how one writer devised a subtle and integrated structural framework to give his religious lyrics further depth of meaning.[62] In reading Herbert's poems Rossetti would have recognized how

[60]See David A. Kent, "W. M. Rossetti and the Editing of Christina Rossetti's Religious Poetry," The Pre-Raphaelite Review 1 (1978): 18–26, and "Sequence and Meaning in Christina Rossetti's Verses (1893)," VP 17 (1979): 259–64. I have since read Festa's dissertation in which he convincingly argues for the carefully planned sequence and unity in Rossetti's "Goblin Market" and Other Poems (1862). Indeed, he argues for the influence of The Temple in particular on the sequencing of poems in this volume (see pp. 201ff.).

[61]Except for, naturally, John Keble's The Christian Year, Rossetti contributed poems to each of these collections: Lyra Eucharistica, ed. Rev. Orby Shipley (London: Longman, 1863); Lyra Messianica, ed. Rev. Orby Shipley (London: Longman, 1864); The Poets' Bible, 2 vols., ed. W. Garrett Horder (London: W. Isbister, 1881 and 1889); and The Illustrated Book of Sacred Poems, ed. Rev. Robert H. Baynes (London: Cassell, Petter, and Galpin, n.d.).

[62]For a concise summary of interpretations of The Temple's structure, see Stanley Fish, The Living Temple: George Herbert and Catechizing (Berkeley: University of California Press, 1978), pp. 8–9.

he had often grouped his lyrics on the basis of recognizable patterns of Christian spiritual experience. To take but one example, she would have seen the logic of the sequential group beginning with "Affliction (I)," followed by "Repentance," "Faith," "Prayer (I)," and "The H. Communion." This almost liturgically ordered sequence is then appropriately succeeded by the celebrative "Antiphon (I)," before a new direction gradually emerges in the next cluster of lyrics. Position within the larger sequence is equally crucial to the lyrics in Rossetti's *Verses*. The first four sections, for instance, enact a meaningful sequence from complaint and petition to God in the first, through dialogue and response in the second, to liturgical celebration (based, like Keble's, on the Church year) in the third, to praise and reflection in the fourth. Although individual sections have not yet received much critical analysis, the presence of paired poems (themselves perhaps a result of Herbert's influence) in, for example, the sixth section of *Verses*, the symmetry of opening and closing sonnets in the fourth section, and the use of sonnets only in the first section all suggest that each section has its own internal thematic coherence in addition to a designated place within the sequential structure of the whole. To condemn Rossetti as escapist and other-worldly—as someone who "cannot accept the conflict and contradictions of man's middle state"—is, at the least, to ignore her concern in *Verses* with placing her devotional lyrics into a balanced, meaningful order.[63]

Cattermole's introduction to his 1835 anthology of devotional poetry helps clarify Rossetti's own effort to order her lyrics. Cattermole describes his collection as a help "to pious thought and devotional feeling" and stresses how wide-ranging he has been: "Few moods of the Christian mind will be found to have been passed over in silence." This comprehensiveness he soon outlines: "In these diversified but mutually concordant pages, the devout soul is supplied with the language of praise and adoration—the penitent with the utterances of a contrite heart: the doubting will find the means of conviction; the sinner will be mildly but solemnly warned of his danger; the worldly and hypocrite, reproved; the proud, humbled; the humble, raised and cheered" (p. xxvi). Cattermole is claiming that his anthology contains something for all sorts and conditions of men. His justification for lyrical expressiveness seems to anticipate Rossetti's own defense of her sometimes melancholy poems to Dr. Heimann in 1858: "they are . . . the record of sensation, fancy, and what not, much as these

---

[63]Mahood, "Two Anglican Poets," p. 37.

came and went."[64] By following the example of Herbert's *Temple*, Rossetti was able to endow her poems with purpose and direction, to put her records of sensation, mood, and imagination into a larger perspective, and also to speak to readers, whatever their spiritual condition might be.

Assessing Herbert's influence on Rossetti is a complex matter because no other two English poets have so much in common, including Christian faith and all that it implies, favorite authors such as Augustine and Plato, poor health, and such temperamental affinities as an inclination to the ascetic and a deep love of music. It would be possible to detect Herbert's influence in aspects of Rossetti's writing I have not already mentioned, except that still other influences would thereby be neglected. For example, Rossetti may share with Herbert a view of experience and nature as parabolic, yet this element of her work is more likely related to her knowledge of Dante, Plato, and Keble, not to mention the emblematic tendencies of Pre-Raphaelitism and the sacramentalism of Anglo-Catholicism. Rossetti's dialogue poems might also be seen as responses to Herbert's example, and yet we cannot exclude the possibility that Browning's dramatic monologues were an important influence. Similarly, since both poets found models for their lyrics of petition and complaint in the Psalms, we can hardly ascribe to Herbert the primary inspiration for Rossetti's poems in these modes. And, while the three-part structure of *The Temple* may be deliberately echoed by the trinitarian associations in the number of poems in *Verses* (331), Rossetti's occasional references to numerological symbolism can be more easily accounted for by her acquaintance with biblical commentaries and interpretations of Dante (including her sister Maria's work *A Shadow of Dante*).[65] Finally, as G. B. Tennyson has argued, the restraint that characterizes so much of Rossetti's verse is as much the product of Anglo-Catholic "reserve" as it is the imitation of the sometimes simple piety of Herbert (*VDP*, pp. 198ff). The presence in Herbert's work of such elements as sacramentalism, dialogue poems, numerology, simplicity, and restraint did, however, serve to reassure Rossetti that these qualities were part of the

[64]Letter quoted by Packer, *Christina Rossetti*, p. 161.
[65]See Sibyl Lutz Severance, "Numerological Structures in *The Temple*" in *"Too Rich to Clothe the Sunne,"* ed. Summers and Pebworth, pp. 229–49. On numerology in Dante, see Maria Francesca Rossetti, *A Shadow of Dante* (London: Rivingtons, 1871), pp. 189–90. On numerology in Revelation, see *FD*, pp. 18, 62–63.

Christian poetic she was trying to follow. In this respect, Herbert was again exemplar and guide.

While it is no longer possible to contrast so sharply Herbert's "true humanist's delight and gratitude for all the earth's gifts" with Rossetti's "false and puritanical asceticism,"[66] some distinctions between these remarkably like-minded poets need to be drawn. Too many writers have exaggerated Rossetti's anxieties and melancholy, her physical and mental weaknesses, and mocked such aspects of her faith as her vision of the afterlife. They choose to ignore the evidence of her humor, intellectual refinement, disciplined industry, courage and forbearance, and her self-consciousness about what she was doing. Herbert's poetry is, on the whole, more explicitly playful, witty, metaphorically dense, and intellectually demanding, but his audience was a comparatively small and sophisticated one. Further, a sense of God's prevenient grace suddenly intervening in one's life is certainly more characteristic of Herbert than of Rossetti, to whom life was so often a test of endurance and faith. We therefore encounter more small dramas in his poems (with their unexpected turns, revelations, and conversions) than in hers. Although Rossetti can also testify to moments of "restitution" and "refreshing" returns of grace (*PW*, p. 156), as Herbert does in "The Flower," it is not surprising to find that the images of the pilgrim and pilgrimage (her debt to John Bunyan) are much more intrinsic to her understanding of experience than to Herbert's. Moreover, while we value her personal lyrics of joy and despair, Rossetti's voice generally speaks in imperatives or exhortations more often than it is overheard in colloquy with God.[67] Her awareness of the reader as a fellow pilgrim might be attributable to a consciousness of the sizable Victorian audience she was addressing. This fact may equally account for the suppression of obvious intellectual complexity in some of her lyrics as well as her attachment to fixed forms such as the roundel and sonnet, since formal poetic repetition can become the equivalent to public, liturgical celebration. Certainly, Rossetti never "*played* at Xtianity."[68] She was an earnest Victorian, serious and self-conscious, and while she learned much from Herbert and admired him, she was not simply George Herbert transplanted into the nineteenth century.

"By thought, word, and deed" may seem a glib expression to suggest

---

[66]Mahood, "Two Anglican Poets," p. 38.

[67]For addresses to the reader, see II, 304; II, 322; and II, 262.

[68]From a letter of 1878 quoted in *Three Rossettis*, ed., Troxell, p. 160.

the scope of Herbert's influence on Rossetti. Drawn from the general confession prior to communion, this phrase from Anglican liturgy does, however, have the advantage of briefly summarizing how, for both Herbert and Rossetti, spirit, language, and action are a unity embraced and governed by Christian values. Despite the veil of obscurity Rossetti appears to have thrown over her indebtedness to Herbert, I have tried to identify major elements in his influence on her and so to confirm the assumptions of many previous readers. First, she learned matters of poetic technique from Herbert, what H. B. Forman described as the "admirable sense of workmanship" in her poetry: how to exploit every resource of language—sound, sense, form—and to offer these back to God.[69] She was also affected by what she read about Herbert's example of holy living and by the prescriptions he set down for a holy life. Finally, Herbert demonstrated how lyric poetry might be fit Christian testimony, and that the manner and style of such poetry—that is, the decorum of a Christian poetic—while it has certain restraints and proprieties, allows considerable liberty for self-expression too, especially within a larger framework designed to contain and illuminate individual poems.

A few years before her death, Rossetti must have been gratified to receive a signed copy of *The Treasury of Sacred Song: Selected From the English Lyrical Poetry of Four Centuries*, an anthology prepared by an old acquaintance of the family, Francis Palgrave, in which her own devotional poetry joined that of Herbert's.[70] Palgrave's note on Herbert in part states: "And here [at Bemerton]—suffering also from advancing consumption—he lived that saintly life of 'detachment' which his poems reveal—say rather, embody." As we recover a clearer perception of Rossetti, we see how her life and art were equally interdependent and that the precedent of Herbert to a considerable degree influenced and guided her achievement.

[69]Forman, "Criticisms on Contemporaries," p. 63.

[70]For Rossetti's ownership of Palgrave's anthology, see *The Pre-Raphaelite Brotherhood* (London: Sebastian d'Orsai, 1973), catalogue no. 36, p. 26.

CATHERINE MUSELLO CANTALUPO

Christina Rossetti: The Devotional Poet
and the Rejection of Romantic Nature

Grant, O Lord,
To the natural man, regeneration . . .

                          Christina Rossetti, *Face of the Deep*

In 1906 Virginia Woolf wrote to Violet Dickinson, "I want to write about Christina Rossetti; so if you can find out what she thought about Christianity and what effect religion had upon her poetry, and will write it on a post card, you will do more for me than if you looked out a train, and bought a new hat."[1] Christina Rossetti called nearly half of her poems "devotional." Yet Woolf's impression that Rossetti's religious ideas and their influence on her work could be discussed on a postcard typifies the dominant twentieth-century attitude. The devotional poems, if studied at all, have been called "uninspired poetic tracts" or even "rubbish";[2] the religious poet has been compared, usually to her disadvantage, with John Donne, George Herbert, and Gerard Manley Hopkins.[3]

Yet the essential fact of Rossetti's work as a poet is that she spent

---

This essay was edited for publication by Charles Cantalupo (Pennsylvania State University) and Barry Qualls (Rutgers University).

[1]Nigel Nicolson, ed., *The Letters of Virginia Woolf*, vol. I, 1888–1912 (Virginia Stephen) (New York: Harcourt Brace Jovanovich, 1977), p. 258; from a letter of December 8, 1906.

[2]See Stuart Curran, "The Lyric Voice of Christina Rossetti," *VP* 9 (1971): 289; and H. N. Fairchild, *Religious Trends in English Poetry*, 6 vols. (New York: Columbia University Press, 1939–1968), vol. IV, *1830–1880* (1957), p. 302.

[3]See B. Ifor Evans, *English Poetry in the Later Nineteenth Century* (1933; rpt. London: Methuen, 1966), p. 103.

her writing life establishing her poetic vocation within a Christian framework. In doing so, she confronted the dominant Romantic aesthetic of nineteenth-century England, especially its emphasis on the primacy of both human imagination and the natural world; out of this lifelong confrontation she evolved her definition and practice of devotional poetry. Of course she wrote much explicitly secular poetry as well. But the secular and religious strains in her writing parallel each other, with the explicitly religious influence increasing until it comes to predominate (most of the explicitly religious poetry was published in *Verses* in 1893). To establish the Christian perspective of Rossetti's poetry, I will first examine her ways of defining "devotional" poetry and then consider two poems—"The thread of life" and "An old-world thicket"—in which she confronts Romanticism and moves to a religious and poetic conversion of the Romantic ideology of nature.

I

For Rossetti, devotional poetry is poetry that records the poet's subjective and incessant spiritual vicissitudes, the emotional waxing and waning of spiritual values such as faith, hope, and love, and the poet's consequent grasp of the appropriate revelation and religious tradition by which to understand these feelings. The devotional poet uses her emotions to lead herself, and her readers, into the meaning of biblical revelation, doctrine, and, for the Anglo-Catholic such as Rossetti, the traditions of the Church. Such devotional poetry is a kind of theology, with each devotional poem in the corpus a fragment of an evolving image of the relationship between the human and the divine. Consistency, completeness, coherence, and clarity are among the qualities of this poetry which distinguish it from religious art that is not so dogged and theological a record of the spiritual life, even as individual poems may reflect the inconsistency, incompleteness, and incoherence of the given spiritual moment. Rossetti's devotional poetry is characterized by its breadth and intensity, and by two other qualities: the use of several forms of biblically founded analogy and a reserved tone and content.

The method of analogy has two specific applications to devotional poetry (though Rossetti is no strict typologist, as she shows in *The Face of the Deep*). The first application is in the form of biblical typology, that is, understanding Old Testament figures and events as prefigurations (types) of New Testament figures and events (antitypes). When

Rossetti's Peter, meditating on Christ's death, cries, "No balm I find in Gilead, yet in Thee / Nailed to Thy palm / I find a balm that wrings and comforts me" ("I followed Thee, my God, I followed Thee," ll. 41–43; II, 242), he is thinking typologically, exactly as he did on a larger scale when he was an apostle of Jesus' New Testament (II, 241–43). The second application, even more pertinent to devotional poetry, is the ancient method of finding in biblical figures and events analogies for the events of the individual spiritual life. Barbara Lewalski has written that one characteristic of seventeenth-century devotional poetry is its special focus "upon the individual Christian, whose life is incorporated within, and in whom may be located, God's vast typological history."[4] This characteristic is responsible for what I described above as the emotional breadth of devotional poetry, a breadth Rossetti shares with Henry Vaughan, Donne, Richard Crashaw, Thomas Traherne, and especially Herbert. Her speaker is variously the Wise Man, Noah's dove, Jacob wrestling with the angel, Peter doubting Christ, Paul being "made perfect in weakness" (2 Cor. 12:9), Christ's spouse, and so on.

Though strict biblical typology is not preeminent in Rossetti's work, the analogical method of seeing one's spiritual life in terms of biblical paradigms does predominate in two forms: first, scriptural quotations and allusions to biblical metaphors are abundant and often conflated in one poem. Second, the Psalms provide a general model for several poems. Lewalski points out that the Psalms were commonly understood in the seventeenth century to "present the entire range of feelings, emotions, adversities, sorrows, joys and exultations pertaining to anyone's spiritual life" and therefore served as model—or *figura*— for the spiritual variety of Herbert's *Temple,* for example. Furthermore, the Psalms present a range of lyric forms, accounting for the variety of forms in books such as *The Temple*—and, I would add, in Rossetti's *Verses.*[5] But since the Psalms are the expression of the old covenant and therefore, from the Christian vantage point, theologically incomplete, Rossetti, like Herbert, continually extends their language and vision into the region of New Testament thought.

The sonnet "Seven vials hold thy wrath," for example, is clearly an exploration of diverse typological relationships, not all obvious ones,

---

[4]Barbara Lewalski, "Typological Symbolism and the 'Progress of the Soul' in Seventeenth-Century Literature," *Literary Uses of Typology from the Late Middle Ages to the Present,* ed. Earl Miner (Princeton: Princeton University Press, 1977), p. 82.

[5]Lewalski, "Typological Symbolism," p. 110.

as well as an assertion of Rossetti's faith in the very process of typological thinking:

> Seven vials hold thy wrath: but what can hold
>   Thy mercy save Thine own Infinitude
>   Boundlessly overflowing with all good,
> All lovingkindness, all delights untold?
> Thy Love, of each created love the mould;
>   Thyself, of all the empty plenitude;
> Heard of at Ephrata, found in the Wood,
> For ever One, the Same, and Manifold.
> Lord, give us grace to tremble with that dove
>   Which Ark-bound winged its solitary way
>   And overpast the Deluge in a day,
>   Whom Noah's hand pulled in and comforted:
> For we who much more hang upon Thy Love
> Behold its shadow in the deed he did.
>   [II, 181–82]

Alternating between New and Old Testament types and allusions, the
speaker refers first to Revelation ("seven vials"), and then to Paul's
concept of God as love overflowing into each creature ("of all the
empty plenitude"). Suddenly she shifts to David as *figura* for the poet,
alluding to his establishing God's presence in an ark ("Heard of at
Ephrata, found in the Wood"). With this typological connection,
Rossetti accepts David's loss and recovery of the ark as a sign of
universal spiritual loss and pursuit. A third image of God is elaborated
in the Old Testament allusion to Noah's ark, a type of God's presence
amid the chaotic "deluge" of divine anger. Noah himself is a type of
God's love: we "behold [Love's] shadow in the deed he did." Together
these several biblical types offer an asymmetrical meditation on divinity derived from what Rossetti held to be the primary authentic
source, Scripture. The large meaning of these compressed rhetorical
shifts between Old and New Testament allusions is clearly stated: God
is "For ever One, the Same, and Manifold." Though the Bible's
narrative is penultimately about God's anger—anger justified by the
continual human denial of God—still, the Bible's typological relationships disclose the divine purpose as each relationship yields its
individual insight.

The devotional poet's exploration of natural analogy parallels her
handling of biblical analogy in its insistence on seeing the natural

world as a declaration of the glory of God. She takes literally Paul's words that "the invisible things of [God] from the creation of the world are clearly seen, being understood by the things that are made" (Rom. 1:20); in other words, *nature* is a storehouse of "types"— symbols of divine attributes, Ruskin's "book of God." The Tractarians rediscovered this doctrine in patristic commentaries and Joseph Butler's *Analogy;* and John Keble's *The Christian Year* (1827) verified it by drawing analogies between liturgical events and their seasons. According to John Henry Newman, Keble's work taught "what may be called, in a large sense of the word, the Sacramental system; that is, the doctrine that material phenomena are both the types and the instruments of real things unseen."[6] As Rossetti's Christianity is essentially an expression of the Oxford Movement, which Newman called "not so much a movement as a 'spirit afloat'" (*Apologia*, p. 85), so her poetry is Tractarian in its elaboration of the belief that "in every creature is latent a memorial of its Creator" (*LS*, p. 130):

> The twig teacheth,
> The moth preacheth,
> The plant vaunteth,
> The bird chanteth.
> ["'Are ye not much better than they?'"; II, 332]

Since the invisible things have been revealed, Scripture and tradition are the subtext of a devotional poetry that, read literally, may seem devoid of religious allusion. Consider, for example, Rossetti's poem with the epigraph "'Balm in Gilead'" (II, 317). Apart from the epigraph and the poem's context—in *Verses* or the religious section of the *Poetical Works* (context offers no small clue to Rossetti's intentions)—the poem itself has no overt religious allusions. Yet if it were not read within the context of strictly Christian meanings, the poem would be baffling:

> Heartsease I found, where Love-lies-bleeding
>   Empurpled all the ground:
> Whatever flowers I missed unheeding,
>   Heartsease I found.
>
>   [ll. 1–4]

---

[6]John Henry Cardinal Newman, *Apologia Pro Vita Sua* (New York: Norton, 1968), p. 28; hereafter cited by page number in the text.

"Heartsease" and "Love-lies-bleeding" are paradoxical synonyms for a single flower, and Rossetti uses them to make an enigmatic poem about the riddle in Christian theology that suffering and consolation (or, more broadly, redemption) are related. Love-lies-bleeding is a natural type of suffering, and specifically of suffering endured by and through *love*; thus, it is also a type of Christ (who bled on the cross to show that God is love). And the suggestion of royalty in "empurpled" reinforces this Christian typology. Just as Christ's suffering led to human redemption (heartsease), so all suffering (including the suffering implied here, romantic loss) may lead to personal consolation (heartsease). The poem's speaker goes on to work out that spiritual transaction in more detail—its dependence on grace, and the stubborn resistance of the suffering soul, for example—all within the confines of natural analogy.

Believing that this single flower was a type of "a real thing unseen," a type of God's love, Rossetti could not accept the implication of some Romantic poetry that God was, for example, *in* the tree rather than the tree's maker. Consequently, she also meditates on the limits of nature in poems such as "The thread of life" (II, 122–23) and "An old-world thicket" (II, 123–28), precisely to avoid glorifying nature. (I explore this meditation more closely in the next section of this essay.) Rossetti recognizes nature's mysteriousness. While she could feel illuminated by nature, she also saw in it a fundamental unintelligibility, as in " 'Hollow sounding and mysterious' " (II, 97–98) where the wind is

> Ever for ever
> Teaching and preaching,
> Never, ah never
> Making us wiser—
> [ll. 20–23]

If nature is at best indirectly communicative and at worst disturbingly mysterious, God has willed it so. The Tractarians saw this mystery as one manifestation of a universal principle of reserve, by which the divine is revealed in part, indirectly, "through a glass darkly." G. B. Tennyson, in *Victorian Devotional Poetry*, explains that the Tractarians revived this principle in conjunction with the doctrine of analogy and that "the idea of Reserve is that since God is ultimately incomprehensible, we can know Him only indirectly; His truth is hidden and given to us only in a manner suited to our capacities for apprehending it. Moreover, it is both unnecessary and undesirable that God and religious truth generally should be disclosed in their fullness at once to all regardless of the differing capacities of individuals to apprehend such things" (*VDP*, p. 45).

We can be sure that Rossetti knew this doctrine of reserve, for she refers to it several times, directly and indirectly, in her poetry and prose. For example, in *Time Flies* she wrote: "any literal revelation of heaven would appear to be over spiritual for us; we need something grosser, something more familiar and more within the range of our experience" (*TF*, p. 42). The reserved devotional poet tries, by simplicity and modest language, to make the essentially mysterious intelligible—"grosser" and "more familiar" than it is—and by typology, analogy, and scriptural allusion to infuse the mundane with sacramental import.

The analogical frame of reference is important to—even inevitable for—Rossetti as a devotional poet because, without the centrifuge of revelation, continual self-scrutiny might lead into a vortex of solipsism. Solipsism would be anathema for the devotional poet, who believes one of her functions is didactic—or at least that she has the duty not to mislead. As Rossetti succinctly, and inscrutably, states in her introduction to *Called to be Saints*: "No graver slur could attach to my book than would be a reputation for prevalent originality" (p. xvii). (Notice that she says "*prevalent* originality.") Scripture shapes emotions into what the poet believes are significant configurations that have an impeccable pedigree and theological validity; the devotional poet's willingness or need to submit her emotions to such typological analyses weaves mystery, risk, variety, and poetic tension into what would otherwise be mundane theology or dull, tensionless religious poetry: emotion is still, in devotional poetry as in all poetry, a primary source for poetry. Thus, rooted in revelation and based on the analogical method, the devotional poet's expression of her own profound intimations of God becomes "poetic" theology, that is: literary art's grasp and expression of the deepest meanings of Scripture and religious ideas, and Scripture's illumination of human life through art.

In the sonnet "It is not death" (II, 184), Rossetti implies that her own poetic silence is a source of personal suffering. Through typological and analogical reasoning, she derives hope and the power to sing. The primary antitype is Christ's death: "It is not death, O Christ, to die for Thee" because our individual deaths, literal and metaphorical, are subject to the same resurrection. This biblical paradox leads Rossetti to a natural analogy: "Nor is that silence of a silent land / Which speaks Thy praise so all may understand." Death and nature's silence are divine negatives, evincing their opposites, and Rossetti concludes:

> Death is not death, and therefore do I hope:
> Nor silence silence; and I therefore sing
> A very humble hopeful quiet psalm,
> Searching my heart-field for an offering;
> A handful of sun-courting heliotrope,
> Of myrrh a bundle, and a little balm.

Rossetti discovers that her poetry can persevere against the press of negatives: nature's coldness, internal silence, mystery, and death. By devotion, self searching, and "a little" art Rossetti hopes to achieve reserved praise that echoes in the silence.

II

The effort to achieve this reserved praise is documented most tellingly in the nature poetry Rossetti wrote throughout her career. This nature poetry as a whole develops within two separate traditions, which I will call the typological and the Romantic. By "typological" nature poem, I mean a poem that reads nature as Christian exegetes have traditionally read the Bible: nature contains "types" or symbols of divine attributes and divine "messages." This view of nature differs significantly from that of the high Romantics in this respect: the Romantics believe in a goal of communion with nature since they see nature as informed by a benevolent spirit (immanence). They have infinite hope in human constructiveness, but they concede that constructiveness and joy finally depend on the individual's, and society's, proper sustaining and ordering relationship to nature. Religious allegorists believe in human constructiveness too, but as a free gift from God, a God much greater than his created nature (transcendence). For religious allegorists, the significance of nature is that God concretely reveals himself through the multitude of nature's signs; nature provides a set of antitypes or analogies.

The devotional art of religious allegorists, however, is not merely the subjective and personal myth-making of the Romantics, but rather analysis guided by the clues of revelation and religious tradition. Rossetti makes this point in *Letter and Spirit:* "To modify by a bound-

281

less licence of imagination the Voice of Revelation, or of tradition, or our own perceptions, concerning the universe, its Ruler, inhabitants, features, origin, destinies, falls within the range of human faculties" (p. 10).

Beyond these boundaries, the religious allegorist—in the confidence that God disposes the will and enlightens—is free to be guided by her own light. A typological reading of creation is a search for analogies, but a search necessarily founded on a sweeping faith in the goodness, or appropriateness, of creation. Rossetti writes:

> In every creature is latent a memorial of its Creator. Throughout and by means of creation God challenges each of us, "Hath not my hand made all these things?" Our prevalent tone of mind should resemble that of the Psalmist when he proclaimed: "The heavens declare the glory of God; and the firmament sheweth His handywork;" . . . Nay, more, we should exercise that far higher privilege which appertains to Christians, of having "the mind of Christ"; and then the two worlds, visible and invisible, will become familiar to us even as they were to Him . . . , as double against each other; and on occasion sparrow and lily will recall God's Providence, seed His Word, earthly bread the Bread of Heaven, a plough the danger of drawing back . . . . Versed in such trains of thought the mind becomes reverential, composed, grave; the heart imbued with such associations becomes steadied and ennobled; and out of the abundance of such a heart the mouth impulsively speaks that which is good and edifying. [LS, pp. 131–33]

Elsewhere in *Letter and Spirit*, Rossetti expresses this doctrine in more fundamental terms: "For if (as I have seen pointed out) God is not to be called like His creature, whose grace is simply typical, but that creature is like Him because expressive of His archetypal Attribute, it suggests itself that for every aspect of creation there must exist the corresponding Divine Attribute" (p. 13).

Rossetti's commitment to this doctrine of analogy makes her ambivalent about the Romantic view of nature. Clearly she inherits the Romantic concern with epistemology; she wonders: "How do subject and object meet in a meaningful relationship? By what means do we have a significant awareness of the world?"[7] Consequently, Rossetti sometimes records the *process* of reading nature as well as the content

---

[7]Earl R. Wasserman, "The English Romantics: The Grounds of Knowledge," in *Romanticism: Points of View*, ed. R. F. Gleckner and G. E. Enscoe, 2d ed. (Detroit: Wayne State University Press, 1979), p. 335.

of that reading, valuing the flux of her experience of nature, with its misrepresentations as well as its insights, just as Wordsworth and Shelley did. The fundamental difference is in what the poets discover, in what they believe nature to represent.

In several major poems Rossetti carries on an argument with Romanticism that is at once a critique of Romanticism and an elucidation of the life and difficulties of her Christian faith. These poems benefit from the Romantic method of describing the introspection of the figure in the landscape, and seem at first glance to deal in Romantic subjectivity.[8] But this impulse toward subjectivity is ultimately mastered by the Christian perspective.

A summary of those Romantic ideas submerged in the arguments of Rossetti's poems is helpful here. As M. H. Abrams has suggested, literary Romanticism's "general tendency was . . . to naturalize the supernatural and to humanize the divine."[9] In other words, in high Romantic art and thought the ground of the divine is nature; there is no literal transcendence—no hell, heaven, or God—to detract from the intellectually acceptable and emotionally exciting idea that man is "of all visible natures, crown . . . / As, more than anything we know, instinct / with godhead" (*The Prelude* [1805 version], VIII:634–39).[10] This concept of nature differs from the doctrine of analogy to the extent that divinity *exists* in Romantic nature, whereas divinity is merely *shadowed* in Christian nature. But the Christian idea of nature as a *sacrament* is easily confounded with pantheism and therefore needs to be carefully distinguished from it. Sacramental nature is, in Christian theology, subject to the action of "grace," which is the self-communication of a transcendent God which allows the mind to recognize and share in the divine presence.[11] The Romantics under-

[8]See C. M. Bowra's discussion of Rossetti in *The Romantic Imagination* (Cambridge: Harvard University Press, 1949).

[9]M. H. Abrams, *Natural Supernaturalism: Tradition and Revolution in Romantic Literature* (New York: Norton, 1971), p. 68.

[10]William Wordsworth, *The Prelude: A Parallel Text*, ed. J. C. Maxwell (Harmondsworth: Penguin, 1975); all references are cited in the text by book and line number, and, unless noted otherwise, refer to the 1805 *Prelude*. Other Wordsworth poems are quoted from *William Wordsworth: The Poems*, ed. John O. Hayden, 2 vols. (Harmondsworth: Penguin, 1977).

[11]Abrams calls Wordsworth's view of nature "sacramental" (*Natural Supernaturalism*, p. 139). To use "sacramentalism" in a Romantic context is to make the word meaningless, emptying it of supernatural content. For a relevant discussion of grace, see *Encyclopedia of Theology: The Concise Sacramentum Mundi*, ed. Karl Rahner (New York: Seabury, 1975), pp. 588–90.

stand nature as imbued with divinity; in other words, God is identified with nature and human self-realization. Wordsworth sometimes reads nature as the projection of the "growth of a Poet's mind," as *The Prelude* suggests, and sometimes as the embodiment of the one soul coextensive with his own.

Rossetti, on the other hand, takes nature as a sign of divine intelligence but not as the intelligence itself.[12] This difference has major consequences. For one thing, Romantic nature contains a "never-failing principle," as Wordsworth writes:

> O Nature! Thou has fed
> My lofty speculations; and in thee,
> For this uneasy heart of ours, I find
> A never-failing principle of joy
> And purest passion.
>
> [II. 462–66]

If nature is, indeed, the "empire we inherit / As natural beings" (III. 195–96 [1850]), then communion with nature is the ultimate spiritual communion. Nature—and no other source—is the source of regeneration of the "godhead" within the dispirited person. The only authority Wordsworth recognizes is nature's inspiration. It is misleading to call this view of nature "sacramentalism" because it does not imply the operation of any intermediate grace linking humanity to God through nature.

Coleridge's early religious thought, influenced by Unitarianism, tended to divest religion of its transcendent and revealed elements: it was, as he described it, "Merely the referring of the mind to its own consciousness for truths indispensable to its own happiness."[13] When he writes in the "Dejection" Ode, "O Lady! we receive but what we give, / And in our life alone does Nature live,"[14] he is referring not to

[12]Owen Barfield, in *Saving the Appearances: A Study in Idolatry* (New York: Harcourt, Brace & World, 1965), pp. 128–30, suggests that Wordsworth's "nostalgic hankering" after what Barfield calls "original participation"—the belief that "there stands behind the phenomena, and *on the other side of them from me*, a represented which is of the same nature as me" (p. 42)—and identifies with pantheism was an answer to the question, What does a "disgodded" (Schiller's term) nature, experienced as a representation of something, represent?

[13]Samuel Taylor Coleridge, Essay 15, *The Friend* (1867; rpt. New York, 1951), p. 64.

[14]Quotations from Coleridge are from *The Poems of Samuel Taylor Coleridge*, ed. E. H. Coleridge (1912; rpt. London: Oxford University Press, 1960).

the paradox of Christian charity, where the reward is all in the giving, but to a way of being happy and complete: "Joy, Lady! is the spirit and the power, / Which wedding Nature to us gives in dower / A new Earth and new Heaven." Joy rooted in the self is the goal.[15] Vivid and morally serious as Coleridge makes the dilemma of spiritual aridity, in the "Dejection" Ode he does not express a transcendental solution to it.

Rossetti does. Her "nature" and her human nature are quite fallen and only partly restored by grace. She is intensely sensitive to the consequences of a fallen nature, to the gap between nature and supernature. She expresses this corollary to the doctrine of analogy quite unequivocally in *Letter and Spirit* when she refers to "the inadequacy of aught temporal to shadow forth that which is eternal" (p. 49). While Rossetti recognizes a "principle of joy" in nature, she is wary of presuming to discover it easily and without fail; consequently, she resists the often strong attraction of nature for fear of "worshipping" nature. In some poems she struggles to the conclusion that God is wholly transcendent, not immanent, and that nature can literally be a hindrance to spiritual progress. Detachment, not communion, is her goal. This quite anti-Romantic stance clearly represents a conservative religious view of nature—a form of asceticism.

The Face of the Deep repeatedly attests that in Rossetti's view idolatry was the besetting sin of the age. She was undoubtedly reacting against Romantic tendencies to idolize the self and nature. Of imagination she writes, "A world of mere opinions and mere fancies, of daydreams and castles in the air, is antagonistic to the true and substantial world of revelation, and is more hollow and unavailing than was Jonah's gourd" (p. 46). Contemplation of nature had been profoundly and subtly appropriated by the Romantic poets as a source of personal revelation— more direct than Scripture and ecclesiastical teachings—and as the foundation for a revived Gnosticism directed toward the reconciliation of man with nature and the consequent reintegration of human personality from its fall into conflicting selves.[16] Nature had become the focus of an "idolatry" of the material world and of imagination, Pan *redivivus*. None of these developments was acceptable to Rossetti, as her poems show.

[15]Or, as Abrams points out, "joy, the necessary condition for 'the shaping spirit of Imagination,' is described as the inner power which unites the living self to a living outer world" (*Natural Supernaturalism*, p. 277). As Abrams shows, Coleridge transposed apocalyptic diction ("the new Earth and new Heaven") to refer to a temporal paradise created by the mind.

[16]Cf. Abrams, *Natural Supernaturalism*, chaps. 3 and 4, pp. 143–252.

In *The Face of the Deep* Rossetti presents nature from two perspectives: as type and as a potentially vital source of energy and knowledge. This second view she rejects. The heavens "are spread out above all humankind as an open scroll declaring the Glory of God" (p. 217), but nature itself is insignificant, not vital, compared with the potential of "heaven":

> Looking forward to this [heaven], what terrestrial sight is worth hankering after because of beauty or majesty? It will pass by and be no more seen; no, nor peered after. . . . I once grieved and grudged because I could not betake myself to a vantage ground whence to watch an eclipse: the grief might have been simply blameless, but the grudge proved that I was in a double sense loving darkness rather than light. [p. 231]

In the language and tropes of this passage Rossetti synthesizes her approach to the typological and Romantic traditions. "Beauty," "majesty," "hankering," and "grieved and grudged" are Romantic coin, which, by implication and assertion, are her own. She has hankered after nature, but now she hankers after heaven. She has grieved at being denied nature's most "transcendent" beauty, but now she makes an absolute distinction between nature and the spiritual. In the act of devaluing nature she crowns her argument with an analogy—wholly characteristic of her poetry and prose—between natural and regenerate behavior: begrudging providence the missed eclipse is "in a double sense loving darkness rather than light."

III

There are in fact two Rossettis in the nature poems, but both are religious. One praises God through a transparent vision of typological nature, through symbols both joyful and gloomy. The other is self-conscious but resists self-tyranny; she questions, complains, and tries to come to terms through the narrow gate of orthodox faith. These two, not mutually exclusive, aspects represent what can be distinguished as the typological and Romantic traditions.[17] In "The

[17]In Rossetti's poetic career the typological aspect emerged first. In 1844 she imitated George Herbert's "Vertue" in her poem "Charity"; Quarles's emblem poems were models for "The end of time" and "Love Ephemeral" (1845), each accompanied by a

thread of life" and "An old-world thicket," Rossetti challenges Romantic assumptions and values.[18] "The thread of life" clearly resembles Wordsworth's "Intimations of Immortality" Ode and "An old-world thicket" Coleridge's "Dejection: An Ode," but Rossetti's poems dramatize the conflict between Romantic "natural supernaturalism" and Christian values of detachment and self-denial.

Ambivalence toward nature—perceiving its "jubilee," as Rossetti's narrator calls it, and yet not being able to share in it—appears in Wordsworth's and Coleridge's poems, when a vibrant nature is apprehended but not experienced by the speaker. Being shut out from nature is felt as a profound deprivation. The speakers of Rossetti's poems feel the pull of nature and so experience a similar isolation, but at the same time they fear nature's hegemony. Rossetti's poems describe her argument with herself and its resolution in a mystical experience of a transcendent God. Attachment to nature, we can deduce, may be a hindrance to spiritual progress; detachment is the ideal. In short, the "natural man" must be regenerated.

To suggest the way to this regeneration, Rossetti quite boldly invents in these poems an alternative to the Romantic communion with nature, a communion based on a theological ideal of individuality. I should say, she reinvents it, for certainly she recalled Dante's paradisiacal vision of "angels with outspread wings making festival, each distinct in brightness and function."[19] Recognizing Rossetti's emphasis on the *individual's* communion, critics have mistakenly aligned Rossetti with Romanticism and even existentialism.[20] But to grasp fully Rossetti's idea of individuality—expressed in these poems and throughout her work—we must recognize the element of self-renunciation, an element repugnant to both the Romantic and existential

---

pictorial emblem. Then Romanticism began to play a role in Rossetti's writing ("Serenade," in 1845). In this early work she was uncritical of Romanticism and joined emblems and Romantic perspectives in single poems. In 1849, for example, she wrote several religious allegories drawn from nature which are distinguished from the more static perspective of the emblem by their empirical method (see, e.g., "Symbols").

[18]Lona Mosk Packer, *Christina Rossetti* (Berkeley: University of California Press, 1963), pp. 320–24, suggests 1877 as a possible date for these poems and discusses Rossetti's reading of Wordsworth's "Intimations" Ode and Coleridge's "Dejection."

[19]*Paradiso*, canto XXI, *The Divine Comedy of Dante Alighieri*, trans. John Sinclair (New York: Oxford University Press, 1977), p. 453; hereafter cited by page number in the text.

[20]See Packer's discussion in *Christina Rossetti*, pp. 320–24.

ideologies. For Rossetti, the individual gains her soul by the seemingly contradictory act of subordinating herself to God.

Two terms describe the distinct religious issues underlying Rossetti's poems: "private judgment" and "authority," both derived from Newman's formulation that "there are two great principles in action in the history of religion, Authority and Private Judgment" (*Apologia*, p. 193). "The thread of life" and "An old-world thicket" are exceptional in their exercise of private judgment, with their blunt cosmic questions and answers about the Romantic unity of mind and nature, a unity from which God has been eliminated; but they are also quite orthodox in their submission to religious authority.

The exercise of private judgment is a central principle in Newman's religious thought, a revitalizing principle, one may argue, when held, as it was by Newman, in conjunction with respect for authority. Newman writes in the *Apologia*: "Catholic Christendom is no simple exhibition of religious absolutism but presents a continuing picture of Authority and Private Judgment alternately advancing and retreating as the ebb and flow of the tide" (p. 193). Rossetti's solutions to these opposing claims of conscience and authority echo Newman's; and, in "The thread of life" and "An old-world thicket," they diverge emphatically from the broad Romantic adherence to private judgment alone. In these two poems the speakers succumb to nature's suggestive power, denying their own feelings of alienation, and denying their spiritual anguish in accordance with the myth of the divinity immanent in nature. Upon that denial, which is an exercise of "private judgment," is built the dramatic reversal, the rejection of Romantic faith in nature. The result, for both speakers, is a religious "conversion." And this conversion is a return to the authenticated revelation of scripture and tradition—in other words, to some of the elements in religion that constitute authority.

In "The thread of life" (II, 122–23) the speaker is nagged by the sense that, as Newman says, nature "remains without its divine interpretation." The poem consists of three stanzas, each in the form of a sonnet. The first stanza describes isolation from an "irresponsive" nature and from a past that had been hopeful. The octave austerely insists that the true relation between man (mind) and nature is indeterminate and free:

> The irresponsive silence of the land,
>> The irresponsive sounding of the sea,
>> Speak both one message of one sense to me:—

288

Aloof, aloof, we stand aloof, so stand
Thou too aloof bound with the flawless band
    Of inner solitude; we bind not thee;
    But who from thy self-chain shall set thee free?
What heart shall touch thy heart? what hand thy hand?—
                        [1.1–8]

It might seem that Rossetti's "irresponsive" nature is synonymous with Coleridge's "inanimate cold world allowed / To the poor loveless ever-anxious crowd" in "Dejection," but this suggestion is misleading. Rossetti violently pulls away from such a view as Coleridge held. Nature simply is irresponsive and aloof; in Rossetti's poem nothing binds nature and humanity, there is no primary thread from God running through nature to the individual soul.[21] Indifferent nature can offer the suffering person no release from "inner solitude": "But who from thy self-chain shall set thee free?" pitiless nature asks. Personality is a circumscribing web that nature cannot penetrate. Furthermore, the speaker is cut off from a former sense of the sympathy of friends and of nature itself:

And sometimes I remember days of old
When fellowship seemed not so far to seek
    And all the world and I seemed much less cold,
    And at the rainbow's foot lay surely gold,
And hope felt strong and life itself not weak.
                      [1. 9–14]

The first stanza, then, depicts the soul's crisis of alienation—Rossetti's gentler word is "aloofness"—and spiritual coldness. By a process the poem does not show, the speaker has been deprived of optimism and a sense of well-being. But these feelings were only semblances, or so the repeated "seem" leads us to believe, ironically undermining the speaker's nostalgia. Furthermore, the rainbow's pot of gold unequivocally mocks her past vision of nature with its implication of naive optimism—as if to demean with a sweeping parody all Romantic conceptions of nature.

[21]Rossetti's conception of nature, so unlike the Romantic ideal of nature's benevolence, may have been influenced by the generally prevalent Darwinian conception of a nature determined by laws of survival, a conception that at first specifically confounded theological assumptions about divine goodness.

The second stanza moderates that denunciation:

> Thus am I mine own prison. Everything
>   Around me free and sunny at ease:
>   Or if in shadow, in a shade of trees
> Which the sun kisses, where the gay birds sing
> And where all winds make various murmuring;
>   Where bees are found, with honey for the bees;
>   Where sounds are music, and where silences
> Are music of an unlike fashioning.
>
> [2. 1–8]

Nature *is* beautiful, "kissed" by God who creates even the shadows (significant to Rossetti as emblems of "invisible things"). In rapid succession the speaker is pulled out of her prison toward nature. But the impulse dies. Both the psychological prison and the placid exterior world are shown to be dead ends, a discovery that leads to the frustrated question:

> Then gaze I at the merrymaking crew,
>   And smile a moment and a moment sigh
> Thinking: Why can I not rejoice with you?
>
> [2. 9–11]

Coleridge and Wordsworth ask this same question, but their answers imply that the subjective self must and will be fulfilled. Coleridge finds his resources within: "I may not hope from outward forms to win / The passion and the life, whose fountains are within" ("Dejection"). In the "Intimations" Ode Wordsworth works back to a reassuring faith in nature's purgative power:

> O joy! that in our embers
> Is something that doth live,
> That nature yet remembers
> What was so fugitive!

In a crucial move Rossetti retreats from her Romantic question and advances to a declaration:

> But soon I put the foolish fancy by:
> I am not what I have nor what I do;
> But what I was I am, I am even I.
>
> [2. 12–14]

The speaker makes a judgment about reality and, radically, rejects the reality of nature. And while the rather biblically redundant passage is an answer Coleridge and Wordsworth might have endorsed—"I am even I"—they would have construed "I" as intimate with nature, sharing its beauty and joy. Rossetti's speaker, however, knows that nature can sing while she grieves, but her grief will not "the season wrong," as Wordsworth says. Isolation from nature is, in Rossetti, the path to detachment from the world and, as the third and last stanza shows, to a new level of spiritual life.

The third stanza is a joyful expression of faith in the doctrine of personal redemption through God alone. It acknowledges each soul's eternal, unique spiritual identity, reveling in the discovery that the Christian scheme not only provides for self-expression but also requires it, since salvation is perceived as the "use of waste" of self, in the sense Newman means: "The day, we know, will come, when every Christian will be judged . . . by what he has done for himself: when, of all the varied blessings of Redemption, in which he was clad here, nothing will remain to him but what he has incorporated in his own moral nature, and made part of himself."[22]

Rossetti's speaker is released from the imprisoning self, not by an attachment to natural beauty, which is always essentially aloof, but by letting that beauty go, by receiving herself from God, and giving herself back to God, freely:

> And this myself as king unto my King
>   I give, to Him Who gave Himself for me;
>   Who gives Himself to me . . .
>
> [3. 9–11]

The image of the soul as king is drawn from Revelation 1:7. In *The Face of the Deep*, Rossetti comments on this passage: "At least and lowest, each of us king with subject self to rule; priest with leprous self to examine and judge." And she prays: "O Good Lord . . . Give us royal hearts to give back ourselves to Thee, and keep back nothing" (p. 16). The sonnet rings with the exuberance of the kingly rather than the priestly soul and with "certitude" as possessive pronouns,

[22]John Henry Newman, Sermon 3, "Evangelical Sanctity, the Completion of Natural Virtue," *Newman's University Sermons, Fifteen Sermons Preached before the University of Oxford, 1826–1843,* intro. D. M. MacKinnon and J. D. Holmes (1871; rpt. London: SPCK, 1970), p. 53.

parallel constructions, and extravagant universal abstractions accumulate.

"The thread of life" makes clear the contrast important to Newman between the "natural" and "regenerate" soul.[23] "Natural man" is attuned to and measured by nature, Wordsworth's "soul of all . . . moral being." Nature is an infallible sign of God's existence, instinct with divinity, a medium of communion with him. Coleridge could thus write about Chamouni: "Who *would* be, who *could* be an Atheist in this valley of wonders!"[24] But Rossetti declares nature mute and separate and ultimately an impediment to her soul's movement toward God. Neither nature's muteness nor its expressiveness is the ultimate reality. For that reality, the poet looks to the austere sacrifice of Christ (always granting that the import of this sacrifice can be grasped only in each soul's active, individual love and faith). The second stanza observes that each person is a unique, powerful soul, but interwoven with that "thread of life" is each Christian's submission to a greater principle than individuality, which might be called "humility." Although both Christian and Romantic aspire to possess their souls in patience, the Romantic would resist such a limit on the self. Glorying in one's self is, of course, far different from giving one's self.

Rossetti believes that, in contrast to the inevitable transience of this natural self, the single soul's strength resides in its eternal identi-

---

[23]See *University Sermons*, especially "The Influence of Natural and Revealed Religion Respectively" and "Evangelical Sanctity the Perfection of Natural Virtue"; and in *An Essay in Aid of a Grammar of Assent* (Notre Dame, Ind.: University of Notre Dame Press, 1979), see "Presumption" (pp. 66ff.), "Belief in One God" (pp. 95ff.), and "Belief in the Holy Trinity" (pp. 109ff.). In *A Grammar of Assent*, although Newman no longer speaks of "natural" man but of "instinct" and "conscience," he still makes the fundamental distinction between "natural" and "revealed" knowledge and belief. He seems to have dropped the word "natural" as imprecise. He discusses the initial apprehension of "One God" as being derived from conscience: "from the perceptive power which identifies the intimations of conscience with the reverberations or echoes . . . of an external admonition, we proceed on to the notion of a Supreme Ruler and Judge" (p. 97). Further on in his argument he writes: "How far this initial religious knowledge comes from without, and how far from within, how much is natural, how much implies a special divine aid which is above nature, we have no means of determining" (p. 105). His point is that at this first level of belief human "nature" is unaided and unshaped by revelation. For knowledge beyond that of the one God, however, revelation must come into play to impress the imagination with such dogmas as that of the Holy Trinity.

[24]From the *Morning Post*, September 11, 1802, introductory note by Coleridge to his "Hymn Before Sun-rise, In the Vale of Chamouni."

ty. In the following image the stable soul is juxtaposed with nature's evolving beauty and corruption:

> Ever mine own, while moons and seasons bring
> From crudeness ripeness mellow and sanative;
> Ever mine own, till Death shall ply his sieve;
> [3. 5–7]

Rossetti follows her conception out along the thread of life to the apocalypse: "And still mine own, when saints break grave and sing." The sonnet—and the poem—end affirming *life*, with the recognition that God's gift of himself has bound the soul to sing "a sweet new song of His redeemed set free." In "The thread of life" the poet's acts of interpreting her spiritual condition and posing her own theological truths are acts of "private judgment"; asserting her humility before God and the redemptive mystery is submission to "authority." Finally, Rossetti's love for Christ leads her to the authority of the Bible. In the poem's last lines, the speaker, with Paul (see 1 Cor. 15:55), is convinced of eternity:

> He bids me sing: O Death, where is thy sting?
> And sing: O grave, where is thy victory?
> [3. 13–14]

In "An old-world thicket" (II, 123–28) the speaker reconstructs another intense spiritual experience, which Rossetti pointedly associates with Dante's conversion in the dark wood of canto I of the *Divine Comedy*: "Una selva oscura," from the second line of *Inferno* I, is the epigraph. The "old-world thicket" is an ironic allusion to the Romantic landscape that is the unique and tangible medium of the poet's purgation—the Keatsian "thicket" of "Ode to a Nightingale."[25] Rossetti's thicket is that and more: a symbolic landscape in which a religious conversion occurs.

The first line of the poem reinforces the conflict between Romantic and religious values (here represented by Dante): "Awake or sleeping (for I know not which)" echoes the last line of Keats's ode: "Fled is that music:—Do I wake or sleep?" Yet it also recalls canto I of the *Inferno*:

[25]Quotations from Keats are from *The Poems of John Keats*, ed. Jack Stillinger (Cambridge: Harvard University Press, Belknap Press, 1978).

Io non so ben ridir com' io v'entrai,
tant'era pieno di sonno a quel punto
che la verace via abbandonai.
[*Inferno*, I.10–12]

(I cannot rightly tell how I entered there, I was so full of sleep at that moment when I left the true way. [p. 23]

Dante and Rossetti enter a dark wood where the "straight way [is] lost." Rossetti's poem opens as an allegory, yet its literal conflict is precisely the Romantic relationship between an individual and nature. Initially, nature may or may not represent a medium of purgation through beauty. Its trees, birds, flowers, light, shade, and water are woven into a slightly skewed vision of spiritual fruitfulness. But all the narrator's impressions are thrown into ironic relief by "seemed" and "as if" and by symbolic associations: for example, the elm, traditionally a Christian symbol for the strength derived from faith, "dies in secret from the core"; and the ivy is "weak and free" (ll. 8, 9).

Irony, however, discredits the narrator only enough to solve the problem of portraying the contrast between the soul before and after conversion.

Such birds they seemed as challenged each desire;
Like spots of azure heaven upon the wing,
Like downy emeralds that alight and sing,
Like actual coals on fire,
Like anything they seemed, and everything.
[ll. 11–15]

Before conversion, the soul is infatuated by "natural piety" and sees nature as infinite in itself. But the implication of "seem" and of the similes and the hyperbolic tone is that nature is *not* all it seems: not as potent as human desires, as heaven, as the creative soul, as the soul inflamed with love of God. The narrator's irony is stronger in these lines:

They [the birds] seemed to speak more wisdom than we speak,
To make our music flat
And all our subtlest reasonings wild or weak.
[ll. 18–20]

294

Again, the "seem" distances the speaker from her earlier ecstatic impressions.

Still, the next three stanzas do describe and declare the pagan beauty of the wood. Perhaps the key to this curiously animate and sensual description of nature is in stanza 6:

> The shade wherein they revelled was a shade
> That danced and twinkled to the unseen sun;
> [ll. 26–27]

Prefigured here is the climactic image of the sun glinting off each leaf, but the emphasis on "shade" is also striking enough to remind us that nature is divinity "seen through a glass darkly," or "uninterpreted," to use Newman's term. Certainly nature seems full of God's glory in these stanzas: Christian symbols such as the butterfly—a sign of resurrection—dew, eyes, water, and the colors of red and gold are interwoven. The earth seems to drink the waters of freshness: "Root fathom-deep and strawberry on its bank" (l. 35), but the soul is dry. Nature reveals God's glory, but—as Newman says in a fine, anti-Romantic distinction—it does not reveal his will. The accomplishment of "An old-world thicket" is its persuasiveness about nature's brilliance, for it never weakens nature's claim while arguing for the spirit. The "evil" implied in Rossetti's poem is not the inability to rejoice with nature, as Wordsworth has it, but to rejoice mistakenly by construing nature as heaven rather than as one sign of heaven.

But the tone of wonder and appreciation changes in stanza 8. Stanza 11 names the "bitter hour" (l. 42) and describes despair that "brimmed full my cup" (l. 50). These allusions to Christ's agony in Gethsemane emphatically give the narrator's suffering a specific theological meaning, identifying her rebellion and pain with the resistance to God's will which resolves in overwhelming contrition. The powerful phrase at the end of stanza 10 expresses impotent self-reflexiveness: "Self stabbing self with keen lack-pity knife" (l. 45). Psychological stages of breakdown and conversion follow this painful awareness. What St. John of the Cross called the "night of sense"[26] descends:

---

[26]St. John of the Cross, *Dark Night of the Soul*, ed. and trans. E. Allison Peers (Garden City, N.Y.: Doubleday Image, 1959), p. 61; hereafter cited by page number in the text.

> Therefore I sat me down: for wherefore walk?
> And closed mine eyes: for wherefore see or hear?
>
> [ll. 56–57]

And later, in stanza 20, the speaker says, "for still my bodily eyes were closed and dark" (l. 92). What happens during this "night of sense," this passive retreat? An unconscious faculty arises:

> Without my will I hearkened and I heard
> (Asleep or waking, for I know not which),
> Till note by note the music changed its pitch;
>
> [ll. 61–63]

until finally,

> Such universal sound of lamentation
> I heard and felt, fain not to feel or hear;
> Nought else there seemed but anguish far and near;
> Nought else but all creation
> Moaning and groaning wrung by pain or fear, . . .
>
> [ll. 71–75]

Contrast these lines with Coleridge's "Dejection" Ode when he hears in the wind a "Devils' yule" "perfect in all tragic sounds" and the "groans, of trampled men, with smarting wounds." In his lines the active faculty is imagination, while in Rossetti's poem the will is passive, yet utterly receptive to the dark moral truth that Paul seized upon: "For we know that the whole creation groaneth and travaileth in pain together until now" (Rom. 8:22). Such passive reception is Rossetti's definition of the action of divine grace.

Coleridge makes nature a "mad Lutanist," an artist. Rossetti makes it a philosopher interpreting existence. But her still-infidel self reacts to the piercing sense of universal suffering in somewhat Miltonic terms:

> My heart then rose a rebel against light,
> Scouring all earth and heaven and depth and height,
> Ingathering wrath and gloom,
> Ingathering wrath to wrath and night to night.
>
> [ll. 77–80]

The dimensions are heroic, the torment internal and self-inflicted. Rossetti's Christian psychology baldly puts responsibility on the rebel self. The self gathers evil to its own evil, which is always primary and present in the form of original sin.

Stanzas 21 to 28 are reminiscent of the *spiritus vertiginis* of St. John of the Cross, the spirit that destroys a person's capacity for private judgment because it "darkens their senses in such a way that it fills them with numerous scruples and perplexities" (*Dark Night of the Soul*, p. 88). Furthermore, theological idea is echoed in poetic device as Rossetti groans in spondees but mocks herself in regular light iambs:

> Wh̆y shŏuld Ĭ bréathe, whóse bréath wăs bút ă sígh?
>
> Wh̆y shŏuld Ĭ líve, whŏ dŕew sŭch páinfŭl bréath?
>
> Ŏh wéarў wórk, thĕ únańswerăblé wh̆y!—
>
> [ll. 101–3]

The slight irony reminds us that the Christian's duty is, in Newman's terms, to try to achieve "certitude" in such questions by private judgment.

The soul desires to achieve passivity and emptiness in a mystical contest between divine and human wills. In this poem the soul finally experiences her full depth of spiritual darkness when she becomes "birthless and deathless, void of start or stop" (l. 125). The turning point is confirmed by the soul's perception that nature does offer consolation: "The wood, and every creature of the wood, / Seemed mourning with me in an undertone" (ll. 131–32). Finally she is filled "with yearnings like a smouldering fire that burned" (l. 138), again like St. John of the Cross, who is "kindled in love with yearnings" (p. 33). If the soul has been purged, is empty, what then is the ensuing music "without, within me" (l. 141) in stanza 24 but mystical grace? Accordingly, the landscape assumes a sacramental character in the sudden pastoral images:

> At length a pattering fall
> Of feet, a bell, and bleatings, broke through all.
> [ll. 144–45]

In canto I of the *Inferno*, Dante prefigures the resolution of his spiritual crisis with an image of the hill "clothed with the beams of the

297

planet that leads men straight on every road" (p. 23). A similar symbol of the sun resolves Rossetti's poem, a fall sunset with oblique rays glittering warmly:

> Then I looked up. The wood lay in a glow
>   From golden sunset and from ruddy sky;
>   The sun had stooped to earth though once so high;
>   Had stooped to earth, in slow
> Warm dying loveliness brought near and low.
>
> [ll. 146–50]

In slow monosyllables Christ is typified as God, the sun whose "warm dying loveliness" is "brought near and low."

It should be clear that the "old-world thicket" is a spiritualized landscape. Throughout the poem we are led to think symbolically by the speaker's imposition of analogies between the evolution of her inner self and nature's mood. We see that the soul is suffused with grace by analogy with the wood which "[lies] in a glow." The image, "Each twig was tipped with gold, each leaf was edged / And veined with gold from the gold-flooded west" (ll. 161–62) might have its source in Coleridge's "Religious Musings":

> Touched by the enchantment of that sudden beam
> Straight the black vapour melteth, and in globes
> Of dewy glitter gems each plant and tree;
> On every leaf, on every blade it hangs!
>
> [ll. 99–102]

But Rossetti has made this image a much more explicit symbol of Christian individuality by placing it in the context of a whole tableau of Christian symbols. Especially significant is the symbol that just precedes it, "Each water drop made answer to the light, / Lit up a spark and showed the sun his face" (ll. 151–52), for these lines suggest the give and take between the soul and God. As in "The thread of life," Rossetti links Christian individuality to faith and love, the loving acceptance that Christ's death saved human souls. The moon, too, symbolizes this reciprocity: she has "put on his glory for the coronet, / Kindling her luminous coldness to its noon, / As his great splendour set" (ll. 157–59). By analogy with human nature, the lines suggest that each soul too is glorified only in relation to God and to Christ's death. Traditional imagery of Christ as the "patriarchal ram"

298

(l. 171) who leads a "homeward flock" (l. 169) perfectly conveys the submission and patience essential to perfected spirituality. From the brillance of gold-threaded nature—implicitly, the glory of the self—the poem subsides into "sun-brightened" (l. 179) patience and hope in revelation.

IV

In 1879 Rossetti published *Seek and Find*, a book that praises creation lyrically and intellectually in its study of the Benedicite. "The thread of life" and "An old-world thicket" both suggest one reason why Rossetti's praise of nature did not overflow into poetry as voluptuously as it did in *Seek and Find*: for her, Romantic poetry dangerously entangled the Christian act of praise with pantheism; its exaltation of nature obscured "the unreality of material phenomena" (*Apologia*, p. 21). Consequently, her conversion poems challenge the Romantic's love of nature with the Christian's faith. By their self-irony the poems acknowledge that to idolize nature and the self is a very subtle distortion of the love of creation that Christianity enjoins. The testimony of each poem is that the soul's sickness is not healed by nature. Instead, the soul symbolically withdraws its faith from creation and places it in God.

Rossetti arrives at this affirmation of religious faith by the exercise "of a private judgment, not formed arbitrarily and according to one's fancy or liking, but conscientiously, and under a sense of duty," to borrow again from Newman (*Apologia*, p. 30). Newman argues that private judgment in religion is necessitated by the principle of probability governing religious truth. In "An old-world thicket" Rossetti cries out against the inconclusiveness of existence and the moral confusion it can lead to, invoking "the unanswerable why." With this question the poem goes beyond the conflict between Romanticism and religious humility to deeper, more univeral questions of meaning. But Rossetti clearly recognizes that there are no answers: there is no "certainty," to use Newman's term, and she knows that, to achieve "certitude," she can at best only discriminate among judgments. In "The thread of life," after posing the question "why can I not rejoice with you?" the speaker immediately recognizes its fatuity: "But soon I put the foolish fancy by." Private judgment in religion is careful to eliminate "fancy or liking."

Rossetti's solution does not, as it might first seem to, eliminate the problem of personal unresponsiveness to nature or to any other form of experience. Instead it places the focus of spiritual enlightenment in the self and the source in God. Nature interposes between the person and God at the risk of this enlightenment. Rossetti writes in *The Face of the Deep:* "The antitype determines the type, not this that. . . . It is pious to contemplate autumn, winter, spring, summer as emblematical of our dear Lord's death, burial, resurrection, ascended glory; but to treat these as if they were a parable of those, is to deny the faith" (p. 380). Rossetti acknowledges that nature, contemplated typologically, may be a mirror of religious mysteries. But she is also sensitive to the contemporary heresy that naturalizes the supernatural and vice-versa. For Rossetti, nature often must be swept aside in order to experience God through Christ. The recollected soul, infused with grace, is then capable of emanating that grace to the world in acts of faith and love.

Rossetti is attracted to the Romantic's ideal of communion with nature; she is attracted to nature itself. But the antithesis of her attraction, obedience to a spiritual value of detachment, triumphs and paradoxically makes possible "holy" (not self-interested) praise. It makes possible her devotional poetry. By such dialectic, many of Rossetti's nature poems resist a Romantic construction of their praise and begin to accomplish what the great Benedicite does: they praise God through his creation.

LINDA SCHOFIELD

Being and Understanding:
Devotional Poetry of Christina
Rossetti and the Tractarians

In the "Postscript" to his *Victorian Devotional Poetry*, G. B. Tennyson suggests looking at Christina Rossetti's poetry in light of Tractarian verse in a way that helps to define the nature of the relationship between these contemporary religious writers. Although in the "Postscript" Tennyson is concerned primarily with revealing the Tractarian inheritance in Rossetti's poetry, his apt description of the Tractarian devotional mode as a "seedfield" that comes to "fruition" in Rossetti's work also points to her distinctive voice in Victorian devotional poetry (*VDP*, pp. 198–99). Certainly, Rossetti and the Tractarians use similar poetic forms, often drawn from metaphysical poetry and the Psalms, to dramatize and encourage Christian devotion. It is when we examine closely the confessional poems[1] found in John Keble's *Christian Year* and the collection *Lyra Apostolica* and those written by Rossetti that we discover fundamental differences in attitude and technique.[2] The purpose of my critical investigation is not

[1] I do not include poems from *Thoughts in Past Years* (Oxford: J. H. Parker, 1838) by Isaac Williams, another prominent Tractarian, for two reasons. The principal one is that none of the short poems contained in the volume falls into the category of confessional poems as I am defining it. The second is that Williams's and Rossetti's interest in writing poetry that could be broadly described as autobiographical deserves a separate full-length study.

[2] For purposes of this study I have defined "confessional poetry" as devotional verse that presents a single speaker conscious of his or her state of sin, that is, in a state of isolation from God. The poem describes a period of meditation during which the penitent reflects on his feelings or on scripture and Christian doctrine. The poem ends in some form of confession of faith.

to point out specific philosophical or theoretical affinities and differences between Rossetti and the Tractarians—such a study is beyond the scope of this necessarily limited essay.[3] Rather, I intend to show how Rossetti, in following a Tractarian practice—illustrating in verse the act of penitential prayer—moves beyond their example to produce a poetry that is a much more intensely personal and innovative rendering of Christian truth.

In poems centering on the religious experience of a single speaker, the "I," the Tractarians and Rossetti depict the process of spiritual renewal in roughly parallel ways. The speaker begins by recognizing his or her isolation from God and lamenting that fact, and ends by invoking and realizing God's mercy. In all cases the speakers learn one or more important Christian truths in the course of their devotional journeys. For Rossetti's speaker, the conversion is an emotional and psychic experience. The entire meditation, from despair to exultation, dramatizes a Christian's appropriation of religious doctrine. When we read the Tractarian equivalent, however, we do not watch the speaker understand and absorb the truth so much as we hear what the truth is.

The stated aims of *The Christian Year* and the *Lyra Apostolica* provide some helpful clues as to why the Tractarians approach the poetry of confession from a standpoint that differs radically from Rossetti's. The varying talents and temperaments of Hurrell Froude, John Henry Newman, and John Keble are less the issue here than the fact that all these poets expected a specific response from their readers. In his "Advertisement" to the original edition of *The Christian Year* Keble explains, "The object of the present publication will be attained, if any person find assistance from it in bringing his own thoughts and feelings into more entire unison with those recommended and exemplified in the Prayer Book."[4] This preface establishes *The Christian Year* as a guide to spiritual reflection, not just as a volume containing poetry inspired by Scripture and the Anglican liturgy. Newman's "Advertisement" to the *Lyra Apostolica* stresses the evangelical nature of the poetry the book contains and emphasizes that the function of the poetry is to guide a reader to a correct understanding of Christian thought: "The following compositions have been reprinted from the

---

[3]Tractarian theories on analogy and reserve and their relation to Rossetti, for instance, would require quite different criteria for a comparison of the poetry.

[4]John Keble, *The Christian Year*, 5th ed., ed. Walter Lock (London: Methuen & Co. Ltd., 1912), p.xxxv. All quotations are from this edition.

'British Magazine,' where they had the advantage of originally appearing, in the humble hope that they may be instrumental in recalling or recommending to the reader important Christian truths which are at this day in a way to be forgotten."[5]

Rossetti is not as explicit about her poetic purpose. She does not tell us in the "Prefatory Note" to *The Face of the Deep*, for instance, what her specific purpose is in juxtaposing biblical commentary with poetry. Nor, when she arranges the devotional poetry in *Verses* (1893) for the Society for Promoting Christian Knowledge, does she choose to write a preface akin to those introducing *Lyra Apostolica* and *The Christian Year*. Her confessional poems affirm this subtle but profound difference from the Tractarians. It is clear that Rossetti writes with Christian readers in mind; her poems require an audience both sympathetic to and knowledgeable about Christian teaching. Yet Rossetti does not direct a message to a community of believers; rather she leads a reader through a personal quest toward union with God and cognizance of his Word. Rossetti focuses on the self in her devotional poetry; the Tractarians focus on the precept.[6]

We see this difference in intention clearly when we juxtapose Keble's "Fourth Sunday in Advent" with Rossetti's "The thread of life" (II, 122–23). We can best determine the divergent emphases of the two poems by first comparing their structural patterns. Both poems begin with a single speaker contemplating the natural world and lamenting his or her isolation from it. There is no hint of a theological theme in either text until the speakers abruptly recollect God's sovereignty over them and the rest of creation. This moment occurs in the fifth stanza of Keble's poem and in the third section of Rossetti's poem. Both poets explore the meaning of specific biblical passages—Keble from Isaiah 32:3 and Rossetti from 1 Corinthians 15:55—by showing how scriptural truth applies to common experience. Both poets weave patterns of words and imagery into the fabric of the meditation in order to imply associations between the divine world and that of the lonely penitent. Sound and light are recurrent themes in Keble's poem; music, freedom, bondage, and the self are themes

[5][J. H. Newman et al.], *Lyra Apostolica*, ed. H. C. Beeching (London: Methuen, 1901), p.vii. All quotations are from this edition.

[6]Dolores Rosenblum also discusses the "self" in Rossetti's poetry in her article "Christina Rossetti's Religious Poetry: Watching, Looking, Keeping Vigil," VP 20 (1982): 33–49, although she places far greater emphasis than I do on the passivity of the persona.

developed in Rossetti's poem. These key words and images all acquire sacred meanings by the final lines of the two poems.

Without directly addressing God, the speakers in both poems move from isolation in the temporal world and ignorance of its meaning to a recognition that the divine reality not only includes them but makes sense of it all. Both speakers reach their conclusions by way of careful contemplation. They observe and consider their position in the universe and gradually reason their way to a realization of Christian truth. In "The thread of life" the words "thus" and "therefore," which begin the second and third stanzas respectively, direct the argument. Keble's speaker progresses from stating his present feeling of isolation (this stage in his contemplations culminates in the iteration of the word "'tis" in the fifth stanza) to asserting God's promise (this stage is directed by the use of the word "shall"). Whereas Rossetti's speaker never moves outside of her interior monologue, Keble's speaker moves from a personal statement to a general one; he applies what he has learned during his reflections to the communal "we."[7]

By tracing the rhetorical direction of "Fourth Sunday in Advent" we see that Keble's prevailing concern is to explore the broader symbolic implications of a scriptural passage for the edification of his implied reader. The central imagery is drawn from the passage in Isaiah which heads the poem, and the poet at no point deviates from an orthodox interpretation of the language in order to plunge into a complex or clever conceit. The average Christian reader easily understands the message and the diction. Indeed, the opening stanza immediately assumes the reader's sympathy:

> Of the bright things in earth and air
> How little can the heart embrace!
> Soft shades and gleaming lights are there—
> I know it well, but cannot trace.

The first two lines are an emphatic statement of fact, the last two, one man's confession about the limitations of his perception. With the passage from Isaiah in mind, the reader expects that somehow the "I" of this poem will explain in detail how Scripture applies to daily

[7] I have distinguished the personae by sex for reasons of clarity, although the use of these pronouns could also be defended on the grounds that Tractarian poetry has a distinctly masculine quality compared with Rossetti's. Certainly, past and recent critics have pointed out the distinctly feminine quality of much of Rossetti's verse.

experience. From the beginning, then, the poem is designed and organized to teach.

In "Fourth Sunday in Advent," Keble is less interested in evoking an empathetic response to the speaker's isolation from the beauties of the "earth and air" than in revealing what has caused his isolation. We are told soon enough. In the second stanza the speaker explains he is "unworthy," although we do not discover until later in the poem that this adjective describes a state of sin. The following stanzas show the speaker looking or listening to nature and failing to respond, not emotionally, but intellectually. He cannot "read" the world's message. By failing to provide concrete references to specific objects in the landscape, the speaker prevents his readers too from clearly "seeing" or "hearing." We are aware of the speaker's surrounding world as a jumble of symbols to be sorted out, not as an environment that dramatizes the feeling of isolation. Phrases such as "bright things," "shades and gleaming lights," "Nature's bounteous book," and "soft Music's cell" are confounding in their vagueness. The phrase "But patience!" therefore comes as a welcome relief from this confusion. We are not disappointed, for by introducing the ideas of spiritual light and sound in the sixth stanza, the speaker takes the metaphoric implications of the language to a plane where symbols can be explained. Heaven not only outrings "Earth's drowsy chime" and "outshines the taper's light," it gives the temporal qualities new meaning. From the seventh stanza to the end of the poem the speaker shows how human understanding of this world depends upon a comprehension of the divine reality, "the concord sweet of Love divine." G. B. Tennyson summarizes the meaning of the poem thus: "It is not enough to be responsive to nature's beauties as things in themselves, or even as vague pointers to a higher power. One must have a Christian understanding of nature as an analogue of God and a Christian understanding of sin as an impediment to seeing God clearly through nature [stanza 2]. . . . The corrective to such a condition is Christian patience and humility [stanza 6]" (VDP, p. 98).

The sound and light imagery in "Fourth Sunday in Advent" conveys religious truth by showing systematically how heaven's superior brightness will redeem the speaker's present experience of alienation. First, the speaker reminds the reader of the problem of sight:

These eyes, that dazzled now and weak,
At glancing motes in sunshine wink,

> Shall see the King's full glory break,
> Nor from the blissful vision shrink.
>
> [ll. 25–28]

The topic of "memory" is a subdivision of the discourse on the senses which also provides an apt subject for comparing the earthly and the heavenly kingdoms:

> If Memory sometimes at our spell
> Refuse to speak, or speak amiss,
> We shall not need her where we dwell
> Ever in sight of all our bliss.
>
> [ll. 37–40]

The poet leaves the reference to sound until the closing stanzas, where he reminds us again that the natural world embodies a lesson that we cannot learn, or read properly, until we are "taught" and "train'd" to achieve a necessary state of spiritual purity:

> The distant landscape draws not nigh
> For all our gazing; but the soul,
> That upward looks, may still descry
> Nearer, each day, the brightening goal.
>
> And thou, too curious ear, that fain
> Wouldst thread the maze of Harmony,
> Content thee with one simple strain,
> The lowlier, sure, the worthier thee;
>
> Till thou art duly train'd, and taught
> The concord sweet of Love divine:
> Then, with that inward Music fraught,
> For ever rise, and sing, and shine.
>
> [ll. 49–60]

In the concluding lines Keble ties up the central metaphors that were initiated and inspired by the biblical passage. The resolution has the effect of a well-constructed sermon. The medium of poetry allows Keble to drive home the full impact of his message by exploring the rich figurative possibilities of the language of scripture.

When juxtaposed to the effusive conclusion of Rossetti's "Thread of life," however, the resolution of "Fourth Sunday in Advent" strikes us as bland and predictable. The poem begins and ends as a lesson on how to regard a verse of Scripture in terms of daily experience. Rossetti works with the same idea, but she leads her speaker not merely to a comprehension of Christian truth but to the speaker's climactic appropriation of God's Word as her own. Unlike Keble's poem, "The thread of life" provides no theological markers to inform us that it is a devotional poem. At the beginning of the poem (which is composed of three stanzas in the sonnet form), the reader is plunged into the speaker's interior landscape without knowing where the imagery will lead. Like Keble's speaker, Rossetti's is isolated from the surrounding world, trying to comprehend what separates her from it. In contrast to the opening stanza of "Fourth Sunday in Advent," though, the first stanza of "The thread of life" focuses not on the speaker's inability to glean a lesson from a welter of natural symbols, but on her sense of solitude:

> The irresponsive silence of the land,
>   The irresponsive sounding of the sea,
>   Speak both one message of one sense to me:—
> Aloof, aloof, we stand aloof, so stand
> Thou too aloof bound with the flawless band
>   Of inner solitude; we bind not thee;
>   But who from thy self-chain shall set thee free?
> What heart shall touch thy heart? what hand thy hand?—
>
> [1. 1–8]

The picture of the outside world in these lines is as sketchy as Keble's vague "Nature's bounteous book." The land and sea merely suggest a landscape. It is their "irresponsive" quality in relation to the speaker that is explained in detail. The paradox of speaking silences and irresponsive sounds is incomprehensible unless we regard the starkness of the landscape as purely a manifestation of the speaker's anomie. Any sense we may have grasped of the shape of the outer world dissipates in the face of the outpourings of the dejected inner self. Since the world has been reduced to a shapeless void, we too are aware only of the speaker's lonely mental world.

The first line of the second stanza in "The thread of life" sums up the speaker's situation—"thus as I my own prison"—and then abruptly changes direction, moving from the inner to the outer world. Suddenly the vague sounds are the specific "singing" of birds and the "murmuring" of winds, and the silences are "music of an unlike fashioning." The scene is described in such loving detail that we wonder that the speaker cannot truly "rejoice" with everything around her. But instead of seeking union with the world of freedom and beauty outside her, the speaker willfully and deliberately rejects the participatory impulse:

> Then gaze I at the merrymaking crew,
>   And smile a moment and a moment sigh
> Thinking: Why can I not rejoice with you?
>   But soon I put the foolish fancy by:
> I am not what I have nor what I do;
>   But what I was I am, I am even I.
>
> [2. 9–14]

In a subdued declaration of her identity and individuality, the speaker chooses to stand apart from the "merrymaking crew," and the subtly derogatory connotations of that phrase should alert us to the changes in her attitude toward her isolation and herself.

It is not until the third stanza, however, that the effects of this change become manifest. The quiet assertion of being becomes an energetic insistence on the indestructibility of the self:

> Therefore myself is that one only thing
>   I hold to use or waste, to keep or give;
>   My sole possession every day I live,
> And still mine own despite Time's winnowing.
> Ever mine own, while moons and seasons bring
>   From crudeness ripeness mellow and sanative;
>   Ever mine own, till Death shall ply his sieve;
> And still mine own, when saints break grave and sing.
>
> [3. 1–8]

The speaker's hopeless isolation in the first stanza is transformed by these lines into a fortunate condition, for now we see the individual imaginatively transcend the limitations of the temporal world. The words "one" and "only" gain positive significance as the speaker methodically reveals the hitherto hidden value of her "sole possession." Nevertheless, it is only when the speaker gives up this newly discovered "possession" that the questions raised earlier in the poem are resolved. The poem has already forced us to change our view of nature, which no longer seems an Edenic terrestrial landscape but a world subject to "Time's winnowing." The sestet of the final stanza, like the last nine stanzas of Keble's poem, places the meaning of key words in a spiritual context. In Rossetti's poem the speaker wills this transformation of meaning to occur:

> And this myself as king unto my King
> I give, to Him Who gave Himself for me;
> Who gives Himself to me, and bids me sing
> A sweet new song of His redeemed set free;
> He bids me sing: O death, where is thy sting?
> And sing: O grave, where is thy victory?
>
> [3. 9–14]

By pledging her being to God, the speaker earns the right to proclaim his truth, his victory over death, as her own. Rossetti's speaker thus goes one step further than Keble's, who merely explains how one must think in order to grasp heaven's offering. When she makes the psychological leap into the realm of Christian promise, Rossetti's speaker is released from her bonds and is able not simply to hear music but to sing "a sweet new song of His redeemed set free." The passage from 1 Corinthians consummates the speaker's devotional experience. The words from Scripture redeem the period of isolation the speaker once suffered. The poem as a whole dramatizes a Christian's spiritual journey toward enlightenment and redemption.

A second pair of poems further demonstrates Rossetti's skill at dramatizing the act of conversion and the appropriation and profession of God's truth. Juxtaposing Rossetti's "Good Friday" (I, 186–87) and Froude's "Trembling Hope" puts Rossetti's achievement into perspective. "Trembling Hope" and "Good Friday" are equally concentrated explorations of Christian doctrine, but even though Froude consistently uses the personal pronoun "I," his poem lacks the intimacy and emotional intensity of Rossetti's. Like Keble, Froude strives for different effects from Rossetti. His poem conforms to the general purpose of the *Lyra Apostolica,* of which it forms a part. Although the supplicant invokes God's mercy directly, as Rossetti's persona does, he never rises imaginatively from his obedient, kneeling position. "Trembling Hope" lies in the background of a poem such as "Good Friday," though Froude does not attempt to establish the same degree of sympathy between the speaker and God.

The "I" in both "Trembling Hope" and "Good Friday" begins by meditating on a religious theme. Froude's speaker contemplates the meaning of Revelation 22:17. Rossetti's speaker contemplates Christ's Passion. The first stanzas of each poem are interrogative, and both disclose the speakers' consciousness of their own spiritual inadequacies. Froude's speaker asks whether he will personally realize Christ's promise of salvation to all believers; Rossetti's speaker asks why, as a believer, she cannot empathize with and thus fully comprehend Christ's sacrifice. Froude and Rossetti develop the theme of the speaker's estrangement from the Deity along parallel lines. In "Trembling Hope" the speaker emphasizes his sense of frustration and feelings of unworthiness by countering each potentially positive statement with a negative one:

> O Lord, I will, but cannot do,
> My heart is hard, my faith untrue;
> The Spirit and the Bride say, Come,
> The eternal ever-blessed Home
>   Oped its portals at my birth,
>   But I am chained to earth.
>
> [ll. 7–12]

Rossetti piles negative upon negative with similar effect:

> Not so those women loved
>   Who with exceeding grief lamented Thee;
>   Not so fallen Peter weeping bitterly;
> Not so the thief was moved;
>
> Not so the Sun and Moon
>   Which hid their faces in a starless sky . . .
>
> [ll. 5–10]

Both poets dramatize the theme of spiritual alienation by referring to specific words and events from Scripture. Froude's speaker hears "the Spirit and the Bride say, Come" and pictures heaven with opened "portals." Rossetti's speaker envisions the mourners at Christ's crucifixion. Both speakers deny their ability to enter into those envisioned scenes.

The speakers of the two poems reach a solution to their seemingly hopeless situations in the same way. When the speakers shed their passive attitudes and invoke the mercy and power of God, they shift to

310

the imperative. Froude's speaker demands "O set my heart at liberty"; Rossetti's speaker, "seek Thy sheep . . . And smite a rock" (ll. 14, 16). The impasse created by self-accusation and confession is overcome by supplication. The contemplation of biblical scenes and symbols reaches a climax in the final petition. After he has pictured himself in chains and with hardened heart, Froude's speaker recognizes that he must appeal to God to liberate his spirit and so allow him, in the words of the epigraph, to "take the waters of life freely." Similarly, Rossetti's speaker calls out to Christ the Shepherd to transform her hardness of heart into an emblem of catharsis and redemption.

Although the language of Scripture guides the progress of both speakers from estrangement from God to union with him, the nature of the final conversion in "Good Friday" is very different from that of the conversion in "Trembling Hope." Froude's poem, like Keble's, is instructive. The title and chapter heading give us clues about the direction the poem will take. Do we have any doubt how the remorseful penitent will answer his initial questions when the title "Trembling Hope" forms a part of the section entitled "Forgiveness"? The "hope" lies in the beckoning passage from Revelation; the poem for the most part stresses "trembling" humility before God. The very tone of the last two lines of the final stanza conveys the cautiously reverential attitude that the speaker has maintained throughout:

> The Golden Keys each eve and morn,
> I see them with a heart forlorn,
> Lest they should Iron prove to me—
> O set my heart at liberty.
>   May I seize what Thou dost give,
>   Seize tremblingly and live.
>   [ll. 13–18]

The most forceful word in these lines, "seize," is robbed of its evocative strength not only because it is modified by the adverb "tremblingly" but also because it is softened by the verb "may," which shifts the entire phrase into the subjunctive mood. God is kept at a distance, at arm's length in fact. Consequently, the poem proves to be a subtle lesson on how to accept God's mercy and forgiveness rather than a study of one man's spiritual journey.

Rossetti, on the other hand, concentrates on that journey. Like "The thread of life," "Good Friday" dramatizes the devotional experience. Through the course of her meditation a single speaker moves from a position of powerlessness and isolation to a state of grace. By holding the speaker, and the reader, in suspense about the outcome of the situation established in the opening lines, Rossetti ensures that the impact of the resolution will be especially forceful. The imagery in the first stanza of "Good Friday," unlike the well-of-life imagery in the first stanza of "Trembling Hope," is organically linked to the poem's concluding stanza. The question beginning "Am I" establishes that the poem will be concerned with identity as much as with sympathy:

> Am I a stone and not a sheep
>> That I can stand, O Christ, beneath Thy Cross,
>> To number drop by drop Thy Blood's slow loss,
> And yet not weep?
>
> [ll. 1–4]

Like "The thread of life," "Good Friday" is about transformation and conversion. The speaker begins by characterizing herself as a stone—an insensate object. She establishes that she is not one of the faithful flock, a "sheep" that can weep freely at the thought of Christ's tribulation for man's sake. This intermediary period of isolation ends much as the second stanza of "The thread of life" does, with an assertion of the self. Through the phrase "I, only I" the speaker arrives at an immediate apprehension of her place in the divine scheme. The final stanza derives its power from its thematic compression:

> Yet give not o'er,
>> But seek Thy sheep, true Shepherd of the flock;
> Greater than Moses, turn and look once more
>> And smite a rock.
>
> [ll. 13–16]

The speaker's empathy with Christ's suffering, her understanding of the Passion in theological terms, and her entrance into the Christian fold are all simultaneous. By appropriating the type for Christ—the rock from Exodus 17:5–6, given typological significance by Paul in 1 Corinthians 10:4—the speaker will be sustained as if by the waters of life, an image implicit in the final symbol of the rock. The conclusion of the poem thus indicates empathy for Christ's suffering and her understanding of the redemptive effect of his death. In contrast to Froude's image of the "Golden Keys," which cannot be readily grasped, the symbol of the rock allows Rossetti to show the speaker's complete assimilation of the Deity she had sought in frustration at the beginning of her prayer. Furthermore, Rossetti keeps the riddle of the stone a mystery until the last moment. In Froude's "Trembling Hope," the repeated phrase "O Lord," which constantly reminds us that God answers the prayers of a penitent, prevents the poem from achieving the same degree of tension and release as Rossetti's "Good Friday." The repeated supplication in Froude's poem assures us of God's presence and softens the impact of the final invocation, whereas in Rossetti's poem Christ does not seem alive to the speaker until she senses her communion with him.

Rossetti's poem "A better resurrection" (I, 68) demonstrates that a supplicatory refrain need not diminish the emotive force of the confessional poem, as it does in "Trembling Hope." In "A better resurrection," Rossetti uses an incantatory prayer to impel the speaker into a conversion as spectacular as that we see in "Good Friday." The phrases "O Jesus, quicken me," and "O Jesus, rise in me" (ll. 8, 16) are not passive reminders of God's power to help. The speaker lends force to these phrases by expressing them in the imperative. Most important, she suggests progress toward her climactic union with Christ by altering the predicate of the refrain. Although the refrains themselves suggest movement, the substance of the lines that precede them suggests stasis. Before we can determine the thematic significance of the incantatory prayer, therefore, we must take account of the lines that show the speaker walking imaginatively through a wilderness of remorse and self-accusation.

"A better resurrection" begins in much the same way as "Trembling Hope" and "Good Friday." The speaker describes her mental state with simile and metaphor and expresses her despair with a repetition of negative phrases:

> I have no wit, no words, no tears;
>   My heart within me like a stone
> Is numbed too much for hopes or fears;
>   Look right, look left, I dwell alone;
> I lift mine eyes, but dimmed with grief
>   No everlasting hills I see;
> My life is in the falling leaf:
>
> [ll. 1–8]

If we ignore for a moment the refrains to this and the following stanzas, we notice that the theme changes little. The speaker merely uses different images, moving from the lifeless plant to a definitively inanimate object, a bowl. The speaker seems fixed in her sense of lifelessness. What is perhaps less obvious on an initial reading is that the pattern of imagery represents the speaker's quest for transformation.[8] The speaker tests each simile and metaphor to describe her "life" until she strikes the right one—the one that can be converted, renewed:

> Cast in the fire the perished thing,
> Melt and remould it, till it be
> A royal cup for Him my King:
>> [ll. 21–23]

The full meaning of the poem does not become clear until the last line: "O Jesus, drink of me" (l. 24). The life the speaker discovers is eternal life, granted by Christ's sacrifice and commemorated in the Eucharist. By identifying herself with the communion chalice and finally the wine, the speaker of "A better resurrection," like the speaker of "Good Friday," becomes one with the Deity and so, in a climactic moment, imaginatively steps into the promise of eternal life.

If we return to the refrain of each stanza we see how this final transformation is implied gradually through the course of the poem. At first, the speaker asks Jesus to "quicken" her, then to "rise in" her, the suggestion being that Christ represents the life that will renew her. With this growing sense that Christ is coming to life within her, the speaker slowly abandons her dejection. In the second and third stanzas she shortens the catalogue of melancholy images to make room for metaphors for renewal (first the "sap of Spring," [l. 15], then the bowl cast into the fire [l. 21]) which prepare us for the final transfiguration. Seen in relation to the lines that precede them, the refrains mark the mind's gradual progress from spiritual emptiness to spiritual fullness. By juxtaposing static indicatives with supplicating imperatives that develop thematically, Rossetti convincingly illustrates the natural process of prayerful meditation—the speaker seems only half aware that God is answering. The refrains impel the devotion to the triumphant conclusion and lend coherence and emotive authenticity to the speaker's entire meditation. Like the "O Lord" iteration in

---

[8]Rossetti modifies this technique in "Long Barren" (I, 180). In this poem the speaker gradually discovers the language that will identify her with symbols of Christ's life-giving quality instead of the objects associated with his Passion. The substance of the refrains remains fairly static, but as Christ is described metaphorically in the introductory lines of the final stanza, the speaker and the Deity appear to merge.

"Trembling Hope," the incantatory "O Jesus" of "A better resurrection" consoles the speaker but, more significantly, drives her toward
the divine embrace. Although Rossetti uses many of the same rhetorical devices in "Good Friday" and "A better resurrection" that
Froude uses in "Trembling Hope," she is able to represent the confessional experience much more evocatively, and largely for this reason
engages the reader's sympathy for the speaker much more effectively
than does Froude.

Ostensibly, the speakers of "Trembling Hope" and "A better resurrection" answer their own prayers, for they will themselves into a
realization of God's grace. Their own voices achieve a resolution to
the problems their introductory entreaties set forth. Both Rossetti and
the Tractarian poets also wrote poems that use a rhetorical structure of
question and answer to explore the comforting qualities of God's
Word. In these poems, the second voice answers the anxious supplica-
tions of the first and in doing so provides a sense of confident finality
appropriate to an ostensibly personal and emotional poem. Several
poems published in Rossetti's *Verses* (1893) under the suggestive heading "Christ our All in all" show the poet experimenting with this kind
of dialogical form. Rossetti's alternation of the voice of the penitent
with a voice that is unmistakably that of God has no exact counterpart
in the Tractarian canon. This difference, as we shall see, is in itself
telling. As devotional dialogue poems, Newman's "Terror" and
Froude's "Weakness of Nature" provide a frame of reference with
which we can assess Rossetti's skill in her most successful use of the
form, in the poem "'Love is strong as death'" (II, 164).

In "Terror" Newman dramatizes a literal confession scene in which
an implied priest speaks alternately with a penitent:

> O Father, list a sinner's call!
> Fain would I hide from man my fall,
>   But I must speak, or faint:
> I cannot wear guilt's silent thrall—
>   Cleanse me, kind Saint!
>
> "Sinner ne'er blunted yet sin's goad;
> Speed thee, my son, a safer road,
>   And sue His pardoning smile
> Who walked woe's depths, bearing man's load
>   Of guilt the while."

[ll. 1–10]

The quotation marks clearly distinguish the two speakers. The words

> "I can but lift the Mercy-sign.
> This wouldst thou? It shall be!
> Kneel down . . ."
>
> [ll. 17–19]

reveal the specific actions that take place during the dialogue. Furthermore, the priest fulfills his proper function as intermediary between God and the confessor. The priest quotes the words "*Absolvo te,*" just as in his first speech, he refers the listener to Christian doctrine. The steady, doctrinally sanctioned words, such as "Sinner ne'er blunted yet sin's goad" and "peace cannot be, hope must be thine," contrast with the anxious entreaties of the penitent. The alternation of the contrasting voices implies that comfort can be found through religious instruction and absolution at the hands of God's representatives on earth. In "Terror," Newman maintains a distinct separation between confession and profession.

Froude's "Weakness of Nature" preserves this separation as well, although the second voice is anonymous. Unlike Newman, Froude does not provide easily interpreted clues to the second speaker's identity. It is possible the second voice is that of God, who responds through the penitent's conscience and memory of Scripture. After all, the penitent addresses God directly. It is equally possible that in his imagination Froude did not assign the words of the second stanza to anyone in particular. The poem may merely present the theologically appropriate response to the questions of a typical seeker after holiness. Certainly Froude, like Newman, avoids what W. David Shaw describes as the "intimacy" of Rossetti's poetry which makes God's identity as speaker clear.[9] As in "Terror," the second voice seems to regard the predicament of the first with knowing detachment. Froude appears more concerned with informing his readers of the correct attitude toward prayer and penance than with dramatizing a personal spiritual struggle.

In stanza one the stress on the autobiographical experience is somewhat deceptive, and the representation of the penitent's emotional state is confusing. The speaker communicates his sense of frustration with his devotional exercises by repeating the phrase "I have." The

---

[9]W. David Shaw, "Projection and Empathy in Victorian Poetry," *VP* 19 (1981): 324.

exclamatory phrase "O God of mercy!" and the expressive verbs
"haunt" and "fly" inform the reader of the speaker's heightened emotional condition. Yet the inversion of normal syntax in the second,
third, and fourth lines formalizes the language in such a way as to
counteract the impression of spontaneously felt emotion:

> "Lord, I have fasted, I have prayed,
> And sackcloth has my girdle been,
> To purge my soul I have essayed
> With hunger blank and vigil keen;
> O God of mercy! why am I
> Still haunted by the self I fly?"
>
> [ll. 1–6]

The epigraph, "Be strong, and He shall comfort thine heart" (Ps.
27:16),[10] seems to be intended as a key to the meaning of the poem,
or at least as an additional descriptive title, but the second speaker
seems uninterested in comforting this troubled heart. Although he
systematically resolves each of the problems introduced by the penitent, he does not actually respond empathetically to his distress. Instead, he uses generalizing indicatives and imperatives to create a
lesson on perseverance and ends with an anticlimactic reference to
biblical doctrine. The final couplet of the second stanza answers the
final couplet of the first, in which the penitent asks—in an emotive
and isolated half line—why he has been singled out for confusion.
The second voice seems to hear only a dispassionate accounting of
religious duties, not the cries of an anxious soul.

Froude and Newman demonstrate how a Christian ought to resolve
feelings of remorse. Rossetti's "'Love is strong as death'" dramatizes
the psychological process of resolution, not by juxtaposing emotion
with reason and remorse with instruction, but by interlocking these
elements of the confessional poem. Like Froude, Rossetti entitles her
poem with a line from Scripture, but in her case the "lesson" it implies
is not so much prescriptive as descriptive. In contrast to Froude's
epigraph—which suggests that God's love is to some degree conditional—Rossetti's title "'Love is strong as death,'" states a reassuring
truth. As a reference to the Song of Songs 8:6, the title alerts us to the
poem's focus on the love relationship between God and his redeemed

---

[10]This line comes from *The Book of Common Prayer* (1662) version of the Psalms,
after the Vulgate.

317

set free. The title also serves as a preface to the dramatization of a personal experience—a voice calls out in the panic and confusion of one on the point of death. The first stanza opens with an iterated *mea culpa* and continues with a stuttering appeal to God's love:

> "I have not sought Thee, I have not found Thee,
>   I have not thirsted for Thee:
> And now cold billows of death surround me,
> Buffeting billows of death astound me,—
>   Wilt Thou look upon, wilt Thou see
>   Thy perishing me?"
>
> [ll. 1–6]

Although the tenor of this stanza resembles that of the opening stanzas in Newman's and Froude's poems, Rossetti establishes a more intimate connection between her two voices than the Tractarians allow, not just by including the personal pronouns "I" and "Thee" but also by placing special emphasis on them. The second voice responds both intellectually and emotionally, like the second voice of Froude's poem, echoing words from the first stanza. But rather than instructing, this voice comforts and informs of truth by categorically reversing the first speaker's negative statements with positive affirmations of love. The word "not" of the first stanza is replaced by the word "yea" in the second. The second voice creates a context for the word "now," whose referent changes from the temporal and perishable to the eternal. A single word thus economically expresses a theological concept and develops the psychic drama; squandered time is redeemed, for through his loving sacrifice, God bound the penitent with love's bands "long ago." Moreover, by duplicating the grammatical structure of the first stanza in the second, Rossetti creates a dialogue in which the two participants appear to be on parallel planes: the Deity not only answers the supplicant's words in kind but transforms her utterances of despair into expressions of joy.

In the poem's resolution Rossetti fuses the muted aspirations of both Froude's and Newman's confessing voices: absolution, denial of self, and realization of God's comfort and mercy. "'Love is strong as death'" is Rossetti's most successful exploration of the I-Thee relationship between the self and God dramatized in many of her dialogue poems. Although we know that the first voice is addressing God, only the capitalized "me" at the very end signals for certain that it is God who answers. Because the structure of the second stanza is identical to that of the first, we read the entire poem up to the final word as if it were uttered by a single speaker. The poet's reasons for assigning the lowercase t to "thee" in the second stanza do not become clear until we reach the end. The true identities of the "thee" and "me" of the poem are thus blended by suggestion. The phrase "and clasp thee to Me" consummates the union between the supplicant and the Deity which has been implied in the preceding lines. Rossetti presents not just the mind in reflection—as we see in Newman's "Dreams," for instance—but the soul hearing God's thoughts as its own and thus profoundly realizing its mystical union with Him. Rossetti does not explicitly state that God seeks out the repentant sinner. Rather, she dramatizes that lesson through the devotional experience of a representative Christian.

For Rossetti, a representative Christian is a fully realized individual, one whose emotions must be vividly drawn, particularized. It is noteworthy that Rossetti published the poems "For Each" and "For All" (II, 279) as companion pieces to conclude *The Face of the Deep*. It is as if she felt compelled to account for the individual experience along with the universal, and did not believe a single poem with a general title would suffice. Rossetti was able to create a highly personal confessional poem even when treating the universal and individual experience together, as in a sonnet such as "If Only" (I, 181). Like the poems by Keble, Newman, and Froude, "If Only" reaches out to the community of believers directly, though the emphasis of the poem is initially on the feelings of a particular individual. The speaker of "If Only" begins in private devotion and ends by projecting her assertion of faith onto the larger "they." The underthought of the poem stresses the necessity for patience, and Rossetti infuses the theme with personality by expressing human emotion in terms of the seasonal cycle. The last line, "they shall sing for love when Christ shall come," is not didactic in tone or intent. Rossetti makes a grammatically impersonal statement into a tonally personal declaration of hope. Although the speaker is asserting the cause for hope through the third person point of view, we understand the "I" of the poem to be included as well. The speaker expresses her acceptance of God's bidding to "love Him and live on" by recalling his promise to all believers.

In "If Only" Rossetti turns the communal experience inward. In contrast, Keble, in "Fourth Sunday in Advent," reaches outward from his personal confession to state Christian truth as it applies to the Christian community. This contrast reveals an essential difference between Rossetti and the Tractarians in their depiction of the confessional experience. The Tractarians focus on what lies outside the sinner, whether it be symbols in the natural world or specific examples of Christian truth. Rossetti centers on the emotions of the self and dramatizes the penitent's spiritual journey toward union with God and acceptance of his Word. Both the Tractarians and Rossetti show the devotional experience as an exploration of being and understanding. In all the poems examined here the speakers open their meditations by expressing what they are not, and end by understanding what they must be or do to enter the realm of Christian truth. Froude's, Newman's, and Keble's speakers see what is the right action or attitude; Rossetti's speakers, however, not only reach the right attitude (by willing the conversion to occur), but they also become one with God and his truth.

Still, these distinctions do not explain completely how Rossetti transcends the Tractarian precedent. A fuller explanation lies in the rhetorical structures of the poems. The forms of the various Tractarian poems are, on one level, like skeletal versions or rough drafts in relation to Rossetti's unified compositions. Keble uses words and symbols from Scripture in "Fourth Sunday in Advent," but the pattern of comparisons between this world and the next is organized in such a predictable way that we are not struck by the final summary lines. Froude's use of symbol in "Trembling Hope" is similarly conventional, and the figurative language does not suggest progress from the beginning of the poem to the conclusion. But Rossetti in, for example, "Good Friday" and "The thread of life," makes scriptural language and "scenery" integral parts of the speaker's meditations, and she organically links the symbolic images of the beginning of the poem with those at the end. Similarly, while the alternation of voices in "Terror" and "Weakness of Nature" lies in the background of Rossetti's " 'Love is strong as death,' " Rossetti's blending of the voice of God and the voice of the penitent produces a more forceful effect than any found in the Tractarian poems, for it suggests the speaker's metaphysical union with God. In addition, though both Rossetti and Newman use conflicting tones, Rossetti orchestrates them more subtly (in the energizing force of God's voice categorically reversing the speaker's negative statements). Froude's use of the imperative to give force to the speaker's supplication, as in "Trembling Hope," is a technique Rossetti uses to full advantage: in "Good Friday" and "The thread of life" she signals the climax of the speakers' search for enlightenment by placing the resolutions in the imperative. The imperative refrain in

"A better resurrection" produces a similar effect. In the final lines of Rossetti's poems the speakers resolve the spiritual tension, interpret the Christian symbols, and redeem the period of isolation tonally, linguistically, and theologically. The dramatic resolutions in Rossetti's poems have no equal in the Tractarian confessional poetry of either *The Christian Year* or the *Lyra Apostolica*.

Many of Rossetti's poems bear closer resemblance to Tractarian verse than those I have examined here. But I have focused on these particular poems because they demonstrate the dramatic and affective potential of the Tractarian poems. In Froude's, Newman's, and Keble's poems the speakers' confessions contain a doctrinal message. Rossetti's speakers, however, live the message. The Tractarian poems are about learning, Rossetti's about being. The Tractarians show what is ignorance and what is truth. Rossetti carries us through the darkness into light. She transforms the language of solitude into the language of salvation.

JEROME BUMP

Christina Rossetti and the
Pre-Raphaelite Brotherhood

The Pre-Raphaelites were perhaps the most famous "school" in English literature. This school was formed partly because, as Barbara Goff has said, "throughout his career, [Dante Gabriel] Rossetti sought to work in groups, and the Brotherhood was not even his first: he had grown up in a group of four, two boys and two girls, educated and encouraged as equals whose individual strengths were encouraged non-competitively. Such mutuality was then second-nature for all the Rossettis and in forming the Brotherhood, Dante Gabriel was substituting for the ultimately capitalistic model of individual artistic enterprise a communal, family model—with and without the religious overtones implicit in the name."[1] Yet something was missing in the "communal, family model" of the Brotherhood, something so obvious it is often overlooked. Half of the family was excluded: the two girls, educated and encouraged as "equals," were apparently no longer considered equal. While it may be argued that one of the girls, Maria, was far more involved in religion than art, there is little doubt that Christina was the artistic equal of most, if not all, of the members of the Brotherhood. Moreover, she was not only the sister of two of the members of the group, she was to be wed to another (James Collinson); and, more important, she considered herself a member of the group.[2] Yet simply by choosing the name "Brotherhood" Dante

---

[1] Barbara Munson Goff, "The Politics of Pre-Raphaelitism," *Journal of Pre-Raphaelite Studies* 2 (1982): 59.

[2] "Writing to Edmund Gosse, Christina says: 'I, as the least and last of the group may remind you that. . . .'" Quoted in Mary F. Sandars, *The Life of Christina Rossetti* (London: Hutchinson, [1930]), p. 88.

Gabriel Rossetti made it clear that there would be no question of including Christina Rossetti or any other woman, no matter how well qualified she might be. I wish to establish here just how qualified Christina Rossetti was for inclusion in this group and to suggest the possibility that she was excluded partly because her brother was at least as oriented to competition as he was to cooperation in art.

While we no longer recognize Christina Rossetti as crucial to the Pre-Raphaelite experiment, she was in fact more visible in Pre-Raphaelite paintings than were John Everett Millais, William Holman Hunt, or her brother Dante Gabriel. She was, for instance, the Virgin Mary in her brother's *Girlhood of Mary Virgin,* the weeping queen in his illustration of Arthur at Avalon for the Moxon *Tennyson,* and she even sat as a model for Hunt so that he could put some of her expression into the eyes of Christ in *The Light of the World.* Further, she shared many of their poetic concerns. For example, she was an early contributor to their set of poems and paintings about Saint Dorothea. Her choice of this saint as a subject for poetry reveals her desire to be a contributing member of the Pre-Raphaelites in poetry even more than in painting, for her brother Dante Gabriel, William Morris, Edward Burne-Jones, and Algernon Charles Swinburne, and even Gerard Manley Hopkins all went on to represent Saint Dorothea in their art.[3]

In fact, during the crucial first two decades of the group's history, until the publication of Dante Gabriel's poems in 1870, Christina Rossetti was their chief literary figure. We tend to think of *The Germ* and Morris's *Defence of Guenevere* as the first successful forays of the Pre-Raphaelites into literature, but both were almost completely ignored. What little praise *The Germ* received was primarily for the poems that Christina Rossetti contributed to it.[4] The first literary victory of the Pre-Raphaelites was the publication of *"Goblin Market" and Other Poems,* and it was written by the member they excluded. Hence her brother William Michael acknowledged her as the "Queen of the Pre-Raphaelites"; Edmund Gosse described her as "the high-priestess of Pre-Raphaelitism"; and Swinburne hailed her as "the Jael

---

[3]See Virginia Surtees, *The Paintings and Drawings of Dante Gabriel Rossetti* (1828–1882): *A Catalogue Raisonné,* 2 vols. (Oxford : Clarendon Press, 1971), I, 12; William Sharp, *Dante Gabriel Rossetti: A Record and Study* (London: Macmillan, 1882), p. 270; *The Swinburne Letters,* ed. Cecil Lang (New Haven: Yale University Press, 1959), 6 vols., I, 38; K. L. Goodwin, "An Unfinished Tale from *The Earthly Paradise,*" VP 13 (1975): 91–102.

[4]Her poems "Testimony," "Sweet Death," and "Dream-Land" were praised and cited in the *Critic* and the *Guardian:* see William Michael Rossetti, ed. *The Germ* (1850; rpt. London: Elliott Stock, 1901), pp. 11–15.

who led their host to victory."[5] The Pre-Raphaelites were indeed the host she led to victory, for in many respects her poetry was as characteristic of their art as any one poet's could be. Diane Apostolos-Cappadona has even described her as the "Pre-Raphaelite poet *par excellence*" and Mary Zaturenska argued that she was "the purest, most characteristic Pre-Raphaelite of them all."[6]

Admittedly, other critics have de-emphasized Rossetti's Pre-Raphaelitism. Betty S. Flowers, for instance, maintains that "When the religious poems are overlooked . . . Rossetti appears to be much more of a Pre-Raphaelite than she really was. . . . the bulk of her work reflects Tractarian rather than Pre-Raphaelite concerns."[7] Flowers cites G. B. Tennyson, who points out that "the linkage of Christina Rossetti with the Pre-Raphaelites [has not] helped to clarify her affinities with Tractarian poetry, though the problem of emphasis and interpretation in respect to the religious element in pre-Raphaelitism [*sic*] is yet more complex than merely her relation to the group" (*VDP*, p. 199). This problem is indeed complex, and how one approaches it depends on one's definitions of the word "Pre-Raphaelite" and the role of the "religious element" in Pre-Raphaelitism.

The Germ, the Pre-Raphaelite manifesto, promulgated four important articles of the Pre-Raphaelites' artistic credo which have been cited by various critics as their dominant features:[8] a love of nature for its own sake, often focusing on nature's richness, bright color, and light; a revolt against simplistic dualisms, especially verbal versus visual and natural versus supernatural, often conveyed in symbolism; deliberate medievalism; and a preference for subjects that, as James Merritt has said, "have an innate poignancy or morbidity."[9] In this essay I attempt to demonstrate that, although Christina Rossetti was excluded from the Brotherhood, all four of these features are central to

[5]William Michael Rossetti, *Some Reminiscences of William Michael Rossetti*, 2 vols. (London: Brown, Langham, 1906), I, 74; Edmund Gosse, *Critical Kit-Kats* (New York: Dodd, Mead, 1896), p. 158; Edmund Gosse, *The Life of Algernon Charles Swinburne* (London: Macmillan, 1917), pp. 136–37.

[6]Diane Apostolos-Cappadona, "Oxford and the Pre-Raphaelites from the Perspective of Nature and Symbol," *Pre-Raphaelite Review* 2 (1981): 110; Mary Zaturenska, *Christina Rossetti* (New York: Macmillan, 1949), p. 74.

[7]Betty S. Flowers, "The Kingly Self: Rossetti as Woman Artist," see p. 160 in this volume.

[8]See, for instance, the introductions in Cecil B. Lang, ed., *The Pre-Raphaelites and Their Circle* 2d ed. (Chicago: University of Chicago Press, 1975); and James D. Merritt, ed., *The Pre-Raphaelite Poem* (New York: Dutton, 1966).

[9]Merritt, *Pre-Raphaelite Poem*, p. 12.

her art. In the process I also explore in more detail some of these criteria of Pre-Raphaelitism. For instance, I point out how the Pre-Raphaelites' preference for melancholy subjects reveals their dominant model of creativity, and how an ascetic, even puritanical, form of religious medievalism is an authentic development of the first principles of the P. R. B.

The Pre-Raphaelites' version of medievalism was clearly related to Romanticism, in particular to that of their major Romantic precursor, Keats. Hence in my conclusion I explore the connections between Rossetti, the Pre-Raphaelites, and Keats. My first and primary comparison, however, is to a poet whose poems were rejected by Dante Gabriel Rossetti: Hopkins. Hopkins is a good subject for comparison here for a number of reasons. First, he was, as Robert Lowell put it, "probably the finest of English poets of nature,"[10] certainly the best Victorian nature poet. Second, in some respects he was *the* poet of the revolt against dualism among the Victorians. Third, it was Hopkins who, in the words of Humphry House, "truly developed Pre-Raphaelite aims."[11] Thus Hopkins provides a good standard by which to measure Rossetti's specific achievements as a poet of nature and of the revolt against dualism, as well as Zaturenska's rival claim that it was Rossetti who was "the purest, most characteristic Pre-Raphaelite." Fourth, I wish to suggest that Rossetti was responsible in no small measure for a number of Hopkins's accomplishments, including his nature poetry and his ability to challenge her title as the quintessential Pre-Raphaelite poet. In this way I illustrate how, of all the Pre-Raphaelites, Rossetti was the one who most successfully embodied their principles in poetry in the crucial first two decades of the Brotherhood.

We first need to recognize that Rossetti was, among other things, a poet of nature. Ruskin insisted that "Pre-Raphaelitism has but one truth in all that it does, obtained by working everything, down to the most minute detail, from nature and from nature only."[12] Yet Gisela Hönnighausen has argued that "it would be pointless to search for an immediate interest in the depiction of nature in Christina Rossetti," and, according to Dorothy Stuart, "nothing is more curious in the

[10]Robert Lowell, "Hopkins' Sanctity" in *Gerard Manley Hopkins: By the Kenyon Critics* (New York: New Directions, 1944), p. 93.

[11]Humphry House, *All in Due Time* (London: Hart-Davis, 1955), p. 158.

[12]John Ruskin, *The Works of John Ruskin*, ed. E. T. Cook and A. Wedderburn, 39 vols. (London: George Allen, 1903–1912), XII, 157.

mentality of Christina Rossetti than her almost complete independence of external stimuli. 'My knowledge of what is called nature,' she
once said, 'is that of the town sparrow.' "[13] Yet precisely because she
was pent up in the city most of her life, the sensations of nature and
country life were particularly powerful for her.[14] Her emblematic use
of nature and the ascetic themes in her religious poetry have tended to
obscure the fact that she, too, felt nature's appeal directly and was
capable of expressing her love for nature without necessarily subordinating it to the demands of art or religion. Indeed, her preference for
nature over art was stronger than that of many other Pre-Raphaelites,
including her brother Dante Gabriel.[15] She did not, for example,
merely share his love of animals; as F. L. Lucas said, she took "refuge
in her dear animal world which she found kindlier than that of
men."[16] She participated in many other aspects of the Pre-
Raphaelites' love of nature as well. Her sympathy for nature is obvious
in a poem such as "Bitter for sweet" (I, 59), in which she feels for the
loss of natural beauty. Even when she is not specifically describing
nature, naturalistic imagery pervades her poetry: in Goblin Market (II,
11–26), for instance, in individual lines such as "Her tree of life
drooped from the root" (l. 260), and especially in the multiple comparisons (ll. 81–86, 184–90, 409–21). Metaphors drawn from nature
dominate in many poems ranging from "Amor Mundi" (I, 213–214)
to "The convent threshold" (I, 61–65) to the first stanza of "A
Birthday" (I, 36–37). The love of nature's plenitude so characteristic
of Pre-Raphaelite art is epitomized in particular by the first stanza of

[13]Gisela Hönnighausen, "Emblematic Tendencies in the Works of Christina
Rossetti," VP 10 (1972): 15; Dorothy Margaret Stuart, Christina Rossetti (London:
Macmillan, 1930), p. 41.

[14]Ironically, not only because she was confined to the city but also because she
fought against the sensations of this world, those sensations were particularly vivid for
her. As Walter Pater put it in his review of the Pre-Raphaelite art of William Morris,
"a passion of which the outlets are sealed, begets a tension of nerve, in which the
sensible world comes to one with a reinforced brilliance and relief—all redness is
turned into blood, all water into tears" (Walter Pater, "Poems by William Morris,"
Westminster Review 90, n.s. 34 [1868]: 303).

[15]For instance, in her letter of 1865 to Anne Gilchrist, Rossetti expressed her
preference for "Nature treasures" rather than "art treasures" (Mackenzie Bell,
Christina Rossetti: A Biographical and Critical Study [London: Hurst and Blackett,
1898], p. 46).

[16]F. L. Lucas, Ten Victorian Poets (Cambridge: Cambridge University Press, 1948),
pp. 127–28.

Goblin Market, in which the plump fullness of each piece of fruit is stressed and an extraordinary sense of abundance is conveyed simply by the list of fruits. This typical Pre-Raphaelite love of abundance is expressed even more explicitly in other poems: for example, in the description of the "thickset" (l. 4) fruit of "A Birthday" and the "thickly" (l. 13) growing flowers of "Amor Mundi," as well as in the "plenteous stars" and "many-leaved" green branches of "Paradise" (ll. 37–38; I, 221–22).

If Pre-Raphaelite paintings are characterized above all by this typically Ruskinian sense of richness of ornament, they are also famous for their brilliance of color. Rossetti's love of color is obvious in *Seek and Find:* "It needs no Solomon to enter into the inexhaustible cheerfulness of 'all green things,' an expression which we may fairly interpret as including the whole vegetable creation. . . . Fancy what this world would be were it prevalently clay-coloured or slate-coloured!" (p. 96). Perhaps the most striking feature of many Pre-Raphaelite paintings, however, is the preternaturally bright light that seems to shine from them, produced by painting the canvas white before laying on the color. Rossetti also tries to reproduce this luminous effect in her poetry. Recall, for instance, the love of gold and silver in "A Birthday," the "golden" sands and "golden" streets of "Paradise," the "eyes as bright / As sunlight on a stream" in "Echo" (ll. 3–4; I, 46), and of course, in *Goblin Market,* the "Bright-fire-like barberries"; Laura's "gleaming" neck and her "tear more rare than pearl"; Lizzie, like a beacon "sending up a golden fire" (ll. 27, 81, 127, 414); as well as the description of the two sisters as two wands of ivory tipped with gold (ll. 190–91), and the many references to their golden hair (ll. 41, 120, 123, 125, 126, 184, 408, 540). The ultimate effect of the preternatural brightness in Pre-Raphaelite painting is similar to the effect described by Rossetti in "Advent" (I, 68–70) and "De Profundis" (II, 94):

> I never watch the scattered fire
> Of stars, of sun's far-trailing train,
> But all my heart is one desire,
> And all in vain:
> ["De Profundis," ll. 9–12]

It is true that this transcendental aspiration led her at times to regard this world as a place of "darkness and corruption" ("Remember," l.

11; I, 37), and to consider love of nature, or at least "amor mundi," as a time-wasting distraction, as she does in "The convent threshold":

> Flee to the mountain, tarry not.
> Is this a time for smile and sigh,
> For songs among the secret trees
> Where sudden blue birds nest and sport?
>
> [ll. 42–45]

Yet, as these lines reveal, even when she tries to repress her love of this world, her feeling produces beautiful nature poetry.

Moreover, even in this otherworldly mood Rossetti could at least use nature as source of imagery for moral allegory and symbolism. We recall the symbolic suggestiveness of "Advent" and the use of natural events as reminders, foreshadowers of death in the second stanza of "Amor Mundi" and the fourth stanza of "The convent threshold." And in *Goblin Market* it is primarily because nature, or at least the artificially perfect fruit, does not foreshadow mortality that it is regarded as a dangerous illusion. Rossetti's presentation of this fruit suggests that she shared the traditional puritan tendency to believe that evil can assail us through our sense of beauty; even natural beauty is a threat because it tantalizes the senses, and they are the bonds that chain us to this world.

Partly because she shared this traditional Judeo-Christian suspicion of nature, Rossetti was not able to embrace the version of the Pre-Raphaelite revolt against dualism which most attracted Hopkins: a vision of the immanence of the supernatural *in* the natural. Raymond Chapman has argued that, because Rossetti was a participant in the Oxford Movement, her vision of nature was superior to that of the secular Pre-Raphaelites, primarily because the Incarnational faith of that movement endowed her with a "Coleridgean sense of the mystical union of all creatures, a belief that love must manifest itself not in human relations alone."[17] Rossetti certainly believed that love must not manifest itself in human relations alone, but I think it should be acknowledged that she did not believe as firmly as many of her contemporaries did in the application of the Incarnational faith of the Oxford Movement to nature, or at least in the related Pre-Raphaelite

[17]Raymond Chapman, *Faith and Revolt: Studies in the Literary Influence of the Oxford Movement* (London: Weidenfeld and Nicholson, 1970), pp. 194–95, 30.

vision of the immanence of the ideal *in* the real.[18] The model for her response to nature was not the Catholic version of the Eucharist, which asserts a genuine incarnation of the Real Presence in this world and is thus a symbol that participates in the reality it names, but rather holy water or palm leaves, natural objects that are blessed with special religious meaning but do not undergo any fundamental change. In other words, for Rossetti, the prototype in nature is but a sign of a higher reality; it does not itself share in that higher reality. Hence it may not be accurate to describe her response to nature as "mystical," as Chapman and Apostolos-Cappadona do, or "sacramental," as Apostolos-Cappadona does, at least as those words are sometimes used in, say, Hopkins criticism.[19]

Nevertheless, as G. B. Tennyson has noted, "Like all Tractarians, [Rossetti] was receptive to nature as a vehicle of divine grace, and especially like Isaac Williams, she was willing to bring an intense personal response to nature as a religious experience" (*VDP*, p. 202). As her hymns of creation suggest, nature can sometimes be enjoyed simultaneously for its own sake and for its symbolization of the ideal: one can rejoice in the opening of mortal flowers at Easter because they also image or shadow forth an eternal flowering, a higher resurrection. In such instances, nature is at once literal and metaphorical. The metaphorical significance is finally the more important. Hence Rossetti produced many allegories, parables, emblems, lessons, fables, and stylized correspondences. Her most extraordinary interpretations of nature in this vein are in prose, especially in *Called to be Saints*, where she worked out complex systems of correspondences usually based on symbolical or allegorical readings of passages in the Bible or other religious texts. Such works imply a medieval worldview in which a vertical correspondence or chain of being connects all things in nature to God, while a lateral correspondence, deriving from the

[18]Of course one's understanding of Rossetti's position depends on one's definition of Tractarian "Incarnationalism." If this term is taken to mean primarily an intense emphasis on Christ, then Rossetti's faith is as strong as anyone's. As G. B. Tennyson puts it, "One of her devotional categories, 'Christ Our All in All', reflects the intense Incarnationalism that the Tractarians cultivated, especially Keble and Isaac Williams. Both the Keblian kind of Christology and the later, more passionate Isaac Williams sort are there" (*VDP*, p. 201). But I am focusing specifically on the sense of Christ *incarnate in* nature. Rossetti resisted this particular revolt against dualism.

[19]Chapman, *Faith and Revolt*, p. 30; Apostolos-Cappadona, "Oxford and the Pre-Raphaelites," p. 100.

vertical, connects each object in nature. Still, even in her most la-
bored spiritual interpretations of nature, whether in the parables or a
single correspondence, she is often original. She usually does not
simply repeat older fables or merely allude to universal symbols. While
she retains the medieval perception of nature as a collection of various
types, surprisingly she often employs the personal, empirical Romantic
approach as well, seeing nature freshly through her own eyes. The
result is a complex, original set of correspondences and natural
sermons.

This approach to nature became quite popular in the second half of
the nineteenth century. Hopkins's "May Magnificat" for instance, is
an exercise in this vein. It is an attempt to explain why a certain
month should have been named for a particular saint, the sort of
preoccupation that dominates Rossetti's reading diary, *Time Flies*, as
well as *Called to be Saints*. Hopkins's "Blessed Virgin Compared to the
Air We Breathe" is even more in the tradition of Rossetti's ingenious
correspondences in prose. While these two poems may not be typical
Hopkins poems, they reveal that Hopkins's response to nature is not as
different from Rossetti's as one might suppose. The variety of Hopkins's responses to nature (especially in the 1860s and 1880s), which
ranged from strong attraction to its beauty to belief that this beauty
must be denied on religious grounds, is in fact congruent with the
range of Rossetti's responses to nature. Indeed, one can argue that a
number of key features of his nature poems originated in the poetry he
composed under her influence. His poetry is but one example of how
she conveyed the program of the Brotherhood to the wider world and
won acceptance for it.[20]

A good example of the influence of Rossetti's typical combination
of nature poetry and religious celebration is Hopkins's "Easter,"
which, as Tennyson has pointed out, "reads almost as though it were
written by Keble and revised for greater impact by Christina Rossetti"

[20] Limited space prevents me from detailing here the full impact of Rossetti's
influence on Hopkins's representation of nature. His "Alchemist in the City" epitomizes the range of parallels between his poetry and hers: it reflects not only her typical
preoccupations with mortality, isolation, shame, idleness, impotence, and her inability to find the ideal in the real but also the city-dweller's longing for nature. The
alchemist's initial emphasis on "new seasons" recalls specifically Rossetti's influence
as the Victorian master of the medieval season poem, a deeply felt but apparently
simple, impersonal song quite unlike most Romantic nature poems, which describe
the complex interactions of subject and object. Rossetti's spring poems, for instance,
clearly influenced Hopkins's "Spring" and "May Magnificat."

(*VDP*, p. 209). The arrival of spring is an integral part of Easter in Hopkins's poem as it is in Rossetti's poems "An Easter carol" (II, 155–56) and "Easter Day" (II, 229–30). Hopkins generally portrays nature in Rossetti's manner in the poem: a sense of richness and brilliance is conveyed by the lists of jewels and the fullness of the word painting, yet this sense is qualified by the generality and unity of the description and the poet's ultimate emphasis on music rather than word painting, on the ear rather than the eye. Rossetti's influence is also obvious in Hopkins's choice of genre in "Easter": the hymn of creation, a traditional genre inspired by Psalm 148. The most joyous synchronic reading of the Bible and the book of nature, this genre inspired many of Rossetti's most felicitous expressions of her feelings for religion and for nature. Her most extensive work in this vein was in prose, *Seek and Find: A Double Series of Short Studies of the Benedicite*, although her poem "'All Thy works praise Thee, o Lord'" (II, 129–38) is a very effective celebration. Most of the themes that appear in this poem appear too in the third stanza of Hopkins's "Easter." For instance, the flowers' discovery of "Spring-time joy" in Hopkins's poem has much in common with the joyful songs in Rossetti's. And Hopkins's "Easter" echoes some of Rossetti's other poems as well: the spring joy of "An Easter carol"; the glad hills and birds of "'What good shall my life do me?'" (II, 294); and all creation in "'And there was no more sea'" (II, 269): "Heaven and earth and sea jubilant, / Jubilant all things that dwell therein" (ll. 7–8).[21]

Hopkins's use of the hymn of creation in "Easter" to teach a lesson to man reminds us, moreover, of the traditional sources of that didacticism which pervades Hopkins's later nature poetry. Rossetti probably provided the best contemporary example of this particular tradition in poetry. Apostolos-Cappadona cites Rossetti's "'Consider the lilies of the field'" (I, 76) as a good example of her didactic use of nature poetry.[22] This poem illustrates Rossetti's mastery of the tropological type, the type used to inculcate a moral or lesson and which was at

[21]Because Hopkins's sonnets are so compact, it is at first difficult to recognize similarities between them and Rossetti's allegorical pageants, for example, "All Thy works praise thee." However, this poem and Hopkins's "God's Grandeur" and "Pied Beauty" clearly share some of the same inspirations. Hopkins's "Hurrahing in Harvest" may also be perceived as being both in the tradition of the songs of the heavens and the hills in hymns of creation and in the context of pleas like those of Rossetti's "'What good shall my life do me?'": "Lift heart and eyes / Up to the hills, grow glad and wise."

[22]Apostolos-Cappodona, "Oxford and the Pre-Raphaelites," p. 100.

least as common as the dogmatic, allegorical type alluding to Christ, or the eschatological, anagogical type that anticipates future reality. The tropological analogy in "'Consider the lilies of the field'" was certainly one of the inspirations for Hopkins's association of flowers with a "lesson" in "Easter": Rossetti's poem begins, "Flowers preach to us if we will hear," and the flowers themselves say, "'Men scent our fragrance in the air, / Yet take no heed / Of humble lessons we would read'" (ll. 15–17); Hopkins's poem advises:

> Gather gladness from the skies;
> Take a lesson from the ground;
> Flowers do ope their heavenward eyes
> And a Spring-time joy have found;
>
> [ll. 13–16]

Rossetti's hymn of creation poems are often echoed in Hopkins's, for she too perceived the unity, the oneness of all things, those moments when "all voices" join in "one loud hymn" (*PW*, p. 306), as in "To what purpose is this waste?" (*PW*, pp. 305–7); or the picture of all things "in oneness of contentment offering praise" in "'And there was no more sea'" (l. 6); or all nature unified by love in "'What good shall my life do me?'"

Rossetti usually expresses such insights into the unity of all nature in rather general terms. This generality in her representations of nature indicates one way in which her poetry differs from that of the P. R. B. and also of Hopkins, some of whose images, especially in his later poems, have led readers to identify his poetry with an emphasis on unique particularity. Although Rossetti's prose, especially *Called to be Saints* and *Time Flies*, reveals her typically Pre-Raphaelite fascination with the minutiae of nature, her poetry, excepting a few catalogues of plants and animals in "An old-world thicket" (II, 123–28) and "To what purpose is this waste?", is conspicuously lacking in collections of details. When she transferred her word painting from prose to poetry, she pruned the details and the result was, as her reviewer in the *Church Quarterly Review* duly noted, a higher level of generality: "It will be seen, we think, by those who study her poetry that, on the one hand, the glories of Nature—retained and revivified by reflection and reading—have deeply affected her imagination; that she has grasped the spiritual significance of ordinary natural phenomena; but that, on the other hand, there is no trace of intimate personal observation, and certainly nothing of the luminous apprehension of details, previously unnoticed, which surprises and delights us in Tennyson."[23] As we have seen, G. B. Tennyson has argued convincingly that Rossetti's response to nature was "intensely personal" (*VDP*, p. 202), but the *Church Quarterly* reviewer is focusing on the *quantity* of detail in her mimesis of nature. Although "no trace" is certainly an exaggeration, the reviewer is fundamentally correct. Yet even in its generality Hopkins's representation of nature in his poetry is closer to Rossetti's than we have recognized.[24] Thus, if Hopkins's example is at all representative, the influence of Rossetti's representation of nature did far more to promote the Pre-Raphaelite return to nature than critics have suspected.

Rossetti also participated in, and successfully exemplified, certain aspects of the Pre-Raphaelite revolt against dualisms.[25] For instance, although she was more interested in overcoming the dichotomy between poetry and music, she participated in several ways in the Pre-Raphaelite attempt to overcome the division between the visual and the verbal arts. She took drawing lessons from Ford Madox Brown and made illustrations for her poems. Her poems were in fact often published with designs. Both her books for children, *Sing-Song* and *Speaking Likenesses*, were illustrated, and her brother's illustrations of *Goblin Market* were mentioned prominently in reviews of that book. Hopkins

[23]"Christina Rossetti," *Church Quarterly Review* 59 (1905): 61.

[24]For all the talk about unique "inscapes" of nature in Hopkins's poetry, the fact remains that he too trimmed many details when he moved from prose to poetry, especially in the poems he composed under Rossetti's influence, from 1864 to 1868. In "Easter," for instance, the only striking or unusual detail is the biblically inspired "nard" and "sard" rhyme. The world is generally represented in relatively simple, unqualified, generic plural nouns such as "flowers," "perfumes," and "dances."

[25]Admittedly, most critics would emphasize instead Rossetti's love of irreconcilable antitheses. Geoffrey Rossetti, for example, wrote that "she seems always aware of dual and opposed attitudes of mind, even in her tiniest poems" and some critics praise her for her expression of counterpoised forces generating dramatic tensions (Geoffrey Rossetti, "Christina Rossetti," *Criterion* 10 [1930]: 107). Yet Hopkins has been praised for the same feature. When we consider his late sonnets, we could compare Rossetti's obsession with such dichotomies as God versus the Devil, right versus wrong, heaven versus earth, to Hopkins's dualisms in a poem such as "Spelt from Sibyl's Leaves." Even if in some respects Rossetti may have been more inclined at times to reductive antitheses than Hopkins or the members of the "Brotherhood," she also had more justification. Her exclusion from the "Brotherhood" was, after all, their enforcement of one of the oldest reductive antitheses: male vs. female.

cited them in his essay "On the Origin of Beauty," and he also noted Arthur Hughes's illustration of Rossetti's poem "A Birthday."[26]

Hopkins was no doubt attracted not only by these illustrations but by the Pre-Raphaelite manner in which the poems themselves occasionally break into a fullness of adjectival description that might be called word painting. The short brush strokes of "Bloom-down-cheeked peaches" and "Bright-fire-like barberries" (l. 27) in the initial list of *Goblin Market*, for instance, recur in Hopkins's own tripartite epithets, "Feel-of-primrose hands," "dappled-with-damson west." In addition, Rossetti used compound adjectives to paint fairly extensive canvases, as in the list of fruits which opens *Goblin Market* or her picture of the young men and women "milk-white, wine-flushed among the vines" in "The convent threshold" (ll. 30–37). Some of these extended passages seem almost gratuitous (e.g., *Goblin Market*, ll. 530–38), thus suggesting the love of word painting for its own sake so pervasive in Keats and the Pre-Raphaelites.

Nor was Rossetti as interested in overcoming the dichotomy between natural and supernatural by representing the supernatural *in* the natural as many of the other Pre-Raphaelites were. In a poem such as "A shadow of Dorothea" (*PW*, pp. 216–17), for example, natural and supernatural certainly do seem to remain an antithetical dualism. In this poem Rossetti stresses the transcendental, otherworldly aspiration embodied in the Dorothea legend, focusing on the celestial origin of Dorothea and her flowers. She concludes the poem by forcing the reader to choose between these flowers and their earthly counterparts, between the supernatural and the natural. The choice she herself often made, reiterated throughout her poetry, is particularly clear in "Three Nuns" (*PW*, pp. 12–16):

> I will not look upon a rose
> Though it is fair to see:

---

[26]For the reference in "On the Origin of Beauty" see Gerard Manley Hopkins, *The Journals and Papers of Gerard Manley Hopkins*, ed. Humphry House (London: Oxford University Press, 1959), p. 103. For the reference to Hughes see *Journals*, p. 142. Humphry House, the editor of the *Journals*, comments: "Hopkins seems to have made some mistake, for this illustration to her poem does not appear in the body or index of the R. A. Catalogue for 1866" (*Journals*, p. 360). Such a painting, however, was in existence in 1866; see *The Letters of Dante Gabriel Rossetti*, ed. Oswald Doughty and J. R. Wahl, 4 vols. (Oxford: Clarendon Press, 1965–1967), II, 586.

The flowers planted in Paradise
Are budding now for me:

[pt. III, ll. 43–46]

Yet these lines could almost as easily have been composed by Hopkins during the six-month custody-of-the-eyes penance he imposed upon himself after joining the Society of Jesus, although he is in many respects the prime poet of the modern revolt against dualism among the Victorians. And in her own time it was recognized immediately that Rossetti had achieved many of the combinations of the natural and the supernatural most characteristic of the Pre-Raphaelites. In an 1863 review, Mrs. Norton, for instance, praised *Goblin Market* "for the vivid and wonderful power by which things unreal and mystic are made to blend and link themselves with the everyday images and events of common life."[27] In "The convent threshold" and many other poems Rossetti transcended the natural-supernatural dichotomy by creating a version of natural supernaturalism similar to the one her brother Dante Gabriel displayed in "The Blessed Damozel": the representation of the natural in the supernatural. She transports her love of this world to the next, enjoying to the fullest the sensations of nature in heaven. Rossetti's in "The convent threshold" seems in some respects even more fleshly than that of her brother, for her poem ends, "There we shall meet as once we met / And love with old familiar love" (ll. 147–48). Unlike Dante Alighieri, she refuses to sublimate human love into divine love. Hence Alice Meynell described this poem as "a song of penitence for love that yet praises love more fervently than would a chorus hymnael."[28]

Perhaps the most succinct summary of Rossetti's natural supernaturalism is the conclusion of her description of heaven in her poem "Paradise" (I, 221):

I hope to see these things again,
    But not as once in dreams by night;
    To see them with my very sight,
And touch and handle and attain:

[ll. 41–44]

[27]Mrs. Norton, " 'The Angel in the House' and 'The Goblin Market,' " *Macmillan's Magazine* 8 (1863): 404.

[28]Alice Meynell, "Christina Rossetti," *New Review* 12 (1895): 201–6.

In other words, the poet renounces the sensations of this world in order to enjoy them again in heaven. She tears down the pleasure-dome of Kubla Khan and Keats's bowers so she can be entitled to reconstruct them in heaven. As she says in "From house to home" (I, 82–88),

> Yea, therefore as a flint I set my face,
> To pluck down, to build up again the whole—
> But in a distant place.
>
> [ll. 206–8]

This version of natural supernaturalism—the natural in the super-natural—was at least as influential, if not more so, than its counter-part, the supernatural in the natural, which we may call supernatural naturalism. Indeed, so pervasive was the influence of Rossetti's brand of natural supernaturalism that it is easily discovered even in the poetry of Hopkins, who of all the Pre-Raphaelites' successors, devel-oped their supernatural naturalism most fully. The poem he finally called "Heaven-Haven," for instance, had several previous titles— "Rest," "Fair Havens; or the Convent," "Fair-Havens—The Nun-nery"—all evocative of Pre-Raphaelite medievalism, especially the convent cemetery scene in Millais's painting *The Vale of Rest*, the nun in the garden in Charles Collins's painting, *Convent Thoughts*, James Collinson's attempt to enter Jesuit monastic life, and the heavily religious flavor of early Pre-Raphaelitism generally. The most obvious Pre-Raphaelite influence, however, is that of Christina Rossetti. Hopkins's final subtitle, "A nun takes the veil," underlines the poem's connection with her art, for nuns and nunlike heroines recur again and again in her poetry, most obviously in "Three Nuns." The con-nection with "The convent threshold," however, is particularly important because of the extraordinary impact it made on Hopkins, who was himself considering crossing the threshold and becoming a religious, a step he finally did take a few years later.

Like most of Rossetti's poems, Hopkins's "Heaven-Haven" is a short, simple lyric, more a song than a picture. Hopkins's diction, like Rossetti's, is conventional and general, with the possible exception of "sided" and "Heaven-Haven," though the latter recalls the com-pounds "heaven-bells" and "heaven-air" in "The convent threshold" (ll. 89, 90) and "haven-rest" in "I do set my bow in the cloud" (*PW*, p. 114). But it is Hopkins's original title, "Rest," that is the most striking connection with Rossetti's poetry. "Rest" is *the* normative word in her poetry, so pervasive that her brother William Michael made it a separate topic in the table of contents of his edition of her poems. As early as 1849 she composed a poem with exactly that title ("Rest"; I, 60–61), and the word dominates other early titles such as "Seeking Rest" (*PW*, p. 296) and " 'There remaineth therefore a rest to the people of God' " (II, 277). The word "rest" is also a normative word in many subsequent poems, including "The convent threshold" (l. 69), "The Dream" (*PW*, pp. 104–5), "The Lotus-Eaters" (*PW*, p. 111), "Yet a little while" (II, 85), and "Sweetest of rest when Thou sheddest rest" (II, 334). The religious inspiration for her preoccupation with rest is made explicit in "Sonnet, from the Psalms" (*PW*, p. 112) and in "I do set my bow in the cloud," in which the imagery of Psalm 23 is associated with the "haven-rest."

Hopkins's poetry has yet another connection with Rossetti's work, a generic connection. Throughout Rossetti's poetry the dream of a garden of heaven (e.g., "As I lie dreaming / It rises, that land" ["Mother Country," ll. 9–10; I, 222–24]) appears so frequently that it becomes a regular genre of her poetry, a genre which Hopkins's "Heaven-Haven" exemplifies in many ways. Hopkins's land of unfailing springs recalls Rossetti's images of "living streams" ("Eye hath not seen"; *PW*, p. 149) in a land where "nor fruit nor waters cease" (" 'The holy city, New Jerusalem,' " l. 23; II, 280); her representation of a "summer rill" beside the lilies in the "sheltered land" in "A shadow of Dorothea"; "the land of love / Where fountains run which run not dry" ("If I had words"; *PW*, p. 371); and "The convent threshold": "Beyond the hills a watered land, / Beyond the gulf a gleaming strand" (ll. 19–20). Hopkins's lily imagery recalls Rossetti's vision of heaven as a place "where the lilies fade not" ("Buried"; *PW*, p. 309) and the pervasiveness of lilies in her poetry generally: in "Paradise," "A shadow of Dorothea," "Sound Sleep" (I, 57), "Thy lilies drink the dew" (II, 256), " 'Thou art fairer than the children of men' " (II, 201), and "To what purpose is this waste?" Further, the desire of Hopkins's speaker to be far from the threatening sea reflects Hopkins's response to the religious longing embodied in Rossetti's prayer in "Heaven overarches": "A little while and we shall be— / Please God—where there is no more sea" (ll. 4–5; *PW*, p. 286) and in her recurrent vision of a place of "our own beyond the salt sea-wall" ("They lie at rest, our blessed dead," l. 12; II, 306), a place " 'beyond the sea, in a green land / Where only rivers are' " ("How one chose," *PW*, pp. 295–96). In

" 'There remaineth therefore a rest for the people of God' " she even uses the same rhyme word, "dumb," that Hopkins uses: "winds and echoes and low songs be dumb" (PW, p. 153).[29]

In addition to this kind of natural supernaturalism and her love of nature, Rossetti conveyed other Pre-Raphaelite principles to Hopkins and his contemporaries. While her vision of heaven seems more like that of Dante Gabriel Rossetti than that of Dante Alighieri, in most other respects Rossetti was far more like Dante Alighieri than his namesake, her brother. Eleanor Walter Thomas stated that "it is evidence of Christina Rossetti's independence [from the Pre-Raphaelites] that she wrote so little at all related to medievalism."[30] Even Thomas, however, compared Rossetti to "the great medieval saints of Italy," cited a parallel with medieval theology in her art, and noted a few of the echoes of Dante in "The convent threshold."[31] Because she was the high priestess of the Oxford Movement as well as of Pre-Raphaelitism, Rossetti embodied a deeper, more genuine medievalism than that represented by Pre-Raphaelitism alone. If, as some critics have suggested, Dante Alighieri was the first Pre-Raphaelite in the broadest sense of the word, Christina Rossetti was a more faithful disciple of his than the members of the Brotherhood. "The convent threshold," for instance, is more truly Dantesque than "The Blessed Damozel" and thus a better model of the definitive genre of the Brotherhood: the medieval dream-vision in which the male lover or beloved is represented as being on a lower spiritual plane than the female in the vision. Despite the rather worldly ending, "The convent threshold" is full of deliberate echoes of the *Divine Comedy*.

Rossetti's medievalism, moreover, is closely related in some respects to another of her Pre-Raphaelite traits, her love of melancholy. In 1895 Alice Law observed that "the keynote of much of Miss Rossetti's

[29]Hopkins's "To fields where flies no sharp and sided hail" recalls his answer to Rossetti's poem "The convent threshold"— "Fling to the convent wicket fast. / Who would not shelter from the hail?" ("A voice from the world," ll. 75–76)—and her many dreams of a place where "there cometh not the wind nor rain / Nor sun nor snow. . . . where no cloud / Darkens the air" ("Eye hath not seen"; PW, p. 149), a place "with no more buffeting winds or tides to stem" ("All Saints: Martyrs," l. 4; II, 245), with "no forked lightnings" and "no thunders" ("The Lotus-Eaters"; PW, p. 111), where one may "Forget . . . the frostful blast" ("Yet a little while"; PW, p. 343).

[30]Eleanor Walter Thomas, *Christina Georgina Rossetti* (New York: Columbia University Press, 1931), pp. 176–77.

[31]Thomas, *Christina Georgina Rossetti*, pp. 33, 166–67, 211, 206, 162–63.

word-music is its aesthetic mysticism and rich melancholy. It is associated here, as in the works of her brother and other Pre-Raphaelites, with the deep medieval colouring, and quaint bejewelled setting of an old thirteenth—or fourteenth-century manuscript."[32] F. L. Lucas discussed this connection at some length:

> Her brother and Morris and Swinburne were moderns seeking inspiration in the mediaeval; she seems, rather, a mediaeval wraith shrinking in shy dismay before the harsh babel of modernity. In the Age of Steam she remained like some quiet anchoress of the Age of Faith—one who might have sat to Giotto, or knelt before St. Francis at Assisi. . . . There clings about this poetess a touch of that mediaeval morbidity which delighted in Dances of Death.[33]

When carried this far it may seem to some that virtue has become vice or, as Dorothy Stuart put it, "if one of the Seven Deadly sins found harbourage in the soul of this mid-Victorian Virgin Saint it was *Accidia*. This word is usually mistranslated 'Sloth', but the thing is, as Professor Saintsbury has said, 'a form or at least a corruption of Melancholy.' "[34]

There are many other connections between Rossetti's medievalism and her melancholy. A poem such as her "Three Stages" (*PW*, pp. 288–90), for instance, illustrates with unusual clarity and simplicity the way in which many Victorian writers managed to free themselves from the dominating influence of their Romantic precursors: they extrapolated Romantic medievalism to the point where the ascetic Christianity of the Middle Ages emerged as an antithesis to Romantic egoism. Evaluating the results of the Romantic experiment over the distance of time, they became particularly conscious of what they thought were the solipistic and nihilistic consequences of the apparently amoral, self-indulgent egoism of their Romantic predecessors. Hence Rossetti's determination, supported by Tennyson's example in "The Palace of Art," to destroy the dome of pleasure Coleridge erected in "Kubla Khan," and the bowers Keats so carefully constructed in "Lamia," "Ode to Psyche," and many other poems in order to rebuild

---

[32]Alice Law, "The Poetry of Christina G. Rossetti," *Westminster Review* 143 (1895): 447.

[33]Lucas, *Ten Victorian Poets*, pp. 117, 132.

[34]Dorothy Margaret Stuart, *Christina Rossetti*, English Association Pamphlet no. 78 (London: Oxford University Press, 1931), p. 5.

them in heaven. Melancholy was almost inevitable, for Rossetti had initially built her dome and bowers in her own soul. In other words, she had internalized her primary precursors, as all poets do, and to deny some of their influence was to deny herself. Like so many other Victorians, however, she felt she had to make the difficult sacrifice of self that her Romantic precursors had not made: she had to give up her cherished secret dream of becoming a Romantic poet in order to set an example, in order to "correct" the dangerous excesses of Romantic egoism. The melancholy which accompanied that ascetic sacrifice of self is particularly evident in her "Dead before death" (I, 59), and its influence is evident in Hopkins's "See how Spring opens with disabling cold," among other poems.

This kind of deliberately anti-Romantic Victorian medievalism was an extrapolation of a form of medieval asceticism sometimes called desert Christianity. The prominent role of Thomas à Kempis even in, say, *The Mill on the Floss,* reminds us that this kind of ascetic medievalism was easily combined with that Victorian revival of Pauline Christianity which has been identified as a resurgence of puritanism. This strain of medievalism and the melancholy associated with its sacrifice of self may seem far removed from what many consider to be characteristic Pre-Raphaelite melancholy, but I would argue that it had its roots in *The Germ,* the crystallization of the common goals of the P. R. B. and the repository of their models of creativity. The aescetic model of the *imitatio Christi* is quite striking in this Pre-Raphaelite manifesto. William Michael Rossetti actually used the term "puritanism" to describe John Orchard's contribution to *The Germ,* "A Dialogue on Art," which was in fact a collaborative effort of Orchard, Dante Gabriel Rossetti, and William Michael himself.

In that journal too Frederic Stephens linked the twin Pre-Raphaelite emphases on purity and on nature in his essay "The Purpose and Tendency of Early Italian Art." Religious diction pervades Stephens's description of painting from nature; for him the "modern school" (the P. R. B.) is devoted to "pure transcripts and faithful studies from nature" done with a "patient devotedness . . . more purely followed by the early Italian painters; a feeling which, exaggerated, and its object mistaken by them though still held holy and pure, was the cause of the retirement of many of the greatest men from the world to the monastery." Stephens's admiration for these monastic painters is as clear as his contempt for sensuality. His basic model, the *imitatio Christi,* soon emerges: " 'My strength is as the stregth of ten, / Because my heart is pure' . . . 'No Cross, No Crown.' " This kind of medievalism is most evident, however, in the speeches of Orchard's

"Christian" who most clearly identifies Jesus as the source of and audience for artistic creativity. Christian recommends art that is "pure, unsensual, and earnestly true." Like Savonarola, Orchard argues that "very few [works of art] are safe from condemnation"—even a poem such as "The Eve of St. Agnes" is unacceptable. To be "instructive, to become a teaching instrument, the art-edifice must be cleansed from its abominations." The artist, "if he desires to inform the people thoroughly, must imitate Christ." In this context, Pre-Raphaelite art emerges as an attempt "to return the sacred edifice to its first purity."[35] Hence the religious melancholy that distinguished Rossetti from her brothers, and from most other members of the Brotherhood, may in fact be regarded as at least as genuine a development from their first principles as their more literary melancholy. Although she may not have regarded "The Eve of St. Agnes" as "unacceptable" as Orchard's Christian did, she did feel the need to revise it.

Rossetti no doubt was more attracted to the religious melancholy in the poem than were the members of the Brotherhood. Like other Pre-Raphaelites, she was very fond of the poetry of Keats, the master of sensuous description in nineteenth-century English poetry. Indeed, Lona Mosk Packer has argued that it was Christina Rossetti "and not Gabriel or Holman Hunt [who] was the first 'Pre-Raphaelite' to appreciate Keats."[36] It is significant, moreover, that the poem Rossetti discovered in an abridged version in William Hone's *Every-day Book* (1830) was "The Eve of St. Agnes," Keats's most famous medieval poem. Her response—"while the chilly shadows flit / Of sweet St. Agnes' Eve"—in "On Keats" (*PW*, p. 291; composed on St. Agnes's Eve, 1849), reveals her attraction to the medieval frame of Keats's poem: the cold, the shadows, and the "patient, holy" (l. 10) Beadsman, the representative of the religious rather than the more purely Romantic strain of medievalism. Yet she must also have sympathized with the Beadsman's attraction to the worldly music nearby, from which, however, he turns away:

> But no—already had his deathbell rung;
> The joys of all his life were said and sung:

[35]*The Germ: A Pre-Raphaelite Little Magazine*, ed. Robert S. Hosmon (Coral Gables, Fla.: University of Miami Press, 1970), pp. 58, 63–64, 151, 155, 153, 157, 160.
[36]Lona Mosk Packer, *Christina Rossetti* (Berkeley: University of California Press, 1963), p. 14. Quotations from Keats are from the *The Poems of John Keats*, ed. Jack Stillinger (Cambridge: Harvard University Press, Belknap Press, 1978).

His was harsh penance on St. Agnes' Eve:
Another way he went, and soon among
Rough ashes sat he for his soul's reprieve,
And all night kept awake, for sinners' sake to grieve.

[ll. 22–27]

Like the ascetic medieval Beadsman, Rossetti was deeply attached to the music of this world but felt that the joys of her life were to be her prayers and poetry. She too tried to turn away from mere enjoyment of this world, seeking another, more difficult way, one that prescribed penance and grief. Like Orchard's "Christian," she wanted to imitate her namesake, Christ, or at least Madeline before the fall:

like a saint:
She seem'd a splendid angel, newly drest,
Save wings, for heaven:—Porphyro grew faint:
She knelt, so pure a thing, so free from mortal taint.

[ll. 222–25]

Barbara Fass has indicated the influence of "The Eve of St. Agnes" on Rossetti in such poems as "Repining" (PW, pp. 9–12) and "For one sake" (PW, pp. 333–34), as well as some of the affinities between Tennyson's "St. Agnes' Eve" and Rossetti's more spiritual versions of Keats's original.[37] I would argue, however, that "The convent threshold" more closely resembles "The Eve of St. Agnes" than do most of Rossetti's other poems: it, too, is about two lovers separated by some kind of blood feud and by differences in temperament (his eyes "look earthward" while hers "look up," l. 17), and it too emphasizes the woman's dreams of her lover who must "flee for [his] life" for "the time is short" (ll. 39, 38).

"The convent threshold" is distinguished from "The Eve of St. Agnes" in much the same way "Repining" is: both poems begin where Keats's poem ends. Rossetti's heroine is a post-seduction Madeline who has decided to repent and atone for her "guilt" and "stain" (ll. 9, 12) and regain her purity in truly medieval fashion by crossing the convent threshold. Rossetti stresses that the storm Keats's lovers flee into is that of the winds of time which destroy all earthly vanities (ll. 63–64). In her version the shadow of death is a more immediate threat to the lovers: the heroine dreams that she is dead (as in Dante

<hr/>

[37]Barbara Fass, "Christina Rossetti and St. Agnes' Eve," VP 14 (1976): 33–46.

Gabriel's "The Blessed Damozel") and envisions a soul flashing up to heaven, in a passage (ll. 85–109) that, like Rossetti's "For one sake," is reminiscent of Tennyson's "St. Agnes' Eve." The heroine's question, "How long until my sleep begin?" (l. 56) projects Madeline's desire to sleep and dream into a death wish like that of the speaker in "Repining." Thus in "The convent threshold" the heroine's death bell has clearly rung, and, like Keats's Beadsman, she needs to kneel, pray, and accept harsh penance. By emphasizing the spiritual medievalism of the Beadsman more than the amorous medievalism of Porphyro in "The convent threshold" and in other poems, Rossetti gave a new direction to Keatsian Romanticism in general and Keatsian melancholy in particular.

Rossetti's "morbid" emphasis on mutability and death is a striking extrapolation of Pre-Raphaelite as well as Romantic melancholy. A reviewer of her 1866 volume for the *Catholic World* stated, "The amount of melancholy is simply overwhelming."[38] That melancholy was overwhelming because Rossetti's ascetic "morbidities" were amplified by a strong literary melancholy and by what we might call the melancholy of the woman's lot in Victorian England. She was moved in part by a consciousness of the triumph of time almost as dominating as Swinburne's and expressed in such lines as "Alas for joy that went before, / For joy that dies, for love that dies" ("The convent threshold," ll. 63–64). These words recall Keats's "Ode on Melancholy," in which he makes clear that melancholy "dwells with Beauty—Beauty that must die; / And Joy, whose hand is ever at his lips / Bidding adieu." Such echoes remind us that Rossetti was also inspired by the primary muse of the Pre-Raphaelites, Romantic melancholy.

Melancholy is a dominant theme in *The Germ*: it pervades all the poems that Rossetti and Thomas Woolner contributed, various poems by Dante Gabriel Rossetti, William Michael Rossetti, James Collinson, and William Bell Scott, as well as Dante Gabriel's prose work, "Hand and Soul." It is true that, as we have seen, Christianity is often represented in *The Germ* as the religion of sorrow, the religion of suffering epitomized in Michelangelo's *Pietà*. (Frederic Stephens, in fact, cites a Pietà in Florence and ascribes the melancholy of the early Italian painters not to typically Romantic sources but to their religious subjects.) Most of the melancholy evident throughout *The Germ*, however, is more typically Romantic. Robert Bridges's definition of this kind of melancholy fits a number of Rossetti's poems. In his essay

[38]Anonymous review of Rossetti's 1866 volume in *Catholic World* 4 (1867): 839.

on Keats, Bridges focuses on "a characteristic attitude of passion, which makes the best occasion to speak of the curiously close similarity which exists between him and the school of painting which had Rossetti for its head. . . . the little 'sweet among much bitterness', the consciousness of something too horrible to speak of behind the scene, . . . have a likeness to the creations of this school so remarkable, that Keats may be safely credited with a chief share of their parentage."[39]

Indeed, the Pre-Raphaelites were apparently more conscious than Keats of the ancient theory of melancholy as the major source of creativity. William Bell Scott, for instance, observed:

> My brother for one completed his works in a state of despair. When I went into D. G. R.'s studio to see his large "Dante's Dream", I found him in a similar state, hidden under a kind of ferocity; and I remember Holman Hunt, the success of whose "Christ in the Temple" was too great to allow of discontent, saying with a haggard expression of face, "It is well for once, but I'll be now found out. I can never do anything more!" The cause of this, which has descended to us from the time of Michel Angelo himself, but is more peculiarly an insular disease nowadays, results mainly from the unpopularity of exceptional genius. The man as well as his work is shied by his professional associates as well as the public: he is not "one of us."[40]

In fact this melancholy theory of creativity is more ancient than Scott recognized. It descends from Aristotle, was revived by the Renaissance Neoplatonists, and adopted by the Romantics, who emphasized the aristocratic superiority and unpopularity of the exceptional genius. Thus, paradoxically, Christina Rossetti's melancholy derived not only from the humble self-abnegation of her ascetic extrapolation of Romantic medievalism but also from the aristocratic Romantic theory of creativity.

In addition, Rossetti suffered from the special melancholy of a creative woman excluded from the creative "brotherhoods" of her time. Hers is the loneliness of the artist in Tennyson's "Lady of Shalott," a

---

[39]Quoted in R. L. Megroz, *Modern English Poetry* (London: Ivor Nicholson and Watson, 1933), pp. 13–14.

[40]William Bell Scott, *Autobiographical Notes of the Life of William Bell Scott*, ed. W. Minton, 2 vols. (New York: Harper and Bros., 1892), II, 86–87.

model she resorts to throughout her poetry, nowhere more obviously than in "Autumn" (I, 143–45):

> I dwell alone—I dwell alone, alone,
>   Whilst full my river flows down to the sea,
>   Gilded with flashing boats
>   That bring no friend to me;
>
>   [ll. 1–4]

To what extent was this fate the result of her brother's decision to name his group the "Brotherhood" and the group's collective decision (or unquestioned assumption) that no women were to be included? Would Dante Gabriel Rossetti have deliberately excluded a highly qualified rival?

In the case of Hopkins he apparently did just that. He blocked the publication of three of Hopkins's better sonnets. But would Dante Gabriel have treated his own sister this way? As David A. Kent has shown, even fraternal assistance, such as William Michael's editing of the posthumous *Poetical Works,* could be deleterious.[41] Sibling rivalry can be one of the fiercest forms of competition we know, and Christina could have been perceived as a dangerous rival to Dante Gabriel's dominance in the group, as well as to other members of the Brotherhood. She had a strong impact even on the fiercest pagan of the century, Swinburne; and we might note the connotations of Swinburne's description of Rossetti as the "Jael" who led them to victory. Jael won fame by deceiving a man into sleeping in her tent and then pounding a tent stake through his temple. Whether Swinburne and Dante Gabriel Rossetti were fully conscious of perceiving her as a dangerous rival, it is clearly possible that such a perception influenced her exclusion from the Brotherhood, even though, or perhaps because, she was the one who would lead them to victory.

[41]David A. Kent, "W. M. Rossetti and the Editing of Christina Rossetti's Religious Poetry," *Pre-Raphaelite Review* 1 (1978): 18–26.

G. B. Tennyson

Afterword: Love God and Die—
Christina Rossetti and the Future

"If I might only love my God and die!"
                                    "If Only"

The modern *lecteur moyen sensuel* who comes upon the poetry of Christina Rossetti is very likely to see it as the cry of an anguished heart. So many of the poems turn on loss, disappointment, sorrow, unworthiness, and above all death, and so many are cast in the first person or employ the feminine third-person pronoun to refer to their subjects that a biographical equation seems called for: the "I" and the "she" must be Christina Rossetti herself. Moreover, the reader normally knows that here he is confronting the poetry of a woman writing in an age when what we see as social restrictions on women were the common rule. A reader who has acquired some biographical information about Rossetti knows that she was the retiring sister of a flamboyant painter and poet who cut a much more visible swath across his society than she did and that she remained, despite some romantic attachments and offers of marriage, a lifelong spinster. Thus the reader may well ask how, other than biographically, can one interpret opening lines such as these:

> I looked for that which is not, nor can be (I, 51)
> The hope I dreamed of was a dream (I, 55)
> The door was shut. I looked between / Its iron bars (I, 56)
> When I am dead, my dearest (I, 58)
> O Earth, lie heavily upon her eyes (I, 60)
> I have no wit, no words, no tears (I, 68)
> She gave up beauty in her tender youth (I, 122)

346

'Oh sad thy lot before I came, / But sadder when I go' (I, 136)
What would I give for a heart of flesh to warm me thro' (I, 142)
Ah woe is me for pleasure that is vain (I, 153)
Give me the lowest place (I, 187)

As though in official confirmation, the scholarship and criticism on Rossetti very largely substantiate one's initial assumptions. The most ambitious modern biography, rich though it is in new and valuable factual information, contends that Rossetti pined away loving an unattainable man, leaving the record of that blighted love in her poetry; and the most recent modern biography of Rossetti follows its eponymous title with the legend "A Divided Life," divided, it would seem, between duty in this world and yearning for another.[1]

It is no wonder, then, that the modern reader of average sensibility, equipped with at least a shorthand knowledge of repression and sublimation, and unequipped with a counterbalancing understanding of the religious impulse, will see in the poetry of Christina Rossetti the record of a miserable and misspent life. Nor can any but the most rigorously antihistorical critic exclude biography from Rossetti's (or any other poet's) writing. Such exclusion works best where we know the fewest facts, as with a Homer or a Shakespeare. And even in such cases the critical impulse has sometimes operated to infer biography from the works or, failing that, to infer another author from the works. Thus we have not only Marlovians, Baconians, and Oxonians contending against Shakespeare but such bemusing curiosities as Samuel Butler's argument that Homer (or more properly the author of the *Odyssey*) was a woman. Given what we do know, and know in some substantial detail, of the life of Rossetti, the temptation to treat her poetry as but thinly veiled autobiography is almost irresistible. Few have resisted. Indeed, the autobiographical has proven to be the dominant approach in scholarship and criticism on Christina Rossetti since her death.

But the time has come to exorcise the demon of false autobiography in the study of Rossetti, and the essays collected here have done so. This volume constitutes a declaration of critical independence for the future study of Rossetti the writer and a subtle recommendation of benign neglect for the narrowly biographical study of Rossetti as an-

[1]The two biographies are Lona Mosk Packer, *Christina Rossetti* (Berkeley: University of California Press, 1963) and Georgina Battiscombe, *Christina Rossetti: A Divided Life* (New York: Holt, Rinehart and Winston, 1981).

guished heart. This is not to say that biography can never again rear its head in the study of Christina Rossetti. It is not even to say that all previous work based on biographical aspects is invalid or that Rossetti was never sad, or yearning, or disappointed. For the intricate connections between a writer's experience and work are always worth investigation, and such investigation often bears useful critical fruit. It is to say, however, that connections between biography and work are indeed intricate rather than transparent and that great tact and subtlety are required in threading the biographical labyrinth. A primer of self-loathing and a handbook of the *contemptus mundi* theme could be assembled from passages and images in the poetry of George Herbert. Yet Herbert counts as our greatest religious poet rather than as our most tormented one. The issue in biographical criticism, as in most other criticism, is how the tool is used.

Feminist critics may say that, because Rossetti was a woman, she has been ill served by biographically centered criticism. There is probably some truth in such a view. A woman and a Victorian woman who was also in later years a semi-invalid is presumed to have been repressed and was so presumed even before the advent of modern feminism. But feminist criticism wants merely to change the terms: such a woman if repressed was so only because she was *op*pressed, but underneath. . . . Unfortunately, Rossetti does not in general lend herself to analysis as a secret rebel or a madwoman in a would-be nunnery. So feminist critics have for the most part passed her by, as they have other similar problem cases such as Charlotte Mary Yonge. (Betty S. Flowers's essay in this volume deals capably with some of these problems.) But in general it is just as well that Rossetti has not been the subject of much doctrinaire feminist criticism, for such criticism is no more the key to her genius than is narrow autobiographical criticism (of which so much modern feminist criticism is but a tendentious variant).

The key to understanding Rossetti is much the same as that to understanding other writers, male or female—a willingness to take her as a writer, coupled with a sensitive reading of the works as they come to us, enhanced as may be by external information, including the biographical, but finally resting in the works as they are. This has been the guiding principle of the present collection and consequently this volume marks the way for the future of Rossetti studies.

What we have for the first time in the more than one hundred years of criticism and scholarship on Rossetti is a full-length volume on Rossetti the *writer*. In his introductory essay Jerome J. McGann strikes the new note in Rossetti studies that helps us to see that the main issue is the kind of writer Rossetti is rather than the kind of life she lived. As McGann points out, not all the contributors to the present volume will agree with his "way of reading" Christina Rossetti, a statement that is manifestly true; but what is equally true is that all the contributors to the present volume do tacitly agree with McGann's approach to Rossetti as in the first instance an author who deserves serious and extensive literary attention. Whether the emphasis in a given essay is biographical, religious, epistolary, feminist, historical, or comparative—and all these emphases are represented in this collection—the authors here approach their subject as a literary phenomenon, not as a case study. This is a distinction with a real difference, a difference that makes possible meaningful future work on Rossetti.

Like many new things, the approach to Rossetti as writer is also old. To read through R. W. Crump's annotated reference guide to writings about Christina Rossetti from 1862, when the first notice appeared, through the year 1973 (when Crump's survey ends) is to note how much more purely critical and literary were the early pieces on Rossetti than those that began appearing after her death and through most of the twentieth century.[2] The early notices were, of course, reviews, and the reviewers had for the most part nothing to go on but the writings themselves. To be sure, there appears early in Rossetti criticism a tendency to couple her with other women poets, especially Mrs. Browning, a tendency that certainly betrays the Victorian disposition (which Victorians surely thought was a courtesy) to set women apart; but even these poetess to poetess comparisons are based on the poetry rather than the biography. And there is a good deal of poet to poet comparisons as well, chiefly of Rossetti to Herbert, Vaughan, and other poets of the Anglican religious tradition. One Thompson Cooper even saw fit to include a notice of Rossetti in his 1879 tenth edition of the compendium *Men of the Time*, a volume instructively subtitled "A Dictionary of Contemporaries, Containing Biographical Notices of Eminent Characters of Both Sexes."[3] The earliest biographical treatment of Rossetti does not appear until 1895, the year after her death, in Ellen Proctor's brief *Memoir* (with a preface by William Michael Rossetti) and of course in the numerous obituary and retrospective notices of that year.[4] (She died on December 29, 1894,

---

[2]R. W. Crump, *Christina Rossetti: A Reference Guide* (Boston: G. K. Hall, 1976).
[3]Ibid., p. 13.
[4]Ibid., pp. 26 and ff.

G. B. Tennyson

so the earliest notices appeared in January 1895). But from then on the biographical, and later the psychological, approaches dominate. It is against the background of the intervening three generations of criticism that the refound literary emphasis of this volume takes on its character of newness and freshness.

By reascending to origins the contributors to this volume have opened anew the literary study of Christina Rossetti. Once we start with the assumption, even if only unconsciously and automatically as we regularly do with most writers, that Rossetti is first of all a writer, we open up a broad, new perspective on her work. This perspective does not exclude the use of those staple concerns of Rossetti criticism, such as biography, religion, Pre-Raphaelitism, and the like—indeed, consideration of these factors is still necessary for a full understanding—but rather the focus on Rossetti as writer uses the traditional considerations and approaches as ways to illuminate the work and not as ways around it. Who, for example, can ever again read *Goblin Market* without seriously entertaining the speculations advanced so brilliantly by D. M. R. Bentley, drawing on known biographical facts about Rossetti? Or who cannot now hope for a complete modern edition of Christina Rossetti's letters, given their potential for biographical and critical illumination of her work, as Antony H. Harrison has shown with some of the early letters? Do we not now look forward (perhaps from the hand of Jerome Bump) to yet further investigation into Rossetti as a shaper of, as well as respondent to, the Pre-Raphaelite impulse? Or to an even fuller study (this surely from David A. Kent) of Christina Rossetti and George Herbert and other predecessors in devotional poetry? And to Rossetti and the Tractarians, to Rossetti as a woman writer, and so on throughout this volume, with its awakening and reawakening of interest in Rossetti's sonnet sequence, her arrangement of poems in collections, her children's poetry, her devotional prose, her treatment of nature, and yet more? All this renewed interest has been made possible by approaching Rossetti as a writer.

The focus, then, for the average modern reader as well as for the modern scholar and critic must henceforth be on Rossetti the writer. Considered as such, Rossetti emerges as a rather more versatile and varied artist than is often realized. In terms of form and genre her work includes a very substantial variety of poetry. The lyric voice predominates, but she also composed dialogues, narrative, allegorical-symbolic, dramatic, and of course devotional poetry, to say nothing of her purely technical mastery of forms such as the sonnet and *bouts-rimés*

350

that appear throughout her poetry. Apart from poetry, Rossetti wrote extensively in prose in the form of short stories and various kinds of non-fiction, much of it uniquely her own in style and substance, such as the devotional prose that is an amalgam of exegesis and commentary, sermonizing and diary, interspersed with verse for the occasion. (P. G. Stanwood's essay here opens up a whole new realm for future scholarship.) The range of Rossetti's writing highlighted by this volume makes us hope for a complete modern edition of the prose to take its place alongside the poetry. Christina Rossetti could then take *her* place, and not the lowest one by any means, among Victorian authors and her place as the premier writer of her variously talented family.

Still, our putative common reader may ask, is there a center to all this literary activity, something around which this variety coheres? Further, why does Rossetti as a writer seem to concentrate so much on loss, deprivation, self-abnegation, unworthiness, and the like, as signaled by, for example, that sequence of opening lines cited earlier? It is at this point that we can and should bring to bear the single most important lens through which to view Rossetti—religion. In so doing we must be willing to see religion not as Rossetti's opiate or her tyrant but as her life.

By saying that religion was Rossetti's life I do not mean to resubsume her again into something else. I mean rather that religion was her life in something of the way that nature was Wordsworth's life. This latter is a proposition much more readily entertained by the modern mind than that religion could absorb anyone as completely as it absorbed Rossetti and many of her contemporaries, such as the Tractarians who influenced her religious ideas so profoundly. But religion can absorb the mind as much as nature, or politics, or sex. In Rossetti's case religion did not dictate in any arbitrary or destructive manner what and how she wrote; it simply informed her thoughts and her sensibility. Just as Wordsworth was formed by his response to nature, that "sense sublime of something far more deeply interfused," so Rossetti was formed by religion, by "Christ our All in all," as she titled one group of poems (II, 188–211). Religious matters were what Rossetti wrote about because these were what she knew and lived, as Wordsworth knew and lived nature. Seen thus, religion is both less important (because it is in a sense raw material for what she wrote) and more important (because it was the ground of her being) than it has been taken to be in Rossetti studies. Therefore one can deal with Rossetti's abundant religious writings as one would deal with Milton's use of the Bible and Christian tradition as the essential material for his epic. One can treat this material as necessary for understanding what Milton was doing, and one can enjoy the results aesthetically, if need be with the help of Coleridge's willing suspension of disbelief. Of course, as with Milton, so with Rossetti: one must ultimately come to judgment about the ideas that are being advanced with so much passion and sincerity. That judgment, however, is not where we start but where we end.

To put this proposition to the test, consider the poem from which my remarks take their title and epigraph, "If Only."

> If I might only love my God and die!
>   But now He bids me love Him and live on,
>   Now when the bloom of all my life is gone,
> The pleasant half of life has quite gone by.
> My tree of hope is lopped that spread so high;
>   And I forget how Summer glowed and shone,
>   While Autumn grips me with its fingers wan,
> And frets me with its fitful windy sigh.
> When Autumn passes then must Winter numb,
>   And Winter may not pass a weary while,
>   But when it passes Spring shall flower again:
> And in that Spring who weepeth now shall smile,
>   Yea, they shall wax who now are on the wane,
>   Yea, they shall sing for love when Christ shall come.[5]

This is an Italian sonnet of conventional rhyme scheme in the octave and slightly unconventional, though not radical, rhyme scheme in the sestet. The sonnet states the "problem" in the octave and "solves" it in the sestet with a traditional "volta" or reversal. The sustaining image is that of the changing seasons, fruitful summer succeeded by somber autumn fading into grim winter, followed by the promise of rebirth in spring. This progression of the seasons in turn parallels and emblematizes a common psychological pattern in humankind. The atheist Shelley felt it as keenly as the pious Rossetti—"If Winter comes, can Spring be far behind?" Leaving aside for the moment the first and last lines of "If Only," we could read the poem as another expression of the age-old awareness that human life, like the

---

[5]William Michael Rossetti (PW, p. 244) gives the first line as "If only I might love my God and die!—" but Crump's more reliable text (I, 181) is taken from the manuscript and earliest editions.

seasons, runs its appointed round and must endure its autumn and winter even as it enjoyed its spring and summer, and that nevertheless the death of the year holds distant promise of renewal. As such the poem is finely expressed, with many effective touches: autumn's "fingers wan" and its "fitful windy sigh," for example, and the telling use of "numb" as a verb. Any but the most callow reader can respond to the poem in these terms, for we have all, unlike Matthew Arnold's Scholar-Gypsy, felt the "lapse of hours" that wears out the life of mortal men.

But, of course, restricting the poem to these terms is justifiable only as an exercise to show how much of it can be apprehended on a nondoctrinal level. The necessary restoration of the first and last lines does not negate what the sonnet contains of conventional wisdom, but it enriches and ultimately transforms it. It makes the sonnet both Christian and uniquely Rossetti's. The first line, "If I might only love my God and die!" is, to be sure, one of those cries of longing and self-negation that readers may be tempted to see as the mark of a burdened or disturbed psyche. But they would be stopping too short. In context it is rather the Christian formulation of a perennial yearning, the desire to rid oneself of the world that is always too much with us in order to enjoy the promised oneness with God that comes with death. But note that Rossetti has not said all when she has said that. On the contrary, the opening line is not the ultimate expression of the sonnet, only the arresting first statement of its problem. Immediately it is followed by "But now He bids me love Him and live on." The key word "love" is linked by divine injunction with "live"; the speaker is saying that it is not God's will that one should at some time convenient for the speaker cease the struggle. His will is that one continue to struggle and to love Him. It is at this point that the speaker links her life to the waning of the year and draws on the traditional associations cited above, almost as though in argument against God's bidding, giving the poem a peculiar tension that makes it anything but complacent *or* resigned.

As the sonnet moves into the sestet the movement of the seasons has reached only to a winter that may endure for a "weary while." Then comes the reversal with the return of spring and the changing of tears to smiles. And at last the two final lines enrich the reversal by fulfilling the promise of the opening two. Each of these last lines repeats the operative word "love" from the opening but transforms it from love through resignation to love through joy. By deft use of her uncommon sestet rhyme scheme Rosetti makes the last line of the sestet rhyme with its first, so that "numb" is anchored and negated by Christ's coming. The final lines have also subtly shifted the focus from the single speaker, the "I" of the first line, to the company of the faithful, the "they": "Yea, they shall sing for love when Christ shall come." The Christ who comes in the spring is the risen Christ of Easter, who in Hopkins's phrase will "easter in us" ("The Wreck of the Deutschland"), the Christ who makes the seasonal renewal and rebirth of nature into a spiritual renewal and rebirth.

When the opening and closing lines are restored to those lines which draw on traditional associations of the seasons with human life and human yearnings, traditional associations are themselves colored by religious perception, and in turn the sonnet as a whole becomes a profession of faith. The seasons as a paradigm of man's life, of his inevitable wearing away and his eternal hope, are subordinated to God and become part of His plan. A moral lesson in Christian acceptance and Christian hope is interwoven with the cycle of nature, so interwoven as to constitute a seamless fabric. The speaker's initial resignation and regretful acceptance that appear at modern first glance to be more self-denial, more sorrow, develop to a final joyous singing that melds the hope of spring with Christian hope. The speaker has ceased to be, if she ever was, the historical person Christina Rossetti and has become the Christian Everyman. It is the same voice that speaks in all the best religious poetry.

The masterly poem "If Only" is far from an isolated example; it is typical. Rossetti's achievement as a writer is that she was able to speak for the Christian Everyman in the Victorian age. In this regard she resembles John Keble and the Tractarians more closely than Gerard Manley Hopkins does (for Hopkins's is an idiosyncratic voice); but in her passion and sincerity she resembles Hopkins more than she does Keble. T. S. Eliot's dictum that the trouble with much religious poetry is that "people who write devotional verse are usually writing as they want to feel, rather than as they do feel" seems quite inapplicable to Rossetti.[6] Too often, in fact, readers have supposed that she is writing *only* as she feels, so intense and persuasive is the voice in her poetry. But I think she was often writing not only as she herself may have felt at one time or another but, beyond that, as she knew imaginatively many had felt. In like manner the modern common reader must make an imaginative leap into the world of faith and belief to appreciate

[6]T. S. Eliot, *After Strange Gods* (London: Faber and Faber, 1934), p. 28.

how completely Rossetti as a writer has captured the mind and heart of that world.

Following William Michael Rossetti, biographers have recorded that the last poem Rossetti wrote, which was found among her papers after her death, was the poignant "Sleeping at last." Two modern biographers have closed their studies of Rossetti using that poem as a kind of epitaph.[7] Perhaps for the person Christina Rossetti it is appropriate. For the writer Christina Rossetti, however, I would adapt the opening line of "If Only" to serve as the motto for her work and a guide for our critical understanding of it. Christina Rossetti was a writer who both preached and practiced the command "Love God and Live."

[7]Packer, *Christina Rossetti*, pp. 407–8, and Battiscombe, *Christina Rossetti*, p. 208. William Michael Rossetti (*PW*, p. 489) writes: "I regard these verses (the title again is mine) as being the very last that Christina ever wrote."

CONTRIBUTORS

D. M. R. BENTLEY is Professor of English at the University of Western Ontario. Founder and editor of the journal *Canadian Poetry: Studies, Documents, Reviews*, he has published on Canadian and Victorian poetry, most pertinently on Dante Gabriel Rossetti, William Morris, and other Pre-Raphaelites. His facsimile edition of the materials leading up to the publication of Dante Gabriel Rossetti's *Poems* (1870) will be published by Garland in 1987.

JEROME BUMP is Professor of English at the University of Texas at Austin and editor of *Texas Studies in Language and Literature*. He is the author of *Gerard Manley Hopkins* and is currently writing a book on creativity which focuses on the Pre-Raphaelites and their contemporaries.

CATHERINE MUSELLO CANTALUPO was born in 1948 and completed her doctoral dissertation, "Continuities of Faith and Style in Christina Rossetti's Poetry," seven months before her death in 1983. Her publications included poetry as well as articles on Alice Meynell, Patrick Kavanagh, and Christina Rossetti.

DIANE D'AMICO is Assistant Professor of English at Allegheny College in Meadville, Pennsylvania. She has published articles on Christina Rossetti in *Victorian Poetry, The Journal of Pre-Raphaelite Studies. The University of Dayton Review, Victorians Institute Journal*, and the *John Donne Journal*.

Contributors

BETTY S. FLOWERS, Associate Professor of English at the University of Texas at Austin, is the author of *Browning and the Modern Tradition* and co-editor of *Daughters and Fathers* (forthcoming). She has published poems, short stories, and articles on poetry and contemporary fiction.

ANTONY H. HARRISON is Professor of English at North Carolina State University, where he teaches nineteenth-century English poetry. His publications include *Swinburne's Medievalism: A Study in Victorian Love Poetry, Christina Rossetti in Context*, and numerous articles on Victorian poetry. He is currently at work on an edition of Christina Rossetti's collected letters.

DAVID A. KENT teaches at Centennial College, Toronto. In addition to articles on Keats, the Rossettis, and Canadian literature, he is the author of *Margaret Avison and Her Works* and the editor of *"Lighting up the Terrain": The Poetry of Margaret Avison* and *Christian Poetry in Canada* (forthcoming).

JEROME J. McGANN is Commonwealth Professor of English at the University of Virginia. One of his recent books, *The Beauty of Inflections*, deals with a number of related Romantic and Victorian subjects. His most recent book is *Building of Loss: The Knowledge of Imaginative Texts* (1987).

RODERICK McGILLIS is Associate Professor of English at the University of Calgary. He has published articles on such writers as Wordsworth, Lewis Carroll, George MacDonald, Charles Dickens, and Sara Coleridge. He is the editor of *The Children's Literature Association Quarterly* and is working on a book on George MacDonald.

DOLORES ROSENBLUM is the author of *Christina Rossetti: The Poetry of Endurance*. She has written on Elizabeth Barrett Browning and Tennyson and has taught at the State University of New York, Albany, and at Indiana University. She is now beginning a second career in social work, having recently graduated from the School of Social Service Administration, University of Chicago.

LINDA SCHOFIELD is a doctoral student in English at the University of Toronto. Her dissertation on Christina Rossetti's poetic identity is a study of the lines of contact between the secular and religious poetry in Rossetti's canon.

W. D. SHAW is Professor of English at Victoria College, University of Toronto, and Fellow of the Royal Society of Canada. He is the author of *The Dialectical Temper: The Rhetorical Art of Robert Browning* (1968), *Tennyson's Style* (1976), and *The Lucid Veil: Poetic Truth in the Victorian Age* (1987).

P. G. STANWOOD is Professor of English at the University of British Columbia. His articles on seventeenth-century literature have been published in many journals, and he is also the editor of five books, including a critical edition of Jeremy Taylor's *Holy Living* and *Holy Dying*.

G. B. TENNYSON is Professor of English at the University of California, Los Angeles. He is the author of books on Thomas Carlyle and of *Victorian Devotional Poetry* and co-editor of *Nature and the Victorian Imagination* and *Victorian Literature: Poetry and Prose*. He is co-editor of the journal *Nineteenth-Century Literature*.

WILLIAM WHITLA is Professor of English and Humanities and Chair of the Division of Humanities at York University, Toronto. He has published *The Central Truth: The Incarnation in Browning's Poetry* and articles on Victorian literature. He is currently working on a book on William Morris and the classical tradition.

INDEX TO THE WRITINGS
OF CHRISTINA ROSSETTI

POEMS

GENERAL INDEX

Aesop, Rossetti's inversions of, 226–27
Alleyn, Ellen. *See* Rossetti, Christina
   Georgina
Analogy, 64, 66, 275–82
Augustine, 67, 103

Baring-Gould, S.: *Lives of the Saints*, 236
Barrett, Elizabeth. *See* Browning, Elizabeth
   Barrett
Bath, Lady (friend of Rossettis), 195, 199–
   200, 203
Battiscombe, Georgina: *Christina Rossetti: A
   Divided Life*, 61, 220–22, 238n, 347
Bell, Mackenzie: *Christina Rossetti: A Bio-
   graphical and Critical Study*, 59–61, 192–
   94, 252–53, 267
Blake, William, 210–11, 221, 252
Brown, Ford Madox, 195, 264, 333
Browning, Elizabeth Barrett, 90–91, 172,
   255
Burrows, Canon (Vicar, Christ Church, Al-
   bany Street), 62, 232
Butler, Alban: *Lives of the . . . Saints*, 236

Caine, Hall T., 91
Carroll, Lewis, 227
Cayley, Charles Bagot, 84, 92 and n; trans-
   lations (Dante, Petrarch), 98–100
Coleridge, Samuel T., 7, 256–57, 284–85,
   287, 289–92, 296, 298, 339
Collinson, Charles, 200–201
Collinson, James, 84, 198–201, 203
Crump, R. W., 36, 132, 349

Dante, 14, 87–88, 97–109 (epigraphs from
   Commedia), 119, 126–27, 166, 172, 203,
   287, 297–98, 338
Dorothea, Saint, 323, 334
Dyce, William, 256 and n

Eliot, T. S., 44, 354
Elizabeth, Saint (of Hungary), 72n, 199–
   200

Forman, H. B., 254, 273
Froude, Hurrell: "Trembling Hope," 309–
   15, 320; "Weakness of Nature," 315–18,
   320
Fuller, Thomas, 237n, 241

Germ, The, 82, 135, 197, 201–2, 323–24,
   340, 343
Gilchrist, Herbert (and Anne G.), 251
Gosse, Edmund, assessments of Rossetti:
   250, 264, 323

Herbert, George, 239, 246, 250; "The
   Call," 258; "Clasping of Hands," 261–62;
   "The Dedication," 268; "Easter Wings,"
   259; influence on Rossetti, 253–73, 276,
   348; "Jesu," 261; "Jordan (II)," 263;
   "Miserie," 263; "Paradise," 261; "Prayer
   (II)," 263; "Sinnes Round," 259; "Trin-
   itie Sunday," 258, 262n; "A True
   Hymn," 265–66; "Vertue," 257–58; "A
   Wreath," 259
Hooker, Richard, 237n

Library of Congress Cataloging-in-Publication Data

The Achievement of Christina Rossetti.

   Includes index.
   1. Rossetti, Christina Georgina, 1830–1894—Criticism and
   interpretation.   I. Kent, David A., 1948–
PR5238.A55   1987   821'.8   87-47548
ISBN 0-8014-1937-9 (alk. paper)